Microsoft SharePoint: Building Office 2003 Solutions

SCOT P. HILLIER

Microsoft SharePoint: Building Office 2003 Solutions
Copyright © 2004 by Scot Hillier

ISBN (pbk): 1-59059-338-3

Printed and bound in the United States of America 9 8 7 6 5

Trademarked names may appear in this book. Rather than use a trademark symbol with every occurrence of a trademarked name, we use the names only in an editorial fashion and to the benefit of the trademark owner, with no intention of infringement of the trademark.

Technical Reviewer: Seth Bates

Editorial Board: Steve Anglin, Dan Appleman, Ewan Buckingham, Gary Cornell, Tony Davis, Jason Gilmore, Chris Mills, Dominic Shakeshaft, Jim Sumser, Karen Watterson, John Zukowski

Assistant Publisher: Grace Wong

Project Manager: Kylie Johnston

Copy Editor: Rebecca Rider

Production Manager: Kari Brooks

Production Editor: Janet Vail

Proofreader: Liz Welch

Compositor: ContentWorks

Indexer: Kevin Broccoli

Artist: Kinetic Publishing Services, LLC

Cover Designer: Kurt Krames

Manufacturing Manager: Tom Debolski

Distributed to the book trade in the United States by Springer-Verlag New York, LLC, 233 Spring Street, Sixth Floor, New York, NY 10013 and outside the United States by Springer-Verlag GmbH & Co. KG, Tiergartenstr. 17, 69112 Heidelberg, Germany.

In the United States: phone 1-800-SPRINGER, email orders@springer-ny.com, or visit http://www.springer-ny.com. Outside the United States: fax +49 6221 345229, email orders@springer.de, or visit http://www.springer.de.

For information on translations, please contact Apress directly at 2560 Ninth Street, Suite 219, Berkeley, CA 94710. Phone 510-549-5930, fax 510-549-5939, email info@apress.com, or visit http://www.apress.com.

The source code for this book is available to readers at http://www.apress.com in the Downloads section.

For Nan, whose heart knows no boundaries

Contents at a Glance

About the Author xi

About the Technical Reviewer................................xiii

Acknowledgments xv

Introduction xvii

Chapter 1   SharePoint Business Solutions 1

Chapter 2   SharePoint Products and Technologies Overview...21

Chapter 3   SharePoint Portal Server Basics..................53

Chapter 4   SharePoint Content Development 97

Chapter 5   Building Web Parts 139

Chapter 6   The Microsoft Single Sign-On Service...........191

Chapter 7   Advanced Web Part Development...................223

Chapter 8   The Microsoft Office System 275

Chapter 9   Programming SharePoint Services.................333

Chapter 10   SharePoint Portal Server
             Administration 391

Chapter 11   Office Solution Accelerators 413

Index 471

Contents

About the Author xi
About the Technical Reviewer.............................xiii
Acknowledgments xv
Introduction xvii

Chapter 1   SharePoint Business Solutions...............1

A Brief History of Portals 1
End-User Challenges 4
Understanding Business Scenarios 8
Analysis and Design Considerations 11
Technical Considerations....................................18

**Chapter 2   SharePoint Products and
             Technologies Overview** 21

Windows Server 2003 Information Worker Infrastructure 21
SharePoint Services 24
Office 2003 26
SharePoint Portal Server 28
Exercise 2-1: Creating a Development Environment 34

Chapter 3   SharePoint Portal Server Basics...........53

Understanding Portal Structure...............................53
Managing Users 61
Libraries..68
Exercise 3-1: SPS Basics 89

Chapter 4   SharePoint Content Development............97

Customizing Portal Content 97
Personalization with My Site...............................113
Customizing with Microsoft FrontPage......................116
Exercise 4-1: Building an Executive Dashboard 128

Chapter 5 Building Web Parts..............................139

Web Part Basics 139
Deploying Web Parts 151
Using Web Part Pages 168
Exercise 5-1: Building a Simple Web Part 171
Exercise 5-2: Adding Child Controls to Web Parts............178

Chapter 6 The Microsoft Single Sign-On Service....191

Setting Up SSO...191
Setting the Security Policy 199
Using SSO in a Web Part 200
Programmatic Administration 205
Viewing the Audit Log...209
Exercise 6-1: Using Single Sign-On 210

Chapter 7 Advanced Web Part Development.............223

Client-Side Web Parts..223
Building Connectable Web Parts 226
Custom Tool Parts 240
Exercise 7-1: Using Terminal Services 243
Exercise 7-2: Connectable Web Parts.........................251
Exercise 7-3: Custom Tool Parts 268

Chapter 8 The Microsoft Office System...............275

Office Integration 275
Developing Office Solutions 286
Exercise 8-1: Building a Smart Document 307
Exercise 8-2: Building a Research Service 322

Chapter 9 Programming SharePoint Services..........333

Document Workflow 333
Accessing Portal Site and User Information..................345
Using SharePoint Web Services...................................349
Exercise 9-1: Creating a Workflow Engine 351
Exercise 9-2: Building a Site Collection Web Part 363
Exercise 9-3: Building a Global Task Web Part 375
Exercise 9-4: Building an Identity Web Part 385

Chapter 10 SharePoint Portal Server Administration 391

Back Up and Restore 391
Site Usage Analysis 393
Cleaning Up Unused Sites 394
Managing the Search Service 397
Exercise 10-1: Establishing Secure Access 403

Chapter 11 Office Solution Accelerators 413

The Microsoft Office System Accelerator for Proposals 414
The Microsoft Office System Accelerator for Recruiting 422
Exercise 11-1: The Accelerator for Proposals 427
Exercise 11-2: The Accelerator for Recruiting 441

Index 471

About the Author

SCOT HILLIER is the Vice President of DataLan Corporation, a Microsoft Gold–Certified partner located in White Plains, New York. Scot is the author of seven books on Microsoft Technologies written over the last ten years. In addition to writing, Scot can often be found presenting to analysts, decision makers, and developers; most recently, he appeared at the NASDAQ stock exchange with Mark Templeton, CEO of Citrix Systems, to support the launch of the MetaFrame Access suite. When not working, Scot can be found at home with his family playing games and taking walks. Scot can be reached at shillier@datalan.com and support for this book may be found at www.sharepointstuff.com.

About the Technical Reviewer

SETH BATES is a Software Architect for DataLan Corporation, a Microsoft Gold-Certified partner in Collaborative Solutions located in White Plains, New York. He has over six years of experience engineering business solutions primarily using Microsoft technologies. With experience in all phases of the software engineering life cycle, Seth provides a broad mix of analysis, design, and implementation expertise to his work. Seth lives in Carmel, New York, with his wife, their new son, and their dog.

Acknowledgments

A BOOK LIKE THIS cannot be created without a significant amount of help from a great team. I'd first like to thank Karen Watterson, who was the first person to ever publish my work—a small technical article—and who was instrumental in getting me thinking about writing again after a two-year break. The book itself was driven by Jim Sumser, who did an outstanding job supporting the effort, editing the text, and generally answering all my little questions. Kylie Johnston functioned as the project manager for the book and made sure everything ran smoothly. I'd also like to give a special thanks to Seth Bates, who was the technical editor for the book. Seth read the book cover to cover and worked every exercise. His patience and attention to detail have gone a long way toward ensuring that the ultimate users of the book—professional developers—will have a smooth road to follow when learning SharePoint Portal Server. Thanks, Seth. Finally, I'd like to thank everyone else at Apress who had a hand in making this book a reality. It was a great experience for me.

I have always said that no one can be successful without the support of their family. In this regard, I am astonishingly fortunate. Nan, your love makes everything possible. You are truly a prayer answered. Ashley, you are a wonderful daughter. Thanks for letting me work and being considerate with requests to "reboot the Internet." Matt, I owe you a few games of "Rise of Nations" to make up for the lost time. Thanks for being such a great son.

Introduction

A LITTLE OVER THREE YEARS AGO, when I completed my sixth book entitled *Scot Hillier's COM+ Programming with Visual Basic* (SAMS, 2000), I thought I was done with technical writing. Since then, I have seen some new technologies emerge, but none that were compelling enough to coax me back to the keyboard. That all changed when I got my hands on the beta of the Microsoft Office System.

Although the Office System certainly has its limitations, several elements really got my attention. The developer in me had a hard time resisting the .NET architecture upon which SharePoint Portal Server (SPS) is based. All true developers love to tinker with products, and the extensive API associated with SPS made development fun again.

From the business perspective, I saw the possibility to create some solutions that would solve real issues that were currently plaguing our business—we needed to organize our file systems and create some light process automation. Both of these tasks are achievable for small and mid-sized organizations using the Office System.

Ultimately, it was the combination of interesting development projects and the promise of improving some business processes that drove me to suggest the book to the Apress staff. In fact, this is really the perspective I tried to bring to the book. I wanted to combine my business needs and programming skills to create a vision of how to use the Office System. You can judge how well that goal was met.

Who This Book Is For

Many years ago, I asked a colleague what professional developers wanted in a book. He responded simply, "Code they can steal." I have never forgotten this advice and it has been the foundation of every book I have written since. This book is therefore targeted squarely at the intermediate to advanced developer in a corporate environment with a pending SPS project. Therefore, readers should be well versed in .NET development with either VB.NET or C# in the Microsoft Visual Studio environment.

How This Book Is Organized

I began my technical career training professional developers in Visual Basic 3.0. As a result, my writing style and chapter organization reflect a training class.

Each chapter in the book begins with an explanation of the appropriate foundational concepts followed by practical exercises to reinforce the explanation. A brief description of each chapter follows.

Chapter 1, SharePoint Business Solutions: This chapter is an overview of SPS and the Office System from a business perspective.

Chapter 2, SharePoint Products and Technologies Overview: This chapter is an overview of SPS and the Office System from a technical perspective, and it contains the detailed instructions necessary to set up the development environment for this book. All of the exercises in the book assume the environment established in this chapter.

Chapter 3, SharePoint Portal Server Basics: This chapter is a detailed look at SPS features and functions and contains detailed instructions on setting up the basic portal.

Chapter 4, SharePoint Content Development: This chapter examines the different ways to create content for SPS that do not explicitly require programming.

Chapter 5, Building Web Parts: This chapter thoroughly investigates the web part life cycle and all the steps necessary to create web parts for SPS.

Chapter 6, The Microsoft Single Sign-On Service: This chapter covers the single sign-on capabilities of SPS and how to use them in web part development.

Chapter 7, Advanced Web Part Development: This chapter examines all of the advanced web part concepts. These include the processes of implementing interfaces for web part interoperability, custom web part properties, and client-side web parts.

Chapter 8, The Microsoft Office System: This chapter focuses on development for Microsoft Office products. In particular, the chapter covers Smart Documents and custom Research Services.

Chapter 9, Programming SharePoint Services: This chapter focuses on programming SharePoint Services through the .NET API. Readers will create a custom workflow engine and create several web parts to overcome limitations found in SharePoint Services.

Chapter 10, SharePoint Portal Server Administration: This chapter presents the basic administration tools associated with SPS.

Chapter 11, Office Solution Accelerators: This chapter examines two of the available *accelerators* for the Office System. Accelerators are solution foundations available as a free download from Microsoft. This chapter examines the proposal and recruiting accelerators.

About the Project Material

This book is intended to give you all of the business and technical background necessary to get a jump start deploying solutions based on Microsoft SharePoint products and technologies. I am assuming that you are an intermediate to advanced technical reader who is involved in an effort to roll out a portal solution. I also assume that you have a reasonable level of business experience to provide context for the work.

Because SharePoint solutions affect the entire enterprise, portions of the book deal with various technical disciplines. In some cases, I will discuss network engineering principles. In other cases, I will write code using Visual Studio .NET. Therefore, readers should have some experience with intermediate networking and a strong understanding of programming concepts.

Throughout the book, I will ask you to participate in the concepts presented. Where a concept is easy to demonstrate, I will provide you with short, hands-on activities. These activities are intended to reinforce basic ideas or demonstrate simple features. You will also find complete exercises at the end of chapters. These exercises are intended as in-depth aids to reinforce several concepts and create a complete vision for a solution. The exercises are a critical part of the book, and readers should complete as many as possible. Additionally, the exercises assume that you have established the development environment defined in Chapter 2. For those who do not want to type in all of the code associated with each exercise, you can access the completed exercises as a download available from the Apress site or `www.sharepointstuff.com`.

I use a wide variety of software products to simulate a true enterprise environment in this book. Throughout, I invite you to try out features and functions of SPS and see how it integrates with other major Microsoft products and technologies. In order to create the basic environment used by this book, you should have the following software available:

- Microsoft Windows 2003, Enterprise Edition

- Microsoft Exchange 2003

- Microsoft Windows Terminal Services

- Microsoft SQL Server 2000

- Microsoft SharePoint Portal Server

- Microsoft Office 2003

- Microsoft InfoPath

- Microsoft Visual Studio .NET

Finally, you should note that I intend this book to be read cover to cover. Unlike some technical books, this one is not intended simply to be a reference that readers access primarily through the index. This book is intended to be an educational experience, and each chapter always assumes that you have read all previous material carefully.

CHAPTER 1

SharePoint Business Solutions

MICROSOFT SHAREPOINT PORTAL SERVER 2003 represents the latest stage in an ongoing workplace evolution that began with the company intranet. This evolutionary process has taken us from simple static HTML pages through dynamic Active Server Pages (ASP) and then Enterprise Information Portals. Throughout this process, the business value of portal technology has not always been clear, but end users have always sensed a level of simplicity within the portal concept that promised a better technology experience. It is the pursuit of this simplicity that has driven the portal market since the mid-1990s.

A Brief History of Portals

My first experience with the Internet was in the early 1990s. I was working for a consulting company writing a traditional fat-client Visual Basic 3.0 application when a colleague called me over to his computer. Although at the time I did not understand, on his screen was an early Internet search engine. He asked me excitedly to watch while he typed in some obscure topic like "Japanese Cuisine." To my amazement a list of documents appeared. He clicked one of the documents and showed me the history of Japanese cooking in America. I was amazed and asked him what application he was running. He said that it wasn't an application; it was the Internet.

That experience opened my eyes not only to the power of the Internet, but to the value of a simplified user interface that places information at your fingertips. These early search engines were really the genesis of the portal market, and that vision influences many of the solutions that we create today. In fact, it was the Internet search engines that first coined the term *portal*. These engines were supposed to be your first stop on the information superhighway.

Intranets

Business organizations were quick to latch on to the idea of the portal. If a search engine worked well on the Internet, then it would also work well for finding information within an organization. Thus the intranet was born.

Early intranet projects represented a significant effort by corporate America to organize information and simplify retrieval. It was not long before most organizations had an intranet site. Typically, these sites were adorned with photos of the company president and a reprint of the current company newsletter. Unfortunately, these intranet sites were built using static content. This meant that a human being had to be responsible for updating the content periodically— a task that turned out to be much more difficult than anyone had originally predicted.

People assigned the task of updating the intranet had to collect information from a variety of sources, assemble that information, and publish it. Often this work required specialized graphics or programming skills that were not readily available within the organization. Soon, updating the intranet became a full-time job. Organizations even went so far as to hire dedicated personnel to maintain these sites.

Often the effort to maintain the intranet site would fail. After a few months, the company headlines and newsletter would remain unchanged as personnel were reassigned and priorities changed. Once the content became stale, end users stopped using the intranet. Enthusiasm waned and the effort was abandoned. Today, most organizations have at least one of these intranet sites that still has the company newsletter from 1997 posted on the home page.

Even though many intranet efforts resulted in failure, organizations continued to believe in the concept of browser-based access to information. The faith of these organizations was grounded in the belief that centralizing information and systems would reduce the total cost of ownership and improve productivity. The intranet failure was attributed to the fact that software development was not the business of these organizations. In order to achieve the promise offered by browsers and portals, organizations would have to turn to software vendors.

Application Portals

In the mid- to late 1990s most software vendors were creating and selling client-server applications. These applications were designed to have a client program installed on the local computer that drew information from a centralized database server. Software vendors, however, were beginning to feel the pressure to create browser-based versions of their products. They were also well aware of the marketing buzz surrounding the use of the word *portal*.

What followed was a significant effort, which is still ongoing, to create these browser-based applications. In nearly all cases where software vendors have created browser-based versions of their applications, they have called them portals. For our purposes, however, this term is inaccurate because most of the products lack the flexibility to truly serve as a portal for an organization. Instead, I will refer to these products as Application Portals.

Enterprise Information Portals

As the Internet bubble continued to expand and "irrational exuberance" gained hold, a new breed of software vendor emerged with a generic portal offering. These generic portals were not built to target a specific application but were intended to be a centralized place for all documents, information, and application access. In order to achieve this generic vision, portal vendors created small programmable units from which you could build any portal you wanted. These small units had lots of clever names that still exist today: parts, nuggets, gadgets, and so on. By the late 1990s, these portal vendors were doing big business migrating entire suites of company applications into the portal. For our purposes, I will refer to these types of portals as Enterprise Information Portals.

Enterprise Information Portals had several flaws that ultimately curtailed their adoption. The first, and most serious, is that they were rushed to market. Because the products were rushed, they were often unstable and always required significant amounts of consulting service work to get them up and running. Enterprise Information Portal projects were always measured in months and sometimes in years.

The second flaw was that many of the vendors mistakenly believed that the Enterprise Information Portal had to ship with document management, collaboration, and customer management features built in. This often led to conflicts within an organization over the fate of existing systems. Customers were often under the impression that they would be stuck using all of the portal features even if they were inferior to their current systems. These flaws led to a sudden stop in the Enterprise Information Portal space. This stop then resulted in consolidation of portal vendors and a reworking of the portal vision.

Microsoft SharePoint Portal Server

Today you can still find examples of all of the various portal offerings. Intranets, Application Portals, and Enterprise Information Portals are still being used, and several vendors are still in business selling these products. The vision, however, has narrowed. Most vendors are no longer touting a complete integration of all company systems. Instead, vendors are focused on smaller accomplishments such as improved collaboration or communication. This is the world in which Microsoft SharePoint Portal Server finds itself.

Microsoft SharePoint Portal Server does not fit neatly into any of the categories I have previously discussed. The primary reason for this is that Microsoft still has a significant commitment to the desktop. In all of the previous portal incarnations, vendors were interested in supplanting the desktop. Microsoft wants to enhance the desktop because it is a significant source of revenue. No one at Microsoft wants to see users move to browser-based computing en masse. Furthermore, Microsoft also has a significant investment in the Office suite. Together the operating system and the Office suite represent a huge part of the Microsoft empire.

As a result, Microsoft SharePoint Portal Server is a hybrid solution that bridges browser-based and client-server concepts. The portal is used to provide collaboration, document management, and searching in harmony with the Microsoft Office suite. Documents located in the portal, for example, are opened, read, and edited with Microsoft Word. Meetings created in the portal are scheduled using Microsoft Outlook. This hybrid solution results in a highly decentralized environment designed to empower the end users to collaborate without restriction. It is indeed a compelling vision, but one that may challenge many organizations that are more comfortable with centralized, "locked-down" desktops.

End-User Challenges

Global competition, or *globalization,* is now the major economic force shaping business decisions. The traditional long-term relationship between companies and their employees is extinct. Companies are constantly looking for ways to make employees more productive in an increasingly competitive marketplace, cut costs, and improve productivity. For their part, employees are typically less loyal to their companies. Today's employees are just as likely to start their own businesses as they are to bring new ideas to their employer. At the same time, technology is creating an increasingly complex work environment. All of these factors combine to create special challenges for businesses and especially end users.

Desktop and Application Complexity

When the desktop metaphor was introduced, it offered a simplified mechanism for interacting with a new, complex, and often scary appliance—the personal computer. The success of the desktop metaphor was that it simplified interaction with a computer. Nontechnical people were not required to learn complex function key combinations in order to use the computer. This metaphor—and above all its simplifying effect—was responsible for the success of graphic operating systems.

Early on, of course, there were several operating systems from several vendors that used the desktop metaphor. Each of these, Apple, IBM, and Microsoft, were competing to dominate the personal computer market. As a result, vendors began to include more functionality in the operating systems. Instead of just a file explorer, computers were loaded with all kinds of applets for managing every aspect of the computer. Vendors even shipped the computer with simple games that became a standard part of the operating system.

Later, after Microsoft had established clear dominance with Windows, it used the operating system to compete against other companies that introduced new technologies. The most famous example of this, of course, is the fight over the Netscape browser. Ultimately, Microsoft was found guilty of using its operating system to unfairly compete against Netscape. However, the constant fear of a small rival suddenly taking over the marketplace has consistently driven Microsoft to add more and more features to its operating system. As a result, the typical desktop is now awash in functionality. You not only have every line-of-business application you need to do your daily job, but you also have CD players, DVD players, and games. You have three or four different document editors available to you. You have two or three ways to get e-mail. Applications have followed suit as well by adding more and more features, reports, and integration points. The desktop and the applications it hosts are complex all over again.

Along with mounting complexity, users are also faced with a lack of standards for application behavior and integration. The most obvious example of this problem can be seen in the use of passwords. Users are now forced to maintain upwards of ten different sets of credentials to access all the client-server, browser-based, and Internet applications they need on a daily basis. Typically, each of these applications has different rules for password length and design. The result is that users are unable to remember all of their credentials without recording them somewhere such as on a Personal Digital Assistant (PDA).

Not only are users forced to manage several sets of credentials, they are also quite often forced to have intimate knowledge of the data sources utilized by applications. A typical example of this intimate knowledge is when an application log-in screen prompts users to select the database or domain they want to access. This seemingly simple request actually forces an end user to understand the network topology of the organization. This is a ridiculous requirement to place on an end user. This same intimate knowledge is also required to access file servers, mapped network drives, and printers.

As if the complexity and variety of information systems were not enough, users are also faced with an explosion of data contained in these systems. A typical organization might have as many as eight customer databases crossing several isolated systems such as Customer Relationship Management (CRM), Enterprise Resource Planning (ERP), multiple spreadsheets, and documents. Each of these systems has a reporting mechanism to access the data, but there is generally no way to see all of the data together to create a single view of a customer, supplier, or partner. Consequently, users are forced to create manual systems to collect and analyze information. This is often done by reentering information into Excel spreadsheets.

In addition to the challenges posed by most information systems, end users have their own personal challenges. Increasingly end users are working from alternate locations other than the central company headquarters. Workers today are highly mobile; they work from home, they work from the road, and they work from other countries. They need constant access to systems even when they are completely disconnected from a network. Many organizations are nothing more than decentralized virtual teams. Working through e-mail and conferences, it is now possible to work with someone for many years and never meet them face to face.

All of this is to say that the computing environment for most end users has become unbearably complicated. In this environment, end users are crying out for simplicity and consolidation. They need tools that give them a more personal view of enterprise resources to cut through the layers of complexity and make them more productive.

Stop for a moment and consider the role of Microsoft Outlook in most organizations. Microsoft Outlook is truly the workhorse of corporate America. Outlook is often the first application an end user opens at the beginning of the day and the last one closed at night. Why? The answer is because end users are trying to impose simplification by using Microsoft Outlook to access their enterprise resources.

Think about it. Your organization may have a document management system, but you generally get your documents as e-mail attachments. Your organization may have an enterprise reporting system, but you get your reports through e-mail as well. This is because end users do not want to use the document management client or wade through the hundreds of reports available in the enterprise reporting system. These systems are too painful to access and too complicated to use. What's more, the end user has probably forgotten her password for the document management system and isn't about to spend 30 minutes on the phone with the help desk to get it reset.

System complexity and variety, overwhelming amounts of data, and work-style challenges have all led end users to a frustrating relationship with their computers. They are begging for simplification, but each new effort rolled out by the IT department only seems to add to the problems. The key to solving this problem lies in creating a user experience that truly consolidates and simplifies.

I should note that it is certainly arguable that SharePoint Portal Server is simply a Microsoft solution to the very complexity the company created in the first place. Although this may be true, the Microsoft foundation in many organizations will not change. It is the rare company indeed that can afford to jettison Microsoft Office and the Windows operating system for a new infrastructure. Therefore, the goal of this book will be to address the issues of complexity head on and try to create a work environment that leads to increased productivity and decreased frustration.

Key SharePoint Features

Although Microsoft SharePoint has a vast numbers of features, a couple are worth mentioning at this early stage because they directly address the issues of consolidation and simplification. First, Microsoft SharePoint allows an organization to consolidate views of enterprise systems directly in the portal through the use of *web parts*. Web parts are programmable elements created using Visual Studio .NET that can access enterprise resources and bring them into the portal. Using these programmable elements, you can create views that cross systems and deliver personalized content to end users. Figure 1-1 shows a typical custom web part accessing a customer database to retrieve phone numbers.

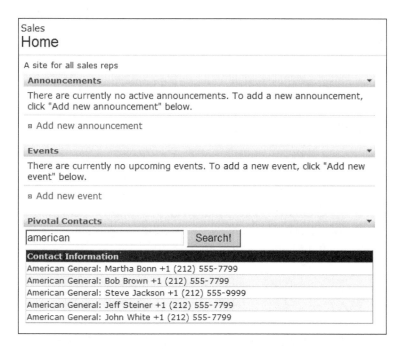

Figure 1-1. A custom web part

Second, when creating these web parts, you can make use of the Microsoft Single Sign-On (SSO) service to act as a proxy for end users when accessing systems. The SSO solution provided by SharePoint stores credentials for line-of-business systems in a centralized data store that can be accessed by authorized web parts. This service reduces the need for end users to remember and enter different credentials for different systems.

The third key element of SharePoint is the *audience* concept. With audiences, you can target content directly to a set of users such as "Sales" or "Customer Service." SharePoint Portal Server allows you to define audiences and recognizes audience members when they enter the portal. Figure 1-2 shows an example of targeted content appearing under the Links for You section of the portal home page.

Figure 1-2. Targeted content in the portal

Understanding Business Scenarios

SharePoint products and technologies form a versatile set of building blocks that you can use to solve a variety of business problems. Like all technical solutions, the success of a SharePoint implementation depends strongly on you understanding the business problem to be solved and creating a cohesive plan to address the issues. In this section, I'll examine some of the common business scenarios in which SharePoint Portal Server can play a role.

Augmenting Personal Productivity

Perhaps the most obvious and straightforward scenario involving a SharePoint deployment is the improvement of personal productivity for employees. I have already addressed in detail the system and data challenges that are facing users of the Windows desktop, but a productivity solution based on SharePoint products and technologies can also be used to make relevant applications, documents, and data available to end users more quickly.

The typical end user spends a significant amount of time searching for documents and information each day. This time is essentially lost productivity during which users browse document management systems, reporting systems, or the Internet. Documents are easily lost on file servers because no standards for file taxonomy, naming, or version control are in use. What's more, business users are often frustrated by technical barriers such as mapped network drives or server names.

A SharePoint solution targeting personal productivity would make relevant content easier to retrieve by creating specific sites for end users. These sites can contain relevant documents, links, and search results for a particular community of users. Such sites eliminate mapped network drives and separate log-ins that hinder productivity. Figure 1-3 shows a document repository targeted at a group of sales professionals.

Figure 1-3. A document repository for sales professionals

Increasing Team Productivity

Along with personal productivity solutions, SharePoint products and technologies can also create team productivity solutions. Increasingly, team productivity is a vital part of business success. Today, most organizations have some combination of formal teams and ad hoc teams. The formal teams are often fixed and departmentalized whereas the other teams may form spontaneously or for a limited time. SharePoint products and technologies support both kinds of teams.

Because formal teams are generally long-lived, a SharePoint solution may contain several fixed sites for these teams. These sites may be created during an initial rollout and then enhanced over time. For these types of teams, SharePoint Portal Server supports both document and meeting workspaces where team members can collaborate even if they are not physically present. Along with meetings and documents, team members can also take advantage of threaded discussion forums that facilitate collaboration even if team members are not present in both time and place. Figure 1-4 shows a typical threaded discussion forum.

Figure 1-4. A threaded discussion forum

Ad hoc teams can benefit from the same collaborative features enjoyed by formal teams, but the sites that host these groups may be created on the fly. SharePoint Portal Server is a truly decentralized model. The philosophy is intended to support team building and productivity from the boardroom to the company softball team. A collaborative solution focused on team building may give site-creation permissions to many individuals who can then easily create team sites directly from within the portal. Figure 1-5 shows a typical site-creation link available within SharePoint Portal Server.

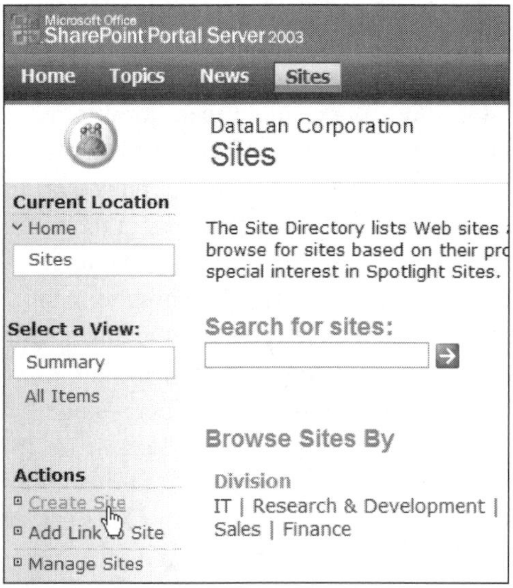

Figure 1-5. A site-creation link

Supporting Remote Workers

Increasingly, the concept of a central place where employees commute to perform work is fading. Organizations today have more telecommuters, outbound offices, and mobile workers than ever before. For an organization, this has typically meant an increase in support costs. Outbound workers often require high-end laptops, remote synchronization, wireless connectivity, and more client-side software. Using a SharePoint solution focused on remote workers, organizations can eliminate some of the maintenance required to support these workers.

Solutions built around SharePoint Portal Server may be made accessible outside of an organization's firewall. Using this type of approach, an organization can make sites and services available to employees as long as they have an Internet connection. This means that telecommuters can easily access required resources with less software installed on their local machine. For mobile workers, such a solution can ease the burden of data synchronization by integrating such operations within the portal.

Integrating with Partners and Customers

Because SharePoint solutions can be safely exposed outside the firewall, they make excellent platforms for integrating with customers and partners. SharePoint Portal Server can host specific self-service sites for key customers and communication sites for partners. This same idea also allows subsidiary companies to communicate and collaborate with parent companies—all without having to integrate at the system level.

Analysis and Design Considerations

SharePoint Portal Server can be remarkably easy to install. In fact, if you follow the single-server deployment strategy, you can have SharePoint Portal Server up and running in 30 minutes. However, that does not mean that it is simple to create an effective business solution using SharePoint products and technologies. The key to properly designing a SharePoint solution is to spend the required time to identify the business problem to be solved and the expected result. Once you understand the solution, then you must document the roles, policies, and systems that constitute the solution. Finally, you must design a solution that incorporates all of the elements in a way that solves the original business problem.

Documenting the Business Vision

For as long as I have been involved in designing software solutions, teams have always agreed in principle that identifying the business problem and understanding the return on investment (ROI) were critical to the success of every project. However, I have rarely seen a team actually engage in these activities, and in the end, this often was a leading factor in the failure of a project.

Shortcutting required analysis is a fact of life in the information technology world, and it is driven equally by managers and engineers. On the management side, project sponsors are frequently unable to articulate the expected return from a technology project. When interviewed, managers are incapable of explaining the productivity increases or cost savings that are expected from a technology effort. Instead, they rely on a vague feeling that the mere presence of a tool, or portal, will surely help the organization be better. This is what I'll call the *tool-only approach*.

On the technical side, most engineers are not trained to look at technology issues as essentially business problems. Instead they look at business issues as primarily technology problems. The typical technical thought process asks the following question: What data does the end user need? Then it asks this: What application provides that data? The solution then is to deploy the application that provides the data and declare the problem solved.

A portal solution based on SharePoint products and technologies is a web of solutions to a myriad of problems. Organizations considering such an implementation would do well to begin by interviewing key project sponsors to document the expected company benefit from such an effort. Sponsors should be clear about the expected productivity increases or cost savings associated with the effort. Use this exercise as a litmus test for the entire project. If a significant return cannot be envisioned for the project, then it may not be worth the effort.

If the return is determined to warrant the project effort, then the correct process is first to create a vision document. The vision document is the first deliverable of the project. This document articulates the business problem, proposed solution, and expected benefit. This document is the highest-level guidance for the project. It acts as the beacon to which the team is headed. In well-run projects, the vision is periodically revisited to ensure that no extraneous effort is expended and that the team is correctly implementing the vision and achieving the desired results.

Documenting Policies and Practices

Once the vision document is completed, the next step is to document the policies and practices that will constrain the use of the solution. Policies and practices act as boundary conditions for the solution. Successful projects exist within these boundaries while solving the original business problem.

Policies are restrictions placed on the organization by its management and articulated as simple statements. For example, the statement "company credit cards are not to be used for personal expenses" is a policy that restricts the use of a company credit card. Similarly, the statement "only port 80 will be open on the firewall" is also a policy. This policy restricts the use and configuration of the company infrastructure. Policies are not easily changed; therefore, a successful project must identify the policies that constrain it.

Practices are similar to policies in that they act as boundary conditions on the solution design. However, practices are more closely associated with the tactical processes used by the organization to do business. For example, the use of an approved vendor list to simplify the purchase process is a practice. Practices are less formal than policies, but they can easily be just as limiting on the final design.

Policies and practices exist at many levels in an organization. Some policies may apply to an entire organization whereas others may be specific to a single process. Initially, you should try to identify the policies and practices that are most likely to constrain the general use of a portal solution. As the portal effort matures, you will identify departmental processes constrained by additional policies and practices. As a starting point, consider the following common areas where policies and practices may affect the initial portal deployment.

Allowing External Access

Determine whether or not personnel will be allowed to access the portal externally. If external access will be allowed, then document the policies for authentication. Determine if a simple user name and password will be sufficient, or whether stronger measures will be required. Specifically, you should determine if Secure Sockets Layer (SSL) and certificates will be required.

Along with system policies, determine if users will be required to access the portal utilizing a two-factor authentication system such as RSA SecurID. SecurID tokens act as virtual ATM cards for the portal. In order to access the portal users must possess the token and know a personal identification number (PIN) number. The passcode generated by the token changes every 60 seconds so a user must be in possession of the token at the time of log-in. The PIN number is a fixed set of numbers known only to the user. The combination of these two elements to complete a log-in request is why it is called *two-factor* authentication. When combined with SSL and certificates, such access schemes are exceedingly hard to hack.

In addition to considerations about personnel access, you should document policies for system deployments. Determine what parts of the system will be deployed behind the firewall or in a Demilitarized Zone (DMZ). All of these issues arise early in a portal development project and will affect the final design significantly.

Negotiating Service-Level Agreements

Based on the business vision, you should determine the expected uptime for the portal. If the portal is functioning as little more than an intranet, perhaps no significant impact occurs if it goes down. On the other hand, some organizations are utilizing the portal as the primary workspace for employees. In this case, a formal service-level agreement should be negotiated for the system.

Along with a service-level agreement, the portal may have to be part of the disaster recovery/business continuity plan. Again, based on the business vision, determine if the criticality of this system warrants a replicated site on the disaster recovery network. If so, make disaster recovery an integral part of the project plan. We have seen many organizations ignore this point and roll out a portal as "just a pilot." These same organizations turn around a few months later and realize they have a single point of failure in their system architecture and a gaping hole in their disaster recovery plan.

Accessing the Application

Determine the policies and practices you will use to provide application access. As I stated earlier, the Microsoft vision of SharePoint solutions incorporates tight integration with Office 2003. If this is in line with your company vision, then you must evaluate your current Office deployment. Give thought to any planned upgrades and how you will handle installation and maintenance on the client machines.

Because the Microsoft vision requires client-side deployments of Office applications, many organizations are combining SharePoint Portal Server with server-based technologies like Windows Terminal Services. Terminal Services is a technology that allows a Windows desktop running on a centralized server to be viewed and operated on a remote computer. Using this technology, organizations can develop significant cost savings by nearly eliminating all client-side installation and maintenance. These server-side installations are then accessed through the Remote Desktop client. Figure 1-6 shows the Remote Desktop client configured to access a server running a SharePoint portal.

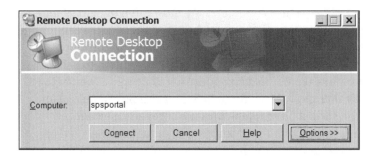

Figure 1-6. Preparing to access Windows Terminal Services

Managing Content

Documents and other content are a significant part of a SharePoint solution. Therefore, organizations must document the policies and practices that determine how the content is created, posted, and managed. Determining the policies and practices surrounding content will have a lot to do with the culture of the organization. In its heart, SharePoint is a distributed solution. This means that it is structured to allow easy content creation and posting. Additionally, sites and subsites can be created without necessarily requiring centralized approval. Many organizations find this philosophy incompatible with the traditional centralized approach to information technology.

Administrators do have significant control over permissions granted to portal users through the use of SharePoint *Roles*; however, every organization will have to determine which people will be responsible for creating and maintaining content. This may be a formal system where each department has a content manager, or it may be a freewheeling approach that lets nearly anyone create a site on the fly and populate it with relevant content. In any case, you should consider these issues carefully before you begin designing the portal.

Working with Audiences, Processes, and Web Parts

One of the most-common mistakes organizations make when deploying a SharePoint portal solution is to structure the constituent sites in a hierarchical fashion that mirrors the departmental structure of the organization. In this design, each department is given a site within the solution and users are expected to find what they need within the site associated with their department. The challenge with this approach is that most people do not work in such a narrow concept. Instead, effective companies are most often organized into cross-discipline teams that consist of members from several departments.

Although somewhat limited in SharePoint Portal Server, the concept of *audiences* is a powerful mechanism for delivering targeted content to people involved in cross-discipline teams. Instead of thinking of people as belonging to a department, classify them by their common needs. A simple example of an audience would be the set of all employees who use company daycare. Obviously this group is independent from any formal organizational hierarchy.

The company departmental hierarchy does have a place in the design of your portal. You can use the departmental structure as a navigation aid for locating the information you need. This is done through the concept of *topics*. Topics provide different organizational views of the portal and its sites. Thus customer information might be a link located under several different topics in the navigational structure, but it exists only once as a site in the solution. Figure 1-7 shows a set of topics within a SharePoint portal home page.

Figure 1-7. Topics are a navigation aid.

After the audiences are identified, you should consider any processes that will be automated within the portal solution. In some cases, you may be trying primarily to create an informational site with all processing occurring outside of the site. In other cases, organizations may want to use the portal solution as a complete work environment that makes the traditional desktop obsolete. Both visions are viable within a SharePoint solution, but creating a true work environment requires a significant investment in web part development to bring system functionality to the portal.

If your portal solution will be automating a significant number of processes, organize the effort by audience. For each audience, list the processes that will be automated within the portal. Then for each process to be automated, create a flowchart that shows how the process will work within the portal.

Automating processes within the portal requires a different mindset than creating full-blown traditional applications. Remember that the automation will occur through the use of web parts. Because web parts are limited in scope and functionality, you should never try to rewrite an entire application to run as a web part. Instead, think of smaller, limited process functionality that you can easily achieve within the portal. Rewriting the sales force automation system as a web part is a bad idea, but creating a web part to display the top ten pending deals is ideal for a web part.

Ultimately, you need a strategy for delivering applications to portal users. Again, this depends upon your vision of the portal solution. If they see your SharePoint solution as an informational site, end users may continue to receive their applications outside of the portal in the traditional way. If you are trying to create a more complete work environment, you may provide links to applications from within the portal. Finally, it is possible to run whole applications within the portal—especially if the applications are web based. Web-based applications can be made to consume an entire page of the portal so that complete access to information and systems is available through a single work environment.

Managing Change

During a presentation, a customer once asked me to describe the most difficult issue surrounding a SharePoint deployment. My answer was immediate. I responded, "It's the same issue as every other project—managing the change for the end users." Change management is the process that helps end users adopt new ways of doing business, and it is never easy. In fact, I would say that change management issues are responsible for more project failures than nearly anything else.

Despite its ability to affect the success of a project, change management is rarely considered in sufficient detail. In my experience, this is because the team is primarily concerned with correctly implementing the technical solution. What's more, technical teams really are not trained to help users through the change management process. Once, I was discussing a portal rollout with an IT director who told me that he was absolutely convinced of the value embodied in our project. His only concern, he said, was how to get the end users to adopt the new environment. Before I could answer him, he muttered under his breath, "I guess we'll just ram it down their throats." Wow!

Successful change management is about educating and assisting end users. Every good portal project must involve some key elements to help end users adapt and be productive. Scheduling end-user training is an obvious first step, but it is rarely enough to ensure success. Instead, consider the entire group of end users and have a complete plan to manage the change.

Begin by mentally dividing the end users into three groups. The first group is the set of people who are excited about the project. This group can be a strong ally in your effort to bring others through the change process. The second group is the set of people who are neutral about the project. This group is waiting to see if the project will be successful before they get behind it. The last group is the set of people who are openly hostile toward the project. This group does not want to change and is typically very vocal about it.

Although the third group is the loudest and cries for the most attention, they should be largely ignored. Instead, I like to start a pilot with the first group. Don't worry about the traditional approach of piloting your project with a particular department. This approach is too narrow and invites people from all three groups into the pilot. This will surely result in someone from group three declaring the project a disaster. Just locate the most enthusiastic people you can—regardless of department—and start a pilot.

Piloting with enthusiastic people guarantees good press. This means that the people in the second group—the ones who are waiting for success—will begin to hear good things about the project. This will result in more people from the second group becoming enthusiastic and joining the first group. Now you can expand your pilot to include more people. In this way, you can continue to build momentum for the project. This strategy can save you a lot of heartache when rolling out something with as much organizational impact as a portal.

Technical Considerations

Along with the business, analysis, and design considerations presented in this chapter, you need to be aware of several technical considerations and limitations. Like all systems, SharePoint products and technologies have minimum hardware requirements. Also, like all software systems, a few compatibility issues may affect your deployment plans.

Server Requirements

When planning for the server installation, both hardware and software requirements must be met. I will address installation in some detail in the next chapter, but this section allows you to start planning your deployment. The following lists the minimum hardware requirements to run SharePoint Portal Server:

- Intel Pentium III–compatible processor

- 512 megabytes (MB) of random access memory (RAM)

- 550 MB of free hard disk space

You should consider a couple of special points when you are setting up SharePoint products and technologies. First, Microsoft SharePoint Portal Server assumes that all the partitions involved in the deployment are formatted as NTFS. Additionally, program and data file paths cannot point to removable or networked storage. Finally, if you are deploying SharePoint Portal Server in a farm using Windows Network Load Balancing (NLB), you should install a second network interface card (NIC) to support communication between servers in the farm.

In addition to the hardware requirements, SharePoint Portal Server has specific software requirements. Most notable is the fact that SharePoint Portal Server requires one of the Windows 2003 operating systems. This does not mean that your entire network has to be upgraded to Windows 2003, but it does mean that you have to have at least one server running the operating system on which you install SharePoint.

You should keep several special considerations in mind when you are deploying the SharePoint software. First, if you choose to run SharePoint Portal Server on Windows Server 2003, Web Edition, you must have Microsoft SQL Server installed on a separate computer. Second, all servers in a server farm must run the same version of Windows 2003, and the same version of SQL Server 2000; however, the computer running SQL Server 2000 does not have to run under Windows 2003. Third, if you are installing SharePoint Portal Server on a domain controller, you must install SQL Server on a separate server. Finally, the following operating system components must be installed on the computer running SharePoint Portal Server:

- Microsoft ASP.NET

- Enabled network COM+ access

- Internet Information Services Manager

- World Wide Web service

Client Requirements

Microsoft SharePoint Portal Server will work with a wide variety of clients. Client machines may be running any operating system from Windows 98 through Windows XP. Client browsers Internet Explorer 5.01 and higher are supported. Although support for previous versions of Office exists, in order to integrate all the functions of SharePoint Portal Server, client machines should have Office 2003 installed.

CHAPTER 2

SharePoint Products and Technologies Overview

THE TERM *SHAREPOINT* REFERS TO MORE than just a portal solution. In fact, the term alone does not refer to any particular product or technology. Instead, it is a catchall term that refers to several different aspects of web-based collaborative solutions. In this chapter, I'll review all of the different products and technologies that are both specific to the term SharePoint as well as related to collaborative solutions in general. This review will help you become familiar with the vocabulary I will use throughout the rest of the book.

Windows Server 2003 Information Worker Infrastructure

With Windows Server 2003, Microsoft has made the productivity of knowledge workers its highest priority. To that end, Windows Server 2003 contains many features designed explicitly to help knowledge workers. The collection of these knowledge worker technologies is known as the Information Worker Infrastructure (IWI). IWI is a set of technologies only loosely related to SharePoint solutions; however, several of these features are worth mentioning because they can be integrated with the collaborative solutions described in this book.

Shadow Copy Folders

In most organizations today, file management is a nightmare. Few organizations beyond the Fortune 1000 truly have a document management system. Instead, most have a set of file servers and mapped network drives that are a chaotic collection of randomly named folders.

On most of these file servers there are few, if any, restrictions on who can create folders, what the names will be, or where files are stored. The result is that end users have a difficult time locating the files that they need to do their job. In fact, most of the time, users simply e-mail documents around the organization— a testament to how difficult it is to find them.

Improving file management, search, and retrieval is a major goal of this book. It is also a major push for Microsoft. Hence, the IWI infrastructure emphasizes file storage improvements. The first of these improvements you'll investigate is the ability to Shadow Copy shared folders.

Shadow Copies are designed to allow end users to recover lost files without any help from a system administrator. A Shadow Copy folder saves the original file and the subsequent changes on a shared file system. Once the changes are saved, end users can recover deleted files and previous file versions with no help from the system administrator. Recovering a lost file or previous version is done by right-clicking a shared file or folder and selecting Properties. From the resulting property sheet, end users can restore files.

To enable Shadow Copies, follow these steps:

1. Open Start ➤ Administrative Tools ➤ Computer Management.

2. In the Computer Management screen, right-click Shared Folders, and select All Tasks ➤ Configure Shadow Copies.

3. Check the box labeled "Enable Shadow Copies".

Folder Redirection

No matter how hard administrators try to centralize computing, end users still use their client machine for many critical tasks. One of the most common uses of the client machine is to save files. The My Documents folder is viewed by most end users as their own personal file system, even when network administrators provide individually mapped network shares to end users.

The Folder Redirection feature of Windows Server 2003 now allows network administrators to redirect client-side folders like My Documents to a server share. This allows the end user to continue to save files into My Documents while guaranteeing that they are properly backed up and shadowed. When redirection is coupled with client-side caching, users can see their documents whether they are connected to the network or mobile.

To enable Folder Redirection, follow these steps:

1. Open Start ➤ Administrative Tools ➤ Active Directory Users and Computers on a domain controller.

2. In the Active Directory Users and Computers screen, right-click the domain or organizational unit (OU) from which you want to redirect the folders and select Properties.

3. In the Properties dialog, select the Group Policy tab.

4. Create a new group Policy by clicking the New button and naming it **Folder Redirection Policy**.

5. Open the new Group Policy object by clicking the Edit button.

6. In the new Group Policy object, expand the tree User Configuration ➤ Windows Settings ➤ Folder Redirection.

7. Right-click the My Documents folder and select Properties.

8. On the Target tab, check "Basic - Redirect everyone's folder to the same location."

9. Under Target Folder Location, select "Create a folder for each user under the root path" and type a Universal Naming Convention (UNC) path for the redirection.

Encrypting File System

Along with improved file management, Windows Server 2003 also supports the encryption of files and folders. Encryption can be applied to files or folders through the Properties dialog. Although encryption is seamless to authorized users, it will prevent unauthorized intruders from viewing the file.

To enable File and Folder Encryption, follow these steps:

1. From Windows Explorer, right-click the file or folder you want to encrypt. The property sheet for the file or folder will appear.

2. On the General tab, click the Advanced button.

3. On the Advanced Attributes screen, check the "Encrypt contents to secure data" box.

Distributed File System

One of the biggest headaches for end users is the collection of mapped network drives that make up the enterprise file system in most organizations. These drive mappings tend to be cryptic and understood only by network engineers. The situation gets even worse if an end user deletes one of the mappings. The result is panic on the part of the end user as files appear to be lost or dependent applications no longer function correctly.

The Distributed File System (DFS) is intended to simplify and consolidate the end-user view of the network file system. DFS allows network administrators to create virtual drives that consolidate several public shares under a single name. This new namespace can look like a single resource to the end user, even if it crosses different servers.

To set up DFS on the server, follow these steps:

1. Open Start ➤ Administrative Tools ➤ Distributed File System.

2. From the Distributed File System screen, select Action ➤ New Root from the menu. The wizard will help you create a new root.

3. After you create a root, you can map multiple shared folders to it to simplify the end-user view of network drives.

SharePoint Services

SharePoint Services are the foundation for all solutions built with SharePoint products and technologies and are considered part of the Windows Server 2003 Information Worker Infrastructure. SharePoint Services are the next version of what was called Team Services under SharePoint 2001. The purpose of SharePoint Services is to provide collaborative services and web sites that support Microsoft Office 2003 and SharePoint Portal Server (SPS). Figure 2-1 shows a conceptual drawing of the relationship between SharePoint Services, SPS, and Microsoft Office 2003.

SharePoint Services is an obvious outgrowth of the same thinking that went into creating the Information Worker Infrastructure of Windows Server 2003. Because SharePoint collaboration often revolves around documents, Microsoft has built in a strong document repository as a central feature. The document repository in SharePoint Services is now SQL-based as opposed to the Web Storage System (WSS) repositories used in the previous version, but it still supports check-in, check-out, and version control.

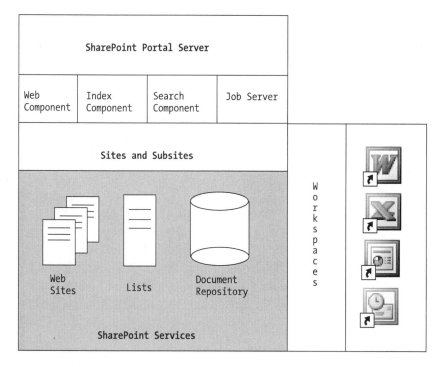

Figure 2-1. Visualizing SharePoint Services

Document repositories are nearly always associated with a web site. SharePoint Services utilizes web sites as ad-hoc virtual conference rooms. If knowledge workers want to collaborate over a document, SharePoint Services will create a web site they can use to exchange information, review the document, and track follow-up actions. All this capability is accessible through either Microsoft Office or SPS.

Web sites created with SharePoint Services contain more than just documents from the repository. Within these sites, SharePoint Services also supports the concept of *lists*. Lists associate the basics of team management with a site. They provide support for inviting members to participate in a meeting, creating task lists, scheduling events, and other fundamentals of collaborative meetings. Figure 2-2 shows a typical SharePoint Services site.

SharePoint Services are designed from the beginning to be extensible. Site creation, lists, and the document repository are all built on a foundation of *web services*. Web services provide the ability for programmers to write extensions to SharePoint Services or whole new applications based on SharePoint Services. Additionally, SharePoint Services supports a built-in framework for extensibility through *web parts*. Web parts are small applets of functionality that may be placed directly into a SharePoint Services site by an end user. Both web services and web parts may be incorporated into solutions by developers using Microsoft Visual Studio .NET 2003.

Figure 2-2. A SharePoint Services site

SharePoint Services have the ability to create and maintain thousands of sites within an organization. Large organizations have the option of creating server farms to support large numbers of sites. Additionally, the SQL-based repository can be clustered to ensure support for business-critical solutions.

Office 2003

With Microsoft Office 2003, Microsoft has made it clear that they envision the Office suite as the primary productivity environment for the knowledge worker. To achieve this end, Microsoft Office 2003 offers complete integration with SharePoint Services. This means that end users can create sites, invite participants, manage lists, and share documents seamlessly using nothing more than Word, Excel, PowerPoint, and Outlook.

The primary mechanisms that interface users with SharePoint Services are two special types of sites called *workspaces*. Office 2003 supports two types of workspaces depending upon the product you are using. If you are primarily interested in collaborating around a document, then Office can create a *document workspace*. On the other hand, if you are more interested in focusing on a meeting with colleagues, then you can use Office to create a *meeting workspace*.

Document workspaces can be associated with any document contained in the SharePoint Services document repository. These workspaces allow multiple people to view and edit documents while keeping track of changes and versions. Along with the document management support, a document workspace also provides related lists such as tasks. Figure 2-3 shows a typical document workspace.

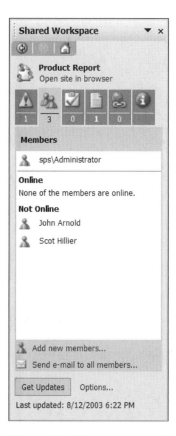

Figure 2-3. A document workspace

Meeting workspaces are associated with meeting requests sent from Microsoft Outlook. When sending out meeting requests, you can set up a meeting workspace for the attendees to use. The workspace keeps track of things like the meeting agenda, assigned tasks, and results. Figure 2-4 shows a typical meeting workspace.

In addition to direct integration with SharePoint Services, Microsoft Office 2003 includes a new form-creation application called InfoPath. InfoPath allows end users to fill out a form online that can be used to programmatically populate a number of line-of-business systems. The idea behind InfoPath is to allow end users to enter information into one form instead of having to rekey the same information into many systems.

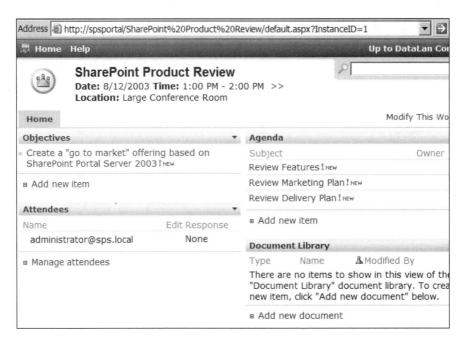

Figure 2-4. A meeting workspace

InfoPath ties neatly into SharePoint Services because the document repository can become the primary storage location for all InfoPath forms. Furthermore, because InfoPath is XML-based, it works well with BizTalk Server to help integrate systems into the SharePoint Services platform.

SharePoint Portal Server

SharePoint Portal Server (SPS) can really be thought of as a specific application built on top of SharePoint Services. Just like the Office suite, SPS can take advantage of sites, membership, lists, and documents. However, the purpose of SPS is different from that of Office. Whereas Microsoft Office uses SharePoint Services primarily to implement ad-hoc collaboration, SPS uses SharePoint Services to implement a more formal and permanent site structure for an organization. Although ad-hoc site creation is still possible, many of the sites in SPS will be long-lived.

The primary entry point into SPS is the portal home page. End users begin at the home page regardless of their role in the organization or place in the company hierarchy. The home page is intended to deliver company announcements and provide tools for locating useful resources. From the portal home page, users can gain access to SharePoint Services sites directly in the browser. From these sites, end users can retrieve documents and lists similar to those available in Microsoft Office 2003.

Installation Considerations

Before beginning your installation of SPS, you need to consider some infrastructure issues. SPS ships with an administrator's guide that has a complete set of planning topics, so I will not try to repeat all of that detail in this section. Instead, I will just go over the major things you should consider.

User Capacity

One of the first issues to consider is the overall capacity of your solution. Although SPS scales well in a test environment, it has some limitations you will want to keep in mind as you plan for deployment. Under most scenarios, these limitations will probably never be reached, but understanding how SPS scales can help keep the solution running trouble-free. All of the test results that are referenced here assume a server-class, dual-processor machine with 1GB of RAM.

Determining the number of concurrent users that can access a SPS installation is tricky at best. The total number of concurrent users is affected not only by the hardware configuration, but also by the activity level of the users themselves. Obviously a system can handle many more simultaneous users that are only occasionally pulling read-only information as opposed to users that are consistently engaged in read-write operations. With that in mind, you can make some statements regarding scalability assuming a moderate level of read-write activity from a group of simultaneous users.

A single web server environment is good for just under 4,000 concurrent users, assuming the required database server is deployed on a separate machine. This number rises to about 6,000 concurrent users when a second web server is added and a farm is created. For three web servers, the number of concurrent users rises to about 7,000.

After four web servers are added to the farm, the number of supported concurrent users does not rise significantly. This is because access to the database server becomes the limiting factor. In order to scale beyond 7,000 concurrent users, a second database server must be added to the infrastructure.

Other Limitations

Along with user capacity, SPS has limits associated with several other key parameters. The limits covered here are not hard limits, but exceeding them can
degrade overall system performance. Generally these limitations are large and
will not affect most organizations; however, they are worth reviewing before you
get started with your installation. Table 2-1 summarizes the key limitations.

Table 2-1. SPS limitations

ITEM	LIMIT
Total web sites in portal	10,000
Total subsites beneath any one web site	1,000
Total documents in any one folder	10,000
Total documents in the repository	2,000,000
Total single document size	50MB
Total entries in any one list	3,000
Total web parts on any one page	100

Deployment Architectures

SPS may be deployed in any of several different scenarios. The business needs of
your organization will largely determine the deployment scenario. In this section, I'll cover each of the deployment scenarios and under what conditions it is
appropriate to implement them.

Each of the available scenarios requires you to deploy several different components that support the portal. SPS itself consists of four major components:
the Web component, Index component, Search component, and the job server.
Additionally, SPS requires a SQL Server installation to support the configuration
of the portal and to act as the document repository. As an option, you can also
choose to install the components to provide backward compatibility between
the SPS 2003 document repository and the SPS 2001 repository.

Stand-Alone Server

The stand-alone server is the simplest deployment option and the one that you will use throughout this book. In a single-server deployment, all four of the SPS components and the SQL Server database reside on a single machine. The SQL Server database may either be a complete installation or the Microsoft SQL Server Desktop Engine (MSDE). The optional components for backward compatibility with SharePoint 2001 may also be installed on the same machine. Exercise 2-1 (at the end of this chapter) will take you through a complete stand-alone server installation that you can use with the rest of this book. Figure 2-5 shows a conceptual drawing of a stand-alone server deployment.

```
┌─────────────────────────────────────────────────────────────┐
│                                                               │
│                   Windows 2003 Server                         │
│                                                               │
├───────────────────────────────────────┬───────────────────────┤
│                                         │                       │
│      SharePoint Portal Server           │    SQL Server         │
│                                         │                       │
├─────────────────┬───────────────────────┤                       │
│                 │                       │                       │
│   Web           │    Index              │                       │
│   Component     │    Component          │                       │
│                 │                       │                       │
├─────────────────┼───────────────────────┤                       │
│                 │                       │                       │
│   Job Server    │    Search             │                       │
│                 │    Component          │                       │
│                 │                       │                       │
└─────────────────┴───────────────────────┴───────────────────────┘
```

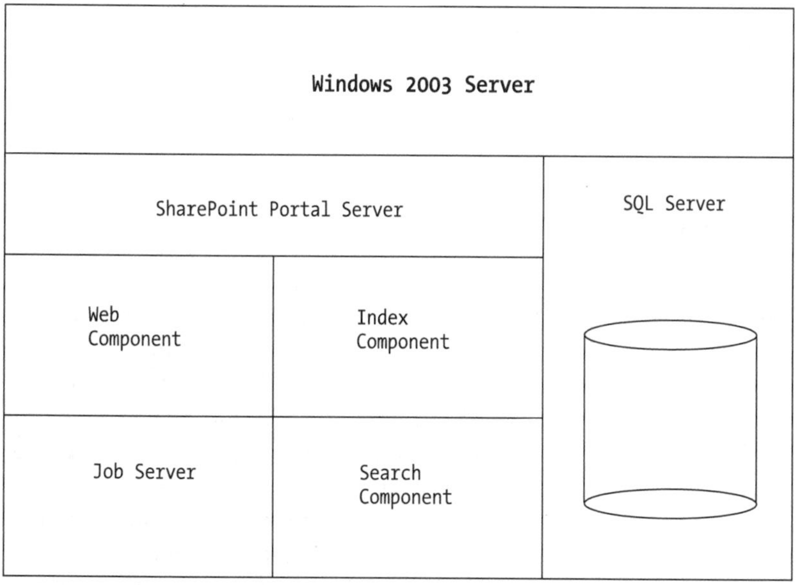

Figure 2-5. A stand-alone server deployment

Small Server Farm

A small server farm is defined as a single web server running the Web component, Index component, Search component, and job server. A second server is used to host SQL Server 2000. In this configuration, you must create an account in the local Power Users group on the web server. This account is then given Security Administrators and Database Creators membership on the SQL Server installation. Detailed installation instructions are available in the administrator's guide and will not be repeated here. Figure 2-6 shows a conceptual drawing of a small server farm deployment.

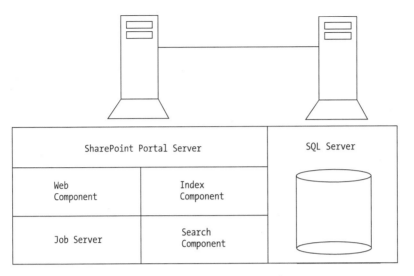

Figure 2-6. A small server farm deployment

Medium Server Farm

A medium server farm is defined as having at least three servers. At least one, but possibly more, servers are set up as web servers with the Search component installed. These servers are joined together using Network Load Balancing (NLB) to function as the front-end web servers that will receive HTTP requests. In this configuration, you must also set up an account in the local Power Users group on each web server. A second server is used to host the Index component and the job server. This server must also have an account set up in the local Power Users group. Finally, a third server hosts SQL Server 2000. Detailed installation instructions are available in the administrator's guide and will not be repeated here. Figure 2-7 shows a conceptual drawing of a medium server farm deployment.

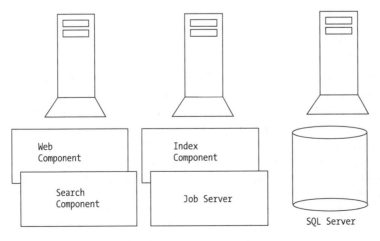

Figure 2-7. A medium server farm deployment

Large Server Farm

A large server farm is defined as having at least six servers. At least two, but possibly more, servers are set up as web servers joined together using NLB. At least two, but no more than four, separate servers are configured with the Search component. At least one, but no more than four, separate servers are configured with the Index component and job server. Finally, at least one separate server hosts SQL Server. Just as in the other scenarios, you must set up an account in the local Power Users group. Detailed installation instructions are available in the administrator's guide and will not be repeated here. Figure 2-8 shows a conceptual drawing of a large farm deployment.

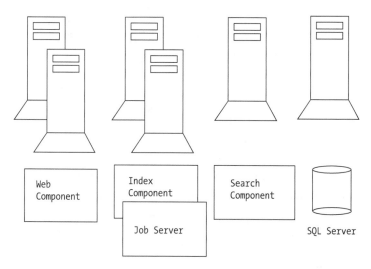

Figure 2-8. A large server farm deployment

Shared Services

In large organizations, you may find it appropriate to create more than one installation of SPS. In these cases, you can simplify deployment and management by using Shared Services. Shared Services allow you to set up a single installation to manage user information, search services, alert services, and single sign-on services. Because these services are likely to be common to all installations within an organization, sharing them makes management and configuration easier.

Upgrading from SharePoint Portal Server 2001

Although it is possible to upgrade an existing SPS 2001 installation to the 2003 version, this is not a process that you should take lightly. First of all, SPS requires Windows Server 2003. This means that you will have to begin the upgrade process by first upgrading all of the web servers in your farm where SPS will be deployed.

During the upgrade process, some of the information contained in SPS2001 is imported into SPS2003, but much of the information is not used. In particular, any portal customizations and web parts you created under SPS2001 will not be used in the upgraded portal. Much of this content is based on fundamentally different technologies with no backward compatibility. Additionally, security roles do not carry over from SPS2001.

Exercise 2-1: Creating a Development Environment

The exercises in this book assume that you have a certain development environment available. This environment includes not only SPS, but also several other products and technologies. In this exercise, you will set up the development environment you will use for the rest of the book.

You should have at least two machines available on which to install Windows Server 2003. For the purposes of this book, you can use almost any edition, but I used the Enterprise Edition. As part of the setup, you will set up one of the servers to act as a domain controller. Therefore, you should be sure that you can dedicate the two machines to your test environment.

This exercise is not intended to walk you through an exhaustive screen-by-screen installation of the required software. Instead, I will focus on special areas of the installation where you need to configure the software or take special care to ensure a correct installation. Generally, I assume that you have some idea of how to install Microsoft server products, but I will try to give enough guidance to keep you from going astray.

Prerequisites

Before beginning your installation, you will want to give some thought to the installation limitations discussed earlier. Although there are certainly pros and cons to any installation, I chose to place Active Directory and Exchange 2003 on one machine and SPS on another. I named the domain controller SPSController and the portal server SPSPortal. Table 2-2 shows a complete list of installed software on each machine.

Table 2-2. Machine configurations

MACHINE	LIST OF SOFTWARE
SPSController	Microsoft Windows Server 2003, Enterprise Edition Active Directory Microsoft Exchange 2003
SPSPortal	Microsoft Windows Server 2003, Enterprise Edition Microsoft SQL Server 2000 Microsoft SharePoint Portal Server 2003 Microsoft Visual Studio .NET 2003
SPSClient	Microsoft Windows XP Professional Microsoft Office 2003 Microsoft InfoPath

Installing Windows Server 2003 on SPSController

In this section, you will install Windows Server 2003 on the SPSController machine and create a domain controller. Although an Active Directory domain is not required for SPS2003 to function, I will assume its presence in exercises throughout the book. When you are finished, you will create a second server and join it to the domain.

 NOTE *The installations of both servers were created using VMware. VMware is a software product that allows a single computer to host multiple operating systems. VMware is not required for the book, but it drastically simplifies the task of managing multiple builds of the operating system. You can obtain VMware from* www.vmware.com.

Getting Started

Boot your computer with the Windows Server 2003, Enterprise Server CD-ROM. Each computer has a different specific method for booting from a CD-ROM. Often you will have to change the boot sequence using the system BIOS. My machines have a special boot menu feature I can select during startup.

Formatting the Partition

When prompted during the installation, be sure to format the installation partition using the NTFS file format. Microsoft SharePoint Portal Server 2003 requires the NTFS file format.

Naming the Server

When prompted during installation, name this machine **SPSController**. I will refer to this name for the domain controller throughout the book, so it is a good idea to stick with the same name I used.

Skip Joining the Domain

When prompted during installation, do not join an existing domain because this server will be promoted later to a domain controller. When you create the second server, you will join it to this new domain.

Creating the Domain Controller

After the initial installation is complete, log on to the local machine as the system administrator. The Manage Your Server applet will open automatically when you log in the first time.

From the Manage Your Server applet, select the right-facing arrow to add or remove a role to the server. After finishing the Preliminary Steps, select to set up the server in a "Typical configuration for a first server". Follow this by entering the name of a new domain (I used **sps.local** and will refer to it throughout the book).

 CAUTION   *When installing a domain controller, Windows will install the DHCP service. If this service is installed, you should not connect this machine to any network with an existing DHCP server. If you do, this server may issue invalid IP addresses to clients on the network! To avoid this, disable the DHCP service after installation by selecting Start ➤ Administrative Tools ➤ DHCP.*

Changing Server Policies

Because the domain controller will largely be used for experimentation, you may want to change the policies for passwords so that they can be simplified and will not expire. This will probably save you some time later because you won't forget the passwords you are using. Select Start ➤ Administrative Tools ➤ Domain Security Policy.

In the Default Domain Security Settings screen, expand the tree under Account Policies and again under Password Policy. Under this node, you can change the definitions for password form and expiration. Figure 2-9 shows the Default Domain Security Settings screen.

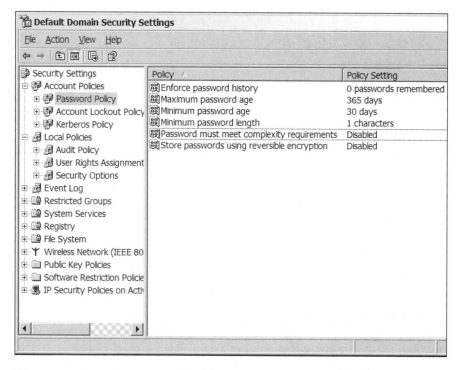

Figure 2-9. Changing password restrictions

Adding Users and Groups to the Domain

After the domain controller is installed, you may add users and groups to Active Directory. Select Start ➤ Administrative Tools ➤ Active Directory Users and Computers. In the management console, select to add a new user or group. Repeat this until you have several users and groups to work with.

Installing Exchange 2003 on SPSController

In this section, you will install Exchange 2003 and set up mailboxes for all the users. Although Exchange 2003 is not specifically required for SPS to run, the collaborative backbone provided by Exchange 2003 significantly enhances the overall business solution. Before you get started installing Exchange 2003, however, you must install a number of prerequisites.

Configuring Prerequisites

Windows Server 2003 is installed without Internet Information Server (IIS) by default. IIS and several of its components are required for Exchange 2003 installation. To add these components, select Start ➤ Control Panel ➤ Add or Remove Programs. Then follow the steps below to add the required prerequisites.

1. On the Add or Remove Programs screen, click the Add/Remove Windows Components button.

2. Select the Application Server component and click Details. Figure 2-10 shows the Application Server screen.

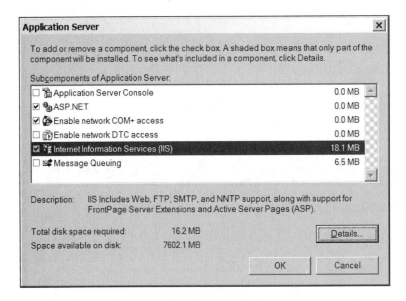

Figure 2-10. Adding required prerequisites

3. On the Application Server screen, check the boxes to install the ASP.NET and Internet Information Services (IIS) components.

4. Highlight the Internet Information Services (IIS) component and click Details. This will bring up the Internet Information Services (IIS) screen shown in Figure 2-11.

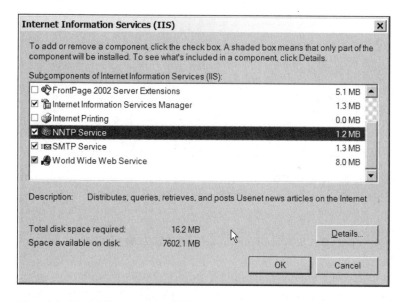

Figure 2-11. Adding required IIS components

5. On the Internet Information Services (IIS) screen, select the NNTP Service and SMTP Service components.

6. Click OK to return to the Application Server screen.

7. Click OK again to return to the Windows Components screen.

8. Click Next to install the components.

Installing Exchange 2003

Once the prerequisites are installed, you may proceed to the installation of Exchange 2003. For the test environment, you can simply choose Typical as your installation type. Figure 2-12 shows the Installation Summary screen.

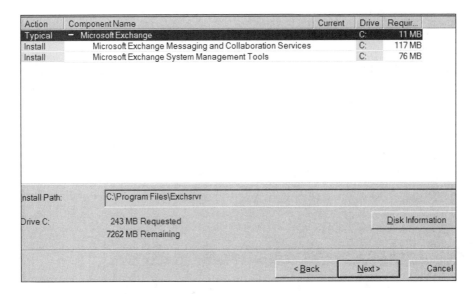

Action	Component Name	Current	Drive	Requir...
Typical	— Microsoft Exchange		C:	11 MB
Install	Microsoft Exchange Messaging and Collaboration Services		C:	117 MB
Install	Microsoft Exchange System Management Tools		C:	76 MB

Install Path: C:\Program Files\Exchsrvr

Drive C: 243 MB Requested   [Disk Information]
              7262 MB Remaining

               [< Back]   [Next >]   [Cancel]

Figure 2-12. Installing Exchange 2003

Configuring Remote Desktop Administration on SPSController

Remote Desktop Administration (RDA) is a handy way to access the SPSController server when you are logged into another machine. This is helpful when you're working the exercises in the book because you can avoid logging into physically separate machines. RDA uses only about 2MB of memory and has little impact on processing power, so Microsoft recommends enabling it for every server.

RDA is enabled from the System Properties dialog on the server. Clients attach to it using the Remote Desktop Connection applet. You can find the client applet at Start ➤ All Programs ➤ Accessories ➤ Communications ➤ Remote Desktop Connection on any Windows XP machine. Follow these steps to enable RDA on SPSController:

1. Select Start ➤ Control Panel ➤ System to open the System Properties dialog.

2. Select the Remote tab.

3. Check the "Allow users to connect remotely to this computer" box, as shown in Figure 2-13.

4. Click OK.

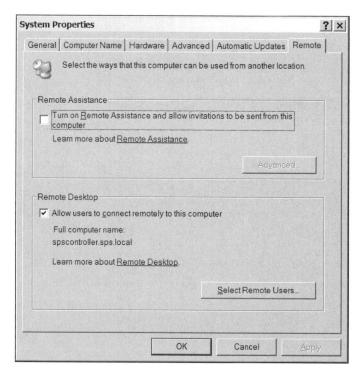

Figure 2-13. Enabling remote desktop administration

Installing Windows Server 2003 on SPSPortal

Follow the same steps as you did for installing Windows Server 2003 on the SPSController server. There are only two differences in the installation process. First, be sure to name this server **SPSPortal**. Second, when prompted during installation, join the sps.local domain that you created earlier.

Configuring ASP.NET

ASP.NET is required on the server where SPS will be installed. In order to install ASP.NET, select Start ➤ Control Panel ➤ Add or Remove Programs. Follow these steps to complete the installation:

1. Click the Add/Remove Windows Components button on the Add or Remove Programs screen.

2. Select Application Server and click the Details button.

3. In the Details screen, select ASP.NET and click OK. Click Next to install the components. Figure 2-14 shows the Details screen.

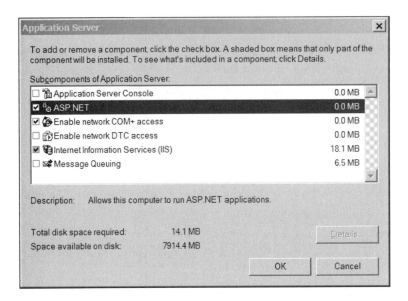

Figure 2-14. Installing ASP.NET

 NOTE *Under Windows Server 2003, Internet Information Server (IIS) is installed in "lock down" mode. This means that only static HTML may be delivered by the web server until dynamic content is explicitly permitted. Generally, when a dynamic content technology like ASP.NET is installed, the installation routine will enable it in the IIS Manager. However, you should be aware of this limitation in case you want to use other types of dynamic content in your solutions.*

Configuring the Internet Explorer

Windows Server 2003 installs Internet Explorer with Enhanced Security activated. Although this is a good default installation for production machines, it can get in the way during testing and experimentation. To disable Enhanced Security, select Start ➤ Control Panel ➤ Add or Remove Programs. Follow these steps:

1. Click the Add/Remove Windows Components button on the Add/Remove Programs screen.

2. Uncheck the "Internet Explorer Enhanced Security Configuration" check box. Click Next to uninstall the components. Figure 2-15 shows the Windows Components screen.

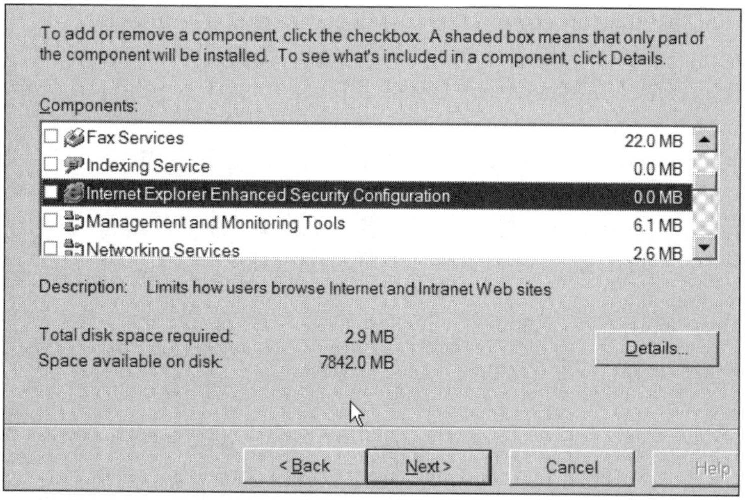

Figure 2-15. Removing Internet Explorer Enhanced Security

Installing SQL Server 2000 on SPSPortal

In a stand-alone server deployment, you may choose to install a separate copy of SQL Server 2000 or use the Microsoft Desktop Database Engine (MSDE). In this installation, I will use a separate copy of SQL Server 2000. The installation of SQL Server 2000 is straightforward with the exception that you will receive a warning indicating that Windows Server 2003 does not support SQL Server 2000. You can continue the installation anyway because you will apply service pack 3 later, which will allow SQL Server 2000 to run on Windows Server 2003. Figure 2-16 shows the warning message.

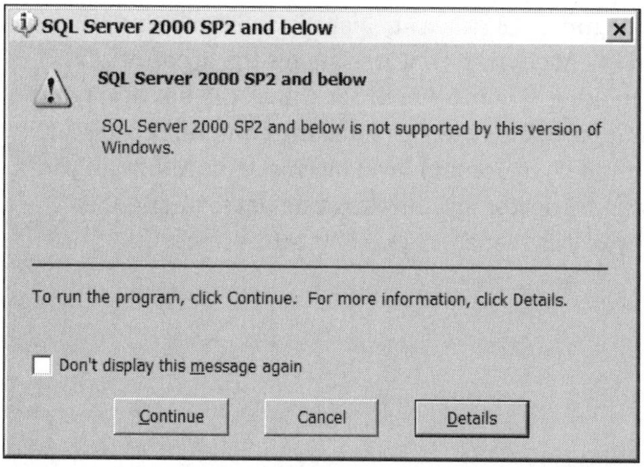

Figure 2-16. SQL Server installation warning

After the initial installation completes, install service pack 3 for SQL Server 2000. During the installation of the service pack, you will be prompted to upgrade the Microsoft Search service. Check the box to perform the required upgrade.

After the installation of the service pack is complete, start the SQL Server service from the SQL Server Service Manager. The Service Manager is accessible by selecting Start ➤ All Programs ➤ Microsoft SQL Server ➤ Service Manager. Be sure that SQL Server is set to start when the server is booted.

Installing SPS on SPSPortal

The installation of SPS2003 follows three phases. First, SharePoint Services are set up on the server. Second, SPS is installed. Finally, proceed through a set of configuration pages to set up the initial portal home. Start by placing the Microsoft SharePoint Portal Server CD in the drive. The installation screen will appear, and you can select "Install Microsoft Office SharePoint Portal Server 2003 components".

When using an existing SQL Server 2000 database, you need to create a domain account for the configuration database administrator. This account needs Create permissions for SQL Server and is also a member of the Local Administrators group for the server where SharePoint is installed. In this installation, I will simply use the Local Administrator account; however, I do not recommend doing so for a production deployment. Figure 2-17 shows the screen where the account information is entered.

Configuring Server Farm Account Settings

Once the initial installation is complete, the browser will open to the Configure Server Farm Account Settings page. This page is part of the SharePoint Portal Server Central Administration site. Figure 2-18 shows the page in the browser.

The Default Content Access Account setting designates the account you should use when creating an index of content sources. Check the box and type the user name of an account that will be used for indexing content. In a typical deployment, this account would have domain-level permissions. Although you would not want to use the administrator account in a true deployment, it is acceptable for your purposes in this scenario (i.e., sps\administrator).

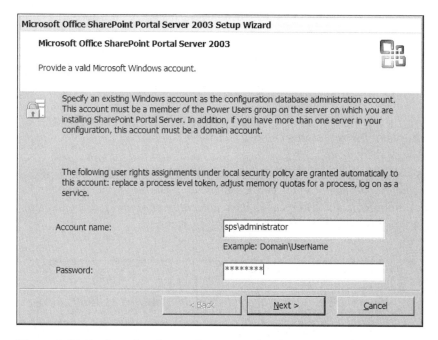

Figure 2-17. Designating the configuration database administrator

Figure 2-18. Configuring server farm account settings

The Portal Site Application Pool Identity setting designates the account under which the portal sites run. This identity determines the permissions associated with the portal sites. In a typical deployment, this account would also have domain-level permissions and would not be an administrator account. Click OK when you have entered the account information.

Configuration Database Settings

The next page that appears is the Specify Configuration Database Settings page for SPSPortal. In this page, select Create Configuration Database. The database server name should be SPSPORTAL. Click OK when you have entered the account information. Figure 2-19 shows the page in the browser.

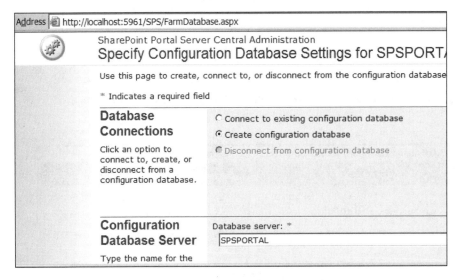

Figure 2-19. Specifying configuration database settings

Configuring Server Farm Account Settings

The next page that appears is the Configure Server Farm Account Settings page for SPSPortal. In this page, add the e-mail address for the administrator in the Contact E-mail Address area (i.e., administrator@sps.local). Click OK when you are done. Figure 2-20 shows the page in the browser.

Figure 2-20. Configuring server farm account settings

Component Assignments

The next page that appears is the Configure Server Topology page for SPSPortal. In this page, examine the section entitled Problems with This Configuration. Typically, this section will indicate that you have not set up the Web component, Search component, Index component, and job server. In the Component Assignments section, you will see the four components listed, but not assigned. To assign these components, click the Change Components button. Figure 2-21 shows part of the page in the browser.

In the Change Component Assignments page, check the boxes for the Web, Search, and Index components. Then select SPSPortal as the job server. This assigns all of the components to the stand-alone server you have created. Click OK when you are done. Figure 2-22 shows the page in the browser.

Global E-mail Settings

After the component assignments are made, you will be returned to the Configure Server Topology page. On this page, click the SPSPortal hyperlink under the Component Assignments section. This link will take you to the SharePoint Portal Server Central Administration page for SPSPortal. On this page, click the hyperlink Server Configuration ➤ Configure E-mail Server Settings. Use this page to specify the global e-mail settings for the Exchange 2003 installation you performed earlier. Figure 2-23 shows the page in the browser.

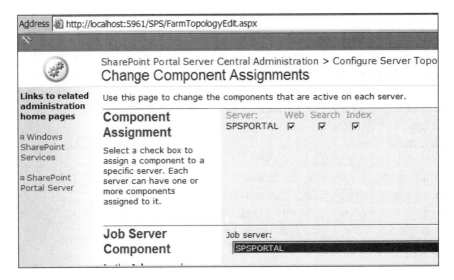

Address | http://localhost:5961/SPS/FarmTopologyView.aspx

View the components currently active on each server. To open SharePoin
Server Central Administration page for each server, click the server name.

Server	Web	Search	Index	Job
SPSPORTAL				

Problems with this Configuration

View current configuration issues with this deployment.

Critical Issues:
No job server has been specified.
The search component is not running anywhere. The portal sites will r
able to search.
The index component is not running anywhere. Search results will bed
out-of-date.
The front-end web server is not running anywhere. No users will be al
access the sites.
The current topology is not supported.

Figure 2-21. Configuring server topology

Address | http://localhost:5961/SPS/FarmTopologyEdit.aspx

SharePoint Portal Server Central Administration > Configure Server Topo
Change Component Assignments

Links to related administration home pages

Use this page to change the components that are active on each server.

Component Assignment

Select a check box to assign a component to a specific server. Each server can have one or more components assigned to it.

Server:	Web	Search	Index
SPSPORTAL	☑	☑	☑

⊞ Windows SharePoint Services

⊞ SharePoint Portal Server

Job Server Component

Job server:
SPSPORTAL

Figure 2-22. Changing component assignments

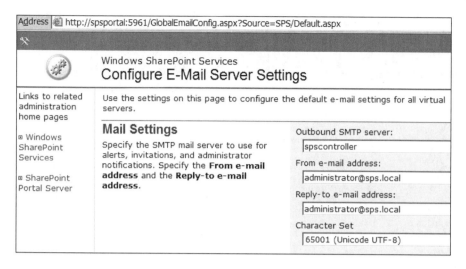

Figure 2-23. Configuring e-mail server settings

Creating the Portal

Once you have finished configuring the e-mail settings, return to the SharePoint Portal Server Central Administration page. On this page click the hyperlink Portal Site and Virtual Server Configuration ➤ Create a portal site. This will open the Create Portal Site for SPSPortal page. In this page, specify a name for the new portal (e.g., DataLan Corporation), and contact information for the portal owner. Click OK to create your new portal. Figure 2-24 shows the new portal home page.

Adding New Users

Once the new portal is created, you will need to give other users permission to access it. You can grant this permission directly from the portal home page. In the lower-right corner of the portal, select Finishing Up ➤ Give Users Access to the Portal. This will open the Manage Users page.

SPS supports several different user roles that I will discuss later. For now, simply add a couple of accounts and assign them as Members. When you add the new members, each user will receive an e-mail letting them know that they have been added to the list of authorized users. Figure 2-25 shows the e-mail in Outlook 2003.

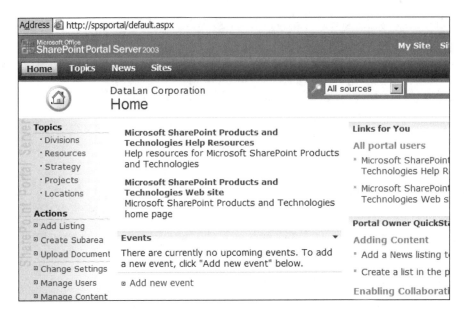

Figure 2-24. Creating the new portal

Figure 2-25. Inviting users to the new portal

Installing Visual Studio.NET 2003 on SPSPortal

Visual Studio.NET 2003 is required to work the code examples and exercises in the later chapters of the book. In your installation, you will set it up directly on the SPSPortal server. There are no major issues with the initial installation of the software; however, you should be sure to install both VB.NET and C# because the book contains examples written in both languages.

Preparing SPSClient

In order to work with the examples in the book, you will need to create at least one client machine running Windows XP Professional. You do not need to have any special concerns for the installation other than to join the client machine to the domain you created earlier. After the operating system is installed, you will need to install Microsoft Office 2003 and Microsoft InfoPath. Both of these installations are straightforward; you can simply use the typical installations.

SharePoint Portal Server Basics

SHAREPOINT PORTAL SERVER (SPS) IS reasonably simple to install, but it is challenging to configure. Not only do you have to plan and implement a suitable site structure, but you must also configure a number of features. In this chapter, I will cover the fundamentals of administration necessary to get the portal deployed to end users.

Understanding Portal Structure

When you first install SPS and view the home page, you will notice that a default structure has been created for you. As with most default portals, you will want to modify the structure significantly before making it accessible to end users. Modifying the structure, however, should not be done lightly. A properly designed portal structure is critical for end-user success. If you spend the time necessary to plan out how the portal will be accessed and searched, end users will readily accept it as valuable. If you fail to implement a strong structure, you run a great risk of having the portal marginalized or simply rejected outright.

Areas

The core structure of the portal is based on the concept of *areas*. Areas in SPS function to accomplish two key objectives. First, areas organize the portal to help users locate information, documents, and resources. Second, areas function like a site map to facilitate browsing of the portal.

In the default portal initially created by SPS, you can view the areas by first clicking the Site Settings link on the portal home page. Site Settings is a link that is available to members of the Administrator site group on almost every page of the portal site. Clicking this link always takes you to an appropriate set of administrative activities for the current site. From the Site Settings page, you can easily view the portal structure. Simply click the link Portal Site Content ➤ Manage Portal Site Structure. Figure 3-1 shows the site structure of the default portal.

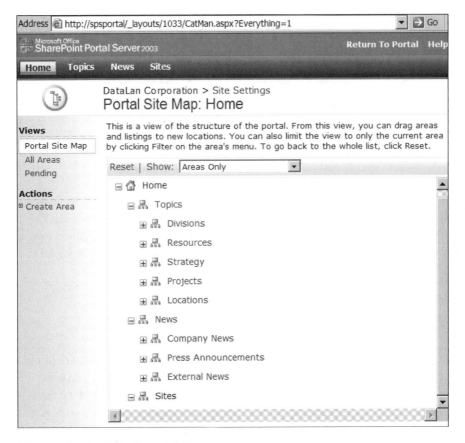

Figure 3-1. The default portal structure

Notice that the default portal structure is divided into a hierarchy of areas. Underneath the Home node are the Topics, News, and Sites areas. Each of these areas may in turn have any given number of subareas. SPS can easily scale to thousands of areas and subareas.

You can create new areas directly from the site map. When you create a new area for the site, you may specify where it should appear in the hierarchy as well as the dates on which it should appear. Creating an area always results in the addition of a new web page to the portal. You can access any of these pages by clicking their name in the site map.

To create a new area, follow these steps:

1. From the site map, click the Create Area link located in the Actions list. This will bring up the Create Area page.

2. On the Create Area page, name the new area **Information Technology** and give it a description.

3. Click OK to create the new area. When you return to the site map, the new area should be visible.

4. Now carefully click and drag the area icon and move the new area onto the existing Divisions area.

5. Expand the Divisions area. Figure 3-2 shows the final site map.

Figure 3-2. Adding a new area

All areas in SPS can contain various elements including links, lists, and documents. From this perspective, all areas are essentially created equal. The difference between the three types of areas is their intended use.

Topics Areas

Topics areas are designed to organize and publish information by subject area. They are intended to be limited to a single subject and to provide specific content on that subject. When using topics, you may either create new content specifically for a topic, or assign existing content to a topic.

Designing the portal topics and properly assigning content to them can be time consuming and error prone. This is especially true if you are trying to migrate a large volume of existing content into a new installation of SPS. Fortunately, SPS ships with a tool to help assign content to topics called the Topic Assistant. The Topic Assistant can be found on the Site Settings page for the portal. Click the link Portal Site Content ➤ Use Topic Assistant.

Before you can use the Topic Assistant effectively, you must enable and train it. Enabling the Topic Assistant is simply a matter of checking the box on the Use Topic Assistant page. Once this is enabled, you can then select the precision with which you want the documents organized. Selecting high precision results in fewer documents being categorized, but it ensures greater accuracy in the results. Low precision will categorize more documents, but the accuracy will suffer as a result. Figure 3-3 shows the page for enabling and training the Topic Assistant.

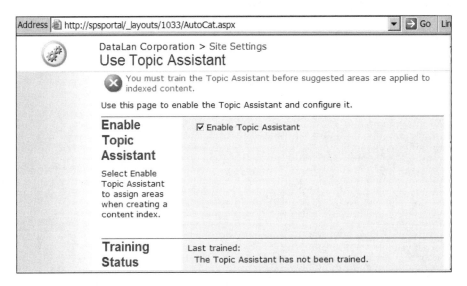

Figure 3-3. Enabling and training the Topic Assistant

Before the Topic Assistant can function correctly, you must have sufficient content available in the portal to properly train it. You can make the required content available either by adding it manually to an existing topic or by crawling existing external content with the Index component. In either case, make sure that you have manually categorized enough content to adequately represent the different topics in the portal. I will detail how to use the Topic Assistant in the exercise at the end of the chapter.

To categorize a document, follow these steps:

1. Navigate to the portal home page.

2. On the home page, click Topics.

3. On the Topics page, click the Human Resources link.

4. On the Human Resources page, click the Upload Document link.

5. On the Upload Document page, click the Browse button and select a file to upload.

6. Fill in the Owner, Description, and Status fields for the new document.

7. Click the Save and Close link.

8. On the Add Listing page, click OK. This will add the document to the current topic.

9. From the Human Resources topic, select Change Settings.

10. On the Change Settings page, click the Search tab.

11. On the Search tab, select the option to include the area when categorizing content with the Topic Assistant.

News Areas

News areas are listings intended to highlight important portal content. When you add news to the portal, it can come from either existing content or new content you type directly into the portal. Once created, a news item then appears as a headline in the portal.

To create a news item, follow these steps:

1. On the portal home page, click the News link. This opens the News page.

2. On the News page, click the Add News link from the Actions list. This opens the Add News page.

3. On the Add News page, enter a title and description for a new news item.

4. In the Content section of the Add News page, select to "Add news listing by entering text."

5. Click the Open Text Editor button.

6. In the text editor, add some content for the news item and click OK.

7. On the Add News page, click OK to finalize the news item.

Sites Areas

Sites areas are designed to facilitate navigation of the sites within the portal. Do not confuse a site area with an actual site. Remember, areas are intended to simplify navigation of the portal. When you create a new site, you can associate it with any number of areas including Topics and News.

Sites

Actual sites in SPS are intended to enhance team productivity. Sites are normally created for cross-functional teams, project teams, and the like. When creating a site, you can select from several different templates depending upon the intended use of the site. Sites can contain various elements including documents, images, tasks, contacts, events, discussions, and surveys.

Portal users can search for sites of interest using the Sites page accessible from the portal home page. End users can also locate sites by using links created on area pages. New sites can be highlighted as special interest sites or just appear as a quick link for a period of time.

Here are the steps to follow to create a site:

1. On the portal home page, click the Sites link. This opens the Sites page.

2. On the Sites page, click the Create Site link from the Actions list. This opens the New SharePoint Site page.

3. On the New SharePoint Site page, fill in the information for title, description, and location.

4. Click the Create button. This opens the Add Link to Site page.

5. On the Add Link to Site page, select the areas to associate with the site.

6. Click OK. This opens the Template Selection page.

7. On the Template Selection page, select Team Site and click OK. Figure 3-4 shows the final site.

Figure 3-4. Creating a new site

Self-Service Site Creation

Normally, users of the portal cannot create new sites in the portal. However, you can configure SPS to allow users to create sites using Self-Service Site Creation (SSSC). When enabled, users can create their own top-level sites without any special permission.

SSSC is part of the Windows SharePoint Services and is configured through the SPS Central Administration page. You can access the Central Administration page by being logged in as an administrator and selecting Start ➤ All Programs ➤ SharePoint Portal Server ➤ SharePoint Central Administration. From this page, you can access the Windows SharePoint Services administration by clicking the link on the top-left side of the page.

From the Windows SharePoint Services page, you can administer your virtual server by selecting Virtual Server Configuration ➤ Configure Virtual Server Settings. This opens a page that lists all the virtual servers. Selecting one opens the Virtual Server Settings page shown in Figure 3-5.

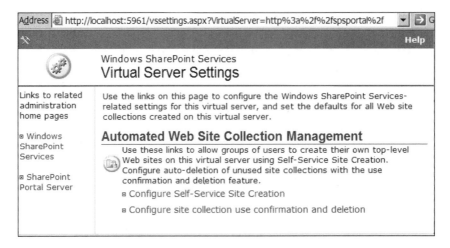

Figure 3-5. Virtual Server Settings

Using the Virtual Server Settings page, you can enable or disable SSSC for the portal. Once enabled, end users will be able to create their own sites directly from the Sites directory. Figure 3-6 shows the Create Site link in the Actions list of the Site directory.

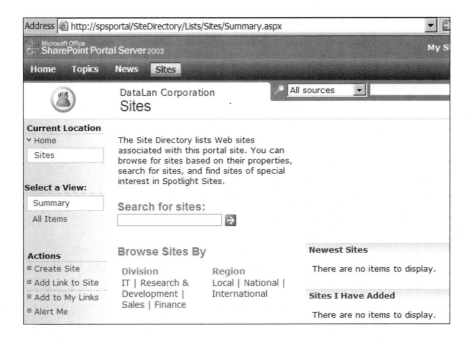

Figure 3-6. Self-Service Site Creation

Managing Users

Once the portal structure is designed and implemented, you will want to assign permissions to portal users. Adding users is relatively straightforward. In fact, you added some users after the portal was installed in Chapter 2. However, determining the permissions that should be granted to each user requires understanding and planning.

Understanding Site Groups

In order to manage users, you must begin by understanding the role-based permissions system upon which SPS operates. SPS refers to the various roles it provides as *site groups*. In SPS, you can assign portal users to the Reader, Contributor, Web Designer, Administrator, Content Manager, or Member site groups.

Each of the site groups in SPS has a corresponding set of rights. These rights are associated with a particular site group initially, but you can easily change the assignments of rights. You can also create your own custom site groups with specific rights you assign.

Before assigning users to site groups, carefully consider their needs. The vast majority of users are likely to be good candidates for the Member site group. This group allows a user to access all of the elements in the portal and personalize their environment.

In a typical portal deployment, 20 to 40 percent of the user community will belong to the Contributor site group. These individuals have additional limited management capabilities associated with lists and can also make use of the document management features of SPS. In some deployments, organizations may even choose to add the majority of users to this group, effectively eliminating the Member site group.

In contrast to the Member and Contributor groups, most organizations will assign less than 10 percent of their users to the Content Manager site group. This group is responsible for reviewing and approving content. In order to properly moderate the posted content, this group should be small.

Generally, the Web Designer and Administrator site groups will have small populations. These groups will be limited to individuals who need special rights to create content or manage the portal. *Web designers* are specialized users responsible for advanced content, formatting, and appearance, whereas *administrators* have complete control over the portal and all its settings.

The least used of all the site groups is the Reader group. This group is useful only for delivering content to specialized groups such as customers or partners. In these cases, only limited functionality is required. Each specific right defined in SPS is explained in the following list, and Table 3-1 summarizes the rights assigned to each site group.

View Area: This right allows a user to view an area and its contents.

View Pages: This right allows a user to view pages within an area.

Add Items: This right allows a user to add items to lists within an area and add documents to libraries.

Edit Items: This right allows a user to edit items in lists, edit documents in a library, and edit web part pages contained in document libraries.

Delete Items: This right allows a user to delete items from a list in an area or a document in a library.

Manage Personal Views: This right allows a user to create, edit, and delete personal views of lists.

Add/Remove Personal Web Parts: This right allows a user to add or remove web parts from a personalized page.

Update Personal Web Parts: This right allows a user to change web part settings to personalize content.

Cancel Check Out: This right allows a user to check in a document to a library without saving the current changes even if they are not the one who checked out the document.

Add and Customize Pages: This right allows a user to use an editor to change HTML pages, web part pages, and portal content.

Create Area: This right allows a user to create a new area in the portal.

Manage Area: This right allows a user to change the properties of an area.

Manage Area Permissions: This right allows a user to change the user rights associated with an area.

Apply Style Sheets: This right allows a user to apply a style sheet to an area or the entire site.

Browse Directories: This right allows a user to browse the directories in an area.

Create Personal Site: This right allows a user to create a personal site in the portal.

Create Sites: This right allows a user to create a new site in the portal if SSSC is enabled.

Use Personal Features: This right allows a user to use alerts and personal sites in the portal.

Manage Alerts: This right allows a user to change alert settings for the portal and users.

Manage User Profiles: This right allows a user to add, delete, and change information associated with the profiles of portal users.

Manage Audiences: This right allows a user to add, delete, and change the membership of an audience.

Manage Portal Site: This right allows a user to manage portal and site settings.

Manage Search: This right allows a user to add, delete, and change index and search settings.

Search: This right allows a user to search the portal site and associated content.

Table 3-1. Site Groups and Rights

RIGHT	READER	CONTRIBUTOR	WEB DESIGNER	ADMINISTRATOR	CONTENT MANAGER	MEMBER
View Area	X	X	X	X	X	X
View Pages	X	X	X	X	X	X
Add Items	—	X	X	X	X	X
Edit Items	—	X	X	X	X	—
Delete Items	—	X	X	X	X	—
Manage Personal Views	—	X	X	X	X	—
Add/Remove Personal Web Parts	—	X	X	X	X	X
Update Personal Web Parts	—	X	X	X	X	X
Cancel Check Out	—	—	X	X	X	—

Table 3-1. Site Groups and Rights, continued

RIGHT	READER	CONTRIBUTOR	WEB DESIGNER	ADMINISTRATOR	CONTENT MANAGER	MEMBER
Add and Customize Pages	—	—	X	X	X	—
Create Area	—	—	X	X	X	—
Manage Area	—	—	X	X	X	—
Manage Area Permissions	—	—	—	X	—	—
Apply Style Sheets	—	—	X	X	—	—
Browse Directories	—	X	X	X	X	—
Create Personal Site	—	X	X	X	X	X
Create Sites	—	X	X	X	X	X
Use Personal Features	—	X	X	X	X	X
Manage Alerts	—	—	—	X	—	—
Manage User Profiles	—	—	—	X	—	—
Manage Audiences	—	—	—	X	—	—
Manage Portal Site	—	—	X	X	—	—
Manage Search	—	—	—	X	—	—
Search	X	X	X	X	X	X

Adding Users

Once you have planned out the membership of each site group, you are ready to add users to the groups. In order to add users to site groups, you should be logged in as a member of the Administrator site group. The simplest way to get started adding users is to navigate to Site Settings ➤ Manage Users.

On the Manage Users page, you can easily add users and groups from the directory. When you select to add users, SPS provides a screen to select users and groups from Active Directory. Figure 3-7 shows the selection page.

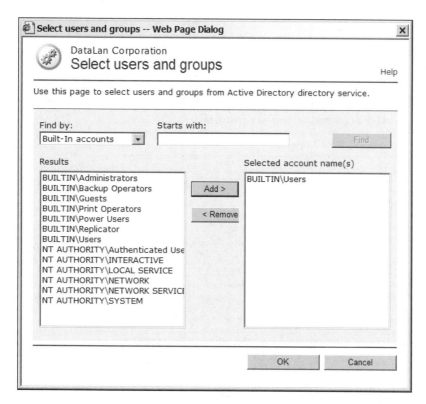

Figure 3-7. Selecting users and groups from Active Directory

In the absence of any separate action, subsites created in the portal will inherit the security settings of their parent. However, you can change the settings to allow customized permissions for any site. Generally, as you move deeper into subsites on the portal, the content targets smaller groups with greater permissions. As an example, sites created specifically for IT projects might allow access to just the project team but with expanded permissions to manage content.

Follow these steps to add users:

1. From the portal home page, click the Site Settings link.

2. On the Site Settings page, select General Settings ➤ Manage Users. This opens the Manage Users page.

3. On the Manage Users page, click the Add Users link. This opens the Add Users page.

4. On the Add Users page, type a user name in the form domain\name and select the site group where the user will be added.

5. Click Next.

6. On the next page, verify the e-mail information for the new user. You can modify the message if you want. Then click Finish. Figure 3-8 shows a typical list of users added to the portal.

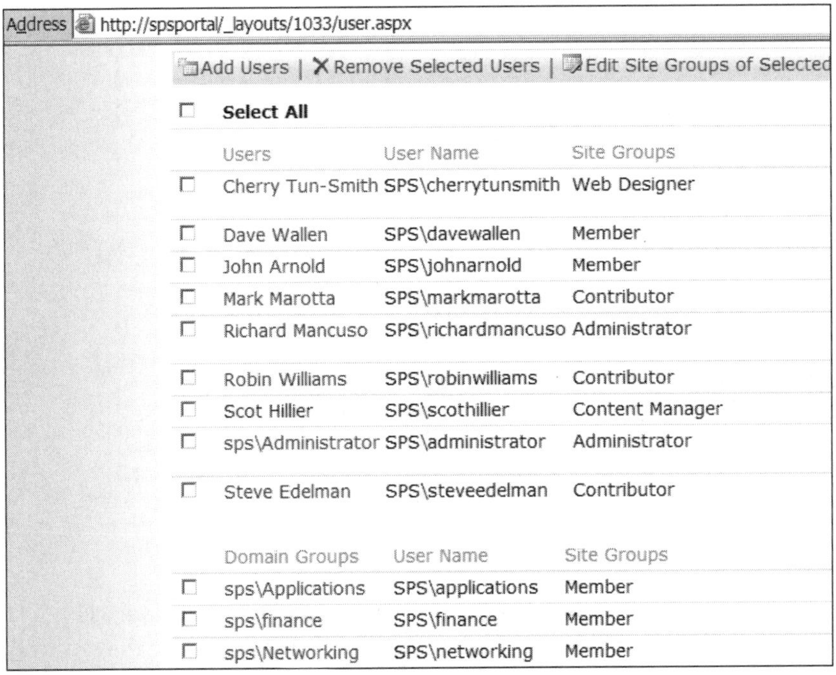

Figure 3-8. Users and groups assigned to site groups

Active Directory Account Creation Mode

Along with the normal domain account mode, SPS also supports a special account mode known as Active Directory Account Creation (ADAC). This mode is intended for use by Internet Service Providers (ISP) who support large constituencies that are not members of the hosting domain. In ADAC mode, users are entered using e-mail addresses instead of domain accounts. In this way, an ISP can host Internet users without having to specifically add them to a domain.

It's important to note that ADAC is incompatible with the normal domain account mode. During the installation of SharePoint Services, you select in which mode the site will operate. After you make the selection, you cannot alter it. Throughout this book, I assume that SharePoint Services are operating in domain account mode.

Understanding User Profiles

One of the primary business reasons for deploying a portal like SPS is to improve employee productivity. Generally this productivity increase is realized through the simplification and personalization of enterprise resources viewed by the end user. If portal users have quick access to the documents, information, and people they need to do their job, they will in turn be more productive.

SPS addresses simplification and personalization through the use of *user profiles*. Whereas site groups are primarily vehicles to address user privileges, user profiles provide detailed information about portal users so that content may be targeted to interested groups of users. Additionally, profiles can be used to include information about people in site searches, which allows a portal user to locate an area expert for assistance.

Before you can investigate the uses of profiles later in the book, you must create them. The simplest way to create a set of profiles for your portal users is to import them directly from Active Directory. You can access the tools for profile management by starting at the portal home page and clicking on the Site Settings link. On the Site Settings page select User Profile, Audiences, and Personal Sites ➤ Manage Profile Database. This opens the Manage Profile Database page.

On the Manage Profile Database page, you can set up a recurring schedule to import profiles from Active Directory. The simplest way to set up the import is to click the Specify Source link, which opens the Configure Profile Import page. On this page, you may specify the source of the profile information and schedule a recurring import.

To import user profiles, take these steps:

1. Log in to the portal in the Administrator site group.

2. From the portal home page, click Site Settings.

3. From the Site Settings page, select User Profile, Audiences, and Personal Sites ➤ Manage Profile Database.

4. From the Manage Profile Database page, select Profile and Import Settings ➤ Specify Source.

NOTE *If you receive this error message, "Failed to retrieve the current domain name from the Active Directory directory services," then you should set up a custom source as described in the paragraph following these steps.*

5.   On the Configure Profile Import page, select Current Domain under the Source section.

6.   Provide an appropriate name and password to run the import.

7.   Set up a full and incremental schedule, if you want one.

8.   Click OK.

9.   On the Manage Profile Database page, click the Start Full Import link.

For more complex environments than I have set up for this book, it may be necessary to define a custom source for the profile import. When you define a custom source on the Configure Profile Import page, you will be prompted to specifically name the domain controller and domain for the import source. You will also have to define a valid search base for the import and a valid Active Directory filter. As an example, a valid search base for my environment is DC=sps,DC=local and a valid filter is objectClass=User.

Once the import is complete, click the View User Profiles link on the Manage Profile Database page to see the results of the import. Examine the list of objects that were imported and delete any that are inappropriate, such as system objects. Once you have the import cleaned up, you can examine a specific profile to see what information is available.

The value of the import will obviously depend upon how much information is available in Active Directory. In any case, the profiles in SPS are more extensive than the entries found in Active Directory, so you will probably have to enter some information by hand. The good news is that portal users can edit their own profile, so you can simply have them update the profile as a first order of business when they use the portal.

Libraries

Once you have defined your site structure and added users to site groups, you will want to begin to make content available. Although SPS can present several different types of content, the backbone of the SPS vision is the sharing of files among site users. In order to share files, SPS makes use of libraries. The three main types of libraries available in SPS are *document libraries, form libraries,* and *picture libraries.*

Document Libraries

In many ways, document libraries are the central feature of SPS. Nearly all site users will be involved with creating, retrieving, and sharing documents. You can create document libraries at any level in the portal hierarchy, and assign different permissions to each one. This makes them very useful for facilitating collaboration among organizational teams. What's more, you'll see later that document libraries are fully integrated with Microsoft Office 2003.

Accessing Document Libraries

By default, every area contains a document library, but when you first visit an area, the area page is largely blank. Many of the content elements are hidden from view, including the built-in document library. The simplest way to make the document library visible is for a member of the Content Manager, Web Designer, or Administrator site group to modify the page by creating a listing of the documents. Every site group except Reader has permission to add documents to the library using the Upload Document link on the Actions list. However, Reader and Member will not be able to see the documents until the library is added to a listing. In theory, a Member site group can also create a listing for the library, but in order to add a listing, you need to know the URL of the item. This will most likely be challenging for a typical Member.

Follow these steps to display a document library list:

1. Log in to the portal as a member of the Content Manager, Web Designer, or Administrator site group.

2. Navigate to any area under Topics.

3. Select Edit Page from the Actions list.

4. Select Modify Shared Page ➤ Add Web Parts ➤ Browse from the upper-right corner of the page.

5. From the Web Parts list click and drag the document library into one of the zones on the page. Figure 3-9 shows the modified page.

6. When you are finished, click View Page on the Actions list.

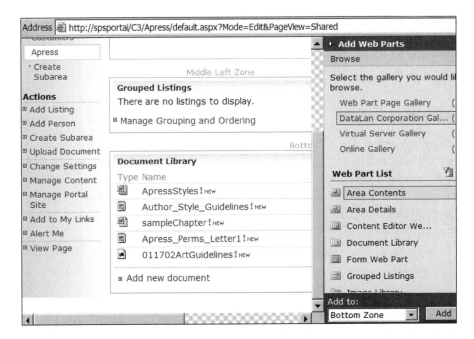

Figure 3-9. Displaying a document library list

When the area page is modified, it creates a listing of all of the documents in the library. Any site group can open a document directly from the list. Every site group except Reader can also add documents using the Add New Document link that appears below the list. They can also access the complete functionality of the document library by clicking Document Library at the top of the list. This link opens the document library page. From this page, you can create or upload new documents.

When new documents are added to the library, a document profile is created. The document profile is a set of properties that forms metadata about the document. This includes not only obvious elements such as name and description, but it also includes a Status field where you can specify the quality of the document as rough, draft, in review, or final. The document profile associated with the library can be modified to include more and different columns. On the Document Library page, clicking the link Modify Settings and Columns will allow you to add and delete properties in the profile.

Document Management Features

Once documents are part of the library, users can take advantage of the document management features built into SPS. These document management features include check-in, check-out, and version control. Although the Member site group can add new documents and set property values for a document profile, it cannot edit the document or change the properties. In fact, most of the document management capabilities of SPS require that you at least belong to the Contributor site group. Access to the document management features is accomplished through a drop-down list associated with each document. Figure 3-10 shows the drop-down list for a document in a library.

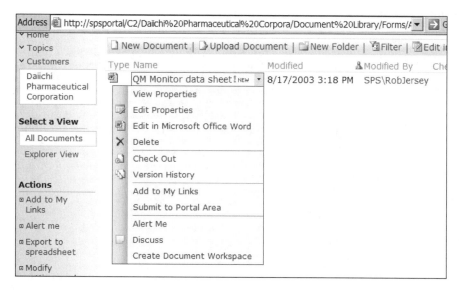

Figure 3-10. Accessing document management features

You can check out documents directly from the document library using the drop-down list. When a document is checked out, it is still listed in the document library and visible to site users. The document can be opened; however, no changes may be saved to the document except by the individual who has it checked out.

Once changes are made to the document, it may be checked back into the library directly from the menu in any Office product by selecting File ➤ Check In. You will also be prompted automatically if you exit the Office application. Web designers, content managers, and administrators have the authority to cancel an existing check-out. This action causes the document to be checked back in to the library immediately; however, all changes made to the document since it was checked out are lost. This feature is primarily used to recover a checked-out document when the holder is unavailable for some reason.

By default, the document library overwrites the old document version with the new version and does not keep any history. If you would like to keep version history, then you must enable it from the Versions page. You can access the Versions page from the drop-down menu associated with a document. You then enable version history by clicking Modify Versioning Settings from the Actions list.

Along with version control, you can also enable content approval for a document library. When document approval is enabled, new documents will not be visible to the general population of site users. Instead, the documents must be approved by a member of the Content Manager site group before they become generally available. Rejections and approvals are issued directly in the portal using the drop-down menu associated with each document. Figure 3-11 shows the menu for rejecting or approving a document.

Figure 3-11. Approving or rejecting a document

To approve content, follow these steps:

1. Log in to the portal as a member of the Administrator site group.

2. Navigate to an area where you have the document library displayed.

3. Click the link Modify Settings and Columns in the Actions list.

4. On the Document Library Settings page, click the Change General Settings link.

5. In the Content Approval section, choose Yes.

6. In the Document Versions section, choose Yes.

7. Click OK.

8. Log in to the portal as a member of the Contributor site group.

9. Navigate to the document library page you just modified.

10. On the Document Library page, click Upload Document. Add a new document to the library.

11. Log in to the portal as a member of the Content Manager site group.

12. Navigate to the document library where the new file is located.

13. Click the Approve/Reject Items link on the document drop-down menu.

14. Change the Approval Status to Approved and click OK.

Backward-Compatible Document Libraries

The document library structure provided in SPS2003 is considerably different than that provided in SPS2001. Perhaps the most significant difference is that SPS2003 uses a SQL Server database as the backbone of the document library, whereas SPS2001 used the Web Storage System (WSS). WSS is a system of enhanced folders that provides document management features to documents that are stored within them.

There are two primary reasons for using the backward-compatible document library feature of SPS2003. First, if you have an existing WSS library from a previous installation of SPS2001, then you may want to use the backward-compatible document library instead of migrating documents to the new library system. Second, organizations that are not immediately moving to Office 2003 can use the backward-compatible library with previous versions of Office to provide enhanced capabilities, which I'll discuss later.

Installation

The components to support the backward-compatible document library are not installed by default. Instead, you must explicitly install them from the SPS installation disk. On the installation start page, the required components appear under the Install Optional Components heading. Figure 3-12 shows the installation screen.

NOTE *The SMTP service is a prerequisite for installing the backward-compatible document library.*

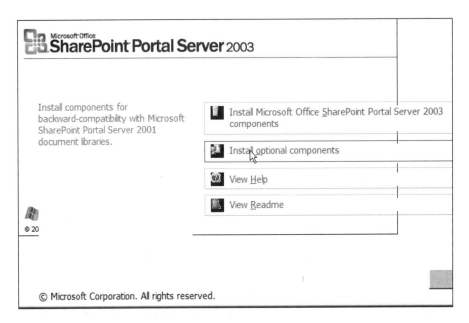

Figure 3-12. Installing the components for backward-compatible libraries

After selecting to install the optional components, you will be given a choice—to install both the client and server components, or just the client components. The server components are necessary to set up the WSS and create the library. The client components are required for Office applications to access the library. Therefore, you will have to install the client components on every machine where a previous version of Office is installed that requires access to the library.

Once installation is complete, you may access basic administrative functions for the library through SPS Central Administration. From here, the first thing to do is specify the server where the document library resides. From the main page, select Server Configuration ➤ Configure Server Topology. On the Configure Server Topology page, click the Change Components button. Reference the server containing the library components here. Figure 3-13 shows the Change Component Assignments page.

Once you have referenced a server hosting a backward-compatible library, a new option will appear on the central administration page. Selecting Component Configuration ➤ Configure Document Libraries (Web Storage System-based) brings up the List and Manage Document Libraries page. From this page you can create a new document library.

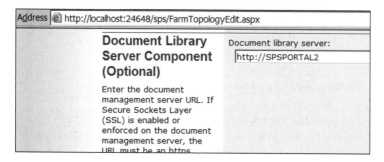

Figure 3-13. Referencing the backward-compatible library server

When a new library is created, SPS builds a structure in the WSS for new documents. This structure is then associated with a Uniform Resource Locator (URL) address. This address is visible in the List and Manage Document Libraries page and may be used to access the document library directly.

The simplest way to examine the new document library is to create a new Network Place in the file explorer. From the file explorer, you can create a new Network Place and use the URL specified for the library. After you create the new Network Place, you can open it and see the basic library structure. You will notice that the structure consists of several administrative folders as well as a specific folder named Documents, which represents the root of the document store. If you are familiar with the document storage features of SPS2001, you will immediately recognize the structure as similar. Figure 3-14 shows a typical backward-compatible library displayed inside the file explorer.

http://spsportal2/accessdocs/			_ □ X
File Edit View Favorites Tools Help			
Back ▾ ⚙ ▾ ⬆ Search Folders ⬆ ⬆ X ⬆ ▥▾			
Address http://spsportal2/accessdocs/			▾ ⬆ Go
Name ▴	Size	Type	Modified
☐ _TEMP_		Web Folder	8/22/2003 8:58 AM
☐ Documents		Web Folder	8/22/2003 8:58 AM
☐ LOCKS		Web Folder	8/22/2003 8:58 AM
☐ Management		Web Folder	8/22/2003 8:58 AM
☐ Portal		Web Folder	8/22/2003 8:58 AM
☐ SHADOW		Web Folder	8/22/2003 8:58 AM
☐ system		Web Folder	8/22/2003 8:58 AM
1 objects selected			

Figure 3-14. Viewing the backward-compatible library

In addition to accessing the backward-compatible document library from a Network Place, you can also access it directly from the portal. Once you have set up and referenced a library, the portal home page will show a new navigation link to the document library. You can perform almost all operations associated with the backward-compatible document library from either the portal or the file explorer.

Administering Users, Roles, and Rights

Once the backward-compatible library is created, you will want to provide access to the portal users. Giving new users permission to access the library is done through SPS Central Administration. From the main page, you can select Component Configuration ➤ Configure Document Libraries (Web Storage System-based) to display the List and Manage Document Libraries page. On this page, click the Edit link to perform basic administration.

On the Change Document Library Settings page, you can perform several administrative tasks. General settings like contact information can be changed directly in the page while three hyperlinks allow you to perform additional tasks. At the bottom of the page, you will see links for managing security, document profiles, and content sources.

When you click the Manage Document Library Security link, the system opens the exact same Network Place that you examined earlier. Within the library structure, you will see a folder named Management. Opening this folder reveals two items: Document Profiles and Workspace Settings. Opening the Workspace Settings item displays a property sheet that allows you to give users access to the entire document library. Figure 3-15 shows the property sheet.

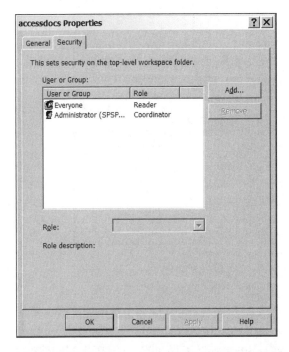

Figure 3-15. Adding users to the document library

New users can gain access to the backward-compatible document library by clicking the Add button and selecting the accounts from the directory structure. When you add a user to the document library, you must assign them to a role. The backward-compatible document library uses roles to assign rights to users. The library supports three roles: Reader, Author, and Coordinator. Table 3-2 lists the roles and their associated rights.

Table 3-2. Rights and Roles in the Backward-Compatible Document Library

RIGHT	READER	AUTHOR	COORDINATOR
Read documents in standard folders.	X	X	X
Read published documents in enhanced folders.	X	X	X
Search public documents.	X	X	X
Add, edit, delete documents.	—	X	X
Submit documents for publication.	—	X	X
Create or modify subfolders.	—	X	X
Add and remove users.	—	—	X
Manage document profiles.	—	—	X
Manage library structure.	—	—	X
Manage approval process.	—	—	X

Document Management Features

Just like the standard document libraries associated with SPS2003, the backward-compatible library supports several document management features, including check-in, check-out, version control, and approval routing. The difference between the standard and backward-compatible libraries is found in the role definitions. Each user's rights are determined by their role in the backward-compatible library as opposed to their rights within SPS2003.

Authors and coordinators may add new documents to the library. New documents can be added either through the portal or using the web folder available through Network Places. When documents are added to the library, metadata is associated with the document in the form of a profile. The document profiles in the backward-compatible library are similar to those available in the standard libraries. When a document is first added to the library, you will be asked to select a profile for the document and fill in the metadata. This metadata is used to retrieve documents during later search operations. Figure 3-16 shows a typical document profile.

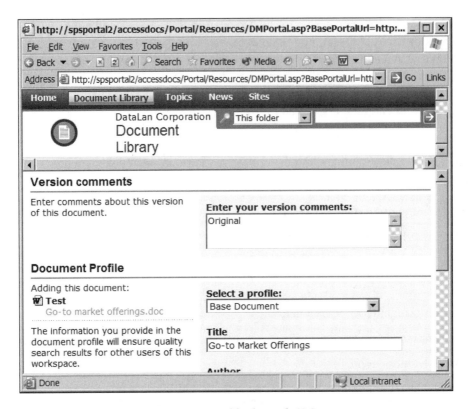

Figure 3-16. Filling in a document profile through SPS

Coordinators can create and edit document profiles for the library. Creating or editing a document profile can be done through the Manage Document Profiles link on the Change Document Library Settings page or directly in the web folder available in Network Places. Either way, you will end up in the Document Profiles folder where you can view all of the current profile definitions. Profiles can be opened and edited, or a new profile can be added by opening the Add Document Profile item. When you add or edit a profile, you may define new metadata fields and specify whether or not they are required.

Once a document is in the library, it may be checked out by authors or coordinators directly from the portal or file explorer. When the document is checked out, no one else can edit it. Additionally, a local copy of the document is downloaded to your computer for you to work on.

After you have made changes to the document, you may check it back into the library directly from the Office application where you edited it by selecting File ➤ Check In. When you check in a document directly from an Office application, you will be prompted to fill in the document profile. You may also make the document available to others by selecting to publish the document immediately. Figure 3-17 shows the document profile from an Office application.

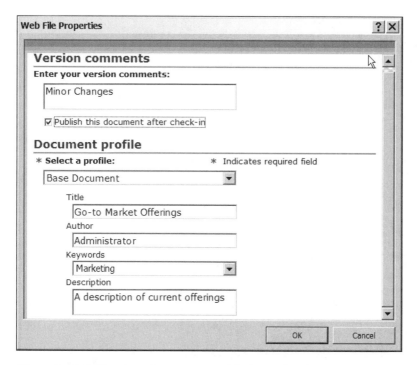

Figure 3-17. Filling in a document profile through Office

Each time a document is checked in, a new version is created. The version history for any document is available directly in the portal where any version can easily be opened for editing. Major version numbers are assigned to documents when they are published. Minor version numbers are assigned to documents when they are checked in.

You can also access version history for any document through the file explorer. In the file explorer, simply locate the document in the library beneath the web folder in Network Places. When you have located the folder, right-click and select Properties from the pop-up menu. The displayed property sheet has a Versions tab that lists the version history. Figure 3-18 shows the property sheet with a typical version history.

Just like the standard document library, the backward-compatible document library supports an approval process for new documents. The approval process for backward-compatible libraries differs from the standard one in that the process is set up using folders contained in the library. Using the Properties tab for any folder in the library, you may specify the users who must approve a document before it can be published. When you specify these users, you may also select whether all of the users must approve in sequence or whether any one of the users can approve a document. Figure 3-19 shows the property sheet where approvers are defined.

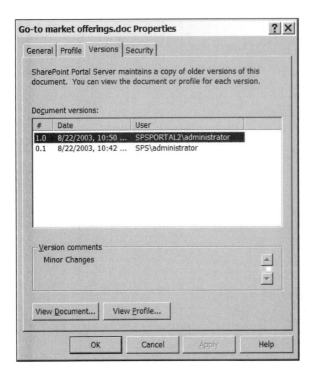

Figure 3-18. Accessing version history

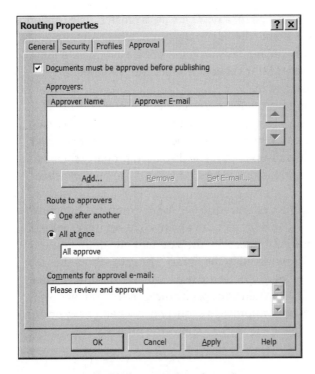

Figure 3-19. Establishing approval routing

Approval routing begins when a new document is saved into a folder with approvers defined. If the routing option on the folder is set to One After Another, then approvers receive an e-mail with a link to the document in the order they are listed on the property sheet. In this case, each approver must approve the document in order before it will be published. If the routing option on the folder is set to All at Once, then every approver receives an e-mail at the same time. Under this scenario, you may specify whether any single approver can approve the document or if it must be approved by everyone before publishing.

Form Libraries

A form library can be thought of as a special document library. The purpose of the form library is to store XML-based forms that can gather similar information. For example, you might create a form library in the Human Resources area of the portal that contains a vacation request form, a 401k change form, or a health insurance change form. In this way, key forms are centralized and easily located through the topic structure of the site.

Although the concept of centralizing forms seems natural enough, you are probably wondering why the forms have to be XML-based. The answer is that these XML-based forms will be used as system integration points to add data to multiple line-of-business systems. The concept is to use an XML-based form to gather data one time and then route the data to all of the systems that require it.

As an example, consider a sales professional returning from a call with a customer. At the end of the day, the sales professional needs to enter several different kinds of data into various line-of-business systems. To start with, the details of the call and status of opportunities must be entered into the Customer Relationship Management (CRM) system. Then, mileage and expenses must be entered into a financial system. Finally, a status report must be created and stored on the file server. In this scenario, the sales professional has to enter data into three different systems, and in all likelihood, much of the data is repeated.

XML-based forms promise to eliminate non-value activities such as redundant data entry by offering a single point for data entry. In the Microsoft view, the sales professional would enter all of the data—customer, expenses, reporting—into a single XML-based form. This form would then be routed to the CRM system, financial system, and reporting system to create the required entries. I will discuss the underlying construction of such systems later in the book. For now, I will simply focus on creating the libraries where the documents will be stored.

Creating a form library can be done directly in the portal. Unlike document libraries, form libraries do not exist by default. When you create a form library, it is given a default form template for use with the library. Typically, a form library is used for only one type of form. Therefore, you will have many different form libraries in a typical portal.

To create a form library, follow these steps:

1. Log in to the portal as a member of the Content Manager, Web Designer, or Administrator site group.

2. Navigate to the Human Resources area of the portal.

3. Click the Manage Content link under the Actions list. This brings up the Documents and Lists page.

4. In the Documents and Lists page, click the Create link. This opens the Create page.

5. On the Create page, click the Form Library link. This opens the New Form Library page.

6. In the New Form Library page, name the new library **HR Forms** and give it a description.

7. Click Create.

Once the form library is created, you can create and upload forms. In Office 2003, XML-based forms are created using Microsoft InfoPath. InfoPath is a product that allows for the design and use of XML-based forms in the business environment. Forms in InfoPath may be designed based on an existing template, a database schema, or from scratch. All of the forms created with InfoPath are interactive with complete control sets like list boxes, options, and text fields. Once the form is created, you can publish it to the form library.

Take these steps to publish an XML-based form:

1. Open Microsoft InfoPath.

2. In Microsoft InfoPath, click the link Design a Form ➤ Design a Form.

3. In the Design a Form window, select Design a New Form ➤ Customize a Sample.

4. In the Customize a Sample window, select Expense Report (Domestic). Click OK.

5. In the Design Tasks window, select Publish Form. This starts the Publishing Wizard.

6. In the Publishing Wizard, select to create a new SharePoint form library.

7. Type in the URL of the form library page you created earlier. Figure 3-20 shows the Publishing Wizard.

8. Name the new library Expense Reports and give it a description.

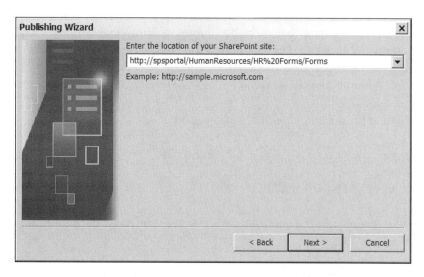

Figure 3-20. Publishing a new form

Image Libraries

Like form libraries, image libraries are a special type of document library. These libraries are specifically intended to manage digital photography and images such as corporate logos. Although images can be stored in any document library, image libraries have special features to view and use graphical content. Just like any library, image libraries can be created at any area or site. In fact, areas have an image library by default.

Uploading pictures into the library is similar to uploading any document or form. Once the images are uploaded, however, they may be presented in special views available only in the image library. The images may also be edited from the portal using Microsoft Picture Manager or sent directly to any Office application for inclusion in a document. The image library can also be accessed directly as a web folder under Network Places in the file explorer.

Lists

Along with document libraries, lists form the foundation of content within SPS. A *list* is a collection of information items displayed in an area or on a site. Everyone who has access to the portal will be able to view lists. Every site group except Reader may also add items to a list. Editing and deleting items in a list can be done by every site group except Reader and Member.

When a list appears on a page, users may add items to the list by using the link that appears immediately below the list. For more comprehensive control of list items, users may click the Manage Content link under the Actions list. This gives complete access to add, edit, or delete list items.

To add a list item, follow these steps:

1. Log in to the portal in the Member site group.

2. On the portal home page, locate the Events list.

3. Click the Add New Event link.

4. Add information for a new event. When you are finished, click Save and Close.

5. The new event will now be visible on the portal home page. Click the event title for more details.

6. From the event detail page, select Export Event. This adds the event to you Microsoft Outlook calendar.

Announcements

The most immediate example of a list is the announcements list that appears on the portal home page. This is the only list created by SPS that is not initially empty. Announcements are useful for presenting headlines to users regarding current events or items of immediate importance.

Links

Link list items are hyperlinks to web pages of interest to a team or organization. A blank list of links typically appears on any new site added to the portal. When users add links to the list, they provide the target URL and a description.

Contacts

Contact list items represent team members associated with an area or site. A blank list of contacts is typically created for any new site added to the portal. The blank list is filled by importing new contacts into the list from Microsoft Outlook or entering them manually.

Here is what you need to do to import contacts:

1. Log in to the portal in the Content Manager site group.

2. From the portal home page, click the Sites link to open the Site Directory.

3. In the Site Directory, click the Create Site link from the Actions list.

4. Create a new site based on the Team Site template.

5. When the new site is created, select Lists ➤ Contacts to open the list.

6. In the new contacts list, click the Import Contacts link.

7. Select the contacts to import from the address book that appears.

Events

Event list items are headlines associated with meetings, seminars, parties, and so on. When you create a new site, a blank event list typically appears on the home page. Users may enter new events directly from the home page and can also associate a document with the event. This is useful for linking directions or agendas with events.

Tasks

Task items form a to-do list for a team. When a new site is created, a blank task list is available. When you create a new task in the list, you may assign it to a team member. The list may then be viewed in summary to track all items for the team.

Issues

Issue items are useful for tracking items such as customer concerns or product defects. When a new site is created, a list of issues is generally not created. You must explicitly create the list for the new site. Once items are added to the list, you may track the response to the issue, its priority, and status.

Alerts

Alerts provide notification to a particular user when an item of interest has been added or updated within the portal. When a new alert is created, the user can define the areas of interest and set up how the notification will occur. SPS can provide alerts pertaining to the following items:

- Areas

- Sites

- Libraries

- Documents

- Lists

- List items

- Search results

- Portal users

Adding an alert is accomplished by the individual user and is generally done using the Alert Me link in the Actions list associated with the item of interest. When a user creates a new alert, they can specify how the alert should be delivered. For more sophisticated alerts, users can specify whether notification should occur for new items, changes, or both. Users can also apply a filter to an alert that will look for key words or phrases before sending an alert.

Once the alert is defined, SPS can deliver the alert to a personalized web site, as an e-mail to Microsoft Outlook, or both. Users can also specify whether they want to be notified immediately of changes or have multiple alerts delivered in a summary notification. Figure 3-21 shows a typical notification e-mail received in Microsoft Outlook.

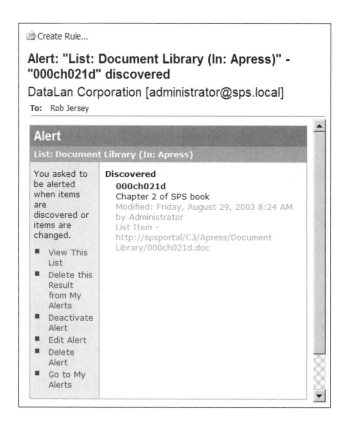

Figure 3-21. Receiving an alert

Discussions

SPS supports two different kinds of discussions: discussion boards and web discussions. Discussion boards in SPS are similar to any newsgroup forum you may have visited on the Internet. Web discussions, on the other hand, are a new way to comment on documents and share those comments with others.

When a new site is created, a discussion board is automatically created. Portal users who have access to the site may start new discussions or participate in existing ones. Discussion boards support expanding and collapsing discussions as well as searching to find postings of interest.

Web discussions allow a way for portal users to view a document online and associate a discussion with the document. Discussions are started using the drop-down list associated with a document in a library. When the discussion is started, the document is opened in the appropriate Office product and a discussion pane appears at the bottom of the document. Figure 3-22 shows an example of a web discussion. I'll cover web discussions in more detail in Chapter 5.

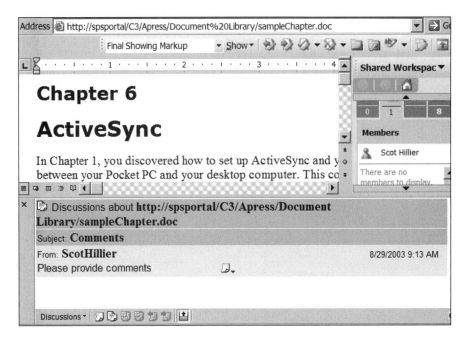

Figure 3-22. Discussing a document

Surveys

Surveys provide a way to poll portal users for input on a subject. When a site is first created, it usually does not have a survey associated with it. Once created, surveys support a wide variety of response types from simple Yes/No answers to free-form text.

You'll need to complete the following steps to create a survey:

1. Log in to the portal in the Administrator site group.

2. Navigate to a site that you created earlier.

3. Click the Create link at the top of the site home page.

4. Select the link to create a new survey.

5. Give your survey a name and description.

6. Click Next.

7. Add a question to your survey and click Finish.

8. Return to the site home page and select your survey from the list.

9. On the survey page, enter a response to the survey.

10. After you have several responses, you can view a summary. Figure 3-23 shows a graphical representation of survey responses.

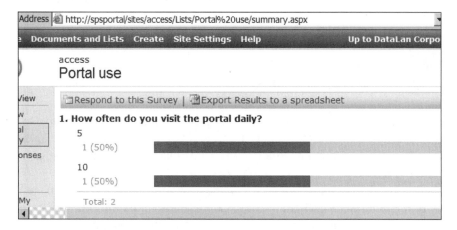

Figure 3-23. Viewing survey results

Searching

Finding information easily is one of the main business benefits of SPS, and the built-in search engine is the primary mechanism for quickly looking across content sources. Searching can be as simple as typing a key word or phrase into the search box located on the portal home page.

The simple search produces a results page initially sorted by relevance and grouped by site. However, the page offers several different views of the results to help users locate information. The available views are sorted by site, author, date, area, or just a simple list of results.

SPS supports an advanced search feature, which is accessed by clicking on the magnifying glass located next to the simple search. The advanced search gives the user much more control over the scope of the search, including where to search and what properties to include.

Exercise 3-1: SPS Basics

In this chapter, I showed you the fundamental features of SPS2003. Now that you have an overview of the product, you can begin to create a more formal portal that you can use to further your investigation. In this exercise, you will clean up the initial portal installation and create a structure based on your business needs.

Clean Up

Assuming you were following along in this chapter, when you first installed SPS, you accepted the default portal. As you investigated the portal features, you also created additional sites and areas that may not be appropriate for the final business vision. Therefore, you start this exercise by cleaning up the portal installation and preparing to create your own structure.

Clearing the Portal Home Page

Start by logging in to the portal as a member of the Administrator site group. On the portal home page, click the Manage Content link under the Actions list. Take note of any items that you have added to the home page during your investigation and remove them.

Now return to the home page and click the News link at the top of the page. On the news home page, click the Manage Content link under the Actions list. Remove all of the news items from the page, including the default items placed there by the initial installation.

Once again, return to the portal home page. Click the Edit Page link under the Actions list. This causes a link to appear in the upper-right corner of the page entitled Modify Shared Page. From this link, select Modify Shared Page ➤ Design This Page. This puts the home page into design mode. In design mode, click the X next to the Portal Owner QuickStart Guide to remove it from the page. When you are finished, click the View Page link under the Actions list. Figure 3-24 shows what my home page looked like after cleaning it up.

Figure 3-24. Cleaning up the home page

Removing Areas

Throughout this chapter, you have created areas and sites to investigate new features. Before you create a more formal portal structure, you should clean up these areas and sites. This can be started by clicking the Manage Portal Site link under the Actions list on the portal home page, which will take you to the portal site map. From the portal site map, select to show all areas and listings. Delete areas and listings that will not be part of your final site structure. You will probably want to delete most of the areas that SPS defined for you in the initial installation with the exception of Topics, News, and Sites.

Removing Sites

Return to the portal home page and click the Sites link at the top of the page to open the Site Directory. From the Site Directory, click Manage Sites under the Actions list. From the Site list, delete any sites that will not be part of your final structure. This action will not actually delete the site; it will just remove the listing. Actual site deletion is an administrative process that requires confirmation from the site owner. Later in the book, you will learn to implement automatic site deletion.

Designing the Area Structure

Perhaps the most important part of the portal design is the area structure. The area structure is critical to locating information and sites. A good area design will make the portal useful. A poor design will result in low adoption rates throughout the organization.

Now is the time for you to think through the initial area structure you want to create for your portal. When developing this structure, keep in mind both the structure of your organization and the structure of your documents. This is because areas are used to navigate through both the hierarchy of your organization and the taxonomy of the document management system.

The easiest place to begin this effort is with your organizational hierarchy. This structure likely already exists in the form of an organizational chart. Using this chart, you can create a similar area structure underneath the Topics area. For my portal, I kept the Departments area and built the company structure underneath.

After considering the company hierarchy, I thought about the document taxonomy I wanted to implement. Because my organization is a services company, most people want to access documents by customer. In fact, the company has a large file server that essentially has a folder for every customer the company has serviced. Because this paradigm is deeply engrained, I decided to create an area for each customer. My plan was then to have a document library associated with each customer's area. Creating this many areas is a large effort, but my experience is that moving documents into a new structure is always a lot of work. My guess is that you will experience the same thing as you migrate to a new portal.

NOTE *Because migrating documents into the portal can be a major undertaking, you may want to consider using third-party tools to assist. One tool that I have used successfully to migrate documents is the Tzunami K-Wise Deployer. You can get information about this tool at* www.k-wise.com.

Along with customers, the other primary way in which my colleagues think about documents is according to which service offering they support. Our service offerings are subsequently broken down into practice areas. Therefore, I created an area for each of the key offerings. Figure 3-25 shows a summary view of my final area structure.

Figure 3-25. Final site map

Adding Users

After you have defined the basic structure, it is time to add users to the portal. Earlier in this chapter, I covered the mechanics of adding users, so I will not go over that in detail again. However, now is the time to give consideration to the membership for each site group. First consider where the bulk of the users will be assigned. For my site, I chose to make most users Members. This gives them reasonable functionality without allowing them to get in trouble. I elevated certain people to the Contributor site group based on their job requirements.

The next thing to do once the main body of users is placed in a group is to assign an owner to each of the areas you created in your portal structure. These owners will be members of the Content Manager site group and will be responsible for the maintenance of their area. Distributing maintenance responsibilities like this is critical for ensuring that the portal does not become a dumping ground full of outdated information. Many a company intranet has succumbed to such a fate because no one maintained the site content.

For each area you defined, visit the home page and click Change Settings under the Actions list. On the General tab of the Change Settings page, add the name of the area contact. Once you have added the area contact, they will appear on the home page of the area with a link for users to send them mail.

The final thing to take care of at this point is to import all of the users into the profiles database. Earlier in the chapter, I covered how to import the users, so I will not go over it again; however, be sure to examine the profiles and fill in any important information that was not provided by the directory service.

Creating the Site Structure

Once the users are added, the next thing to consider is the structure of team sites you want available in the initial portal rollout. Whereas areas exist to support information retrieval, sites exist to facilitate team collaboration. Therefore, you should give consideration to the teams that exist within your organization. Typically, some teams are long-lived while others are more ad-hoc. A company board of directors is an example of a long-lived team, whereas organizers of the holiday party usually belong to an ad-hoc team. In your initial rollout, you will probably want to create sites for long-lived teams while providing SSSC for ad-hoc teams.

In my portal structure, I created team sites for each of the service offerings my example company represents. In my organization, these teams meet weekly to investigate new technology and develop sales and marketing materials. I also enabled SSSC mode so that individuals could create their own team sites. For each site I created, I linked them back to the areas so that the sites could be easily located. Figure 3-26 shows how three of my sites appear under different areas in the site map.

Figure 3-26. Mapping sites to areas

Loading Documents

Easily the largest job of all in rolling out SPS is migrating documents into the new structure. Later in the book, you'll see how it is possible to leave content sources in place and crawl them so they can be searched, but for now I'll focus on getting documents into the portal. This all begins by assembling representative documents that you can use to train the Topic Assistant.

Pick an appropriate place in your area structure and upload representative documents into the document library. I selected to start with a single customer and upload various documents that related to sales and project deliverables. In my strategy, the documents live in a specific customer area, but they are categorized by other areas such as Sales or Delivery. Therefore, I changed the settings to prevent the Topic Assistant from using the customer area for categorization. This is done from the Search tab of the Area settings page as shown in Figure 3-27.

After the representative documents were loaded into a single customer area, I went through each one and submitted them to multiple portal areas. In this way, the documents are associated with areas in your structure so that the Topic Assistant can be properly trained. Submitting the documents to various areas is done through the drop-down list associated with each document. When you submit to an area, you can use a replica of the site map to select the areas to associate with the document. Figure 3-28 shows the site map replica with areas selected.

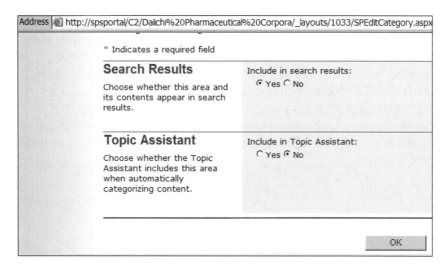

Figure 3-27. *Excluding an area from Topic Assistant*

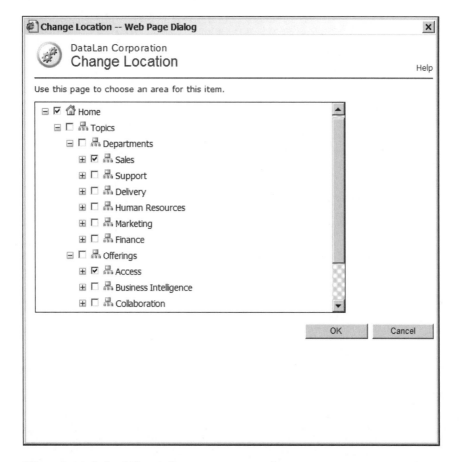

Figure 3-28. *Submitting a document to several areas*

Once you have submitted a representative sample of documents to the various areas, you are ready to train the Topic Assistant. From the Site Settings page select Portal Site Content ➤ Use Topic Assistant. On the Use Topic Assistant page, click the link Train Now. The Topic Assistant will then examine the documents you have loaded and the areas associated with them. After training is complete, you will get a report as to whether or not the Topic Assistant had enough information to successfully complete training. If you are successful, then the Topic Assistant will automatically categorize content the next time a content source is crawled.

CHAPTER 4

SharePoint Content Development

Although the default installation of SharePoint Portal Server (SPS) looks attractive right out of the box, you will undoubtedly want to customize the appearance and behavior of the portal to match your organization. SPS supports this type of customization directly in the portal as well as through external products like Microsoft FrontPage. Additionally, individual users can personalize the portal to support their own needs. In this chapter, I will cover the various customization and personalization techniques that will help you integrate the portal into your organization.

Customizing Portal Content

As I have said before, one of the major objectives of SPS is to improve the productivity of the knowledge worker. With this in mind, SPS provides a number of ways to customize the portal and target content at groups of knowledge workers. These mechanisms include the ability to create targeted team sites, but also the ability to modify pages, use custom templates, and define groups that receive specific content.

Site Membership

One of the first ways in which you can target content to portal users is through the structure of the portal sites. In the previous chapter, you created several sites for use by various teams in the organization. After creating these team sites, you can then grant access to them so that only team members can use them. Applying these restrictions effectively targets the site content to a particular group of portal users.

Top-level sites that are created directly from the portal initially have no members, and no one is allowed access to them. Modifying access rights to a site can only be done by a member of the Administrator site group for that site. Access rights can subsequently be granted by clicking the Site Settings link at the top of the site home page.

On the Site Settings page, selecting Administration ➤ Manage Users opens the Manage Users page for the particular site. Typically, the first thing to do is grant administration rights to someone who will be responsible for the overall site and its content. After naming the administrator, you can add team members to the site. Typically, these team members will be added to the Contributor site group. Once the initial set of permissions is established, administration of a site should be turned over to the designated administrator. This person, in turn, can control the access rights for team members.

Once the new site administrator takes responsibility for the site, the next thing to do is ensure that all requests for access to the site are properly directed. This is done by selecting Administration ➤ Go to Site Administration from the Site Settings page. This opens the Top-Level Site Administration page. On this page, the administrator should select Users and Permissions ➤ Manage Access Requests. On the page that opens, the new administrator can direct access requests to his or her own mailbox. Figure 4-1 shows the Manage Request Access page.

Access Team
Manage Request Access: Access Team

Allow users to request access to this site. All requests for access will be sent to the e-mail address listed in the following field. The owner of the e-mail address should be a member of the Administrator site group.

☑ Allow requests for access

Send all requests for access to the following e-mail address: ScotHillier@sps.local

OK   Cancel

Figure 4-1. Directing access requests

Throughout the portal, whenever a user attempts to access a restricted feature, SPS responds with an access request page. This page allows the user to send an access request by e-mail to the administrator of a site or area. Figure 4-2 shows a typical access request page in the portal.

Once the access request is made, the administrator for the resource receives an e-mail containing links to approve or reject the access request. Clicking one of the links takes the administrator directly to the appropriate page in the portal. From the portal, access can be granted and an e-mail response generated. Figure 4-3 shows a typical e-mail request received by an administrator.

Sites in SPS can be created at the top level or as subsites underneath any existing site. When subsites are created, they inherit the permissions of the parent site above them. Although this system of hierarchical site groups is appropriate for most uses, SPS will allow a site to be separated from the hierarchy and have its own unique set of permissions. Unique permissions are useful whenever you need to completely change the permission set of a site.

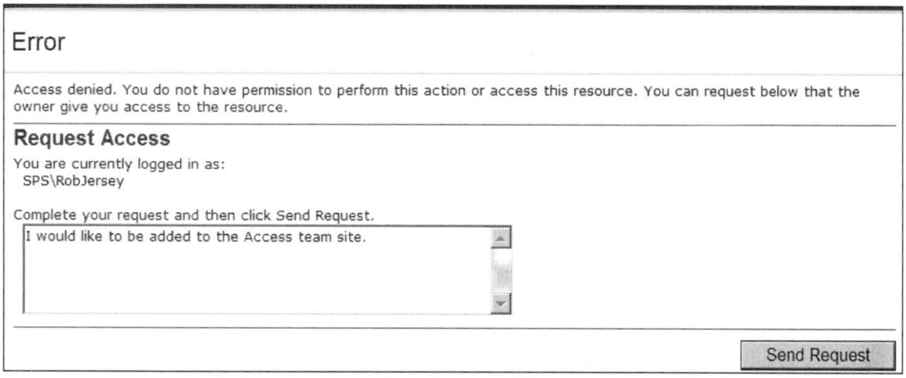

Error

Access denied. You do not have permission to perform this action or access this resource. You can request below that the owner give you access to the resource.

Request Access

You are currently logged in as:
SPS\RobJersey

Complete your request and then click Send Request.

I would like to be added to the Access team site.

[Send Request]

Figure 4-2. Requesting access to a resource

Access request for a site

administrator@sps.local

To: Scot Hillier

SPS\RobJersey is requesting access to:
http://spsportal/sites/access

Click one of the following links:

- Grant SPS\RobJersey access to the site

- Manage request access setting for the site

Message from SPS\RobJersey:
I would like to be added to the Access team site.

Note: Do not reply to this message. It is sent from an unmonitored account.

Figure 4-3. Receiving a request

To set up unique permissions, you need to follow these steps:

1. Log in to the portal as a member of the Administrator site group.

2. From the portal home page, click the Sites link to open the Site Directory.

3. From the Site Directory, navigate to a top-level site you created earlier.

4. On the home page of the site, click Create.

5. On the Create page, click Sites and Workspaces.

6. Name the new site and give it a description.

7. Select Use Unique Permissions.

8. Click Create.

9. On the Template Selection page, select the Team Site template.

10. Click OK.

11. When the site home page appears, click Site Settings.

12. On the Site Settings page, select Administration ➤ Manage Users.

Along with changing the access permissions, you can also determine whether or not to allow anonymous access to a site. Anonymous access allows anyone who is a registered domain user to access the site even without specific permission. You can change this setting for each site you create.

Here is what to do to allow anonymous access:

1. Log in to the portal as a member of the Administrator site group.

2. From the portal home page, click Sites.

3. Navigate to an existing site you created earlier.

4. From the Site home page click Site Settings.

5. On the Site Settings page, select Administration ➤ Go to Site Administration.

6. On the Top-Level Site Administration page, select Users and Permissions ➤ Manage Anonymous Access.

7. On the Change Anonymous Access Settings page, adjust the settings as desired. Figure 4-4 shows the Change Anonymous Access Settings page.

8. Click OK.

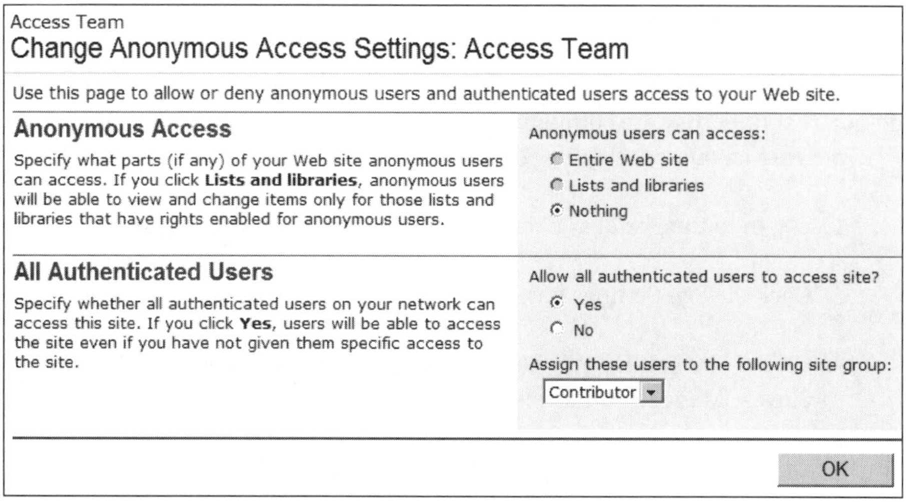

Access Team
Change Anonymous Access Settings: Access Team

Use this page to allow or deny anonymous users and authenticated users access to your Web site.

Anonymous Access

Specify what parts (if any) of your Web site anonymous users can access. If you click **Lists and libraries**, anonymous users will be able to view and change items only for those lists and libraries that have rights enabled for anonymous users.

Anonymous users can access:
- ○ Entire Web site
- ○ Lists and libraries
- ● Nothing

All Authenticated Users

Specify whether all authenticated users on your network can access this site. If you click **Yes**, users will be able to access the site even if you have not given them specific access to the site.

Allow all authenticated users to access site?
- ● Yes
- ○ No

Assign these users to the following site group:

[Contributor ▼]

[OK]

Figure 4-4. Allowing anonymous access

In addition to all of the site-level permissions, SPS also allows you to control access at the list level. This means that you can give access to a site while restricting access to a particular list on the site. From any list on a page, you can select Modify Settings and Columns to reach the customization page for a list. On this page, click "Change permissions for this list" to restrict access.

Audiences

Portal users can be classified in many different ways to identify groups that are interested in particular content. So far, you have used site groups and access rights to target content to portal users. However, SPS supports a more granular approach to content direction using *audiences*. Audiences allow you to group portal users by similar characteristics—such as membership in an Active Directory group—and then display specific content to the audience.

When SPS is first installed, a single audience is defined called All Portal Users. This audience targets content at anyone with permission to view the portal home page. Initially, the only way to view any of the targeted content is either on the portal home page, or through the My Site link. However, you can go much further by creating your own audiences.

You create audiences by specifying membership rules. These rules are associated with properties found in the Active Directory. You may specify one or many rules to determine membership. When you define membership, you may specify that all the rules must be met or that any of the rules can be met.

Once you have created an audience, it must be compiled. Compilation is done periodically to ensure that audience membership is always up to date. You can set up a compilation schedule, or force a compilation manually. Audiences do not exist until they are compiled.

To create an audience, follow these steps:

1. Log in to the portal as a member of the Administrator site group.

2. Click the Site Settings link.

3. On the Site Settings page, select User Profile, Audiences, and Personal Sites ➤ Manage Audiences.

4. On the Manage Audiences page, click Create Audience.

5. Give the audience a name and description. Choose whether the audience candidates must satisfy all the rules you specify or any of them.

6. Click OK.

7. On the Add Audience Rule page, specify a rule for audience membership. Figure 4-5 shows a typical rule definition.

8. After the new audience and rule are created, return to the Manage Audiences page.

9. On the Manage Audiences page, click Start Compilation.

10. After the compilation is complete, view the audience membership to verify the results.

Once an audience is created and compiled, you may target content to the group it represents. SPS allows you to target content to audiences using any of three different mechanisms. First, you may direct the content to the Links for You section of the home page. Alternately, you may direct the content to My Site in either the Links for You section or the News for You section.

When targeting content to an audience, you must typically select a link, listing, or document. You cannot target entire areas or sites. When you first add a link, listing, or document at the portal level, you can choose to target it to an audience. You can also choose to target the content after it is added to the portal by dragging the content to the Home or News area.

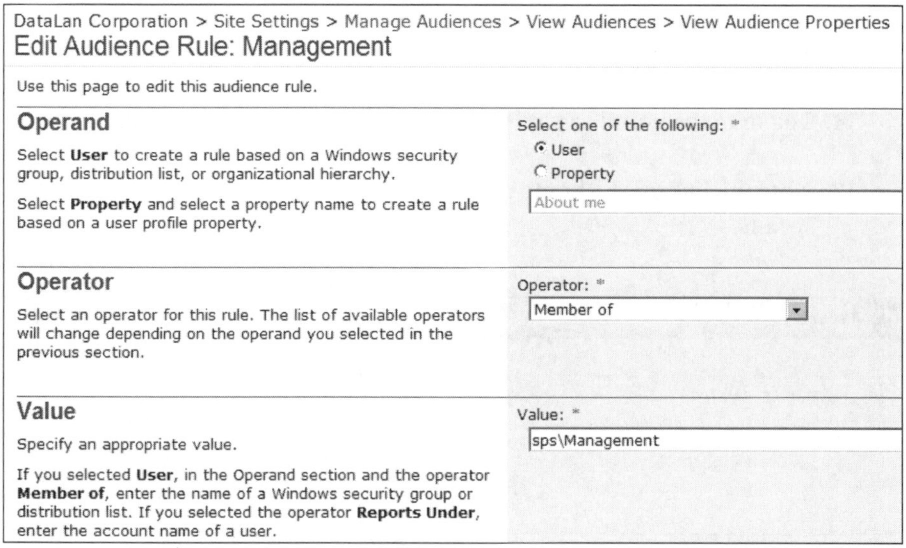

DataLan Corporation > Site Settings > Manage Audiences > View Audiences > View Audience Properties
Edit Audience Rule: Management

Use this page to edit this audience rule.

Operand

Select **User** to create a rule based on a Windows security group, distribution list, or organizational hierarchy.

Select **Property** and select a property name to create a rule based on a user profile property.

Select one of the following: *
- ⦿ User
- ⦾ Property

    About me

Operator

Select an operator for this rule. The list of available operators will change depending on the operand you selected in the previous section.

Operator: *

    Member of

Value

Specify an appropriate value.

If you selected **User**, in the Operand section and the operator **Member of**, enter the name of a Windows security group or distribution list. If you selected the operator **Reports Under**, enter the account name of a user.

Value: *

    sps\Management

Figure 4-5. Creating an audience rule

Here are the steps to target content:

1. Log in to the portal as a member of the Administrator site group.

2. From the portal home page, click Manage Portal Site from the Actions list.

3. From the portal site map, select to show All items.

4. Expand the site map and locate a link, listing, or document.

5. Select Edit from the drop-down menu associated with the link, listing, or document.

6. On the Change Settings page, click the Display tab.

7. On the Display tab, select the audience to target.

8. Click OK.

9. Return to the portal site map.

10. On the site map, drag the targeted link, listing, or document to the Home area.

11. Log in to the portal as a member of the audience you targeted.

12. Note the link on the home page of the portal. Figure 4-6 shows the results.

Figure 4-6. Targeted content in the portal

In order to show the targeted content on My Site, you select Portal Site Content ➤ Manage Targeted Links on My Site from the Site Settings page. This opens a list where new items can be added. You can add existing items to the list or create new ones.

Targeting content to a specific audience is a powerful concept, but its default implementation is limited. With only three places to place the targeted material, audiences may seem to be more trouble than they're worth. However, the concept of audiences reaches its true value when it is incorporated into custom web parts that are able to display information and change behavior based on audience membership. I'll examine web part development later in the book and make extensive use of the programmable classes found in the `Microsoft.SharePoint.Portal` namespace.

Understanding Web Parts

SPS not only provides a solid structure to assist end users in locating information, it also provides a strong framework to assist content developers in presenting information. The SPS content framework is built on a set of customizable software components known as *web parts*. Web parts are visible immediately upon entering the portal. They are responsible for generating all of the lists and views that make up the portal. Without web parts, nothing would appear on a portal web page.

For end users, the web part framework is seamless. Although each page in the portal is made up of several web parts, end users experience them as a single page of content. The distinction between web parts and web pages becomes significant, however, for designers and programmers responsible for the portal content.

Modifying Web Part Pages

Members of the Web Designer, Administrator, and Content Manager site groups have the right to add and customize shared pages within the portal. Users with this right can customize a web page by selecting Edit Page from the Actions list. Selecting to edit the page causes a drop-down to appear on the page entitled Modify Shared Page. Selecting Modify Shared Page ➤ Design This Page causes the page to enter web-part mode. In this mode web parts can be added or removed and their behavior can be altered. Figure 4-7 shows a typical portal page in web-part mode.

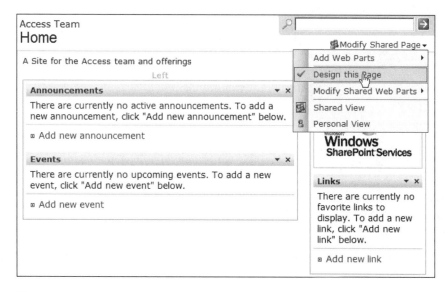

Figure 4-7. Entering web-part mode

Shared pages in the portal represent the content seen by all portal users. However, all site groups except Reader can modify their own Personal View for most pages. Modifying the Personal View of a page affects the way the content is displayed to the user who modified the page but does not affect the rest of the portal users. Before modifying a page, you should clearly understand whether your changes will be globally applied to the Shared View or just your Personal View.

Once the Shared or Personal View is in web-part mode, you can easily remove any web part by clicking the X located in the upper-right corner of the web part. Web parts can also be added to the page by selecting Modify Shared View ➤ Add Web Parts. From this menu item, you can select to browse, search, or import web parts.

Web parts are stored in one of several *galleries* that you can browse or search. These galleries are listed directly on the page when you select to add web parts to a page. The available galleries include the Web Part Page Gallery, the [sitename] Gallery, the Virtual Server Gallery, and the Online Gallery. Figure 4-8 shows the galleries available for use in a page.

Figure 4-8. Accessing web part galleries

The Web Part Page Gallery contains all of the web parts that are available specifically to the web page that is being modified. If you close web parts by clicking the X, then the web part disappears from the page and becomes available in the Web Part Page Gallery. Once it is in the gallery, it may be moved back to the page by dragging it from the gallery and onto the page.

The [sitename] Gallery is named after the site where the current page is located. If your site is named Board of Directors, then the [sitename] Gallery will be named Board of Directors Gallery. This gallery contains the bulk of the general-purpose web parts that may be used throughout the current site. Later, you will add your own custom web parts to this gallery for use in the portal.

The Virtual Server Gallery is a gallery intended for large enterprise deployments of SPS with many sites. In these cases, the Virtual Server Gallery acts as an enterprise-level repository for web parts. Using this gallery entails a special deployment model for web parts called a web-part package file that I will cover later in the book.

The Online Gallery is a special gallery of web parts created and maintained by Microsoft. Initially, you will find some news and stock web parts in this gallery. Over time, Microsoft expects to add more web parts for general use.

Regardless of where you get the web part, placing it on the page is always accomplished in the same manner. Each page is divided into several zones that can contain web parts, and the number and layout of the available zones depends upon the template used to create the current page. To move a web part onto the page, you click and drag the web part from the selected gallery into an available zone. Each zone on the page may contain more than one web part. Figure 4-9 shows a web part being dragged into a zone.

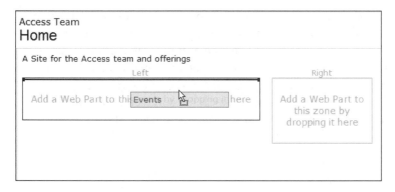

Figure 4-9. Placing a web part in a zone

Once the web parts are placed in the desired zones, they can be modified. This is accomplished by selecting Modify Shared Web Part from the drop-down menu associated with the web part. Figure 4-10 shows how to access the properties for the web part.

Web part properties are typically grouped together in logical categories such as Appearance or Layout. You can examine the individual properties by expanding the categories in the properties pane. Once you have the properties set, click Apply to see your changes immediately on the page.

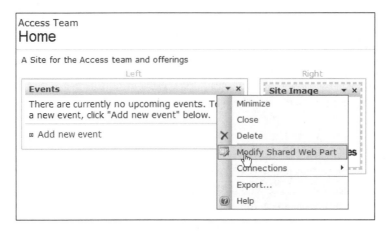

Figure 4-10. Modifying a web part

Connecting Web Parts

Although web parts are useful for displaying information, links, and lists, so far we have only seen them acting as islands of information. The content presented by multiple web parts on a page may be related, but the web parts are unaware of the related information. The connection is only made in the mind of the end user. With connected web parts, however, you can relate multiple web parts functionally. For example, an image on a site can be connected to an image viewer. Figure 4-11 shows an example of selecting an image link as the source for an image on a site home page.

Figure 4-11. Connecting web parts

You need to follow these steps to connect web parts:

1. Log in to the portal as a member of the Administrator site group.

2. On the portal home page, select Edit Page from the Actions list.

3. Now select Modify Shared Page ➤ Add Web Parts ➤ Browse.

4. Drag the Contacts web part from the Site Gallery to the middle-left zone of the portal home page.

5. Click View Page on the Actions list to leave web-part mode.

6. Now click the Contacts link to open the detail page.

7. On the Contacts page, click Import Contacts.

8. Import the contacts from Microsoft Outlook for the personnel that you assigned as area or site administrators.

9. On the Contacts page, click Modify Settings and Columns.

10. On the Customize Contacts page, select Views ➤ Create a New View.

11. On the Create View page, click Standard View.

12. Name the new view Experts and check the box "Make this the default view."

13. In the Columns section, uncheck every box except Last Name and First Name.

14. Click OK.

15. On the portal home page, select Edit Page from the Actions list.

16. Now select Modify Shared Page ➤ Design This Page.

17. Using the drop-down list for the Contacts web part, select Modify Shared Web Part.

18. In the List Views pane, change the current view to Experts.

19. Click OK.

20. Now select Modify Shared Page ➤ Add Web Parts ➤ Browse.

21. Drag another Contacts web part from the Site Gallery to the bottom zone of the portal home page.

22. Using the drop-down list from the first Contacts Web Part, select Connections ➤ Provide Row To ➤ Contacts [2].

23. When the transformer dialog appears, follow the prompts to select the fields to connect between the web parts.

24. Click View Page from the Actions list. You should now have a master-detail contacts display on the home page of the portal.

If you spend some additional time working on the list views, you can create exactly what you want. I added an additional hyperlink field to my list so that I could name an expert for each area in the portal. Figure 4-12 shows the final view perfected to associate an expert with each area and provide contact information to the portal user.

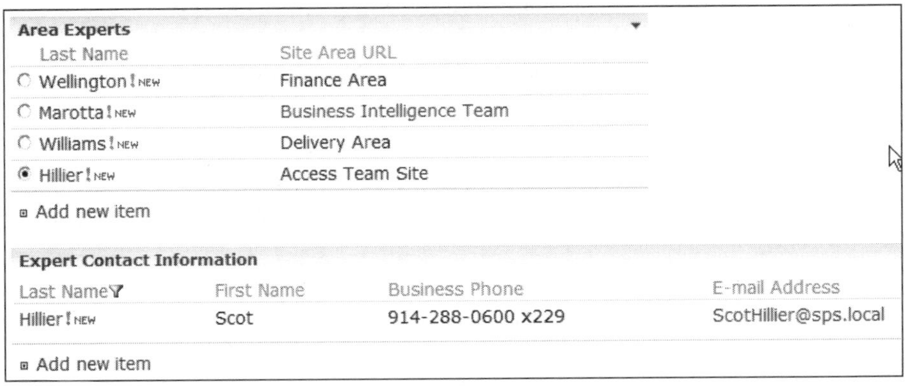

Figure 4-12. Creating a master-detail connection

Templates

Templates are a foundational element of SPS and allow for rapid structure and content creation. Although you are initially limited to the default templates offered by SPS, you do have some capability to create new templates within the portal. Later you will see that you can gain much more flexibility using an external editor, but for now, you will focus on creating templates within the portal environment.

Site Templates

Whenever you create a new site, SPS uses predefined templates to simplify the creation of the new elements for the site. You have already seen the list of templates in use several times. These templates allow you to create everything from a specialized team site to a blank site you can use to create content from scratch. Although SPS comes with several templates already defined, you can create your own templates and then make them available to others for use. These new templates can be created directly in the browser and saved through the SPS interface.

SPS defines a Site Collection as the top-level site and all of the sites beneath it in the hierarchy. You have already seen that permissions granted at the top of a site collection are inherited by sites lower in the collection. Using the same organizational structure, SPS maintains a Site Template Gallery for each Site Collection. A new site template can be created and added to the gallery by any member of the Administrator site group.

Site templates may be created outside of SPS using an authoring tool like Microsoft FrontPage, but the simplest way to create a template is to use an existing site within the portal framework. Creating a template from an existing site is done through the Site Settings page for the site you want to save. Generally, you will save only the structure of a site as a template; however, SPS does allow you the option of saving content along with the structure.

To create a site template, follow these steps:

1. Log in to the portal as a member of the Administrator site group.

2. From the portal home page, click the Sites link.

3. From the Site Directory, click the Create Site link under the Actions list.

4. Name the new site **Softball Team** and give it a description.

5. Type in a web site address for the new site and click Create.

6. On the Add Link to Site page, click OK.

7. On the Template Selection page, select to base this site on the Team Site template and click OK.

8. When the new site is created, select Modify Shared Page ➤ Add Web Parts ➤ Browse in the upper-right corner of the page.

9. On the Web Parts pane, drag the Members web part onto the page.

10. When you have finished modifying the site, click the Home link.

11. From the Home page, click Site Settings.

12. On the Site Settings page, select Administration ➤ Go to Site Administration.

13. On the Top-Level Site Administration page, select Management and Statistics ➤ Save Site as Template.

14. On the Save Site as Template page, name the new template Sports Team. Give it a file name and description.

15. Note that this page would allow you to save the site content as part of the template, if you wished. Click OK to finish.

Once you have created saved templates for a site collection, you can go back and manage the templates. Accessing the set of templates for a site collection is done through the Top-Level Site Administration page. On this page select Site Collection Galleries ➤ Manage Site Template Gallery. This will show you a list of all templates for the site collection excluding the default templates. From this list, you can edit the template properties or delete the template altogether.

List Templates

Just as you can create site templates from existing sites, SPS allows you to create list templates from existing lists. A list template consists of the fields that you define for the list and any views you define. Just like site templates, you also have the option of saving the list content as part of the template.
Follow these steps to create a list template:

1. Log in to the portal as a member of the Administrator site group.

2. Navigate to the Softball site that you created earlier.

3. On the site home page, click the Create link.

4. On the Create page, select Lists ➤ Contacts to create a new list for the site.

5. Name the new list **Players** and give it a description.

6. Click Create.

7. When the new list is displayed, select Modify Settings and Columns from the Actions list.

8. On the Customize page, select Columns ➤ Add a New Column.

9. Name the new column **Position** and give it a description.

10. Click OK to return to the Customize page.

11. On the Customize page, select General Settings ➤ Save List as Template.

12. On the Save as Template page, name the template **Players**. Give it a file name and description.

13. Click OK.

14. If you now return to the Create page, you will see that the new list template is available.

Area Templates

Just like sites, areas in SPS also utilize templates to control their appearance. When you create an area within the portal, it is assigned a default template; however, you can change the assignment by selecting Change Settings from the Actions list. This link opens a tabbed page that controls most of the aspects associated with an area.

The template for an area is designated on the Page tab. On this tab, you can specify that the area inherits its template from its parent, uses a default template, or uses a custom template based on another web page. Additionally, you can specify how subareas underneath this area will appear.

Personalization with My Site

Along with all of the information, documents, and links provided through the area structure of SPS, end users are also provided with a personal site known as *My Site*. My Site is easily accessed by clicking the associated link directly on the portal home page. When first accessed, SPS takes a moment to format the initial site, which contains a calendar, news, links, and alerts.

Using My Site

My Site consists of both a private and public view. The private view is intended as a personal workplace for the individual end user. The public view, on the other hand, acts like a business card that can be accessed by other portal users. You can see the different views by clicking either Private or Public under the Select View list. Figure 4-13 shows a public view of My Site.

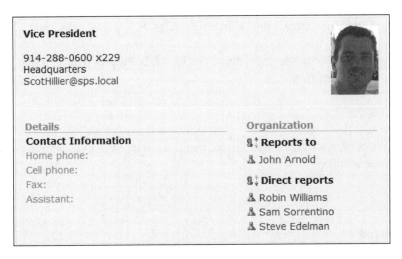

Figure 4-13. The public view of My Site

One of the first things to do when a user initially accesses My Site is update their profile. Profile information is available by clicking the Edit Profile link under the Actions list. The profile page allows end users to include enhanced contact information and even a paragraph of information about themselves.

You will notice that the profile items on My Site are a subset of the items available in the profile database. This is because the administrator determines which properties in the profile database can be edited by the end user directly. The administrator also determines which properties will appear in the public view of My Site. Administrators can access the profile database through the Site Settings page under the section User Profile, Audiences, and Personal Sites.

When the private view is first accessed, you will notice a reference to My Calendar. My Calendar is a web part that you can connect to an Exchange 2003 server so that your calendar will be visible on My Site. To display your calendar, you must modify the properties of the web part. This will require end users to know the exact name of the Exchange server. If you have created the test environment outlined in Chapter 2, you can easily set up the calendar web part.

Here is how you would set up My Calendar:

1. Log in to the portal as any end user.

2. From the portal home page, click the My Site link.

3. On the home page of My Site, ensure that you have the private view selected.

4. Select Modify My Page ➤ Design This Page.

5. On the My Calendar web part, select Modify My Web Part from the drop-down menu.

6. Under the Mail Configuration section, enter the mail server address as `http://spscontroller/exchange`.

7. Enter the appropriate mailbox name for the account you are currently logged in under.

8. Click OK.

Along with the calendar, the private view provides a place for you to add your own personal links to key information under My Links Summary. You will also see any targeted content under the Links for You list. (Links for You on My Site is exactly the same as the web part that appears on the portal home page.) Finally, any alerts that you have set throughout the portal are summarized in the My Alerts Summary list, which can also be managed from a link on the Actions list.

Customizing My Site

End users have full control over the items that appear on My Site. At any time, a user can customize My Site by using the Modify My Page menu. This menu allows end users to add or remove web parts from the page. In this way, end users can make My Site a personalized workspace that shows them the information, documents, and links that they most care about.

In addition to modifying the web parts that appear on My Site, users may also add new lists and pages directly by clicking the appropriate link under the Actions list. Selecting to create a new list opens a Create page similar to any area or site in the portal. From this page, end users have a wide choice of elements to add to My Site.

Although the administrator retains control over the appearance of the public view of My Site, end users can utilize the public view to share documents, sites, and links with other users. Under My Lists, users have access to both a private document library and a shared document library. The shared library is used for posting documents that you want to make available to others. For example, the portal administrator may post a document describing the procedures to personalize My Site. This way, portal users can engage in self-service rather than sending all their questions directly to the portal administrator. The type of sharing can be done with the Shared Links and Shared Workspace Sites web parts that appear on the public view of My Site.

Customizing with Microsoft FrontPage

Because SPS is built on top of SharePoint Services, most of the items in SPS are accessible in some way from Microsoft Office 2003. Later in the book, I will go into detail about exactly how the standard products like Word, Excel, and Outlook integrate with SharePoint Services. But for now, I will focus primarily on the content-creation capabilities that Microsoft FrontPage 2003 brings to your portal solution.

 CAUTION *If you must support browsers other than Internet Explorer, you should work closely with those browsers to ensure that pages appear correctly when created with FrontPage.*

Although SPS offers several ways to create and manage content, if you are a web developer, you will likely find them too limiting. In my experience, companies want their intranets to look and feel much like their existing corporate site on the Internet. This means that we need more control over the content and the layout of pages. This is the real reason to use Microsoft FrontPage in conjunction with SPS.

You can open the portal site directly from a URL by selecting File ➤ Open Site. When you open the URL, FrontPage displays a folder list view that shows all of the areas, sites, libraries, and lists defined in the portal. Figure 4-14 shows a typical folder list for a portal.

Opening the portal home page within FrontPage will give you an idea of the structure and elements available for editing. From the folder list, you can right-click a file and select Open from the pop-up menu. If you do this, you will see the same portal home page you are used to, but all of the elements are exposed for editing. You'll see, for example, that you could easily type directly into the page to edit content. You'll also notice that the landscape is complicated. Before you start making significant changes, you'll need to understand several aspects of page design; however, my goal is to provide only a brief overview of the major design tools you will need to work with pages in the portal.

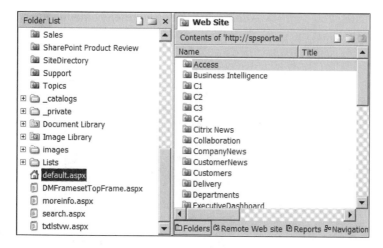

Figure 4-14. Viewing the portal structure

Designing a New Page

Adding a page to an existing web site is a simple matter of selecting File ➤ New from the menu. When you make this selection, FrontPage opens a *task pane* with a list of new items you can create. This introduces one of the most important new metaphors in FrontPage. Many of the tasks in FrontPage are accomplished through task panes. Task panes are similar in functionality to a dialog box, but they remain visible even after you finish the immediate operation. Multiple task panes stack up in a queue like web pages in a browser. You can navigate the task panes by using the back, forward, and home buttons within the pane or the drop-down menu at the top of the pane.

Once the new page is added, you may start designing it. Before you start creating sites that integrate directly with SharePoint Services, you'll review some of the basic page-creation tools in FrontPage. These tools will be useful later when you are working with more complicated pages.

When starting a new page, many web designers will create a prototype page using a graphics program such as Adobe Photoshop. Then they cut the image apart to create the graphics for the new page. This is especially helpful if you have an existing web site and are trying to make the new page match that look and feel. As I mentioned earlier, this is often the case with intranets—they must match the look and feel of the corporate Internet site. You can get help with this effort by making use of a tracing image in FrontPage.

Tracing images allow you to take a JPEG, GIF, PNG, or BMP file and use it like tracing paper to help with the layout and design of a page. In order to set a tracing image, you must have the page in design view, which is controlled by a set of buttons underneath the page, as shown in Figure 4-15. Once in design view, the tracing image is set by selecting View ➤ Tracing Image ➤ Configure from the

FrontPage menu. When you configure the tracing image, you select the file to act as the image, its position on the page, and its opacity.

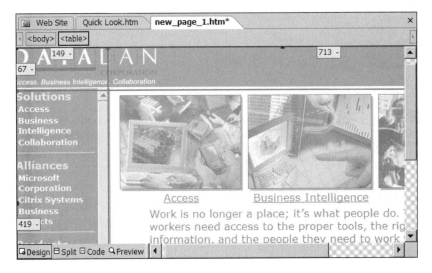

Figure 4-15. Setting a tracing image

Once you have a tracing image in place, you will want to construct the layout of the page to define the areas where content will be placed. Microsoft FrontPage allows you to set up multiple complex regions for content using layout tables. Layout tables are similar to any HTML table, but they are specifically intended to help layout content regions on the page. Inserting a layout table into a page is done by using a task pane. The layout table task pane can be opened by selecting Table ➤ Layout Tables and Cells.

Within the task pane, you can choose to create your own layout tables or use the predefined layouts in the pane. Generally, the predefined layouts are sufficient because several different kinds are available. Even if these are not exactly what you want, you can modify the layouts once they are applied to the page.

To utilize Layout Tables and Cells, take these steps:

1. Select Start ➤ All Programs ➤ Microsoft Office ➤ Microsoft Office FrontPage 2003 to open Microsoft FrontPage.

2. From the main menu, select File ➤ Open Site.

3. In the Open Site dialog, type `http://spsportal` and click Open.

4. When the site opens, make sure the folder list is visible by selecting View ➤ Folder List from the main menu.

5. Using the folder list, examine the sites, lists, and libraries defined in the site.

6. Open the New task pane by selecting File ➤ New from the main menu.

7. In the New task pane, click Blank Page to add a new page to the site.

8. Open the Layout Tables and Cells task pane by selecting Table ➤ Layout Tables and Cells.

9. In the Layout Tables and Cells task pane, click a new layout from the Table Layout section with a top title row that spans the entire page and a navigation column that spans the left side of the page.

10. Click your mouse inside the top row.

11. In the task pane, select New Tables and Cells ➤ Insert Layout Cell.

12. In the Insert Layout Cell dialog, accept the default values and click OK to insert the new cell.

13. When the new cell appears, click Cell Formatting.

14. In the task pane, click Cell Properties and Borders.

15. In the task pane, change the BgColor drop-down list to blue.

16. Click the sizing handle and make the cell fill the entire available area within the layout table.

17. In the task pane, click Cell Corners and Shadows.

18. Select to round the upper-right corners of the cell.

19. Place cells in the layout so that the page has a blue title area and blue navigation area. Figure 4-16 shows my final page.

Once the initial layout is complete, adding text is a simple matter of typing directly into the cells. You can format the font style directly from the editor using the same approach as you would in Microsoft Word. For images, you may either place the image directly in a cell, or make use of layers to position images. Layers are floating frames that can be positioned anywhere on the page. You can add a new layer from the Insert menu. Once added, you can drag the layer around the page and position it exactly where you want it. Using the layouts and layers, you can rapidly put a page together over a tracing image.

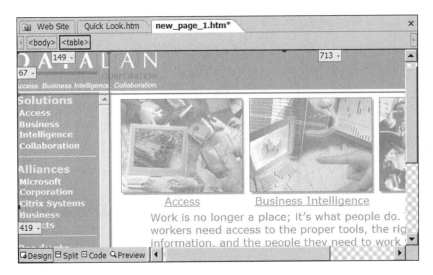

Figure 4-16. Table and cell layout

Working with Data Sources

Once you have an idea of how to use the basic layout tools, you will want to be able to add more interesting content than just text and graphics. Microsoft FrontPage in conjunction with SharePoint Services supports the ability to create XML data sources that you can use in your web pages. This capability allows you to connect directly with SQL databases, XML sheets, SharePoint lists, and other sources to display dynamic data sets. Using FrontPage, you can display the data without ever writing code.

The key to using dynamic data sets in your web pages is to make use of the Data Source Catalog and the Data View web part. The Data Source Catalog acts as an agent for mapping access to any number of data sources that can provide XML data sets. The Data View web part is the component that displays those data sets on the page.

When the Data View web part is displaying an XML data set, it has the ability to format the data set based on the eXtensible Stylesheet Language Transform (XSLT). This means that you can use the FrontPage what you see is what you get (WYSIWYG) editor to format columns, colors, and styles for a data set. You can also use conditional format to change the style of a data cell when it reaches certain parameters. In this way, you can call attention to outlying data in the set.

Using XML data sets begins with the Data Source Catalog. You can access the Data Source Catalog by selecting Data ➤ Insert Data View from the main menu in Microsoft FrontPage. The catalog lists all of the available XML data sources. If you have an existing SharePoint Service site open in FrontPage, you'll notice that all of the lists and libraries in the site are available for use as data sources. In addition to these sources, you'll also see support for database connections, XML files, server-side scripts, and web services. Figure 4-17 shows a typical Data Source Catalog.

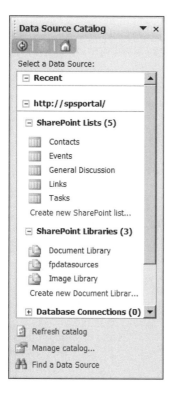

Figure 4-17. The Data Source Catalog

When using the Data Source Catalog, you are not limited to the lists and libraries associated with the site that is currently open. You can either create new lists and libraries directly or utilize list and libraries from other sites within the portal structure. If you click either the Create New SharePoint List or the Create New Document Library link, you will open a dialog that allows you to add a new list, library, or survey to the Data Source Catalog. If you instead want to add an element from another site, you can click the Manage Catalog link to add a new source. From this link, you can add a reference to another SharePoint site, which will import all of the data sources defined for that site.

If the data source you want to use is not a SharePoint element already, you will have to spend some time setting up the source before it can be used. Most of the data sources are set up in a similar fashion that begins by clicking the Add to Catalog link, which appears just below the data source type you want to use.

To add a database connection, follow these steps:

1. From the FrontPage main menu, select Data ➤ Insert Data View to open the Data Source Catalog pane.

2. In the Data Source Catalog, expand the Database Connections node.

3. Click the link Add to Catalog just beneath the node to open the Data Source Properties dialog.

4. On the General tab, name the connection **pub authors**.

5. On the Source tab, click the Configure Database Connection button.

6. In the Configure Database Connection dialog, enter **spsportal** in the Server Name text box.

7. In the Authentication section, enter a valid user name and password to access the SQL Server installation.

8. Click Next.

9. On the next step, select the Pubs database from the drop-down list and select the Authors table from the list.

10. Click Finish.

11. On the Source tab, click Fields.

12. In the Displayed Fields dialog, remove the field au_id from the set of displayed fields and click OK.

13. On the Source tab, click Sort.

14. In the Sort dialog, select to sort the fields by au_lname and click OK.

15. In the Data Source Properties dialog, click OK to complete the definition of the new data source.

When using a database connection as a data source, it is generally not a good idea to save the credentials directly in the database connection. Instead you can use Windows authentication to verify access credentials at the time the data is accessed in the web site. However, if you go down this path, you will have to set up credentials in the database for each user. A better mechanism for authentication is to use the Microsoft Single Sign-On (SSO) service. This service allows you to set up a master set of credentials just for accessing such data sources. Later in the book, I'll cover the setup and usage of SSO when I discuss creating custom web parts.

Once the data source is defined, adding it to the page is a simple matter of dragging the source from the catalog to the page. Once you drop the data source onto the page, FrontPage adds the server-side code necessary to access the data source and display the data. Because the page now contains server-side code, you may be prompted to rename the page to contain an ASPX extension. The ASPX extension is required for the page to be recognized as containing server-side code.

Working with Data Views

Once the data set is visible on the page, you can make changes to the presentation directly in the page. Changing font styles, font sizes, and column header names can be done using the same techniques as in a word processor. A drop-down menu also becomes available in the upper-left corner of the table. This drop-down menu gives you the ability to sort and filter the data as well as change the presentation style. From this menu, you can also apply conditional formatting to call out values in the data set that need attention.

Selecting Style from the drop-down menu opens the View Styles dialog. In this dialog, you may choose to apply one of several predefined styles that arrange the tabular data in various reporting formats. You can also change the paging, add headers and footers, as well as add a sort/filter toolbar to the header of the table. This gives your data view some flexibility to support the reporting needs of the intended users.

Selecting Sort and Group from the drop-down menu opens the Sort and Group dialog. In this dialog, you can select the fields to sort the tabular data. You can pick multiple fields for the sort and apply a grouping to the sorted data.

Selecting Filter from the drop-down menu opens the Filter Criteria dialog. In this dialog, you can specify the filter to apply when the page is viewed. Using this dialog, you may apply several different criteria nested together. As you might expect, this is essentially a SQL query tool that applies to the data view.

Using conditional formatting, you can highlight a cell when it has values that meet certain criteria. To get started, you have to select the table, column, or cell where you want to apply the formatting. After selecting the values, you can pick Conditional Formatting from the drop-down menu. This in turn opens the Conditional Formatting pane. In the pane, you click Create to build the conditions.

Building conditional formatting rules is very similar to building filter rules. You can specify the fields and conditions that trigger the formatting. Once the rules are defined, FrontPage opens a style dialog that you can use to change the font, size, and color of the data to call it out in the table.

Not only can you apply sorts, filters, groups, and formatting in the data view, but you can apply them to the data source as well. In the Data Source Catalog, you can use the drop-down list associated with a data source and select Show Data. This action opens the data in the task pane and presents the same options as you find in the drop-down menu on a page.

Although data views can stand alone on a page like a report, they also have the ability to interact with other data sources. For example, you can have one data view that displays names and another data view that displays contact information. Selecting a name from the first data view causes the contact information to show in the second data view. This is the same concept of connecting web parts that you saw when you modified pages directly in SPS. The biggest difference between connecting web parts in FrontPage versus SPS is that FrontPage can connect web parts from two different web pages. SPS can only connect web parts that are on the same page.

You can connect two data views by selecting Web Part Connections from the drop-down menu associated with either of the views. Microsoft FrontPage responds by running a wizard that helps you make the connection. The wizard walks you through the process of selecting the fields to connect and the behavior for each part. The wizard also allows you to select a connection with a web part that is on a different page.

One of the major challenges of portal development is the integration of systems within the portal. I have found that data views are the easiest way to take data from disparate systems and present them together in a meaningful way. Furthermore, because they do not require any programming, they are pretty simple to get up and running. This capability is the single biggest reason to use FrontPage in your portal development.

Here is what you need to do to work with data views:

1. In Microsoft FrontPage, select File ➤ New.

2. In the New pane, click Blank Page.

3. Open the Data Source Catalog by selecting Data ➤ Insert Data View.

4. From the Data Source Catalog, drag the Pub Authors data source onto the new page and drop it.

5. Select the table on the page and locate the drop-down menu.

6. From the drop-down menu, select Style to open the View Styles dialog.

7. On the Options tab, check the box Show Toolbar Options For:.

8. Click OK.

9. From the table's drop-down menu, select Filter to open the Filter Criteria dialog.

10. In the Filter Criteria dialog, click the link "Click here to add a new clause."

11. In the Field Name list, select au_lname.

12. In the Comparison list, select Begins With.

13. In the Value list, select [Input Parameter].

14. Click OK.

15. Select File ➤ Save and save the new page.

16. Select File ➤ Preview in browser to see the new page.

Creating and Consuming a Web Service in FrontPage

Earlier in this chapter, I noted that web services were one of the data sources that could be used by Microsoft FrontPage. It turns out that web services are useful in many other aspects of portal development. Later, you will find that they can be integrated with InfoPath to create mechanisms to input form data into multiple systems. Although complete coverage of web services is beyond the scope of this book, I will cover the basics of web service development and show you how to use it as a data source in FrontPage.

The easiest way to think of web services is as a component accessible over a network using standard Hypertext Transfer Protocol (HTTP). In this way, a web service is not unlike its predecessor, the Distributed Component Object Model (DCOM). DCOM was designed to allow components on different machines to communicate across a network. The fundamental problem with DCOM is that it was proprietary and was easily blocked by corporate firewalls. The driving force behind web services is essentially to create an open protocol for distributed components that won't be blocked by firewalls.

Although creating a web service in Visual Studio is simple, creating one on the same virtual server where SharePoint Services is installed is difficult. This is because SharePoint Services essentially takes over the virtual server where it is installed, making it difficult to run any other kind of web application, including Active Server Pages (ASP) and web services. The simplest way around this dilemma is to create a new virtual server on a different port. Once the new virtual server is created, you can easily build web services on it. The exercise at the end of this chapter shows in detail how to create a new virtual server.

When you create a new web service project in Visual Studio, the project template provides most of what you need immediately. The key file you need to examine is `Service1.asmx`, which contains the code for the web service. The code in a web service is not much different from any Visual Studio project you create. The biggest area of concern lies in the decorations used in the code.

Like all Visual Studio projects, web services are based on class definitions; however, the classes in a web service are decorated with a Namespace attribute that references a unique URL instead of just a simple name. The structure of the URL itself is not critical, but it does provide a way to organize the web services you create and make them discoverable by external components. In this case, you do not need to go through discovery because you already know about the web service. The following code shows a typical class definition for a web service.

```
<System.Web.Services.WebService _
(Namespace:="http://www.datalan.com/pubs/authors")> _
Public Class Authors
    Inherits System.Web.Services.WebService

End Class
```

Inside the class definition, you may define functions that accept input parameters and return values. The only difference between any normal function you create and a web service is once again found in the attributes. Every function must have a `<WebMethod()>` decoration. The following code shows a typical definition for a web service method.

```
<WebMethod()> _
Public Function GetData() As String

End Function
```

A web service can accept and return any kind of data type; however, Microsoft FrontPage deals best with `DataSet` objects returned directly from the web service. If you return a `DataSet` object, you will be able to use the sorts and filters more easily. Listing 4-1 shows a complete example of a web service returning a list of author last names as XML from the Pubs database.

Listing 4-1. A Web Service Returning XML

```
Imports System.Web.Services
Imports System.Data
Imports System.Data.SqlClient

<System.Web.Services.WebService _
(Namespace:="http://www.datalan.com/pubs/authors")> _
Public Class Authors
    Inherits System.Web.Services.WebService


    <WebMethod()> _
    Public Function GetData() As DataSet

        'Dataset for query
        Dim objDataSet As DataSet


        'Set up connection string from custom properties
        Dim strConnection As String = _
        "Password=;Persist Security Info=True;User ID=sa;" _
        + "Initial Catalog=pubs;Data Source=(local)"

        'Query database for phone numbers"
        Dim strSQL As String = "select au_lname from authors"

        'Try to run the query
        Try
            With New SqlDataAdapter
                objDataSet = New DataSet("root")
                .SelectCommand = New _
SqlCommand(strSQL, New SqlConnection(strConnection))
                .Fill(objDataSet, "Contacts")
            End With
            Return objDataSet
        Catch ex As Exception
            Return Nothing
            Exit Function
        End Try
    End Function

End Class
```

Once the web service is written, it can be added to the Data Source Catalog in Microsoft FrontPage. From the Data Source Catalog, you would click the Add to Catalog link below the XML Web Services node to open the Data Source Properties dialog. In this dialog, you must provide the URL that points to the web service description. The web service description is the definition of the methods, parameters, and return values provided by the web service. You access the web service description using the URL of the web service followed by ?WSDL. For this example, the following URL points to the web service description:

```
http://spsportal:8080/pubs/service1.asmx?WSDL
```

Once the web service description URL is defined, you can connect to the web service. Connecting to the web service will make the returned data available in the Data Source Catalog, where you can drag it onto a page. Once on the page, it functions like any other data view.

Using Web Components

Another useful component for creating portal content is the FrontPage web component. FrontPage web components are essentially web parts that do not have knowledge of the web part infrastructure. FrontPage web components have properties and can display data, but they cannot connect to other web components. In fact, it is easy to see that web components controls are really the predecessor to web parts.

If web components are just light versions of web parts, then why would you use them? The answer is that there are many web components available that were created before web parts. Therefore, you might find some useful functionality that is not immediately available in a web part. A prime example of this is the spreadsheet and chart control. Web components also exist for Java applets, ActiveX controls, and Flash movies. All of the web components are accessible from the menu by selecting Insert ➤ Web Component.

Exercise 4-1: Building an Executive Dashboard

Key Performance Indicators (KPI) are measurements that indicate the state of an organization. KPIs can either present data from the past (revenue from the previous quarter) or they can predict into the future (likely number of units that will sell in the Southeast). Both types of KPIs have value to managers running the organization; however, most managers have a difficult time getting access to KPIs. In this exercise, you will create an Executive Dashboard that presents some mock KPIs using a SharePoint site created with Microsoft FrontPage.

Preparing Data Sources

Although SharePoint sites are excellent for presenting information to end users, you must still do the work necessary on the back end to provide appropriate data sources for SharePoint Services to access. Sites built with Microsoft FrontPage can use several different kinds of data sources, including XML, SQL databases, and web services. In this exercise, you will make use of some different data sources, including direct access to SQL databases, Microsoft Excel spreadsheets, and SQL XML.

The concept of making services available remotely across the Internet is now affecting nearly every aspect of the enterprise. The same is true with SQL Server. SQL Server 2000 supports directly accessing databases through HTTP using SQL XML. This means that you can make SQL calls directly from a browser.

In order to set up SQL Server to deliver data over the web, you must first configure a virtual directory for clients to access. Interestingly, your installation of SharePoint Services has a global impact on the SPSPortal server. This means that SharePoint Services has really taken over the entire web site where it was installed. Therefore, you first have to create a new web site for the client to access the functions of SQL XML.

To create a new web site, follow these steps:

1. Log in to SPSPortal as the local administrator.

2. Select Start ➤ Administrative Tools ➤ Internet Information Services (IIS) Manager.

3. In the IIS Manager, expand the tree until the Web Sites folder is visible.

4. Right-click the Web Sites folder and select New ➤ Web Site. This starts the web site wizard.

5. In the Description text box, type **SQLXML** and click Next.

6. In the "TCP port this Web site should use (Default 80)" text box, type **8080** and click Next.

7. Click Browse to search for a new directory.

8. In the Browse for Folder dialog select the root of the C: drive and click Make New Folder.

9. Name the new folder **SQLXML Web** and click OK.

10. Finish the rest of the wizard to create the new web site.

11. In the IIS Manager, click the Web Service Extensions folder.

12. Select the web service extension All Unknown ISAPI Extensions and click Allow.

13. Close the IIS Manager.

Once the new web site is created, you must now create a virtual directory beneath the new web site. The virtual directory will act as the access point for the SQL Server data. You will utilize existing data from the Northwind database for your exercise.

Here is what you will do to create a virtual directory:

1. Select Start ➤ All Programs ➤ Microsoft SQL Server ➤ Configure SQL XML Support in IIS.

2. In the IIS Virtual Directory Manager, expand the tree until the SQLXML web site is visible.

3. Right-click the SQLXML web link and select New ➤ Virtual Directory; this opens the New Virtual Directory Properties dialog.

4. On the General tab, name the new virtual directory **Northwind**.

5. Under the Local Path section, click Browse. Browse to the SQLXML Web folder you created earlier and select it.

6. Click Make New Folder and create a directory underneath named **Northwind**.

7. Click OK.

8. On the Security tab, enter credentials that will be used to log in to SQL Server.

NOTE *If you use Windows Integrated Security, you will need to give permissions to access the folder you created on the General tab. This is because you created a new web outside of the default web site.*

---

9. On the Data Source tab, select the Northwind database.

NOTE *If you use Windows Integrated Security, you will need to give appropriate permissions to access the Northwind database.*

10. On the Settings tab, check the box "Allow sql=... or template=... URL queries." Uncheck any other boxes.

11. Click OK to exit the property sheet.

12. Test the setup by logging into SPSClient and opening Internet Explorer.

13. In the browser, type the following URL:

```
http://spsportal:8080/northwind?
sql=select * from categories for xml auto&root=data
```

Building the Team Site

Now that the data sources are prepared for use, you can move on to creating the site itself. In this part of the exercise, you will use Microsoft FrontPage to create a new SharePoint Services site. This site will use different data sources to present KPIs in a dashboard format. After you create the site, you will make it accessible from SPS.

To create a new team site, follow these steps:

1. Log in to SPSClient as the administrator.

2. Once logged in, select Start ➤ All Programs ➤ Microsoft Office ➤ Microsoft Office FrontPage 2003.

3. In FrontPage, select File ➤ New. This opens the New pane.

4. In the New pane, select New Web Site ➤ SharePoint Team Site.

5. In the Web Site Templates dialog, select the General tab.

6. On the General tab, select to create a new SharePoint Team Site.

7. Specify the location of the new site as http://spsportal/ExecutiveDashboard.

8. Click OK.

9. When the new site is created, select View ➤ Folder List to display the site contents.

10. In the folder list, right-click `default.aspx` and select Open from the pop-up menu. This makes the page appear in design view.

11. In the designer, change the name of the web site by highlighting the text Team Web Site and changing it to Executive Dashboard.

Adding the Data Sources to the Catalog

Using the folder list, you can explore the contents of the new site. You notice that the new site is identical to one that you create in SPS using the Team Site template; however, you have much more control over the layout and functionality of the site when you edit it in FrontPage. Specifically, you can add custom data sources that are not available in SPS.

1. Select Data ➤ Insert Data View to open the Data Source Catalog.

2. In the Data Source catalog, expand the Database Connections node.

3. Click the Add to Catalog link underneath the node to open the Data Source Properties dialog.

4. On the Source tab, click the Configure Database Connection button.

5. In the Configure Database Connection dialog, type **spsportal** in the Server Name text box.

6. In the Authentication section, select "Save this username and password in the data connection." Type valid credentials into the User Name and Password boxes.

 NOTE *It is not a best practice to save the credentials in the data connection. Normally, you would use the Microsoft Single Sign-On (SSO) service or Windows authentication. I cover the SSO later in the book.*

---

7. Click Next.

8. Select the Northwind database from the drop-down list of databases.

9. Select the Sales By Category view.

10. Click Finish to return to the Data Source Properties dialog.

11. Click the Fields button.

12. In the Displayed Fields dialog, remove the CategoryID field from the list of displayed fields.

13. On the General tab, name the connection **Overall Category Sales**.

14. Click OK.

15. Click OK again to exit.

16. Verify that you have typed the query correctly by opening the drop-down menu associated with the new connection and selecting Show Data.

Along with traditional direct connections to the database, you can also make use of the SQL XML connection to return data. These connections are made under the Server-Side Scripts section.

1. In the Data Source Catalog expand the Server-Side Scripts node.

2. Click the Add to Catalog link beneath the node to open the Data Source Properties dialog.

3. In the URL box, type the following URL:

```
http://spsportal:8080/northwind?
sql=select * from [Category Sales for 1997] for xml auto&root=summary
```

4. On the General tab, name the connection **Category Sales for 1997**.

5. Click OK.

6. Verify that you have typed the query correctly by opening the drop-down menu associated with the new connection and selecting Show Data.

Creating the Data Views

Once the data sources have been added to the catalog, you can use them to create content for the management dashboard. In this section of the exercise, you will clean up the default page and then add the new content. You'll create both tables and charts for the dashboard.

1. In design view, select each web part on the page and delete it by right-clicking and selecting Cut from the pop-up menu. You should have two empty zones remaining: Left and Right.

2. With the Data Source Catalog open, carefully drag the connection labeled Overall Category Sales onto the page; drop it onto the left Web Part Zone. A data table will appear as a result.

3. In the upper-left corner of the data table, locate the arrow used to access the Data View Options drop-down menu and click it. Figure 4-18 shows the arrow.

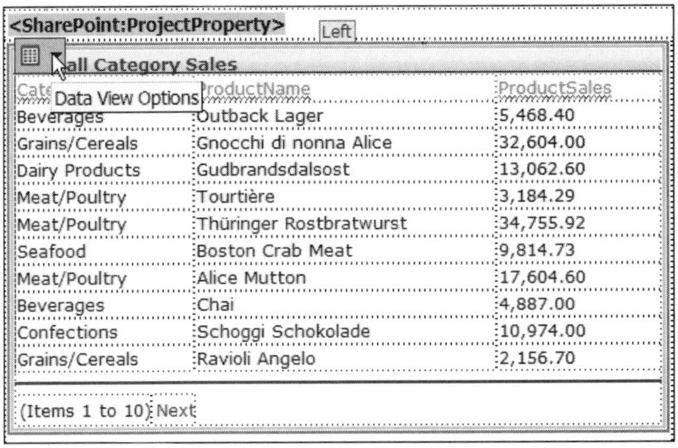

`<SharePoint:ProjectProperty>`	Left	
all Category Sales		
Cat Data View Options	ProductName	ProductSales
Beverages	Outback Lager	5,468.40
Grains/Cereals	Gnocchi di nonna Alice	32,604.00
Dairy Products	Gudbrandsdalsost	13,062.60
Meat/Poultry	Tourtière	3,184.29
Meat/Poultry	Thüringer Rostbratwurst	34,755.92
Seafood	Boston Crab Meat	9,814.73
Meat/Poultry	Alice Mutton	17,604.60
Beverages	Chai	4,887.00
Confections	Schoggi Schokolade	10,974.00
Grains/Cereals	Ravioli Angelo	2,156.70
(Items 1 to 10) Next		

Figure 4-18. Accessing the Data View Options menu

4. Select Data View Options ➤ Sort and Group.

5. Select to sort the data by CategoryName.

6. Click OK.

7. Carefully drag the connection labeled Category Sales for 1997 and drop it onto the right Web Part Zone.

Once both of the data views are in the page, you can connect them to make them more effective. In this exercise, you will connect the Category Sales for 1997 web part to the Overall Category Sales web part. In this way, you can filter the larger data set by using the smaller data set. This is a typical master-detail relationship between web parts.

1. In the right Web Part Zone, select the Category Sales for 1997 web part.

2. Select Data ➤ Web Part Connections from the FrontPage menu. This starts the Web Part Connections wizard.

3. In the first step, accept the default value of Provide Data Values To and click Next.

4. In the next step, accept the default value of "Connect to a web part on this page" and click Next.

5. In the next step, accept the default values for Target Web Part and Target Action. Click Next.

6. In the next step, choose to filter on CategoryName by selecting it from both columns and clicking Next.

7. In the next step, accept the default value of "Create a hyperlink on CategoryName" and click Next.

8. Click Finish.

9. Select File ➤ Save to save your work.

10. In the folder list, right-click default.aspx and select Preview in Browser from the pop-up menu. Verify the filter behavior by clicking hyperlinks in the category list.

Along with data sources and web parts, you can also use server-side web components to display data. Web components allow you to access other interesting sources of data, such as Excel spreadsheets, and incorporate them into the page. In this section, you'll add a chart to the dashboard.

1. Carefully click in the area just below the right Web Part Zone. You will place the next component below the zone, not inside it.

2. In Microsoft FrontPage, select Insert ➤ Web Component.

3. In the Insert Web Component dialog, select Spreadsheets and Charts from the Component Type list.

4. In the Choose a Control list, select Office Chart.

5. Click Finish. A new chart space will be added to the page and the Commands and Options dialog will open.

6. On the Data Source tab, click the option to display "Data typed into a data sheet".

7. In the data sheet, type the information contained in Table 4-1.

Table 4-1. Data for the Web Component

CATEGORY	SALES
Beverages	102074
Condiments	55277
Confections	80894
Dairy Products	114749
Grains/Cereals	55948
Meat/Poultry	81338
Produce	53019
Seafood	65544

8. On the Type tab, select the column chart.

9. Close the Commands and Options dialog.

10. In the web page, size the chart to fit comfortably in the available space.

11. Select File ➤ Save to save your work.

12. Select File ➤ Exit to close Microsoft FrontPage.

Accessing the Site from SPS

Once the new site is completed, you can add a reference to it in SPS. Adding a linked reference will make the site available in the Site Directory and through searches. You can also manage many aspects of the site using standard SPS management tools.

1. Log in to SPS as a member of the Administrator site group.

2. On the portal home page, click the Sites link.

3. On the Site Directory, click the Add Link to Site link under the Actions list.

4. On the Add Link to Site page, name the site **Executive Dashboard** and give it a description.

5. In the URL field, type `http://spsportal/ExecutiveDashboard`.

6. In the Areas section, click the Change Location link.

7. In the Change Location site map, expand the nodes and check the areas Sites and Topics ➤ Departments.

8. Click OK to close the site map.

9. Click OK again to add the new site link.

10. Using the site map, navigate to the area where you placed a link to the new site.

11. On the home page, verify that the web parts are working correctly and then click the Site Settings link.

12. On the Site Settings page, select Administration ➤ Go to Site Administration.

13. On the Site Administration page, select Users and Permissions ➤ Manage Permission Inheritance.

14. On the Manage Permission Inheritance page select Use Unique Permissions.

15. Click OK to return to the Site Settings page.

16. On the Site Settings page, select Administration ➤ Manage Users.

17. Adjust the permissions so that only appropriate management and financial personnel can access the new dashboard.

CHAPTER 5

Building Web Parts

THROUGHOUT OUR INVESTIGATION OF SharePoint Portal Server (SPS), we have used web parts to integrate systems and display information. Although SPS ships with a number of useful web parts, the included set is unlikely to handle every situation because each organization has a different set of systems to integrate. Therefore, you will inevitably have to create your own web parts.

In this chapter, we will examine the fundamental construction and deployment of web parts. Before we begin, however, you will want to make sure that you have all the required tools in place to create web parts. If you followed the instructions in Chapter 2, you should already have Microsoft Visual Studio .NET 2003 installed on SPSPortal.

Along with Visual Studio, you should download and install the web part template for SharePoint Services. The template is available from msdn.microsoft.com and is named WebPartTemplatesforVSNetSample2.exe. The templates provide both C# and VB.NET projects.

Although you do not have to have the template to create the web part, it simplifies the process by providing a new project type and some starter code. The examples in this chapter assume you are using the template, but I will explain all of the code requirements in detail whether they are generated by the template or coded by hand. Throughout the examples, I will use both C# and VB.NET so that you can get the fundamentals regardless of your language preference.

Web Part Basics

You create a new web part project in the same way that you create any other project. When you select File ➤ New Project from the Visual Studio menu, you are presented with a set of project types from which to choose. Regardless of whether you choose C# or VB.NET, the project type is named "Web Part Library." When you create this project, the template generates four key files for you: the assembly information file, the manifest file, the code file, and the web part description file.

The assembly information file, AssemblyInfo.cs or AssemblyInfo.vb, contains assembly information such as the version. This information will be important when you are giving the web part permission to run inside of SPS. The manifest file, Manifest.xml, contains information important to the distribution of the web part. The code file, WebPart.cs or WebPart.vb, contains all of the code necessary for the web part to function. The web part description file, `WebPart.dwp`, contains metadata about the web part that SPS needs to upload the part and make it available for use in page design.

The WebPart Class

Creating a web part in Visual Studio is possible because Microsoft has provided an extensive set of .NET classes that allow access to nearly every facet of SharePoint Services. These classes are all defined within the `SharePoint` namespace. Throughout the book, we will be examining various pieces of the `SharePoint` namespace, but for now we will look closely at a single class: `Microsoft.SharePoint.WebPartPages.WebPart`. All web parts you construct must inherit from `Microsoft.SharePoint.WebPartPages.WebPart`, and depending upon the exact functionality you are trying to implement, you will have to override various methods of this class.

The first thing to note about the `WebPart` class is that it inherits from the `System.Web.UI.Control` class. This is exactly the same class from which the class `System.Web.UI.WebControls.WebControl` inherits. This is significant because developers use the `WebControl` class to create custom ASP.NET controls that live in the Visual Studio toolbox. In fact, web parts behave almost exactly like custom ASP.NET controls. Both types of controls are accessible from a toolbox, both have properties that are set during the design of a user interface, and both have runtime behavior that is affected by the values of the properties. Figure 5-1 shows the class hierarchy that relates web parts and custom controls.

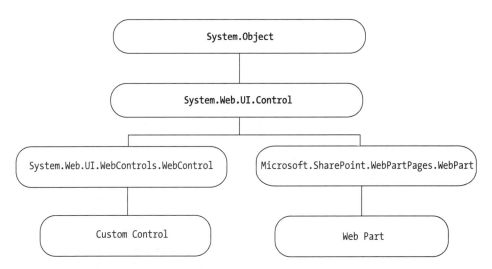

Figure 5-1. The WebPart class hierarchy

When you create a new web part project in Visual Studio .NET, a new class is generated that inherits from the WebPart class. The project also decorates the class with three attributes that affect its behavior. The following code shows a template class declaration in C#.

```
[DefaultProperty("Text"),
ToolboxData("<{0}:WebPart1 runat=server></{0}:WebPart1>"),
XmlRoot(Namespace="HelloCS")]
public class WebPart1 : Microsoft.SharePoint.WebPartPages.WebPart
{
}
```

The DefaultProperty and ToolboxData attributes are exactly the same attributes found in an ASP.NET custom control. These attributes exist to govern the behavior of the control in a full-scale design environment such as Visual Studio .NET. These attributes show clearly that web parts are a specialized version of exactly the same components that Visual Studio developers drag onto ASP.NET web pages. Compare the previous code with the following code, which is a class declaration for an ASP.NET custom control written in VB.NET.

```
<DefaultProperty("Text"), _
ToolboxData("<{0}:WebCustomControl1 runat=server> _
</{0}:WebCustomControl1>")> _
Public Class WebCustomControl1
    Inherits System.Web.UI.WebControls.WebControl

End Class
```

A close examination of the two code fragments will reveal that the web part code has one additional attribute not found in the ASP.NET custom control code— the XmlRoot attribute. This attribute is specific to web parts and is used as the root element when an instance of the web part is serialized to XML. This serialization maintains the state of the control and is part of the web part framework found in SharePoint Services.

The relationship between web parts and ASP.NET custom controls just demonstrated is so strong that you can actually add web parts to the toolbox in Visual Studio .NET. Once in the toolbox, the web parts can be dragged onto a web page in an ASP.NET project. However, this is really not the recommended use for a web part because Visual Studio .NET does not support the same infrastructure as SharePoint Services. Therefore, although an ASP.NET application is similar to a SharePoint Services site, it is not capable of providing all of the features such as web part connections or in-browser page design.

The Web Part Life Cycle

Just like ASP.NET controls, web parts participate in a server-side request/ response sequence that loads a page in the portal each time it is requested and unloads the page once it is sent to the client. Web parts, therefore, follow the same control life cycle that ASP.NET controls follow. This life cycle supports a state management system that makes the portal appear to the end user like they are interacting with a stateful system, when in fact each request for a page is a separate operation.

When a page from a SharePoint Services site that contains web parts is requested for the first time—or when it is submitted to the server—the web part life cycle begins. The first phase in this life cycle is *initialization*. The initialization phase is marked by a call to the OnInit method of the WebPart class. During initialization, values from the web part storage system are loaded into the web part. These values are created when the web part page is designed.

SharePoint Services supports either a single set of shared values that are applied to all portal users or a set for each individual user. Each property in a web part may be designated to support shared or personal values. Additionally, web parts may be modified in a shared or personal view by end users with appropriate permissions. All of these elements combine to determine the initial set of property values that will be loaded into the web part.

After the web part is initialized, the ViewState of the web part is populated. ViewState is a property inherited from System.Web.UI.Control. The ViewState is filled from the state information that was previously serialized into a hidden field in the web page. Once the ViewState property is populated, the control returns to the same state it was in when it was last processed on the server. The ViewState is populated through a call to the LoadViewState method.

Once the web part has returned to its previous state, the server can make changes to the properties of the web part based on values that were posted by the client browser. Any new values that were posted during the request—such as text field values—are applied to the corresponding property of the web part. At this point, the web part has reached the state intended by the end user.

After all of the new property values are applied to the web part, the page may begin using the information to process the end user request. This begins through a call to the OnLoad event of the WebPart class. The OnLoad event fires for every web part regardless of how many properties have changed. Web part developers use the OnLoad event as the basis for the functionality embodied in the web part. During this event, web parts may access a database or other system to retrieve information for display. The key thing to remember about this event is that it always fires after the posted data has been applied to the web part.

Once the OnLoad event completes, any events triggered by the client interaction with the web part are fired. This includes all user-generated events such as the Click event associated with a button. It is critical for the web part developer to understand that the user-generated events happen after the OnLoad event. This means that you must be careful not to rely on the results of user-generated events when you write code for the OnLoad event.

Once the web part has finished handling the user-generated events, it is ready to create the output of the control. The web part begins creating this output with a call to the OnPreRender event of the WebPart class. The OnPreRender event gives the web part developer the opportunity to change any of the web part properties before the control output is drawn. This is the perfect place to run a database query that relies on several user-supplied values because all of the values will be available at this point in the life cycle.

After the OnPreRender event is complete, the ViewState of the web part is serialized and saved to a hidden field in the web page. The ViewState is saved through a call to the SaveViewState event, which is inherited from the System.Web.UI.Control class.

Once the ViewState is saved, the web part output may be drawn. Drawing begins through a call to the RenderWebPart event. In this method, the web part must programmatically generate its HTML output. This output will be rendered in the appropriate zone on the page in the portal.

After the output is rendered, the control web part can be removed from the memory of the server. Web parts receive notification that they are about to be removed from memory through the Dispose event. This method allows the web part developer to release critical resources such as database connections before the web part is destroyed.

The web part life cycle ends when it is finally removed from memory. The last event to fire is the OnUnload event. This event notifies the web part that it is being removed from memory. Generally web part developers do not need access to this event because all cleanup should have been accomplished in the Dispose event.

Understanding the complete life cycle helps significantly when developing web parts. In particular, understanding when certain values are available to the web part will ensure that you create components with consistent behavior. Figure 5-2 summarizes the life cycle in a flowchart.

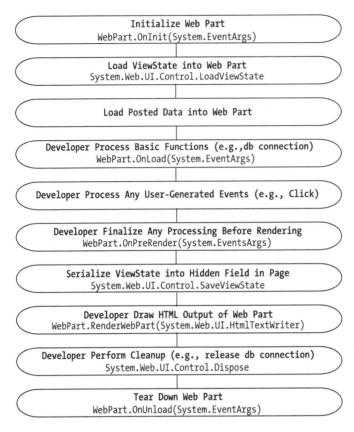

Figure 5-2. The web part life cycle

Web Part Properties

Well-designed web parts function in a variety of different pages because they are configurable by an administrator or end user directly in the portal. This configuration is possible because each web part supports a series of properties that can be set in the portal and read by the web part at runtime. In code, these properties are created in the same manner as any property for any class with the exception that they have special decorations that determine their behavior within the design environment of SPS. The process of creating a property begins with a standard property construct. This involves declaring a member variable to hold the value and a get/set construct to set and retrieve the value. Listing 5-1 shows a typical property defined using C#.

Listing 5-1. Creating a Property in C#

```csharp
private string m_text;

public string Text
{
    get
    {
        return m_text;
    }

    set
    {
        m_text = value;
    }
}
```

Property Basics

Most properties are designed to be configured directly in the portal. Therefore, you must decorate the property with different attributes to define its behavior when a page is designed. These property values are subsequently serialized and saved when the page is processed so that the property values can be read later when an end user accesses the page. Each of the properties you define is decorated with the Browsable, Category, DefaultValue, WebPartStorage, FriendlyName, and Description attributes.

The Browsable attribute is a Boolean value that determines whether or not the property appears in the tool pane during design time. You may set this value to either True or False. Although most of your properties will be browsable, you may have sensitive properties that should not be accessible by general portal users. The advantage of using a nonbrowsable property is that the value is still serialized and saved even though it cannot be set in the portal. In these cases, the web part itself is setting the value in code.

The Category attribute is a String value that determines the category in the tool pane where the property should appear. Using this attribute, you may have the property appear in a standard category like Appearance or you may create your own custom category. Generally, you should try to observe a logical placement that corresponds to the way most of the standard web parts work.

The DefaultValue attribute specifies the value of the property when the web part is first placed on a page. The exact value of the attribute is dependent upon the data type of the property itself. When setting a default value in the attribute, recognize that this does not actually change the value of the property itself. In order to ensure that the actual default value is in sync with the DefaultValue attribute, be sure to set the value of the member variable in code.

The WebPartStorage attribute is an enumeration that determines whether the property values are saved for an individual or for all users of the page on which the web part sits. This attribute may be set to Storage.None, Storage.Personal, or Storage.Shared. When the attribute is set to Storage.None, the property is not serialized and saved to the web part storage system. When the attribute is set to Storage.Personal, the property value may be set for each user of a page. The web part infrastructure serializes and saves the values separately for each user. Finally, when the attribute is set to Storage.Shared, the web part infrastructure saves only a single value of the property that is applied to all users of the page on which the web part sits.

The FriendlyName and Description attributes are both String values that are used to display a name and description for the property in the tool pane. These are both straightforward attributes that are obvious in their use. The only thing to watch out for here is consistency. Use the same names and descriptions for the same properties across all web parts you create. This will make them much easier to understand and configure.

Once you understand the property definition scheme, you can create as many as you need to properly configure the web part. Although they are easy to change, I recommend that you spend some time designing your web part before implementing the property set. If you think through the intended use of the web part, you will save yourself a lot of wasted time writing and rewriting property structures. As a final example, Listing 5-2 shows a complete property structure in VB.NET.

Listing 5-2. Defining a Web Part Property

```
Dim m_DatabaseName As String

<Browsable(true),Category("Miscellaneous"), _
DefaultValue(""),WebPartStorage(Storage.Personal),FriendlyName("Database"), _
Description("The database to access")> _
Property DatabaseName() As String
    Get
        Return m_DatabaseName
    End Get

    Set(ByVal Value As String)
        m_DatabaseName = Value
    End Set
End Property
```

Rendering Web Parts

Because the WebPart class inherits from System.Web.UI.Control, the entire user interface for a web part must be created through code. There is no drag-and-drop user interface design in a web part. This approach is definitely a drawback and can slow your ability to create web parts. Be that as it may, it becomes less of an issue once you have created a few web parts and learned the techniques for generating the user interface.

Properly rendering a web part requires that you first create any ASP.NET controls that you will need in code. The required ASP.NET controls are then added to the controls collection of the web part by overriding the CreateChildControls method of the base class. Finally, you can draw the output by overriding the RenderWebPart method.

You may use any available ASP.NET control found in Visual Studio .NET or any ASP.NET control you have written to create the user interface for a web part. Remember, however, that these controls cannot be dragged onto a page. Instead, they must be declared in code.

When you declare ASP.NET controls in code, be sure to set a reference to the appropriate namespace. Nearly all of the ASP.NET controls that you could want belong to the System.Web.UI.WebControls namespace. Therefore, you should reference them in code using the following C# or VB.NET declaration.

```
//C#
using System.Web.UI.WebControls;

'VB.NET
Imports System.Web.UI.WebControls
```

Once the appropriate namespace is referenced, you may create instances of the controls. When you create these instances, be sure to create them with their associated events. This way, you will have access to all of the events for any control you use. The following code shows an example of declaring several ASP.NET controls in VB.NET using the WithEvents keyword.

```
'Controls to appear in the web part
Protected WithEvents txtSearch As TextBox
Protected WithEvents btnSearch As Button
Protected WithEvents lstData As ListBox
Protected WithEvents lblMessage As Label
```

Once the controls are declared, you can set their properties and add them to the Controls collection of the web part. You can do this by overriding the CreateChildControls method. In this method, set property values for each control and then add it to the Controls collection using the Controls.Add method. Listing 5-3 shows several controls being added to a web part.

Listing 5-3. Adding ASP.NET Controls to a Web Part

```
Protected Overrides Sub CreateChildControls()

    'Purpose: Add the child controls to the web part

    'Text Box for Search String
    txtSearch = New TextBox
    With txtSearch
        .Width = Unit.Percentage(100)
        .Font.Name = "arial"
        .Font.Size = New FontUnit(FontSize.AsUnit).Point(8)
    End With
    Controls.Add(txtSearch)

    'Button to initiate searching
    btnSearch = New Button
    With btnSearch
        .Text = "Search!"
        .Font.Name = "arial"
        .Font.Size = New FontUnit(FontSize.AsUnit).Point(8)
    End With
    Controls.Add(btnSearch)

    'List to display results
    lstData = New ListBox
    With lstData
        .AutoPostBack = True
        .Width = Unit.Percentage(100)
        .Font.Name = "arial"
        .Font.Size = New FontUnit(FontSize.AsUnit).Point(8)
        .Rows = 5
    End With
    Controls.Add(lstData)

    'Label for error messages
    lblMessage = New Label
    With lblMessage
        .Width = Unit.Percentage(100)
        .Font.Name = "arial"
        .Font.Size = New FontUnit(FontSize.AsUnit).Point(10)
```

```
        .Text = ""
    End With
    Controls.Add(lblMessage)

End Sub
```

When coding a web part in C#, you follow the same general ideas; however, you must manually connect events to the ASP.NET controls in the web part. Once the event is connected, you must also define an event handler in code. Listing 5-4 shows a simple example of declaring an ASP.NET TextBox and Button.

Listing 5-4. Adding ASP.NET Controls in C#

```
protected TextBox txtDisplay;
protected Button btnGo;

protected override void CreateChildControls()
{
    this.btnGo.Click += new System.EventHandler(this.btnGo_Click);
    this.Controls.Add(btnGo);

    txtDisplay.Width=Unit.Percentage(100);
    this.Controls.Add(txtDisplay);

}

private void btnGo_Click(object sender, System.EventArgs e)
{
    txtDisplay.Text=Text;
}
```

Once the controls are all configured and added to the web part, you are ready to draw the output. When rendering the user interface of the web part, you use the HtmlTextWriter class provided by the RenderWebPart method. This class allows you to create any manner of HTML output for the web part. The following code fragments show how to override the RenderWebPart method in both C# and VB.NET.

```
//C#
protected override void RenderWebPart(HtmlTextWriter output)
    {

    }
```

```
'VB.NET
Protected Overrides Sub RenderWebPart _
(ByVal output As System.Web.UI.HtmlTextWriter)

End Sub
```

As a general rule, you should render your user interface within an HTML
<TABLE>. The reason for this is that you can never be sure what the web part page
layout will look like. As you saw in the last chapter, layouts and web part zones
can take almost any form. Therefore, you should use the relative layout offered
by the <TABLE> tag to respect the width defined by the zone where the web part
appears. Listing 5-5 shows how to render a table containing ASP.NET controls.
You should take particular note of the WIDTH definition within the table.

Listing 5-5. Rendering ASP.NET Controls in an HTML Table

```
With output
    .Write("<TABLE BORDER=0 WIDTH=100%>")
    .Write("<TR>")
    .Write("<TD Width=70%>")
    txtCompany.RenderControl(output)
    .Write("</TD>")
    .Write("<TD>")
    btnSearch.RenderControl(output)
    .Write("</TD>")
    .Write("</TR>")
    .Write("<TR>")
    .Write("<TD COLSPAN=2>")
    grdNames.RenderControl(output)
    .Write("</TD>")
    .Write("</TR>")
    .Write("<TR>")
    .Write("<TD COLSPAN=2>")
    lblMessage.RenderControl(output)
    .Write("</TD>")
    .Write("</TR>")
    .Write("</TABLE>")
End With
```

Deploying Web Parts

After you have finished coding the web part, you are ready to begin the process of deploying it for use in SharePoint Services. Unfortunately, deploying web parts is not a simple matter. You must complete several detailed steps in order to successfully use a web part in a new page.

Understanding Strong Names

Because SPS is a web-based application with potential ties to sensitive organizational information, web part security is a significant concern. These security concerns encompass not only access to information, but also potential malicious behavior by web parts. In order to ensure that no unsafe web parts are allowed to run in SPS, you must digitally sign all web parts with a strong name.

You can create a strong name by combining the text name of the web part, its version number, culture information, digital signature, and a public key. When you create a strong name for your web part, you guarantee that its name is globally unique. This ensures that your web part is not confused with any other web part that might happen to have the same text name.

Along with uniqueness, a strong name also guarantees the version lineage of the web part. This means that no one can create a new version of the web part without access to the private key that created the initial strong name. This is important, because it ensures that every subsequent version of the web part came from the same developer—or independent software vendor (ISV)—who created the initial version. This protection establishes trust with SPS and the end users.

Additionally, strong names also ensure that the web part has not been modified since it was originally compiled. The .NET Framework applies several security checks to web parts that have strong names. It is this series of tests that ensure that the web part has not changed. Once again, this creates trust within the SPS deployment, which helps an organization feel confident deploying and using web parts for even sensitive business needs.

One thing to keep in mind about strongly named web parts is that they are only allowed to reference other strongly named assemblies. This is because security is only assured when the entire chain of calls is protected by strong naming. Most of the time this will not be an issue, but occasionally you might run into a third-party component that you want to use in a web part that is not strongly named. In this case, Visual Studio will notify you during the build process.

Before you can give your web part a strong name, you must generate a public/private key pair to use when signing the web part. You create a key pair using the Strong Name tool (sn.exe). In order to use the Strong Name tool, you must open the command-line interfaces and navigate to the directory where the tool is located. From that location, you must run the Strong Name tool with the syntax sn.exe -k [file name].

To create a key pair file, follow these steps:

1. Open a command window by selecting Start ➤ All Programs ➤ Accessories ➤ Command Prompt.

2. In the command window, navigate to \Program Files\Microsoft Visual Studio .NET 2003\SDK\v1.1\Bin.

3. In the command-line window, create a key file by executing the following line:

```
sn.exe -k c:\keypair.snk
```

Once the key pair is created, you can use it to sign the web part by referencing it in the AssemblyInfo file. Within this file, three attributes determine how the web part is signed: AssemblyKeyFile, AssemblyKeyName, and AssemblyDelaySign.

Using the AssemblyKeyFile attribute, you may reference the key pair directly by an absolute path or a path relative to your project directory. This is the most likely mechanism you will use to sign your web parts. The following code shows an example of how to reference the key file.

```
' VB.NET Syntax
<Assembly: AssemblyKeyFile("C:\keypair.snk")>

//C# Syntax
[assembly: AssemblyKeyFile("C:\\keypair.snk")]
```

Using the AssemblyKeyName attribute, you can reference an existing key that has been installed on your machine. Organizations might choose to do this if they have a digital certificate from a provider such as VeriSign that they already use to sign code. In this case, you would provide the name of the key to use.

If an organization already has a digital certificate, then it may not be made generally available to developers who need to sign code. In this case, the developer may choose to delay signing the web part. When you delay signing, the web part space is reserved for the final signature, but you can still use the web part during development.

In order to delay signing the web part, you must set the `AssemblyDelaySign` attribute to `True`. You must then get the public key portion of the certificate and reference it using the `AssemblyKeyFile` attribute. Finally, you must instruct the .NET Framework to skip the strong-name verification test for the web part by using the Strong Name tool with the following syntax:

```
sn -Vr [assembly.dll]
```

 CAUTION   *Skipping the strong-name verification opens a security hole in SPS. Any web part that uses the same assembly name can spoof the genuine web part. Reserve this technique solely for development in organizations where the digital certificate is not provided to developers. Otherwise, always reference a valid key pair.*

Regardless of how you choose to sign the web part, you should make sure that the version number specified in the `AssemblyInfo` file is absolute. Visual Studio .NET has the ability to auto-increment your project version using wild cards; however, this is not supported by strong naming. Therefore, you must specify an exact version for the web part. The following code fragment shows an example.

```
//C# Syntax
[assembly: AssemblyVersion("1.0.0.0")]

'VB.NET Syntax
<Assembly: AssemblyVersion("1.0.0.0")>
```

Building the Web Part

After the assembly file is edited, you have just a couple of steps left before you can build the web part. The first of these steps is to modify the web part description file—with the `.dwp` extension—in order to update it with the assembly information. SPS uses the web part description file to upload the web part into one of its galleries. The last step is to designate the proper build directory for the final assembly.

The web part description file is an XML file that contains the title, description, assembly name, and type name for the web part. If you use the web part template to start a project, then you are provided with a mock web part description file. To successfully upload the web part, you must modify the entries to reflect the information related to your web part. Although the `<Title>` and `<Description>` elements are self-explanatory, the rest of the file requires some explanation.

The `<Assembly>` element consists of the assembly name without the `.dll` extension followed by the `Version`, `Culture`, and `PublicKeyToken`. The assembly name is generally the same as the web part project name, and the `Version` is found in the `AssemblyInfo` file. The `Culture` is also found in the `AssemblyInfo` file in the `AssemblyCulture` attribute. However, this attribute is often left empty. In this case, use the value `Neutral` to indicate that no culture information is supplied. The `PublicKeyToken` is a truncated version of the public key, which is obtained by using the Strong Name tool.

Once you have generated a key file using the Strong Name tool, you can extract the `PublicKeyToken` from the file. The `PublicKeyToken` is important in not only the web description file, but also later in SPS as you will see. To extract the `PublicKeyToken`, run the Strong Name tool using the following syntax:

```
sn.exe -T assembly.dll
```

The `<TypeName>` element consists of a fully qualified name for the web part. The fully qualified name is the namespace followed by the class name.

Along with the required elements of the web part description file, you may also set properties of the web part using the description file. To set a property, simply add an element that has the same name as the property you wish to set. When the web part is uploaded, the property values are set by the SPS web part infrastructure. The following code shows a complete web part description file.

```
<?xml version="1.0" encoding="utf-8"?>
<WebPart xmlns="http://schemas.microsoft.com/WebPart/v2" >
    <Title>Page View</Title>
    <Description>A web part to embed pages in the portal</Description>
    <Assembly>SPSPageView, Version=1.0.0.0, Culture=Neutral,
     PublicKeyToken=5959aab8a976a104</Assembly>
    <TypeName>SPSPageView.Container</TypeName>
    <Width>100</Width>
</WebPart>
```

Once the web part description file is properly modified, you must set the build directory for the project. All web parts must be installed in the `\inetpub\wwwroot\bin` directory. Although you can certainly copy your assembly to this directory after it is built, you may find it easier to simply set the build directory so that the assembly is automatically compiled to the correct spot.

> **NOTE** *The* \bin *directory is not created by default; you must create it manually.*

You can set the build directory for your project by right-clicking the project in Visual Studio and selecting Properties from the pop-up menu. This will open the Property Pages dialog. In this dialog, select Configuration Properties ➤ Build. Locate the Output Path option and set it to point to \inetpub\wwwroot\bin. Now you can build the web part successfully. Figure 5-3 shows the output path in the Property Pages dialog for a C# project.

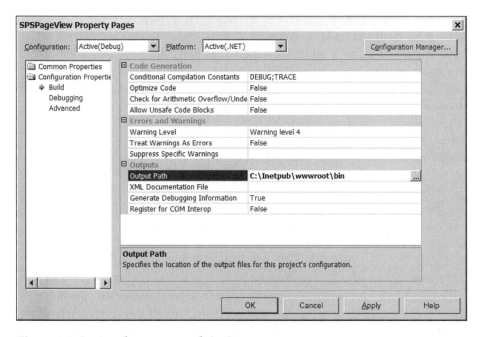

Figure 5-3. Setting the output path in C#

Code Access Security

SPS is based on ASP.NET technology. As such, it is bound by the same security limitations that apply to any ASP.NET application. Practically speaking, this means that web parts are often restricted from accessing enterprise resources such as databases and web services unless you specifically configure SharePoint Services to allow such access. Managing how code can access enterprise resources is known as *code access security*.

Understanding Configuration Files

Code access security is implemented by a series of configuration files. The first configuration file of concern is `machine.config` located in `C:\Windows\Microsoft.NET\Framework\v1.14322\CONFIG`. This file specifies master settings that will be inherited by all SharePoint Services sites that run on the server. This particular file is densely packed with information, and a complete discussion of the contents is beyond the scope of this book. However, one section—`<securityPolicy>`—is of immediate importance.

The `<securityPolicy>` section defines five levels of trust for ASP.NET applications: Full, High, Medium, Low, and Minimal. The trust level definitions allow you to assign partial permissions to an ASP.NET application that determine what resources the application can access. For example, applications with High levels of trust can read and write to files within their directory structure whereas an application with a Low trust level can only read files. The permissions allotted by each level of trust are defined within a separate policy file designated by the `<trustLevel>` element. The following code shows the `<securityPolicy>` section for the `machine.config` file associated with an installation of SPS.

```
<securityPolicy>
    <trustLevel name="Full" policyFile="internal"/>
    <trustLevel name="High" policyFile="web_hightrust.config"/>
    <trustLevel name="Medium" policyFile="web_mediumtrust.config"/>
    <trustLevel name="Low" policyFile="web_lowtrust.config"/>
    <trustLevel name="Minimal" policyFile="web_minimaltrust.config"/>
</securityPolicy>
```

The security policy files referenced by the `<trustLevel>` element are also XML files. These files contain a separate section for each policy that the file defines. Examining each of the files referenced in the `machine.config` file results in the complete picture of the trust levels and permission shown in Table 5-1.

Table 5-1. Trust Levels and Permissions in ASP.NET

PERMISSION	FULL	HIGH	MEDIUM	LOW	MINIMAL
AspNetHosting-Permission	Full	High	Medium	Low	Minimal
Environment	Unlimited	Unlimited	Read TEMP, TMP, OS, USERNAME, COMPUTER-NAME	None	None

PERMISSION	FULL	HIGH	MEDIUM	LOW	MINIMAL
FileIO	Unlimited	Unlimited	Read, Write, Append, PathDiscovery: Application Directory	Read, PathDiscovery: Application Directory	None
IsolatedStorage	Unlimited	Unlimited	Assembly-Isolation-ByUser, Unrestricted	1MB quota Assembly-Isolation-ByUser	None
Reflection	Unlimited	ReflectionEmit	None	None	None
Registry	Unlimited	Unlimited	None	None	None
Security	Unlimited	Execution, Assertion, Control-Principal, ControlThread, Remoting-Configuration	Execution, Assertion, Control-Principal, ControlThread, Remoting-Configuration	Execution	Execution
Socket	Unlimited	Unlimited	None	None	None
WebPermission	Unlimited	Unlimited	Connect to Origin Host	None	None
DNS	Unlimited	Unlimited	Unlimited	None	None
Printing	Unlimited	Default	Default	None	None
OleDBPermission	Unlimited	None	None	None	None
SqlClient-Permission	Unlimited	Unlimited	Unlimited	None	None
EventLog	Unlimited	None	None	None	None
Message Queue	Unlimited	None	None	None	None
Service Controller	Unlimited	None	None	None	None
Performance Counters	Unlimited	None	None	None	None
Directory Service	Unlimited	None	None	None	None

The `machine.config` file represents the highest level of configuration for ASP.NET applications; however, each application may have a supplemental configuration file named `web.config`. This file is typically found in the root directory of an application, and for SPS it is located in `\inetpub\wwwroot`. Opening this file will reveal that it also has a `<securityPolicy>` section that defines two additional levels of trust known as WSS_Medium and WSS_Minimal. The following code shows the `<securityPolicy>` section from the file.

```
<securityPolicy>
  <trustLevel name="WSS_Medium"
  policyFile="C:\Program Files\Common Files\Microsoft Shared\
Web Server Extensions\60\config\wss_mediumtrust.config" />
  <trustLevel name="WSS_Minimal"
  policyFile="C:\Program Files\Common Files\Microsoft Shared\
Web Server Extensions\60\config\wss_minimaltrust.config" />
</securityPolicy>
```

The security policy files defined by SPS are based on the files defined by ASP.NET. As a result, they define permissions for the same functions plus two additional functions. Table 5-2 shows the trust levels and permissions added by SPS.

Table 5-2. Trust Levels and Permissions in SPS

PERMISSION	WSS_MEDIUM	WSS_MINIMAL
AspNetHostingPermission	Medium	Minimal
Environment	Read TEMP, TMP, OS, USERNAME, COMPUTERNAME	None
FileIO	Read, Write, Append, PathDiscovery: Application Directory	None
IsolatedStorage	AssemblyIsolationByUser, Unrestricted	None
Reflection	None	None
Registry	None	None
Security	Execution, Assertion, ControlPrincipal, ControlThread, RemotingConfiguration	Execution
Socket	None	None
WebPermission	Connect to Origin Host	None

PERMISSION	WSS_MEDIUM	WSS_MINIMAL
DNS	Unlimited	None
Printing	Default	None
OleDBPermission	None	None
SqlClientPermission	Unlimited	None
EventLog	None	None
Message Queue	None	None
Service Controller	None	None
Performance Counters	None	None
Directory Service	None	None
SharePointPermission	ObjectModel=true	None
WebPartPermission	Connections=true	Connections=true

The default installation of SharePoint Services defines a trust level of WSS_Minimal for all sites. Because web parts are deployed to the \inetpub\ wwwroot\bin directory, they are affected by the trust level set in the web.config file. This means that web parts associated with a SharePoint Services site have significant limitations. Most importantly, web parts running under WSS_Minimal cannot access any databases nor can they access the objects contained in the SharePoint object model.

The Common Language Runtime (CLR) will throw an error if a web part attempts to access an unauthorized resource. Therefore, you must always implement appropriate error handling in a web part during attempts to access resources. Exception classes for these errors can be found in the Microsoft.SharePoint.Security namespace.

Customizing Policy Files

Because one of the major reasons to write a web part is to integrate line-of-business systems with the portal, you will undoubtedly want to raise the trust level under which certain web parts will run. You have three options for raising the trust level for assemblies in the \inetpub\wwwroot\bin directory. All three have strengths and weaknesses you need to consider depending upon whether you are in a development, testing, or production environment.

The first option is simply to raise the trust level for all SharePoint Services sites by modifying the web.config file directly in a text editor. The trust level for SharePoint Services is set in the <system.web> section of the web.config file. To raise the level of trust, modify the <trust> tag to use any one of the seven defined levels. The following code shows an example with the trust level set to WSS_Medium.

```
<trust level="WSS_Medium" originUrl=""/>
```

Although making a global change to the trust level is simple, it should only be done in development environments. Generally, you should strive to limit access to resources to only essential web parts in a production environment. The default WSS_Minimal level is recommended for production.

The second option is to deploy all of your web parts into the Global Assembly Cache (GAC). The GAC grants the Full level of trust to web parts installed there without requiring a change to the web.config file. Once again, this is a fairly simple way to solve the problem, but it does make the web part available to all applications and servers. This is a potential problem because a highly trusted component is now more widely accessible. As a side note, you will also have to restart Internet Information Server (IIS) each time you recompile a web part into the GAC.

Web parts can be added to the GAC in several ways. First, you can use the command-line tool gacutil.exe with the following syntax:

```
gacutil -i [assembly.dll]
```

You can also simply navigate to the directory \Windows\assembly to view and modify the contents of the GAC. Finally, you can use the Microsoft Windows Installer to install the web part to the GAC during distribution. The latter method is the recommended best practice for production environments, whereas the first two are generally acceptable for development and testing environments.

The final option for raising the trust level associated with a web part is to create your own custom policy file. Although this approach requires the most effort, it is easily the most secure. This approach should be considered the recommended best practice for production environments.

To create a custom policy file, follow these steps:

 NOTE *If you are strictly following this text, you may not have developed your first web part yet. If this is the case, complete this series of steps after you finish the exercise at the end of the chapter.*

1. Open the Windows File Explorer and navigate to \Program Files\Common Files\Microsoft Shared\Web Server Extensions\60\config.

2. Copy wss_minimaltrust.config and paste it back to create a copy of the file.

3. Rename the copied file **wss_sqltrust.config**.

4. Open wss_sqltrust.config in Visual Studio for editing.

5. In the <SecurityClasses> section, add a reference to the SqlClientPermission class so web parts can access SQL databases.

```
<SecurityClass Name="SqlClientPermission"
Description="System.Data.SqlClient.SqlClientPermission, System.Data,
Version=1.0.53383.0, Culture=neutral,
PublicKeyToken=b77a5c561934e089"/>
```

6. In the <NamedPermissionSets> section, add a new permission set that grants all of the rights you want to define for your new policy, including access to SQL databases.

7. Extract the public key for the assembly from a web part you have developed by using the Security Utility tool with the following syntax:

```
secutil.exe -hex -s [assembly.dll]
```

8. Create a new <CodeGroup> section to apply the policy to the web part. This <CodeGroup> must precede the existing <CodeGroup> section defined for ASP.NET because once a policy is assigned, processing stops. The following code shows an example:

```
<CodeGroup
    class="UnionCodeGroup"
    version="1"
    PermissionSetName="wss_sqltrust">
    <IMembershipCondition
        class="StrongNameMembershipCondition"
        version="1"
PublicKeyBlob="0x00243383004838300943383338
30602338333832433830525341313383433830013383100
0936E3CD84B98E97825E63A7DBD7C15C10893315D16B5D9
8E7B7F38814BF0861D0BB5279A710EFFA
CA29A01BB745136FA2DDCAF8F5105C5F429DFF904A0B94
F0A4A8D27D3F8329CA4E7B44962D8764B8
D8A38D9F16859A035C23AC69D39D2969D03680C791C4D7
5B38BBE4D12C30467B6FE8F41131FC859E
D3B9B6F0D432478DC"
        Name="SPSPivotalContacts"
/>
```

9. Save and close the file.

10. Open the `web.config` file in Visual Studio.

11. Edit the `<securityPolicy>` section to add a reference to the new policy as shown here:

```
<securityPolicy>
  <trustLevel name="WSS_Medium" policyFile="C:\Program Files\
Common Files\Microsoft Shared\Web Server
Extensions\60\config\wss_mediumtrust.config" />
  <trustLevel name="WSS_Minimal" policyFile="C:\Program Files\
Common Files\Microsoft Shared\Web Server
Extensions\60\config\wss_minimaltrust.config" />
  <trustLevel name="WSS_SQL" policyFile="C:\Program Files\
Common Files\Microsoft Shared\Web Server
Extensions\60\config\wss_sqltrust.config" />
</securityPolicy>
```

12. In the `<system.web>` section, modify the `<trust>` element to use the new policy as shown here:

```
<trust level="WSS_SQL" originUrl="" />
```

13. Save and close the file.

14. Restart IIS and the new policy will be in effect.

Listing 5-6 shows the final XML.

Listing 5-6. Defining a New Policy

```
<PermissionSet
    class="NamedPermissionSet"
    version="1"
    Name="wss_sqltrust">
        <IPermission
            class="AspNetHostingPermission"
            version="1"
            Level="Minimal"
        />
        <IPermission
            class="SecurityPermission"
```

```
            version="1"
            Flags="Execution"
        />
        <IPermission class="WebPartPermission"
            version="1"
            Connections="True"
        />
        <IPermission
            class="SqlClientPermission"
            version="1"
            Unrestricted="true"
        />
</PermissionSet>
```

The predefined security policies available to SharePoint Services lack templates for defining access to several key resources. These resources include the SharePoint object model and web services. Therefore, I will review the necessary modifications you must make to policy files in order to access these resources.

If you want your web part to be able to access the classes in the SharePoint namespace, you must define a new <IPermission> element in the policy file similar to what was done above for SQL access. The following code shows how to define the element.

```
<IPermission
    class="SharePointPermission"
    version="1"
    ObjectModel="true"
/>
```

Similarly, if you want your web part to be able to call a web service, you must also define a new <IPermission> element. In this element, you specify the Uniform Resource Identifier (URI) of the web service to access. This URI may be in the form of a regular expression, which means you can set it up to match more than one available web service. The following code shows how to define the element.

```
<IPermission class="WebPermission" version="1">
<ConnectAccess>
<URI uri="http://localhost/services/callreport.asmx?WSDL"/>
</ConnectAccess>
</IPermission>
```

Remember that in any case where a strongly named web part is in use, all of the other components must also be strongly named. This can cause problems when you are accessing web services or other libraries. In these cases, you must either install your web part to the GAC or implement a custom security policy.

Marking Web Parts As Safe

Adding a new web part to the inetpub\wwwroot\bin directory or the GAC handles the code access security issues for the part, but it is not sufficient to allow the part to be imported into SPS. In addition to permission to access resources, web parts also need permission to be imported into SPS. This permission is granted by marking the web part as "Safe" in the web.config file.

The web.config file contains not only the code access security policy, but also the list of all assemblies allowed to run in a web part page. This information is kept in the <SafeControls> section of the file. Before a web part can be imported into SPS, it must be listed in the section. Listing 5-7 shows a truncated example of a <SafeControls> section.

Listing 5-7. Controls Marked As Safe

```
<SafeControls>
<SafeControl Assembly="SPSMaskTool, Version=1.0.0.0, Culture=neutral,
PublicKeyToken=eb3e58846fb2ac2b" Namespace="SPSMaskTool" TypeName="*" />
<SafeControl Assembly="SPSPageView, Version=1.0.0.0, Culture=neutral,
PublicKeyToken=eb3e58846fb2ac2b" Namespace="SPSPageView" TypeName="*" />
<SafeControl Assembly="SPSDataList, Version=1.0.0.0, Culture=neutral,
PublicKeyToken=eb3e58846fb2ac2b" Namespace="SPSDataList" TypeName="*" />
<SafeControl Assembly="SPSDataSet, Version=1.0.0.0, Culture=neutral,
PublicKeyToken=eb3e58846fb2ac2b" Namespace="SPSDataSet" TypeName="*" />
<SafeControl Assembly="SPSPivotalContacts, Version=1.0.0.0, Culture=neutral,
PublicKeyToken=eb3e58846fb2ac2b" Namespace="SPSPivotalContacts" TypeName="*" />
<SafeControl Assembly="Citrix, Version=1.0.0.0, Culture=neutral,
PublicKeyToken=eb3e58846fb2ac2b" Namespace="Citrix" TypeName="*" />
</SafeControls>
```

In the <SafeControls> section, you must add a <SafeControl> element for each web part that you want to use in SPS. In the <SafeControl> element, you must specify several attributes. These attributes are similar to those attributes that you specified in the web part description file.

- The `Assembly` attribute contains the fully qualified assembly name along with the `Version`, `Culture`, and `PublicKeyToken` attributes.

- The `Version` attribute contains the assembly version as it appears in the manifest file.

- The `Culture` attribute contains the culture designation or "neutral" if none is provided.

- The `PublicKeyToken` attribute contains the token generated from the Strong Name tool.

- The `Namespace` attribute contains the namespace as defined in the web part project.

- The `TypeName` attribute contains the fully qualified name of the type or an asterisk to denote every web part in the assembly.

- `Safe` is an optional attribute that is normally set to `True`, but can be set to `False` to deny permission to a specific web part.

SharePoint Services reads the `<SafeControls>` section at runtime to load web parts dynamically into the appropriate web page. Essentially, SharePoint Services uses late binding to load the control, and the `<SafeControls>` section contains the information necessary to load the web part and test it for security. If a web part is not listed in the `<SafeControls>` section, SharePoint Services throws an exception notifying you that the control is not safe. Figure 5-4 shows a typical error message for an unsafe web part.

Figure 5-4. Identifying unsafe web parts

Deployment Packages

Setting the output path for the web part project to inetpub\wwwroot\bin is a simple way to ensure that the final web part assembly is deployed to the right location; however, this technique is only useful in a development environment. For production environments, you will want to build a distribution package that can be deployed independent of Visual Studio.

Creating a deployment package is done inside Visual Studio .NET as a new cabinet project in the same solution where the web part project is located. When you create the cabinet, you need to include the manifest file and the web part description file. Along with the assembly, these files are required to successfully deploy the web part.

Here are the steps to follow to create a deployment package:

 NOTE *If you are strictly following this text, you may not have developed your first web part yet. If so, complete this series of steps after you finish the exercise at the end of the chapter.*

---

1. Start Visual Studio .NET.

2. Open a solution containing a web part project.

3. From the Visual Studio main menu, select File ➤ Add Project ➤ New Project to open the Add New Project dialog.

4. Click the Setup and Deployment Projects folder.

5. Select to create a new Cabinet Project.

6. Name the project and click OK.

7. In the Solution Explorer, right-click the Cabinet project and select Add ➤ Project Output from the pop-up menu.

8. In the Add Project Output Group dialog box, select the web part project you want to deploy.

9. In the configuration drop-down list, select Release .NET.

10. In the project list box, select Primary Output.

11. Click OK.

12. In the Solution Explorer, right-click the Cabinet project again and select Add ➤ Project Output from the pop-up menu.

13. In the Add Project Output Group dialog box, select the web part project you want to deploy.

14. In the configuration drop-down list, select Release .NET.

15. In the project list box, select Content Files.

16. Click OK.

17. Build the Cabinet project.

Once the cabinet file is created, you may deploy it onto any server running SharePoint Services by using the administration tool StsAdm.exe. The tool is located in the directory \Program Files\Common Files\Microsoft Shared\web server extensions\60\bin. Using this tool, you can add a web part to SharePoint Services, delete one, or see a list of all the web parts that are available. Table 5-3 lists the available command-line switches for the tool and the following examples show you how to use it.

To add a web part package:

```
Stsadm.exe -o addwppack -filename c:\mypart.cab
```

To delete a web part package:

```
Stsadm.exe -o deletewppack -name mypart.cab
```

Table 5-3. Command-Line Switches for StsAdm

SWITCH	USAGE
o	addwppack, deletewppack, enumwppacks
filename	The name of the Cabinet file
name	The name of the package
url	The URL of the virtual server; if not specified, applies to all virtual servers on the machine
globalinstall	Installs the package to the GAC
force	Forces an overwrite of an existing package

Using Web Part Pages

Once the web part is compiled and deployed, it is ready for use in SPS; however, web parts are intended to be added and configured by end users—not developers. Therefore, the tools to manage web parts are an intrinsic part of SPS and are accessible directly to portal users who have sufficient permissions assigned. These permissions allow users to import web parts directly to a page or add them from a gallery.

Adding Web Parts to a Page

Perhaps the easiest way to add a new web part to a page is to simply import it directly into SPS. If the end user has permission to customize pages, then they may select Modify Shared Page ➤ Add Web Parts ➤ Import to open the Import pane. From the Import pane, users can browse for web part description files that correspond to the web part they want to upload. Figure 5-5 shows the menu selection required to import a web part.

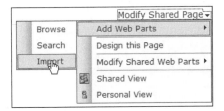

Figure 5-5. Importing web parts

Once the web part is imported, it appears in the Import pane. Users may then drag the web part out of the pane and drop it in a zone on the page. After it is dropped in a zone, you may configure it by setting the available properties. Importing is a simple way to add new parts, but you can make your new web parts more accessible to end users by creating a gallery for them, which you will learn to do later in the book.

Debugging Web Parts

As with any component, you will undoubtedly need to debug your web parts to get them to function correctly; however, because web parts are late-bound components—meaning they are added to SPS at runtime—they cannot be run alone in Visual Studio for testing. Therefore, you will need to hook into SPS to properly debug them. Fortunately, this is a fairly straightforward process.

Before you can begin debugging, you must accomplish all of the steps we discussed earlier to give the web part appropriate permissions. This means that you should ensure that the correct policy file is in use and that the web part is added to the `<SafeControls>` section of the `web.config` file. Additionally, you should set the project configuration to Debug and be sure that the output path is set to compile the assembly into the `\bin` directory. Once this is done, you can set breakpoints in your code.

The best strategy for debugging a web part is to select a site within SPS where you intend to add the web part and hook Visual Studio into that page. Hooking into the page is done from the Property Pages dialog. You then set debugging options by selecting Configuration Properties ➤ Debugging in the dialog.

Once the debugging options are set, you must modify the `web.config` file to allow debugging. This requires you to open the `web.config` file in Visual Studio and modify the `<trust>` and `<compilation>` elements. The first thing to do is to change the active policy from WSS_Minimal to at least WSS_Medium because debugging is not allowed under WSS_Minimal. Then you must modify the `<configuration>` element to have a debug attribute set to True.

To set up debugging in C#, take these steps:

1. Open a web part project in Visual Studio .NET.

2. Set the build configuration to Debug.

3. Right-click the project in the Solution Explorer and select Properties from the pop-up menu.

4. In the Property Pages dialog, select Configuration Properties ➤ Debugging.

5. Under Debuggers set Enable ASP.NET debugging to True.

6. Under Start Action set Debug Mode to URL and click the Apply button.

7. Set the Start URL to the URL for the SharePoint Services site where you will add the new web part.

8. In the Property Pages dialog, select Configuration Properties ➤ Build.

9. Set the Output Path to `\inetpub\wwwroot\bin`.

10. Click OK.

11. Open the `c:\inetpub\wwwroot\web.config` file in Visual Studio.

12. In the `<system.web>` section, modify the `<compilation>` element as follows:

    ```
    <compilation batch="false" debug="true" />
    ```

13. Modify the `<trust>` element as follows:

    ```
    <trust level="WSS_Medium" originUrl="" />
    ```

14. Save the file and close it.

15. Select Start ➤ Administrative Tools ➤ Internet Information Server (IIS) Manager to open the IIS Manager.

16. In the IIS Manager, right-click SPSPORTAL and select All Tasks ➤ Restart IIS.

17. In the Stop/Start/Restart dialog, click OK to restart IIS and apply the new security policy.

18. In Visual Studio, set the web part project as the start-up project by right-clicking it in the Solution Explorer and selecting Set As Startup Project from the pop-up menu.

19. Select Debug ➤ Start from the menu to begin debugging.

20. When the SharePoint Services site appears in the browser, click Edit Page from the Actions list.

21. Select Modify Shared Page ➤ Add Web Parts ➤ Import from the menu in the upper-right corner of the page.

22. In the Import pane, click Browse.

23. Navigate to the web part description file and click OK.

24. In the Import pane, click Upload.

25. Drag the web part into any zone on the page. Your breakpoints should work now.

Exercise 5-1: Building a Simple Web Part

When properly designed, web parts may be used in a variety of situations. In this exercise, you will create a page viewer web part that accepts a URL and displays a web site. This is a convenient way to embed external web pages in your portal, and will offer you a chance to use many of the concepts we have discussed in the chapter.

Creating the New Project

Before beginning, make sure that you have the web part template installed. This template will be the foundation of your project. For this exercise, you will create the web part using C#.

1. Open Visual Studio .NET 2003.

2. Select File ➤ New ➤ Project from the menu.

3. In the New Project dialog, select the Visual C# Projects folder.

4. From the project items, select Web Part Library.

5. Name the new project **SPSPageView**.

6. Click OK.

7. In the Solution Explorer, locate the file WebPart1.cs.

8. Rename this file **PageView.cs**.

9. In the Solution Explorer, locate the file WebPart1.dwp.

10. Rename this file **PageView.dwp**.

11. Open the file Manifest.xml for editing.

12. In the DwpFiles section, change the web part description file name to **PageView.dwp**.

Modifying the Web Part Description File

The web part template that you are using creates a default web part description file with a .dwp extension. This file contains information that is used by SPS to upload the web part and make it available. However, you need to change the information to reflect the names you will use in this project.

1. Open the file PageView.dwp in Visual Studio .NET.

2. Change the <Title> tag to contain the name **PageView**.

3. Change the <Description> tag to contain the text "**A web part to embed pages in the portal.**"

4. Change the <Assembly> tag to contain **SPSPageView**. You may come back later and create a complete entry including Version, Culture, and PublicKeyToken, but this entry alone should work for this exercise.

5. Change the <TypeName> tag to contain **SPSPageView.Container**.

6. Save the file and close it.

Listing 5-8 shows the final contents of the web part description file.

Listing 5-8. The Web Part Description File

```
<?xml version="1.0" encoding="utf-8"?>
<WebPart xmlns="http://schemas.microsoft.com/WebPart/v2" >
    <Title>PageView</Title>
    <Description>A web part to embed pages in the portal</Description>
    <Assembly>SPSPageView</Assembly>
    <TypeName>SPSPageView.Container</TypeName>
    <!- Specify initial values for any additional base
class or custom properties here. ->
</WebPart>
```

Coding the Web Part

Writing the code for the web part entails several steps. First, you will clean up the template code to make it easier to understand. Second, you will define the properties for the web part. Finally, you will write the code to render the web part in the portal.

1. Open `PageView.cs` in Visual Studio .NET.

2. In the code, rename the class from `WebPart1` to **Container**. Be sure to make the changes both in the name of the class and the attributes that decorate the class.

3. Change the `DefaultProperty` decoration of the class from Text to **URL**.

4. Remove the code from the `RenderWebPart` function.

5. Go through the class and strip out all of the comments and the one predefined property.

Listing 5-9 shows how the code should appear in the file.

Listing 5-9. Starting the Web Part in PageView.cs

```
using System;
using System.ComponentModel;
using System.Web.UI;
using System.Web.UI.WebControls;
using System.Xml.Serialization;
using Microsoft.SharePoint;
using Microsoft.SharePoint.Utilities;
using Microsoft.SharePoint.WebPartPages;

namespace SPSPageView
{

    [DefaultProperty("URL"),
    ToolboxData("<{0}:Container runat=server></{0}:Container>"),
    XmlRoot(Namespace="SPSPageView")]
    public class Container : Microsoft.SharePoint.WebPartPages.WebPart
    {
        protected override void RenderWebPart(HtmlTextWriter output)
        {
        }
    }
}
```

Defining the Properties

The basic design of your web part is going to be a division in the web page created by an `<IFRAME></IFRAME>` tag. Using this tag, you can embed a web page into the portal. The only thing you need to know is the URL of the page to embed. However, the URL is not enough to create a professional web part with good fit and finish.

When web parts are used on a page, the designer can never know the available height and width of the display area. Typically, the height is not an issue and can be set using a property because the browser produces scroll bars if the specified height exceeds the available display height. However, the web part designer should be respectful of the available width by specifying the required width as a percentage. With this in mind, you will define two properties for your web part: one for the URL and the other for the page height. Listing 5-10 shows the code you should add to the class to define the properties.

Listing 5-10. Defining the Properties

```
private string url="";
private int pageHeight = 400;

[Browsable(true),Category("Miscellaneous"),
DefaultValue(""),
WebPartStorage(Storage.Personal),
FriendlyName("URL"),Description("The address of the page to display")]
public string URL
{
    get
    {
    return url;
    }

    set
    {
    url = value;
    }
}

[Browsable(true),Category("Miscellaneous"),
DefaultValue(400),
WebPartStorage(Storage.Personal),
FriendlyName("Page Height"),Description("The height of the page in pixels.")]
public int PageHeight
```

```
{
    get
    {
    return pageHeight;
    }

    set
    {
    pageHeight = value;
    }
}
```

Rendering the Web Part

In order to render the web part display, you must override the RenderWebPart function. Because there is no drag-and-drop tool for creating the web part interface, you must code it by hand. The RenderWebPart function provides an HTMLTextWriter that outputs HTML to create the interface. Add the following line of code to the RenderWebPart function to create the display.

```
output.Write("<div><iframe height='" + pageHeight + "'
width='100%' src='" + URL + "'></iframe></div>");
```

Deploying the Web Part

Once the web part is coded, you must prepare the project to be compiled. In order to run in SPS, the web part assembly must have a strong name and be deployed in the \bin directory underneath the root of the web site. Additionally, the web part must be marked as safe in the web.config file. In this section, we'll take all the steps necessary to deploy the web part.

Creating a Strong Name

Web parts need a strong name in order to run in SPS. In order to give the web part a strong name, you have to create a key pair file using the Strong Name tool, sn.exe. Once the strong name is created, you must create a reference to it in the assembly file.

1. Open a command window by selecting Start ➤ All Programs ➤ Accessories ➤ Command Prompt.

2. In the command window, navigate to `\Program Files\Microsoft Visual Studio .NET 2003\SDK\v1.1\bin`.

3. In the command-line window, create a key file by executing the line `sn.exe -k c:\keypair.snk`.

4. In Visual Studio .NET, open the `AssemblyInfo.cs` file.

5. In the `AssemblyInfo.cs` file, scroll to the bottom of the file and add a reference to the key file by editing the `AssemblyKeyFile` entry to read as follows:

```
[assembly: AssemblyKeyFile("c:\\keypair.snk")]
```

6. Save and close `AssemblyInfo.cs`.

Compiling the Web Part

Once the strong name is defined and referenced in the key file, you are ready to compile the code. Because web parts must run in the `\bin` directory underneath the root of the web site, it is easier if you simply compile your assembly into the required directory. This makes it easier to get the web part working.

1. Right-click the `SPSPageView` project in Visual Studio .NET and select Properties from the pop-up menu.

2. In the Property Pages dialog, select Configuration Properties ➤ Build.

3. Set the Output Path property to `\inetpub\wwwroot\bin`.

4. Click OK.

5. Compile the web part by selecting Build ➤ Build SPSPageView.

6. When the web part compiles successfully, close Visual Studio .NET.

Marking the Web Part As Safe

Even though the web part has compiled successfully, it cannot run in SPS until it is marked as safe. To mark the web part as safe, you need to make an entry in the web.config file under the <SafeControls> section. Furthermore, this section requires an entry for the PublicKeyToken, which is embedded in the key file.

1. Open a command window by selecting Start ➤ All Programs ➤ Accessories ➤ Command Prompt.

2. In the command window, navigate to \Program Files\Microsoft Visual Studio .NET 2003\SDK\v1.1\Bin.

3. In the command-line window, display the PublicKeyToken by running the following line:

   ```
   sn.exe -T c:\inetpub\wwwroot\bin\SPSPageView.dll
   ```

4. Record the value of the PublicKeyToken for use in the web.config file.

5. Using a text editor, open the web.config file, which is located under \inetpub\wwwroot.

6. Locate the <SafeControls> section of the file. In this section, you must add a new <SafeControl> entry for your web part. The following example shows the form, but you must substitute your particular PublicKeyToken.

   ```
   <SafeControl Assembly="SPSPageView, Version=1.0.0.0,
   Culture=neutral, PublicKeyToken=ba635e9bfab94eac"
   Namespace="SPSPageView" TypeName="*" />
   ```

7. When the changes are complete, save and close the file.

Using the Web Part

Once the web part is properly compiled, placed in the \bin directory, and marked as safe, it can be used in a portal page. To use the web part, you will import it into a gallery. Once it's imported, you can drag it onto a page and set its properties.

1. Log into SPS as a member of the Administrator Site Group.

2. Navigate to any site that you have previously created.

3. On the site home page, select Modify Shared Page ➤ Add Web Parts ➤ Import.

4. In the Import pane, click Browse.

5. Locate the file `PageView.dwp` and click Open.

6. In the Import pane, click Upload.

7. Drag the PageView web part from the pane to any zone on the page.

8. When the web part appears, select Modify Shared Web Part from its drop-down menu.

9. Under the Miscellaneous section, enter a value for the URL field in the form `http://[address]`.

10. Click OK.

Exercise 5-2: Adding Child Controls to Web Parts

One of the challenges associated with creating web parts is using existing ASP.NET controls in your user interface. This is because the controls are not dragged onto a design surface from the toolbox. Instead, you must create them programmatically. This exercise introduces you to the basic techniques required to utilize existing controls in your web part.

Creating the New Project

Before beginning, make sure that you have the web part template installed. This template will be the foundation of your project. For this exercise, you will be creating a web part that accesses the `pubs` database using VB.NET.

1. Open Visual Studio .NET 2003.

2. Select File ➤ New ➤ Project from the menu.

3. In the New Project dialog, select the Visual Basic Projects folder.

4. From the project items, select Web Part Library.

5. Name the new project **SPSPubsAuthors**.

6. Click OK.

7. In the Solution Explorer, locate the file `WebPart1.vb`.

8. Rename this file **PubsAuthors.vb**.

9. In the Solution Explorer, locate the file `WebPart1.dwp`.

10. Rename this file **PubsAuthors.dwp**.

11. Open the file `Manifest.xml` for editing.

12. In the `DwpFiles` section, change the web part description file name to **PubsAuthors.dwp**.

Modifying the Web Part Description File

The web part template that you are using creates a default web part description file with a `.dwp` extension. This file contains information that is used by SPS to upload the web part and make it available. However, the information needs to be changed to reflect the names you will use in this project.

1. Open the file `PubsAuthors.dwp` in Visual Studio .NET.

2. Change the `<Title>` tag to contain the name **PubsAuthors**.

3. Change the `<Description>` tag to contain the text "**A web part to access the pubs database.**"

4. Change the `<Assembly>` tag to contain **SPSPubsAuthors**. You may come back later and create a complete entry including `Version`, `Culture`, and `PublicKeyToken`, but this entry alone should work for the exercise.

5. Change the `<TypeName>` tag to contain **SPSPubsAuthors.View**.

6. Save the file and close it.

Listing 5-11 shows the final contents of the web part description file.

Listing 5-11. The Web Part Description File

```
<?xml version="1.0" encoding="utf-8"?>
<WebPart xmlns="http://schemas.microsoft.com/WebPart/v2" >
    <Title>PubsAuthors</Title>
    <Description>A web part to access the pubs database</Description>
    <Assembly>SPSPubsAuthors</Assembly>
    <TypeName>SPSPubsAuthors.View</TypeName>
    <!- Specify initial values for any additional
base class or custom properties here. ->
</WebPart>
```

Coding the Web Part

Writing the code for the web part requires some extra steps to utilize the ASP.NET controls. In addition to creating properties and rendering the output, you must instantiate and configure the additional controls.

1. Open `PubsAuthors.vb` in Visual Studio .NET.

2. In the code, rename the class from `WebPart1` to **View**. Be sure to make the changes both in the name of the class and the attributes that decorate the class.

3. Change the `DefaultProperty` decoration of the class from "Text" to "".

4. Remove the code from the `RenderWebPart` function.

5. Go through the class and strip out all of the comments and the one pre-defined property.

Listing 5-12 shows the how the code should appear in the file.

Listing 5-12. Starting the Web Part in PubsAuthors.vb

```
Imports System
Imports System.ComponentModel
Imports System.Web.UI
Imports System.Web.UI.WebControls
Imports System.Xml.Serialization
```

```
Imports Microsoft.SharePoint
Imports Microsoft.SharePoint.Utilities
Imports Microsoft.SharePoint.WebPartPages


<DefaultProperty(""), ToolboxData("<{0}:View runat=server></{0}:View>"), _
XmlRoot(Namespace:="SPSPubsAuthors")> _
 Public Class View
    Inherits Microsoft.SharePoint.WebPartPages.WebPart

    Protected Overrides Sub RenderWebPart _
    (ByVal output As System.Web.UI.HtmlTextWriter)

    End Sub

End Class
```

Defining the Properties

The design of your web part is going to use a DataGrid control to display the
authors table from the pubs database. In this web part, you will set up properties
for the server, user name, and password. You will enter these properties directly
into the web part to make the database connection. Listing 5-13 shows the properties to define for the web part.

 CAUTION *You should never design a web part to accept user names
and passwords as properties. We are doing it in this exercise to simplify the development of the web part. Later in the book, you will
learn to incorporate the Microsoft Single Sign-On (SSO) service into
the web part. SSO is the correct mechanism for handling all user
names and passwords for web parts.*

Listing 5-13. Defining the Properties

```
Private strSQLserver As String = ""
Private strDatabase As String = ""
Private strUserName As String = ""
Private strPassword As String = ""

'SQL Server Name
<Browsable(True), Category("Miscellaneous"), DefaultValue(""), _
```

```
WebPartStorage(Storage.Shared), FriendlyName("SQLServer"), _
Description("The server where pubs is installed.")> _
Property SQLServer() As String
    Get
        Return strSQLserver
    End Get

    Set(ByVal Value As String)
        strSQLserver = Value
    End Set
End Property

'Database Name
<Browsable(True), Category("Miscellaneous"), DefaultValue(""), _
WebPartStorage(Storage.Shared), FriendlyName("Database"), _
Description("The database where the Enterprise Data is located.")> _
Property Database() As String
    Get
        Return strDatabase
    End Get

    Set(ByVal Value As String)
        strDatabase = Value
    End Set
End Property

'User Name
<Browsable(True), Category("Miscellaneous"), DefaultValue(""), _
WebPartStorage(Storage.Shared), FriendlyName("UserName"), _
Description("The account to use to access the database.")> _
Property UserName() As String
    Get
        Return strUserName
    End Get

    Set(ByVal Value As String)
        strUserName = Value
    End Set
End Property

'Password
<Browsable(True), Category("Miscellaneous"), DefaultValue(""), _
```

```
WebPartStorage(Storage.Shared), FriendlyName("Password"), _
Description("The password to access the database.")> _
Property Password() As String
    Get
        Return strPassword
    End Get

    Set(ByVal Value As String)
        strPassword = Value
    End Set
End Property
```

Defining the Child Controls

In order to use existing ASP.NET controls in your new web part, you must override the CreateChildControls method. In this method, you programmatically create a new instance of each child control, adjust its properties, and add it to the Controls set for the web part. Listing 5-14 shows how to create the child controls for the web part.

Listing 5-14. Creating Child Controls

```
Protected WithEvents grdNames As DataGrid
Protected WithEvents lblMessage As Label

Protected Overrides Sub CreateChildControls()

    'Grid to display results
    grdNames = New DataGrid
    With grdNames
        .Width = Unit.Percentage(100)
        .HeaderStyle.Font.Name = "arial"
        .HeaderStyle.Font.Size = New FontUnit(FontSize.AsUnit).Point(10)
        .HeaderStyle.Font.Bold = True
        .HeaderStyle.ForeColor = System.Drawing.Color.Wheat
        .HeaderStyle.BackColor = System.Drawing.Color.DarkBlue
        .AlternatingItemStyle.BackColor = System.Drawing.Color.LightCyan
    End With
    Controls.Add(grdNames)
```

```
'Label for error messages
lblMessage = New Label
With lblMessage
    .Width = Unit.Percentage(100)
    .Font.Name = "arial"
    .Font.Size = New FontUnit(FontSize.AsUnit).Point(10)
    .Text = ""
End With
Controls.Add(lblMessage)

End Sub
```

Rendering the Web Part

Because your web part is displaying just the rows from the authors table, you will not need to accept user input for search criteria. Therefore, you can simply query the database and generate the display directly in the RenderWebPart method. However, if you were accepting user input, you would have to be concerned with the web part life cycle and when the input becomes available as discussed in the beginning of this chapter. Listing 5-15 shows how to render the web part output.

Listing 5-15. Rendering the Web Part

```
Protected Overrides Sub RenderWebPart _
(ByVal output As System.Web.UI.HtmlTextWriter)

    Dim objDataSet As System.Data.DataSet

    'Set up connection string from custom properties
    Dim strConnection As String
    strConnection += "Password=" & Password
    strConnection += ";Persist Security Info=True;User ID="
    strConnection += UserName + ";Initial Catalog=" + Database
    strConnection += ";Data Source=" + SQLServer

    'Query pubs database
    Dim strSQL As String = "select * from authors"

    'Try to run the query
    Try
```

```
        With New System.Data.SqlClient.SqlDataAdapter
            objDataSet = New DataSet("root")

            .SelectCommand = _
            New System.Data.SqlClient.SqlCommand(strSQL, _
            New System.Data.SqlClient.SqlConnection(strConnection))

            .Fill(objDataSet, "authors")
        End With
    Catch ex As Exception
        lblMessage.Text = ex.Message
        Exit Sub
    End Try


    'Bind to grid
    Try
        With grdNames
            .DataSource = objDataSet
            .DataMember = "authors"
            .DataBind()
        End With
    Catch ex As Exception
        lblMessage.Text = ex.Message
        Exit Sub
    End Try


    'Draw the controls in an HTML table
    With output
        .Write("<TABLE BORDER=0 WIDTH=100%>")
        .Write("<TR>")
        .Write("<TD>")
        grdNames.RenderControl(output)
        .Write("</TD>")
        .Write("</TR>")
        .Write("<TR>")
        .Write("<TD>")
        lblMessage.RenderControl(output)
        .Write("</TD>")
        .Write("</TR>")
        .Write("</TABLE>")
    End With

End Sub
```

Deploying the Web Part

Once the web part is coded, you must prepare the project to be compiled. In order to run in SPS, the web part assembly must have a strong name and be deployed in the \bin directory underneath the root of the web site. Additionally, the web part must be marked as safe in the web.config file. If you have already completed Exercise 5-1, you will find these steps nearly identical.

Creating a Strong Name

Web parts need a strong name in order to run in SPS. In order to give the web part a strong name, you have to create a key pair file using the Strong Name tool, sn.exe. Once the strong name is created, you must create a reference to it in the assembly file. If you have already completed Exercise 5-1, you can use the same key file for this web part. Although it's true that you can use the same key file pair for every web part, the recommended practice is to use a new one for each web part.

1. Open a command window by selecting Start ➤ All Programs ➤ Accessories ➤ Command Prompt.

2. In the command window, navigate to \Program Files\Microsoft Visual Studio .NET 2003\SDK\v1.1\Bin.

3. In the command-line window, create a key file by executing the following line:

   ```
   sn.exe -k c:\keypair.snk
   ```

4. In Visual Studio .NET, open the AssemblyInfo.vb file.

5. In the AssemblyInfo.vb, add a new line as follows:

   ```
   <Assembly: AssemblyKeyFile("c:\keypair.snk")>
   ```

6. Save and close AssemblyInfo.vb.

Compiling the Web Part

Once the strong name is defined and referenced in the key file, you are ready to compile the code. Because web parts must run in the \bin directory underneath the root of the web site, it is easier if you simply compile your assembly into the required directory. This will make it easier to get the web part working.

1. Right-click the SPSPubsAuthors project in Visual Studio .NET and select Properties from the pop-up menu.

2. In the Property Pages dialog, select Configuration Properties ➤ Build.

3. Set the Output Path property to \inetpub\wwwroot\bin.

4. Click OK.

5. Compile the web part by selecting Build ➤ Build SPSPubsAuthors.

6. When the web part compiles successfully, close Visual Studio .NET.

Modifying the web.config File

Even though the web part has compiled successfully, it cannot run in SPS until it is marked as safe. Marking the web part as safe requires that you make an entry in the web.config file under the <SafeControls> section. You will also have to change the trust level for the site because web parts cannot access databases under the default trust level of WSS_Minimal.

1. Open a command window by selecting Start ➤ All Programs ➤ Accessories ➤ Command Prompt.

2. In the command window, navigate to \Program Files\Microsoft Visual Studio .NET 2003\SDK\v1.1\Bin.

3. In the command-line window, display the PublicKeyToken by running the following line:

```
sn.exe -T c:\inetpub\wwwroot\bin\SPSPubsAuthors.dll
```

4. Record the value of the PublicKeyToken for use in the web.config file.

5. Using a text editor, open the web.config file, which is located under the \inetpub\wwwroot directory.

6. Locate the `<SafeControls>` section of the file. In this section, you must add a new `<SafeControl>` entry for your web part. The following example shows the form, but you must substitute your particular `PublicKeyToken`.

```
<SafeControl Assembly="SPSPubsAuthors, Version=1.0.0.0,
Culture=neutral, PublicKeyToken=ba635e9bfab94eac"
Namespace="SPSPubsAuthors" TypeName="*" />
```

7. Locate the `<system.web>` section of the file. In this section, change the `<trust>` element so that the security policy is set to WSS_Medium as shown here:

```
<trust level="WSS_Medium" originUrl="" />
```

8. Save the file and close it.

9. Select Start ➤ Administrative Tools ➤ Internet Information Server (IIS) Manager to open the IIS Manager.

10. In the IIS Manager, right-click SPSPORTAL and select All Tasks ➤ Restart IIS.

11. In the Stop/Start/Restart dialog, click OK to restart IIS, and apply the new security policy.

Using the Web Part

Once the web part is properly compiled, placed in the `\bin` directory, and marked as safe, it can be used in a portal page. To use the web part, you will import it into a gallery. Once it's imported, you can drag it onto a page and set its properties.

1. Log in to SPS as a member of the Administrator Site Group.

2. Navigate to any site that you have previously created.

3. On the site home page, select Modify Shared Page ➤ Add Web Parts ➤ Import.

4. In the Import pane, click Browse.

5. Locate the file PubsAuthors.dwp and click Open.

6. In the Import pane, click Upload.

7. Drag the PubsAuthors web part from the pane to any zone on the page.

8. When the web part appears, select Modify Shared Web Part from its drop-down menu.

9. In the Miscellaneous section, enter a value for the SQLServer, UserName, and Password properties.

10. Enter the value **pubs** for the Database property.

11. Click OK. The records should now appear in the grid.

CHAPTER 6

The Microsoft Single Sign-On Service

IN THE PREVIOUS CHAPTER, YOU CREATED a basic web part that accessed a database using credentials retrieved from properties of the web part. Although this made for a simple design, it required users to type their credentials in clear text directly into the property pane. As we stated several times, this technique is unacceptable for a production environment. This is where the Microsoft Single Sign-On (SSO) service comes in to play.

You should note right at the outset that configuring SSO is complicated and getting it to work correctly is tricky. The configuration steps require several cryptic hand edits to configuration files that impact code access security. The overall experience can be frustrating, but the rewards are worth the effort when you finally eliminate all the annoying secondary log-ins required by your enterprise applications.

Setting Up SSO

SSO is a combination of a Windows 2003 service, a SQL Server data store, and web-based administration tools that provide credential storage and retrieval services to your web parts. SSO is installed by default along with SharePoint Portal Server (SPS); however, the service is stopped and set to manual start-up. In order to begin working with SSO, you must configure and start the service.

Before the SSO service can be started, you must create a new global security group that will contain an account used to run the service. This same group will contain the accounts that are authorized to administer the SSO service. The account used to run the SSO service will also be a member of this group. This group must meet several requirements:

- Belong to the local administrators group on the job server.

- Belong to the local administrators group on the server running the configuration database.

- Belong to the STS_WPG and SPS_WPG groups—which run all of the pooled SharePoint components and resources—on every server in the farm where SPS is installed.

- Have db_owner and public rights for the SharePoint Services configuration database.

- Belong to the Server Administrators role for the SQL Server instance where the SSO database is located.

Once you have defined a security group with an account, you can configure the SSO service to run under the specified account. Additionally, you can add users to the security group so that they can define credentials in the data store. Designated users may then define sets of applications and credentials for enterprise applications.

To set up the SSO account and start the service, follow these steps:

1. Log in to SPSController as the domain administrator.

2. Select Start ➤ Administrative Tools ➤ Active Directory Users and Computers.

3. In the Active Directory Users and Computers dialog, right-click the Users folder and select New ➤ Group from the pop-up menu.

4. In the New Object dialog, type **MSSSOAdmins** in the Group Name. Any member of this group will be allowed to administer the SSO service.

5. Click OK.

6. In the Active Directory Users and Computers dialog, right-click the Users folder and select New ➤ User from the pop-up menu.

7. In the New Object dialog, type **MSSSOService** in the Full Name and User Logon Name boxes.

8. Click Next.

9. Type a password for the account.

10. Uncheck the "User must change password at next logon" box.

11. Check the "User cannot change password" box.

12. Check the "Password never expires" box.

13. Click Next.

14. On the next screen, uncheck the "Create an Exchange mailbox" box.

15. Click Next.

16. On the next screen, click Finish.

17. Right-click the MSSSOService object and select Properties from the pop-up menu.

18. On the Member Of tab, click Add.

19. Type in the account name **sps\MSSSOAdmins** and click the Check Names button.

20. Once the account name is validated, click OK.

21. Click OK again.

22. Log in to SPSPortal as the domain administrator.

23. Select Start ➤ Administrative Tools ➤ Computer Management.

24. In the Computer Management dialog, expand the Local Users and Groups node and open the Groups folder.

25. In the Groups folder, right-click Administrators and select Add to Group from the pop-up menu.

26. In the Administrators Properties dialog, click Add.

27. Type in the account name **sps\MSSSOAdmins** and click the Check Names button.

28. Once the account name is validated, click OK.

29. In the Administrators Properties dialog, click OK.

30. In the Groups folder, right-click SPS_WPG and select Add to Group from the pop-up menu.

31. In the SPS_WPG Properties dialog, click Add.

32. Type in the account name `sps\MSSSOAdmins` and click the Check Names button.

33. Once the account name is validated, click OK.

34. In the SPS_WPG Properties dialog, click OK.

35. In the Groups folder, right-click STS_WPG and select Add to Group from the pop-up menu.

36. In the STS_WPG Properties dialog, click Add.

37. Type in the account name `sps\MSSSOAdmins` and click the Check Names button.

38. Once the account name is validated, click OK.

39. In the STS_WPG Properties dialog, click OK.

NOTE *Because this book utilizes a single-server configuration, you do not have to add the MSSSOAdmin account to any other local groups. If you deploy a multiple-server configuration, be sure to add the account to the appropriate group for each server that meets the requirements outlined earlier.*

40. Select All Programs ➤ Microsoft SQL Server ➤ Enterprise Manager.

41. In the SQL Server Enterprise Manager, expand the tree and select Console Root ➤ Microsoft SQL Servers ➤ SQL Server Group ➤ (local) (Windows NT) ➤ Security ➤ Logins.

42. Right-click the Logins node and select New Login from the pop-up menu.

43. In the Name field type **sps\MSSSOAdmins**.

44. On the Database Access tab, check the box associated with the configuration database (e.g., SPS01_Config_db).

45. In the list of database roles, check db_owner and public.

46. On the Server Roles tab, check the Server Administrators box.

47. Click OK.

48. Select Start ➤ Administrative Tools ➤ Services.

49. In the Services dialog, right-click the Microsoft Single Sign-On Service and select Properties from the pop-up menu.

50. On the Log On tab, select the option This Account and type in **sps\MSSSOService**.

51. Enter the password you set for this account.

52. Click Apply.

53. On the General tab, change the Startup Type to Automatic.

54. Click Start to start the service.

Before you can access credentials using SSO, an application definition must be created for the credentials. Application definitions consist of a unique name for the application and the definition of the logon fields to accept. SSO is capable of managing a number of fields beyond user name and password. In fact, you can define any custom field for the service, such as domain or database name.

Accessing the administrative pages for SSO is done by selecting Start ➤ All Programs ➤ SharePoint Portal Server ➤ SharePoint Portal Server Single Sign-On Administration. When you first access the administration pages, only one option is available. You must complete the setup of the MSSSO service by clicking the Manage Server Settings link. The server settings require you to specify the accounts that will be used to manage the SSO service and define new applications. Until these settings are complete, you cannot define new applications. Figure 6-1 shows what the page should look like the first time you access it.

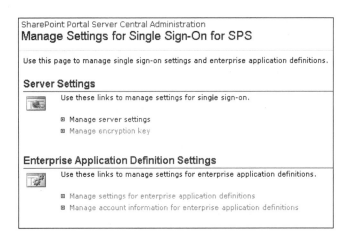

SharePoint Portal Server Central Administration
Manage Settings for Single Sign-On for SPS

Use this page to manage single sign-on settings and enterprise application definitions.

Server Settings

Use these links to manage settings for single sign-on.

▣ Manage server settings
▣ Manage encryption key

Enterprise Application Definition Settings

Use these links to manage settings for enterprise application definitions.

▣ Manage settings for enterprise application definitions
▣ Manage account information for enterprise application definitions

Figure 6-1. The Manage Server Settings page

To specify server settings, take these steps:

1. Log on to SPSPortal as member of MSSSOAdmins.

2. Select Start ➤ All Programs ➤ SharePoint Portal Server ➤ SharePoint Portal Server Single Sign-On Administration.

3. On the Manage Settings for Single Sign-On page, click Manage Server Settings.

4. On the Manage Server Settings page, type **sps\MSSSOAdmins** into the Account Name box for both the Single Sign-On Settings and Enterprise Application Definition Settings sections.

5. Click OK.

Once the initial settings are entered, you may return to the Manage Settings for Single Sign-On page where the additional hyperlinks will be available. Selecting Enterprise Application Definition Settings ➤ Manage Settings for Enterprise Application Definitions opens a page where you may define new applications. This page allows you to name the application, define the fields that should be managed, and determine whether the application will use a group or individual log-in. Figure 6-2 shows the available configuration options.

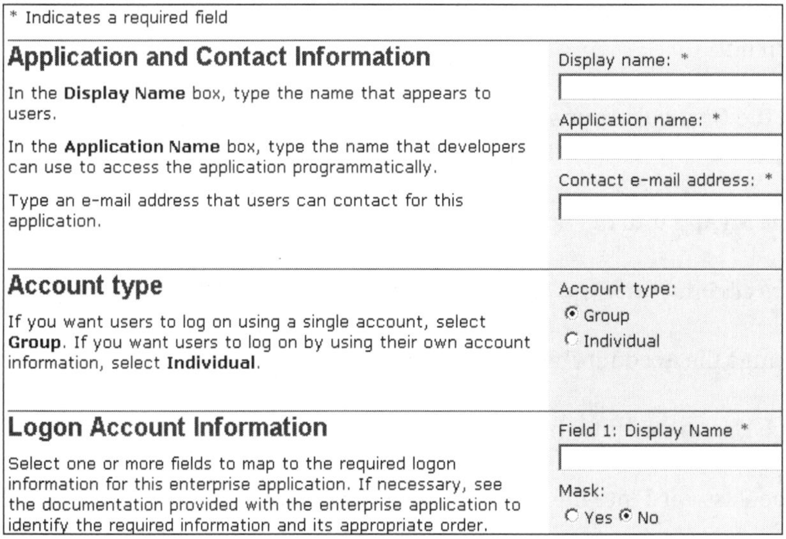

```
* Indicates a required field
```

Application and Contact Information	Display name: *
In the **Display Name** box, type the name that appears to users.	
	Application name: *
In the **Application Name** box, type the name that developers can use to access the application programmatically.	
	Contact e-mail address: *
Type an e-mail address that users can contact for this application.	

Account type	Account type:
If you want users to log on using a single account, select **Group**. If you want users to log on by using their own account information, select **Individual**.	⦿ Group ○ Individual

Logon Account Information	Field 1: Display Name *
Select one or more fields to map to the required logon information for this enterprise application. If necessary, see the documentation provided with the enterprise application to identify the required information and its appropriate order.	Mask: ○ Yes ⦿ No

Figure 6-2. Defining an application

You should use a group log-in when you want a single set of credentials to be used by web parts regardless of what user is accessing the system. This design is often associated with read-only information where users do not normally need separate identification. An organization might use this, for example, to give employees access to public information regarding corporate performance. In this scenario, it is not important which employee is accessing the system because the read-only information will not change.

Where you are more concerned about access and permissions, you should use an individual log-in. Applications defined with an individual log-in will require that each end user have their own set of credentials. SSO is capable of prompting individuals for credentials the first time they use a web part; after this, the service automatically stores the credentials for future use.

To create an enterprise applications definition, follow these steps:

1. Log on to SPSPortal as a member of MSSSOAdmins.

2. Select Start ➤ All Programs ➤ SharePoint Portal Server ➤ SharePoint Portal Server Single Sign-On Administration.

3. On the Manage Settings for Single Sign-On page, select Enterprise Application Definition Settings ➤ Manage Settings for Enterprise Application Definitions.

4. On the Manage Enterprise Application Definitions page, click the New Item link.

5. On the Create Enterprise Application Definition page, type **My Application** into the Display Name box.

6. Type **MyApp** into the Application Name box.

7. Type `administrator@sps.local` into the Contact E-mail Address box.

8. Change the Account Type to Individual.

9. Type **User name** into the Field 1: Display Name box.

10. Type **Password** into the Field 2: Display Name box.

11. Choose the Yes option for Mask under Field 2 to mask the password when it is entered.

12. Click OK.

Although SSO is capable of prompting users for credentials, you can set them up ahead of time by using the administrative web pages. Because you will not know individual log-in information, this capability is clearly most useful when an application is defined to utilize a group log-in. Individual log-ins will generally prompt users for credentials when they first use the web part. We'll see how to utilize this capability in code later on.

Here is what you need to do to define log-in credentials:

1. Log in to `SPSPortal` as a member of the MSSSOAdmins group.

2. Select Start ➤ All Programs ➤ SharePoint Portal Server ➤ SharePoint Portal Server Single Sign-On Administration.

3. On the Manage Settings for Single Sign-On page, select Enterprise Application Definition Settings ➤ Manage Account Information for Enterprise Application Definitions.

4. In the User Account Name box enter `sps\administrator`.

5. Click OK.

6. On the Account Information page, type **sa** into the User Name box.

7. Type the **sa** password into the Password box for your SPSPortal installation of SQL Server.

8. Click OK.

Setting the Security Policy

The Microsoft SSO service uses a SQL Server database to store application credentials, and web parts attempting to access this data store are subject to code access security restrictions determined by the active policy. By default, WSS_Minimal and WSS_Medium do not allow access to SSO functionality. In order to grant access, you must modify the policy files or create a custom policy file.

SSO uses a ticketing system for accessing credentials. Web parts can request a ticket from SSO that can subsequently be used to access credentials within the data store. Permission to access SSO is determined by the SingleSignonPermission class. This class accepts an enumerated value that determines the level of access the code is granted. Table 6-1 lists the possible values for the SingleSignonPermission class.

Table 6-1. The SingleSignonPermission Class

PERMISSION	DESCRIPTION
Minimal	The web part can reserve a ticket to redeem credentials later but cannot access credential information.
Credentials	The web part can redeem a ticket for credentials and access credential information.
Administer	The web part has full access to SSO for credential information and application administration.

Whether you choose to modify an existing policy file or create a new one, you must make an appropriate entry in both the <SecurityClasses> and <PermissionSets> sections of the file. In the <SecurityClasses> section, you must add a reference to the SingleSignonPermission class. The following code shows the appropriate entry.

```
<SecurityClass Name="SingleSignonPermission"
Description=
"Microsoft.SharePoint.Portal.SingleSignon.Security.SingleSignonPermission,
Microsoft.SharePoint.Portal.SingleSignon.Security, Version=11.0.0.0,
Culture=neutral, PublicKeyToken=71e9bce111e9429c"/>
```

Once the entry is made to reference the `SingleSignonPermission` class, you must add an entry to the wss_sqltrust `<PermissionSet>` to grant the appropriate level of permission. As with all other permissions, you grant the access using the `<IPermission>` element setting `Minimal`, `Credentials`, or `Administer` as the value. Additionally, the specific permission grant must appear within the permission set for wss_sqltrust. As always, remember to restart Internet Information Server (IIS) once your policy changes are complete. The following code shows the entry for granting access to SSO within the wss_sqltrust permission set.

```
<PermissionSet
    class="NamedPermissionSet"
    version="1"
    Name="wss_sqltrust">
    <IPermission
        class="SingleSignonPermission"
        version="1"
        Access="Credentials"
    />
```

Using SSO in a Web Part

Once the service is running and the policy is established, you are ready to create a web part. In order to use the Microsoft SSO service in a web part, you must first set a reference to the `SingleSignOn` assembly in Visual Studio. After starting a new web part project, set a reference to the `Microsoft.SharePoint.Portal.SingleSignon.dll` assembly. Once this reference is set, you can import the library into your code by using one of the following formats for C# or VB.NET.

```
//C#
using Microsoft.SharePoint.Portal.SingleSignon;

'VB.NET
Imports Microsoft.SharePoint.Portal.SingleSignon
```

The `Microsoft.SharePoint.Portal.SingleSignon` namespace provides several classes that provide complete access to all of the administration functions of SSO. You can use these classes not only to access enterprise systems, but also to create your own separate administration interface. You can even go so far as to build a web part that allows portal users to perform self-service on their own credentials. Table 6-2 summarizes the classes available in the `SingleSignon` namespace.

Table 6-2. Classes in the SingleSignon Namespace

CLASS	DESCRIPTION
Application	Retrieves, adds, and deletes application definitions
Credentials	Retrieves, adds, and deletes application credentials
SSOReturnCodes	Enumerates the results of a SingleSignonException
SingleSignonException	Thrown when an SSO error occurs

Access to the entire set of stored credentials managed by SSO is accomplished through the Credentials class. Using this class, you can store, retrieve, and delete credentials for any application stored in the configuration database. Table 6-3 lists the members of the Credentials class.

Table 6-3. The Credentials Class

MEMBER	DESCRIPTION
DeleteAllUserCredentials(String Account)	Deletes all the credentials for a user or group Account for every application definition.
DeleteUserCredentials(String Application, String Account)	Deletes the credentials for a user or group Account for a specific Application definition.
GetCredentials(UInt32 Flag, String Application, String[ ] Credentials)	Returns a reference to an array of Credentials given an Application name. If the Flag is set to 0, then the cache is checked for the credentials before the database is accessed directly. If the Flag is set to 1, then the cache is not checked.
GetCredentialsUsingTicket(UInt32 Flag, String Application, String Ticket, String[ ] Credentials)	Returns a reference to an array of Credentials given an Application name and an access Ticket. If the Flag is set to 0, then the ADO.NET data cache is checked for the credentials before the database is accessed directly. If the Flag is set to 1, then the cache is not checked.

Table 6-3. The Credentials Class, continued

MEMBER	DESCRIPTION
ReserveCredentialTicket(SingleSignOn-TicketType.Default, String Ticket)	Returns an access Ticket that may be used by a member of the SSO administrator account to access credentials.
SetCredentials(UInt32 Flag, String Application, String [ ] Credentials)	Sets the Credentials for a specific Application for the current user.
SetGroupCredentials(String Application, String Group, String[ ] Credentials)	Sets the Credentials for a specific Application for the specified Group.
SetUserCredentials(String Application, String Account, String[ ] Credentials)	Sets the Credentials for a specific Application for the specified Account.

When a web part needs to access an external system, it calls the GetCredentials method. Any user is allowed to call GetCredentials; however, the active security policy determines the level of access allowed. If the credentials exist in the data store, then they are returned as an array of Strings. The order of the data returned in the array is the same as the order in which the application fields were defined by the administrator. The following code shows the basic technique using VB.NET.

```
Dim Username As String
Dim Password As String
Dim strCredentials() As String
Dim uintFlag As New UInt32

Credentials.GetCredentials(UInt32.Parse("1"), "AppName", strCredentials)
Username = strCredentials(0)
Password = strCredentials(1)
```

If the web part attempts to retrieve credentials and fails, then the GetCredentials method throws a SingleSignonException. The exact reason for the failure is subsequently determined by examining the LastErrorCode property of the SingleSignonException object. Table 6-4 lists the possible return values for the LastErrorCode property.

Table 6-4. Single Sign-On Return Codes

NAME	DESCRIPTION
SSO_E_ACCESSDENIED	Access is denied to the SSO resource.
SSO_E_ALREADY_SS	The computer is already set up as a secret server.
SSO_E_APPLICATION_ALREADY_EXISTS	The Enterprise Application Definition already exists.
SSO_E_APPLICATION_CANNOT_OVERWRITE	The operation is unable to overwrite the Enterprise Application Definition.
SSO_E_APPLICATION_CREATION_DISPOSITION_UNKNOWN	Disposition is unknown.
SSO_E_APPLICATION_NOT_FOUND	The Enterprise Application Definition cannot be found.
SSO_E_APPLICATION_TYPE_UNKNOWN	The Enterprise Application Definition type is unknown.
SSO_E_CREDS_NOT_FOUND	The credentials could not be found.
SSO_E_DB_ALREADY_EXISTS	The database specified already exists.
SSO_E_EXCEPTION	This is a general SSO exception.
SSO_E_GET_CREDS_FLAG_UNKNOWN	The GetCredentials flag is unknown.
SSO_E_INVALID_AUDIT_PURGE_DAYS	The purge audit days specified are invalid.
SSO_E_INVALID_NUMBER_OF_CRED_FIELDS	The number of credential fields specified is invalid.
SSO_E_INVALID_NUMBER_OF_CREDS	The number of credentials is invalid.
SSO_E_INVALID_TICKET_TIMEOUT	The access token time-out specified is invalid.
SSO_E_MASTER_SECRET_NOT_EXIST	The encryption key does not exist.
SSO_E_REENCRYPTING	SSO is reencrypting the SSO database.
SSO_E_SECRET_ALREADY_EXISTS	The base system key already exists.
SSO_E_SET_CREDS_FLAG_UNKNOWN	The SetCredentials flag is unknown.
SSO_E_SHAREPOINT_VROOT_CANNOT_BE_FOUND	The virtual root for SPS could not be found.

Table 6-4. Single Sign-On Return Codes, continued

NAME	DESCRIPTION
SSO_E_SSO_DB_NOT_INSTALLED	The SSO database does not exist.
SSO_E_SSO_NOT_CONFIGURED	SSO is not configured.
SSO_E_SSO_NOT_INSTALLED	The SSO service is not installed.
SSO_E_SSO_WRONG_VERSION	The wrong SSO database version is being used.
SSO_E_TICKET_TYPE_UNKNOWN	The access token type is unknown.
SSO_E_WRONG_SS	This is the wrong secret server.

Your web part should treat the SSO resource exactly as it would any protected resource limited by code access security policies. This means that you should always implement error handling when attempting to access the data store. In most cases, you will be attempting to retrieve credentials and should be concerned that the credentials do not exist. This situation can happen frequently with application definitions that contain an individual log-in. In fact, it is almost guaranteed to happen the first time a user invokes a web part that accesses a new application definition.

Because an administrator will not know individual credentials, your web part should expect to handle SSO_E_CREDS_NOT_FOUND the first time any user accesses your web part. In response, you must help the user enter the correct credentials into the data store for future use. SSO supports the user by providing a web page where the user can enter their credentials if they are not found.

Users access the logon form provided by the SSO by clicking a hyperlink that you build in code. The hyperlink is generated by the SingleSignonLocator class. This class supports the GetCredentialEntryUrl method, which takes the application name as an argument. The following code shows how to build a simple hyperlink in the RenderWebPart method to redirect users to the logon form.

```
Try

Catch x As SingleSignonException

    'If we cannot get the credentials, then show a link to log in
    If x.LastErrorCode = SSOReturnCodes.SSO_E_CREDS_NOT_FOUND Then

    'Get the URL to save SSO credentials
    Dim strURL As String
    strURL = SingleSignonLocator.GetCredentialEntryUrl("MyApp")
```

```
'Display a link
output.Write("<a href=""" + strURL + """>Please log in</a>")

    End If

End Try
```

CAUTION   *The* GetCredentialEntryUrl *method will fail if the current user has no credentials in the SSO database. Talk about a catch-22! The workaround is to first define dummy credentials for each user and then delete them. This will associate the user with an application definition while ensuring that the* SSO_E_CREDS_NOT_FOUND *exception occurs when the web part is first accessed.*

The SingleSignonLocator class belongs to the Microsoft.SharePoint.Portal namespace. Therefore, you will have to set a reference to the Microsoft.SharePoint.Portal.dll assembly before you can use the class. Additionally, you will want to import the namespace into your code using one of the following examples.

```
//C#
using Microsoft.SharePoint.Portal;

'VB.NET
Imports Microsoft.SharePoint.Portal
```

Programmatic Administration

The basic approach to single sign-on described earlier requires that every user provide credentials the first time they use a web part. Although this approach will work, you may run into some challenges. For example, enterprise applications may require users to change passwords periodically. In this case, the retrieved credentials may not work and you would have to redirect the user to the logon page. As an alternative approach, you may want to give users the ability to manage all of their credentials directly from the portal.

The Application class is the primary class used to administer SSO. This class has a number of subclasses that form collections of information contained in the data store. Table 6-5 lists the subclasses of the Application class.

Table 6-5. Subclasses of the Application Class

CLASS	DESCRIPTION
ApplicationCollection	A collection of all Enterprise Application Definitions
ApplicationInfo	A single application definition from a collection of definitions
ApplicationFieldCollection	A collection of all fields defined in an application
ApplicationField	A single field from a collection of fields

When creating any administrative tool for credentials, you will most likely want to begin by listing the available application definitions. Using the ApplicationCollection class, you can gain access to the entire collection of application definitions and display them. You can access the collection by simply creating the ApplicationCollection object. You can then enumerate the collection to retrieve the definitions. Listing 6-1 shows how to access the collection and display the results in a list box.

Listing 6-1. Listing Application Definitions

```
Try

    'Get collection of all application definitions
    Dim objCollection As New Application.ApplicationCollection
    Dim objApp As Application.ApplicationInfo

    For Each objApp In objCollection

        'List only the individual applications, not group apps
        If objApp.Type = Application.ApplicationType.Individual Then

            'Create the new listing
            Dim objItem As New ListItem
            With objItem
                .Text = objApp.ApplicationFriendlyName
                .Value = objApp.ApplicationName
            End With

            'Add the new listing
            lstApps.Items.Add(objItem)
```

```
        End If

    Next

Catch x As SingleSignonException
    lblMessage.Text = x.Message
Catch y As Exception
    lblMessage.Text = y.Message
End Try
```

After the available applications are listed, users will want to select an application and enter their credentials. The `ApplicationFieldCollection` class provides access to all of the fields that are defined for an application. Using this class, you can label a set of text boxes with the required fields for entry. Because each application definition is limited to a maximum of five fields, creating a display where users can enter information is relatively easy to handle. Listing 6-2 shows an example of configuring five `TextBox` and `Label` controls to display the field names and a place for the user to type the credentials.

Listing 6-2. Displaying Field Information

```
Try

    'Get the collection of fields
    Dim objFields As New _
Application.ApplicationFieldCollection(lstApps.SelectedValue)
    Dim objField As Application.ApplicationField
    Dim i As Integer = 0

    'Show fields
    For Each objField In objFields
        i += 1
        Select Case i
            Case 1
                Text1.Visible = True
                If objField.Mask = True Then
                    Text1.TextMode = TextBoxMode.Password
                Else
                    Text1.TextMode = TextBoxMode.SingleLine
                End If
                Label1.Visible = True
                Label1.Text = objField.Field
```

```
            Case 2
                Text2.Visible = True
                If objField.Mask = True Then
                    Text2.TextMode = TextBoxMode.Password
                Else
                    Text2.TextMode = TextBoxMode.SingleLine
                End If
                Label2.Visible = True
                Label2.Text = objField.Field
            Case 3
                Text3.Visible = True
                If objField.Mask = True Then
                    Text3.TextMode = TextBoxMode.Password
                Else
                    Text3.TextMode = TextBoxMode.SingleLine
                End If
                 Label3.Visible = True
                Label3.Text = objField.Field
            Case 4
                Text4.Visible = True
                If objField.Mask = True Then
                    Text4.TextMode = TextBoxMode.Password
                Else
                    Text4.TextMode = TextBoxMode.SingleLine
                End If
                Label4.Visible = True
                Label4.Text = objField.Field
            Case 5
                Text5.Visible = True
                If objField.Mask = True Then
                    Text5.TextMode = TextBoxMode.Password
                Else
                    Text5.TextMode = TextBoxMode.SingleLine
                End If
                Label5.Visible = True
                Label5.Text = objField.Field
        End Select
    Next

    'Show button
    btnSubmit.Visible = True
```

```
Catch x As SingleSignonException
    lblMessage.Text = x.Message
Catch y As Exception
    lblMessage.Text = y.Message
End Try
```

After the credentials are entered into the TextBox controls, the credentials must be updated. This is accomplished by calling the SetCredentials method of the Credentials class. This method updates the SSO data store for the current user. Listing 6-3 shows the code for updating the credentials from the data entered in the TextBox controls.

Listing 6-3. Updating Credentials

```
Dim strFields(4) As String
strFields(0) = Text1.Text
strFields(1) = Text2.Text
strFields(2) = Text3.Text
strFields(3) = Text4.Text
strFields(4) = Text5.Text

Try
    Credentials.SetCredentials(Convert.ToUInt32(1), lstApps.SelectedValue, _
strFields(0), strFields(1), strFields(2), strFields(3), strFields(4))
    lblMessage.Text = "Successfully added credentials."
Catch x As SingleSignonException
    lblMessage.Text = x.Message
Catch y As Exception
    lblMessage.Text = y.Message
End Try
```

Viewing the Audit Log

Every action performed against the Microsoft SSO service is logged in the data store associated with the service. Each action is logged with a member of the ServiceAction enumeration. This enumeration identifies the operation that was attempted. The log also captures relevant information such as the identity of the user who performed the action and the application that was accessed. You can find the audit log defined under the SSO database in the SSO_Audit table. Figure 6-3 shows a sample log.

AuditID	UserAuthorityName	ActionType	ActionResultCode	Application	UserName	I
{6644D1BF-0FF2-49	<NULL>	28	0	<NULL>	sps\MSSOAdmin	
{E769BF80-BBEB-4B	<NULL>	1	0	PubsAuthors	sps\MSSOAdmin	
{61B5C1DF-1F38-44	<NULL>	22	0	<NULL>	sps\MSSOAdmin	
{196B270C-90BF-43	<NULL>	1	0	PubsAuthors	sps\MSSOAdmin	
{B08AE89E-8ABD-46	<NULL>	29	0	<NULL>	sps\MSSOAdmin	
{8058425D-396C-4C	<NULL>	29	0	<NULL>	sps\MSSOAdmin	
{A77CFB31-31AA-43	<NULL>	29	0	<NULL>	sps\MSSOAdmin	
{8C60B571-13DB-41	<NULL>	26	0	MSSSOAudit	sps\MSSOAdmin	
{BACD4796-D6C3-4:	sps\MSSOAdmin	2	0	MSSSOAudit	sps\MSSOAdmins	
{C4C8A583-8A6E-49	<NULL>	29	0	<NULL>	sps\MSSOAdmin	
{F361958F-AF3F-48	<NULL>	29	0	<NULL>	sps\MSSOAdmin	
{1961D87F-B4C2-41	<NULL>	29	0	<NULL>	sps\MSSOAdmin	
{60C42695-DF91-41	<NULL>	22	0	<NULL>	sps\MSSOAdmin	
{C710F876-37B6-47	<NULL>	29	0	<NULL>	sps\MSSOAdmin	
{106120E6-FB70-4F|	<NULL>	29	0	<NULL>	sps\MSSOAdmin	
{57CB0D70-9CBF-4F	<NULL>	28	0	<NULL>	sps\MSSOAdmin	
{CF870C04-402E-40	<NULL>	29	0	<NULL>	sps\MSSOAdmin	
{71126090-8982-4F	<NULL>	22	0	<NULL>	sps\MSSOAdmin	
{30B62399-C712-41	<NULL>	1	0	PubsAuthors	sps\MSSOAdmin	
{85BE9B9E-0804-47|	<NULL>	1	-2140995583	MSSSOAudit	sps\MSSOAdmin	

Figure 6-3. A sample audit log

Exercise 6-1: Using Single Sign-On

The Microsoft SSO service is useful for allowing web parts to access line-of-business systems without prompting for a separate log-in. In this exercise, you will create a simple web part that displays the audit log from SSO.

Prerequisites

Before beginning this exercise, be sure that you have properly configured the Microsoft SSO service on SPSPortal. This means you should have a global security group named MSSSOAdmins defined, and it should contain an account named MSSSOService. Additionally, MSSSOAdmins must be a member of the required local groups on SPSPortal. The SSO service should be running under MSSSOService. If you have not properly configured SSO, refer to the steps earlier in the chapter.

Creating the Application Definition

This exercise retrieves all necessary information from the SSO service that you need to connect to the SSO database and retrieve the audit log. You will use a group account definition to access the data store. Therefore, you must create an enterprise application definition and store the credentials for the definition.

1. Log on to SPSPortal as a member of MSSSOAdmins.

2. Select Start ➤ All Programs ➤ SharePoint Portal Server ➤ SharePoint Portal Server Single Sign-On Administration.

3. On the Manage Settings for Single Sign-On page, select Enterprise Application Definition Settings ➤ Manage Settings for Enterprise Application Definitions.

4. On the Manage Enterprise Application Definitions page, click the New Item link.

5. On the Create Enterprise Application Definition page, type **MSSSO audit log** into the Display Name box.

6. Type **MSSSOAudit** into the Application Name box.

7. Type administrator@sps.local into the Contact E-mail Address box.

8. Ensure the Account type is set to Group.

9. Type **Username** into the Field 1: Display Name box.

10. Type **Password** into the Field 2: Display Name box.

11. Choose the Yes option for Mask under Field 2 to mask the password when it is entered.

12. Click OK.

Entering the Credentials

Most often when you use SSO, you will not enter credentials directly. Instead, you will allow users to enter their own credentials the first time they use a web part. In this exercise, however, we will start with defined credentials to ensure that your web part is working correctly. Later you will implement a separate log-in form for first-time users.

1. Log on to SPSPortal as a member of MSSSOAdmins.

2. Select Start ➤ All Programs ➤ SharePoint Portal Server ➤ SharePoint Portal Server Single Sign-On Administration.

3. On the Manage Settings for Single Sign-On page, select Enterprise Application Definition Settings ➤ Manage Account Information for Enterprise Application Definitions.

4. In the Enterprise Application Definition list, select MSSSO Audit Log.

5. In the Group Account Name enter **sps\MSSSOAdmins**.

6. Click OK.

7. On the Account Information page, type values in that will allow access to the pubs database.

8. Click OK.

Creating the Web Part

At this point, you have built a couple of web parts and should understand how to start a project. Rather than repeat all the steps here again, simply open Visual Studio .NET and create a new web part library project in C#. Name the new project **MSSSOAudit**. After the new project is created, make appropriate modifications to the web part description file as you have done in previous exercises.

Setting References

Before you can get started writing code, you must set a reference that will allow you to use SSO and access SQL databases. Because you will be using the Credentials class and a DataSet, you must set a reference to the Microsoft.SharePoint.Portal.SingleSignon.dll assembly and the System.Data.dll assembly.

1. In Visual Studio, select Project ➤ Add Reference from the menu.

2. In the Add Reference dialog, click Microsoft.SharePoint.Portal.SingleSignon.dll and System.Data.dll.

3. Click Select and then OK to add the reference.

4. Add the following lines to `MSSSOAudit.cs` to reference the SSO assembly in your code along with the references necessary for database access.

```
using Microsoft.SharePoint.Portal.SingleSignon;
using System.Data;
using System.Data.SqlClient;
```

Defining the Properties

The design of your web part is going to use a `DataGrid` control to display the SSO_Audit table from the SSO database. In this web part, you will set up properties for the user name and password, but you will not allow them to be `Browsable` in the portal. Listing 6-4 shows the complete web part as it should appear after the properties are defined.

Listing 6-4. Defining the Properties

```
using System;
using System.ComponentModel;
using System.Web.UI;
using System.Web.UI.WebControls;
using System.Xml.Serialization;
using Microsoft.SharePoint;
using Microsoft.SharePoint.Utilities;
using Microsoft.SharePoint.WebPartPages;
using Microsoft.SharePoint.Portal.SingleSignon;
using System.Data;
using System.Data.SqlClient;

namespace MSSSOAudit
{

    [DefaultProperty(""),
        ToolboxData("<{0}:Log runat=server></{0}:Log>"),
        XmlRoot(Namespace="MSSSOAudit")]
    public class Log : Microsoft.SharePoint.WebPartPages.WebPart
    {
```

```csharp
//PROPERTIES
private string m_userName="";
private string m_password="";

[Browsable(false),Category("Miscellaneous"),
DefaultValue(""),
WebPartStorage(Storage.Shared),
FriendlyName("UserName"),
Description("The account name to access the SSO database")]
public string userName
{
    get
    {
        return m_userName;
    }

    set
    {
        m_userName = value;
    }
}

[Browsable(false),Category("Miscellaneous"),
DefaultValue(""),
WebPartStorage(Storage.Shared),
FriendlyName("Password"),Description("The password to access the SSO
database")]
public string password
{
    get
    {
        return m_password;
    }

    set
    {
        m_password = value;
    }
}
}
}
```

Defining the Child Controls

Your web part will show the audit table in a grid; therefore, you must override the CreateChildControls method to add the new DataGrid control. In this method, you programmatically create a new instance of the grid, adjust its properties, and add it to the Controls collection for the web part. Listing 6-5 shows how to create the child controls for the web part.

Listing 6-5. Creating Child Controls

```
//CHILD CONTROLS
protected DataGrid grdAudit;
protected Label lblMessage;

protected override void CreateChildControls()
{
    //DataGrid
    grdAudit = new DataGrid();
    grdAudit.Width = Unit.Percentage(100);
    grdAudit.HeaderStyle.Font.Name = "arial";
    grdAudit.HeaderStyle.ForeColor = System.Drawing.Color.Wheat;
    grdAudit.HeaderStyle.BackColor = System.Drawing.Color.DarkBlue;
    grdAudit.AlternatingItemStyle.BackColor = System.Drawing.Color.LightCyan;
    Controls.Add(grdAudit);

    //Label
    lblMessage=new Label();
    lblMessage.Width = Unit.Percentage(100);
    lblMessage.Font.Name = "arial";
    lblMessage.Text = "";
    Controls.Add(lblMessage);
}
```

Rendering the Web Part

Because your web part is displaying just the rows from the audit table, you can place your single sign-on code directly in the RenderWebPart method without concern for the state of any of the child controls. If you were relying on user interaction, you would have to consider the web part life cycle and event firing order to determine the best place to retrieve credentials. Listing 6-6 shows how to render the web part output.

Listing 6-6. Rendering the Web Part

```
//RENDERING
protected override void RenderWebPart(HtmlTextWriter output)
{
    string[] strCredentials=null;
    string strConnection=null;
    SqlDataAdapter objAdapter;
    SqlCommand objCommand;
    SqlConnection objConnection;
    DataSet objDataSet;

    //Try to get credentials
    try
    {

    // Call MSSSO
    Credentials.GetCredentials(Convert.ToUInt32(1),
        "MSSSOAudit",ref strCredentials);

    //save credentials
    userName=strCredentials[0];
    password=strCredentials[1];

    //Create connection string
    strConnection += "Password=" + password;
    strConnection += ";Persist Security Info=True;";
    strConnection += "User ID=" + userName + ";Initial Catalog=SSO;";
    strConnection += "Data Source=(local)";

    }
    catch (SingleSignonException x)
    {
    if (x.LastErrorCode==SSOReturnCodes.SSO_E_CREDS_NOT_FOUND)
        {lblMessage.Text="Credentials not found!";}
    else
        {lblMessage.Text=x.Message;}
    }

    //Try to show the grid
    try
    {
```

```
    //query the SSO database
    objAdapter=new SqlDataAdapter();
    objDataSet=new DataSet("root");

    objConnection=new SqlConnection(strConnection);
    objCommand=new SqlCommand("Select * from SSO_Audit",objConnection);
    objAdapter.SelectCommand=objCommand;
    objAdapter.Fill(objDataSet,"audit");

    //bind to the grid
    grdAudit.DataSource=objDataSet;
    grdAudit.DataMember="audit";
    grdAudit.DataBind();
}
catch (Exception x)
{
    lblMessage.Text+=x.Message;
}
finally
{
    //draw grid
    grdAudit.RenderControl(output);
    output.Write("<BR>");
    lblMessage.RenderControl(output);
}
}
```

Deploying the Web Part

Just like all of the web parts you have created previously, this one requires a strong name and must be marked as safe in the web.config file. Additionally, you must grant this web part permission to access both SQL Server databases and the Microsoft SSO service. You will grant these permissions by modifying the web.config and wss_mediumtrust.config files.

Creating a Strong Name

At this point, it should be clear that accessing the Strong Name tool is a common operation when creating web parts. Therefore, you may want to make it more easily available in Visual Studio. Follow these steps to add the Strong Name tool to the Visual Studio environment:

1. In Visual Studio select Tools ➤ External Tools from the menu.

2. In the External Tools dialog, click Add.

3. Change the Title for the new tool to **Strong Name Tool**.

4. Near the Command box, click the ellipsis (...) button.

5. Navigate to `\Program Files\Microsoft Visual Studio .NET 2003\SDK\v1.1\bin` and select `sn.exe`.

6. In the Open file dialog, click Open.

7. Check the "Use output window" box.

8. Check the "Prompt for arguments" box. Figure 6-4 shows the completed tool definition.

9. After you complete the definition, click OK.

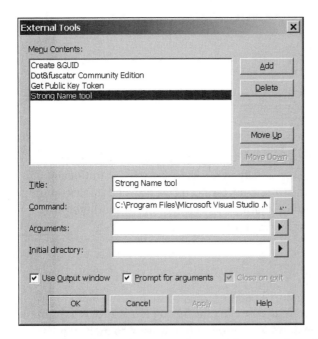

Figure 6-4. Adding the Strong Name tool to Visual Studio

10. To use the Strong Name tool, select Tools ➤ Strong Name Tool from the Visual Studio menu.

11. In the Strong Name Tool window, type **-k c:\keypair.snk** into the Arguments box.

 NOTE   *This operation overwrites any previously defined key pair at the same location. To avoid this problem, you can either continue with the existing key pair, or define a new key in another location.*

---

12. Click OK.

13. In Visual Studio .NET, open the `AssemblyInfo.cs` file.

14. In `AssemblyInfo.cs` modify the `AssemblyKeyFile` attribute as follows:

    ```
    [assembly: AssemblyKeyFile(c:\\keypair.snk)]
    ```

15. Save and close `AssemblyInfo.cs`.

Compiling the Web Part

Once the strong name is defined and referenced in the key file, you are ready to compile the code. Because web parts must run in the `\bin` directory underneath the root of the web site, it is easier if you simply compile your assembly into the required directory. This will make it easier to get the web part working.

1. Right-click the `MSSSOAudit` project in Visual Studio .NET and select Properties from the pop-up menu.

2. In the Property Pages dialog, select Configuration Properties ➤ Build.

3. Set the Output Path property to `\inetpub\wwwroot\bin`.

4. Click OK.

5. Compile the web part by selecting Build ➤ Build MSSSOAudit.

Modifying the web.config File

For the web part to successfully access the SQL database, you must make an entry in the web.config file under the <SafeControls> section. You will also have to change the trust level for the site because web parts cannot access databases under the default trust level of WSS_Minimal.

1. In Visual Studio, select Tools ➤ Strong Name Tool from the menu.

2. In the Strong Name Tool window, type the following into the Arguments box:

   ```
   -T c:\inetpub\wwwroot\bin\MSSSOAudit.dll
   ```

3. Click the OK button to display the PublicKeyToken.

4. Open the web.config file in Visual Studio.

5. Locate the <SafeControls> section of the file. In this section, you must add a new <SafeControl> entry for your web part. The following example shows the form, but you must substitute your particular PublicKeyToken:

   ```
   <SafeControl Assembly="MSSSOAudit, Version=1.0.0.0,
   Culture=neutral, PublicKeyToken=ba635e9bfab94eac"
   Namespace="MSSSOAudit" TypeName="*" />
   ```

6. Locate the <System.web> section of the file. In this section, change the <trust> element so that the security policy is set to WSS_Medium as shown here:

   ```
   <trust level="WSS_Medium" originUrl="" />
   ```

7. Save the file and close it.

Assigning Permissions

Before SPS will authorize the web part to interact with SSO, you must grant permission by modifying the policy file. You could create your own custom file as I described in the previous chapter, or simply modify the current policy. For this exercise, you will modify the wss_mediumtrust.config file.

1. Open `wss_mediumtrust.config` in Visual Studio for editing.

2. In the `<SecurityClasses>` section, add the following entry to reference the permission class:

```
<SecurityClass Name="SingleSignonPermission"
Description=
"Microsoft.SharePoint.Portal.SingleSignon.Security.SingleSignonPermission,
Microsoft.SharePoint.Portal.SingleSignon.Security, Version=11.0.0.0,
Culture=neutral, PublicKeyToken=71e9bce111e9429c"/>
```

CAUTION   *The code above should appear on a single line within the configuration file. If it is not written on a single line, SharePoint Services may throw errors.*

3. In the policy file, locate the `<PermissionSet>` element with the `Name` attribute of ASP.NET. Add the following `<IPermission>` element directly beneath the `<PermissionSet>` element to grant access to the SSO service.

```
<IPermission
    class="SingleSignonPermission"
    version="1"
    Access="Administer"
/>
```

4. Save the file and close it.

5. Restart IIS to have the new policy take effect.

Using the Web Part

Once the web part is properly compiled, placed in the \bin directory, marked as safe, and given permission to access SSO, it can be used in a portal page. To use the web part, you will import it into a gallery. Once it's imported, you can drag it onto a page and set its properties.

1. Log in to SPS as a member of the MSSSOAdmins security group.

2. Navigate to any site that you have previously created.

3. On the site home page, select Modify Shared Page ➤ Add Web Parts ➤ Import.

4. In the Import pane, click Browse.

5. Locate the file `MSSSOAudit.dwp` and click Open.

6. In the Import pane, click Upload.

7. Drag the MSSSOAudit web part from the pane to any zone on the page. The audit records should immediately appear in the grid.

CHAPTER 7

Advanced Web Part Development

ALTHOUGH BASIC WEB PARTS ARE USEFUL for customizing the display of information and some light system integration, they have some limitations. I noted, for example, that properties were limited to simple values of types like String, Integer, and enumerations. Also, the web parts you created in Chapters 5 and 6 were isolated from one another and could not take advantage of web part connections. Additionally, all of my examples only operated as server-side code. In this chapter, you'll examine advanced web part concepts that allow you to overcome the limitations found in the basic web part.

Client-Side Web Parts

When I began our discussion of web parts, I made it clear that they were essentially ASP.NET controls running in a special infrastructure. This definition is significant because all of the web parts you have written so far have been designed to operate on the server. They have relied upon post-back processing to access data and integrate other systems. This fundamental processing model is unchangeable in SharePoint Services; however, you can utilize some new techniques to introduce client-side processing to your web parts.

Using ActiveX Controls

The most-likely reason to use client-side processing is to incorporate an ActiveX control into your web part. In some cases, by using an ActiveX control, you can provide functionality that is not easily created through server-side processing. A good example of such functionality is found in the Office Web Components (OWC).

OWC is a set of ActiveX controls that implement spreadsheet and charting functionality that is compatible with Office products like Excel. The controls have a rich interface that allows end users to interact with data sources, pivot spreadsheets, and change chart characteristics. This functionality is not present in ASP.NET and would be difficult to implement through server-side processing.

You can include ActiveX controls in a web part by writing an appropriate `<OBJECT>` tag in the `RenderWebPart` method. As far as the web part is concerned, `<OBJECT>` tags are no different than any other HTML element. When the web part appears to the client, however, the referenced ActiveX control will load into the portal. The following code shows an example of creating an `<OBJECT>` tag in a web part.

```
output.Write ("<OBJECT id=""myobj""" & _
" style=""VISIBILITY: hidden; WIDTH: 0px; HEIGHT: 0px""" & _
" classid=""clsid:238F6F83-B8B4-11CF-8771-00A024541EE3""" & _
" VIEWASTEXT>" + vbCrLf)
output.Write("</OBJECT>" + vbCrLf)
```

The most challenging part of incorporating an ActiveX control is correctly constructing the `<OBJECT>` tag. Fortunately, you can easily lift the required HTML from Microsoft FrontPage. Whenever you add an ActiveX control to a page, FrontPage generates the appropriate code. Simply use this code as a template for your `RenderWebPart` method.

Although the `<OBJECT>` tag is sufficient for incorporating the ActiveX control into the user interface, most ActiveX controls rely on a client-side script to make them fully functional. This means that you may have to generate client-side script routines in the `RenderWebPart` method. This can be a bit tricky, especially when the client-side script uses a large number of quotation marks. Listing 7-1 shows an example of creating a JavaScript block using VB.NET in the `RenderWebPart` method.

Listing 7-1. Creating a Client-Side Script

```
With output
    .Write("<script language=""javascript"" type=""text/javascript"">")
    .Write("<!--")
    .Write("function windowLoad()")
    .Write("{")
    .Write("//Code goes here")
    .Write("}")
    .Write("-->")
    .Write("</script>")
End With
```

Using Script Files

In Listing 7-1, I showed you how to generate your own script code directly in the RenderWebPart method. However, you can also create separate script files that can be accessed at runtime by your web parts. There are two techniques for accessing such scripts: linking and embedding.

Linking a script file allows you to create your script in a separate file and put it on the web server. When a web part references the script, it is loaded into the browser cache. All future references to the script then utilize the cached code. Linking a script requires you to first create the script in a separate text file. Once this file is created, it is placed under a special folder and referenced in your web part.

To make a script available to web parts for linking, follow these steps:

1. Open the Windows Explorer, navigate to \Inetpub\wwwroot, and create a new sub folder named \wpresources.

2. In this folder, create a new folder with the name of the web part assembly (e.g., SPSPageView).

3. Under the new folder, create another folder consisting of the Assembly, Version, Culture, and PublicKeyToken (e.g., 1.0.0.0_en-us_eb3e58846fb2ac2b).

NOTE *Although the correct format for the new folder is version_culture_token, you may leave out the culture information when the culture is neutral.*

4. Create a script file in a text editor.

5. Save this file under the folder you just created.

Once the file is saved in the appropriate location, you may use the RegisterClientScriptBlock method of the Page object to load the script at runtime. This method takes as arguments a unique identifying name and a String for the script. Because you are linking the script, you only need to reference the location of the script file. The following code shows how to link a script file.

```
String scriptKey = "MyKey";
String scriptFile = this.ClassResourcePath + "\\myscript.js";
```

```
String scriptBlock = "<script language='javascript' src='"
+ scriptFile + "'></script>";

Page.RegisterClientScriptBlock(scriptKey,scriptBlock);
```

Embedding a script differs from linking it in that the script is not stored in a separate file. In this case, the script is simply created in code and then loaded using the `RegisterScriptBlock` method. Regardless of which method you choose, however, you should always check to see if the script has been loaded previously before you attempt to load it. You can do this using the script key and the `IsClientScriptBlockRegistered` method of the `Page` object. Although no error will occur if you attempt to reload a script, doing so will reduce the efficiency of your overall loading process.

Building Connectable Web Parts

The philosophy behind the use of web parts in SharePoint Portal Server (SPS) is that end users should be able to access information and assemble views without having to rely upon programmers to create custom web pages. One of the ways that this philosophy is put into action is through the use of web part *connections.* Connecting web parts in the portal allows a value from one web part to be used as an input, sort, or filter for the display of another web part.

Earlier in the book, you saw this functionality from the end-user perspective. In that example, you created a master-detail view of a contact list by using one web part to select a contact name and a second web part to display the detailed contact information. One of the main uses of connected web parts is creating these types of master-detail views, which allows end users to customize how information appears on their portal pages.

Behind the scenes, SPS uses the web part infrastructure to determine which web parts on a page are suitable for connection. Connectable web parts are then given a special Connections item on their drop-down menu that lists all of the other web parts to which it can connect. If you want to create connectable web parts that can be used in SPS, you must understand how to integrate your web parts with the connection infrastructure.

Connection Interfaces

The primary mechanism for integrating web parts with the connection infrastructure is through a set of interfaces. These interfaces expose methods and events that allow the connection infrastructure to query your web parts for appropriate connection information and provide notification when another web part wants to connect. The available interfaces support passing a single piece of data, a row of data, an entire list of data, or custom data sets between web parts. Table 7-1 lists the available interfaces and their purposes.

Table 7-1. Connection Interfaces

INTERFACE	PURPOSE
ICellProvider	Implemented by a web part that can provide a single value to other web parts
ICellConsumer	Implemented by a web part that can consume a single value from other web parts
IRowProvider	Implemented by a web part that can provide an entire row of data to other web parts
IRowConsumer	Implemented by a web part that can consume an entire row of data from other web parts
IListProvider	Implemented by a web part that can provide an entire list to other web parts
IListConsumer	Implemented by a web part that can consume an entire list from other web parts
IFilterProvider	Implemented by a web part that can provide a value for filtering to other web parts
IFilterConsumer	Implemented by a web part that can use a provided value from other web parts for filtering a view
IParametersInProvider	Implemented by a web part that can provide arbitrary input values to other web parts
IParametersInConsumer	Implemented by a web part that can consume arbitrary input values from other web parts
IParametersOutProvider	Implemented by a web part that can provide arbitrary output values to other web parts
IParametersOutConsumer	Implemented by a web part that can consume arbitrary output values from other web parts

Connection interfaces are provided in complementary pairs that can be implemented to pass data such as ICellProvider and ICellConsumer. However, connection interfaces can often allow connections that are not immediately obvious. For example, a web part that provides an entire row can be connected to a web part that only consumes a single field. This is because the web part infrastructure implements a selection dialog that allows end users to select which field from the row will be consumed. This means that there are many possible combinations of compatible interfaces. Figure 7-1 shows a typical field selection dialog in SPS.

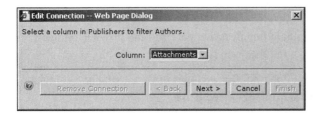

Figure 7-1. Connecting web parts in SPS

Determining which interfaces are compatible is handled by the web part infrastructure according to several rules. The first, and most obvious, rule is that all complementary interface pairs are compatible. This means that `ICellProvider/ICellConsumer`, `IRowProvider/IRowConsumer`, and `IListProvider/IListConsumer` are always compatible. For interfaces that are not complementary, extended connections—known as *transformers*—are allowed where they make sense; however, some of these connections are not supported directly in SPS and can only be achieved when you are editing the page in Microsoft FrontPage. Table 7-2 lists these interfaces and their restrictions.

Table 7-2. Extended Connection Compatibility

	IFILTERPROVIDER	IROWPROVIDER	IPARAMETERS-INPROVIDER	IPARAMETERS-OUTPROVIDER
ICellConsumer	—	SPS[1]/FP[2]	—	—
IFilterConsumer	CPC[3]	SPS/FP/CPC	—	—
IParametersIn-Consumer	—	FP/CPC	FP/CPC	FP/CPC

[1] **SPS:** Connection creation allowed directly in SPS

[2] **FP:** Connection creation allowed in Microsoft FrontPage

[3] **CPC:** Cross-page connections allowed in Microsoft FrontPage

During the design of your web part, you determine the interfaces to implement based on its intended use. Keep in mind that your web part must be easily understood by portal end users. Your goal is to avoid the need for detailed training or help files associated with your web part. To the greatest extent possible, the purpose of your web part should be understood through its display and the options provided on the connection menu.

Once you have determined which interfaces will be implemented by your web part, you are ready to begin development. You can start your web part using the same web part templates that you used in earlier chapters. Although the web part templates have some specific templates available just for connectable web parts, they are generally geared toward simple single-value connections. You will find them lacking if you want to create more sophisticated web parts.

Regardless of how you start the project, you must specify the interfaces to implement in your web part. All of the interfaces for connecting web parts are located in the Microsoft.SharePoint.WebPartPages.Communication namespace. Declaring that a class implements an interface from this namespace requires that every method and event in the interface be declared. Each of the interfaces available for connecting web parts has a somewhat differing set of events and methods; therefore, you should be careful with the declarations. Listing 7-2 shows an example of declaring the IRowProvider interface in VB.NET.

Listing 7-2. Declaring Interfaces

```
Imports Microsoft.SharePoint.WebPartPages.Communication

<DefaultProperty("Text"), ToolboxData("<{0}:WebPart1
runat=server></{0}:WebPart1>"),
XmlRoot(Namespace:="SPSDataSet")> _
Public Class WebPart1
Inherits Microsoft.SharePoint.WebPartPages.WebPart

    Implements IRowProvider

    Public Event RowProviderInit(ByVal sender As Object, ByVal e As
Microsoft.SharePoint.WebPartPages.Communication.RowProviderInitEventArgs) Implements
Microsoft.SharePoint.WebPartPages. _
Communication.IRowProvider.RowProviderInit

    Public Event RowReady(ByVal sender As Object, ByVal e As
Microsoft.SharePoint.WebPartPages.Communication.RowReadyEventArgs)
Implements Microsoft.SharePoint.WebPartPages. _
Communication.IRowProvider.RowReady
End Class
```

Connection Life Cycle

Correctly implementing the interfaces to support communication is a painstaking process that you need to understand thoroughly to be successful. Each of the methods and events you must code are directly connected to the process used by the web part framework to connect the target web parts. Before you begin development, you need to examine the sequence of events that happen when two web parts are connected.

Consider the scenario in which two web parts are on a page in SPS but are not yet connected. Assume that the web parts have implemented complementary interfaces. The exact interfaces are not critical to the discussion, so I will simply refer to the web parts as the provider part and the consumer part.

The connection process begins when the end user selects to connect the provider and consumer using the drop-down menu associated with either web part. When this happens, the web part infrastructure responds by querying both the provider and consumer web parts to get a reference to interfaces they implement. This information allows the web part infrastructure to begin using the interfaces to create the connection.

Once the web part infrastructure has access to the interfaces, the next thing it does is ask the web parts whether they support connecting on the client, the server, or both. This information is provided to the connecting web parts so that they can correctly prepare for the connection.

Once the web part architecture determines where the web parts run, it connects the web parts. Each web part is notified that the connection has taken place and is passed relevant information regarding the pending data transfer. This way each of the web parts can react to the connection and prepare for the transaction.

Once the web parts are connected, the infrastructure instructs the web parts to fire any preparatory events. Typically, these events involve broadcasting schema information regarding the transfer to the other web part. The provider part web part might broadcast a list of field names that represent the columns in a row, or it may simply send a single field name associated with a cell depending upon the implemented interface. For its turn, the consumer part will broadcast similar schema information to specify what data it is expecting to receive.

At this point in the process, the provider web part is waiting for some user interaction that will signal the start of a transfer. Generally, this involves the selection of an item or row. Such a selection causes the web part infrastructure to notify the provider part that the data transfer has begun. The provider part then fires an event within the consumer part that sends the selected data. When the consumer part receives the data, it responds by modifying its view in accordance with its designed functionality. Once the transfer of data is complete, the web part infrastructure redraws both web parts. Figure 7-2 shows a diagram of the connection life cycle.

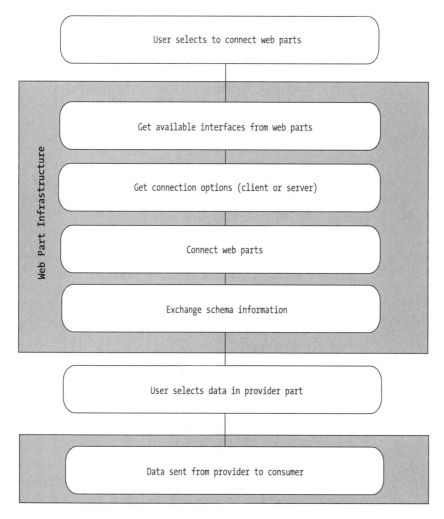

Figure 7-2. The connection life cycle

Each of the steps in the connection life cycle is associated with a method or event in the interface implemented by a web part. The process of creating connectable web parts is one of coding the methods and events to achieve the correct functionality. As an example, we'll investigate the simplest form of data transfer—a single field. A single field can be transferred using the complementary interfaces ICellProvider and ICellConsumer.

Registering Interfaces

Before connections can be made between web parts, the web part infrastructure must know what interfaces are implemented by each web part. Using this information, the web part infrastructure can ensure that only compatible web parts are connected. This prevents end users from making connection errors that could cause strange behavior in the portal.

Web parts tell the infrastructure about the interfaces they support by overriding the EnsureInterfaces method. EnsureInterfaces is a member of the WebPart class and is called by the infrastructure whenever it needs updated information regarding supported interfaces. Within this method, web parts make a call to the RegisterInterface method for each interface they support regardless of whether the interface is a provider or a consumer. Table 7-3 lists the parameters for the RegisterInterface method.

Table 7-3. RegisterInterface Parameters

PARAMETER	TYPE	DESCRIPTION
InterfaceName	String	A friendly name for the interface. This name should be unique within the web part and not contain any special characters (e.g., MyInterface).
InterfaceType	String	The text name of the interface (e.g., ICellProvider, ICellConsumer).
MaxConnections	Enumeration	The parameter that specifies that the web part can connect to only one web part (WebPart.LimitOneConnection) or any number of parts (WebPart.UnlimitedConnections).
RunAt	Enumeration	The parameter that specifies whether data is transferred on the client (ConnectionRunAt.Client), the server (ConnectionRunAt.Server), or both (ConnectionRunAt.ServerAndClient).
InterfaceObject	Object	A reference to the object that implements this interface (typically Me or this).
ClientReference	String	A unique identifier used only for client connections. This name should contain the token _WPQ_, which is replaced at connection time with a guaranteed unique identifier.
MenuItem	String	The text that will appear in the connection menu.
Description	String	A description of the interface.

The ability to register an interface for the purpose of connecting web parts is subject to code access security requirements. By default, web part connections are supported in both the WSS_Minimal and WSS_Medium policies. If you use a custom policy, however, you will have to add the permission as we discussed in Chapter 5. Because of the potential for an error, you should call the RegisterInterface method inside of a try/catch block and trap for the SecurityException class. Listing 7-3 shows an example of calling the RegisterInterface method using C#.

Listing 7-3. Registering an Interface

```
public override void EnsureInterfaces()
{
    try
    {
        RegisterInterface("MyInterface",
            "ICellConsumer",
            WebPart.UnlimitedConnections,
            ConnectionRunAt.Server,
            this,
            "",
            "Get a company identifier from...",
            "Receives a company identifier");
    }
    catch(SecurityException e)
    {
        //Must implement "WSS_Minimal" or "WSS_Medium"
        //Show exception message in a label
        lblMessage.Text += e.Message + "<br>";
    }
}
```

Running on Client or Server

Once the web parts have notified the infrastructure that they are connectable, they must specify whether they can connect on the server, the client, or both. All web parts, regardless of the particular interfaces they implement, must provide this information. The infrastructure queries the web part by calling the CanRunAt method. The web part then returns one of the enumerated values ConnectionRunAt.Client, ConnectionRunAt.Server, or ConnectionRunAt.ServerAndClient. The following code shows an example in VB.NET.

```
Public Overrides Function CanRunAt() As ConnectionRunAt
    Return ConnectionRunAt.Server
End Function
```

Although the code above is quite simple, some situations may require more processing. For example, pages with an ActiveX component installed for client processing may switch to server processing if the control is not installed.

Connection Notifications

Once the web part infrastructure understands where to connect the parts and on what interfaces, the connection is made. Both the provider and consumer web parts are notified that the connection has been established through a call to the PartCommunicationConnect method. This method passes along relevant information that each web part may care to track including a reference to the other web part, the interface that is connected, and where the data transfer will occur. Table 7-4 lists the arguments of the PartCommunicationConnect method.

Table 7-4. PartCommunicationConnect Arguments

ARGUMENT	TYPE	DESCRIPTION
InterfaceName	String	A friendly name for the interface. This should be the same as the value you provided in the RegisterInterfaces method.
ConnectedPart	WebPart	A reference to the other web part in the connection.
ConnectedInterfaceName	String	The friendly name of the interface on the other web part in the connection.
RunAt	Enumeration	Specifies where the data transfer will take place.

When the PartCommunicationConnect method is called, your web part should validate all of the information that it receives. This includes checking to see if the friendly interface name sent in is the same as the one that was sent out when RegisterInterfaces was called. Additionally, you should call EnsureChildControl to force the CreateChildControls method to run. This ensures that your user interface is ready to respond to the data transaction. Listing 7-4 shows an example of coding the PartCommunicationConnect method in VB.NET.

Listing 7-4. Receiving Connection Notification

```
Public Overrides Sub PartCommunicationConnect( _
ByVal InterfaceName As String, ByVal connectedPart As _
Microsoft.SharePoint.WebPartPages.WebPart, _
ByVal connectedInterfaceName As String, ByVal runAt As _
Microsoft.SharePoint.WebPartPages.Communication.ConnectionRunAt)


'Purpose: To inform this web part that the infrastructure has connected it to
'another part

    'This part only connects on the server
    If runAt = ConnectionRunAt.Server Then

        'Add the child controls for the part
        EnsureChildControls()

        'Increment the connection counter
        If InterfaceName = MyInterfaceName Then
            intConnectionCount += 1
        End If

    End If

End Sub
```

Broadcasting Schema Information

Once the connection is made, each part is allowed to broadcast relevant schema information to the other part. This broadcast functions to allow each web part to receive more detailed information about the data before it is transferred. Typically this schema information includes one or more field names that identify the data to be transferred. Web parts can use this information to validate the expected data before the transaction begins.

The web part infrastructure starts the broadcasting process by calling the PartCommunicationInit method on each web part involved in the connection. When a web part receives this call, it then executes specific initialization events that broadcast the information to interested listeners. The listeners may then take any necessary action to prepare for the pending data transfer based on the schema information sent.

Up to this point, your web parts have behaved largely identically regardless of whether they were providers or consumers. When it comes to broadcasting initialization events prior to the actual data transfer, however, each web part has its own custom events. This means that the implementation of the PartCommunicationInit method will be different in each web part.

Although the behavior of each web part will vary, Microsoft engineers have followed a convention that dictates events ending with the Init suffix are candidates for firing in the PartCommunicationInit method. This convention makes it easier to decide how to code the method. Listing 7-5 shows an example of a web part that implements ICellConsumer that broadcasts schema information via the CellConsumerInit event.

Listing 7-5. Broadcasting Schema Information

```
public override void PartCommunicationInit()
{
    if(m_connectionCount > 0)
    {
        CellConsumerInitEventArgs initArgs = new CellConsumerInitEventArgs();

        initArgs.FieldName = myCellName;
        initArgs.FieldDisplayName = myCellTitle;

        CellConsumerInit(this, initArgs);
    }
}
```

In many simple web parts, the broadcasting of schema information adds little value. If, for example, a web part can only accept a Company Name field, it will be powerless to do anything if it is connected to a Customer Name field instead. Because these situations are possible, it is important to validate the schema information, but also to provide sufficient error handling to deal with meaningless values when they are received. Often this is simply a matter of showing no results in the consumer web part until a valid value is sent by the provider web part.

Exchanging Data

Once the web parts have broadcast their schema information, they are ready for the actual data exchange. The web part infrastructure initiates this exchange by calling the PartCommunicationMain method. This method allows web parts to fire any other events that are necessary to complete the transaction.

Although it is possible for both a provider and consumer web part to fire events from the PartCommunicationMain method, most often you will use it in a provider part to send the actual data to the consumer part. Following the event naming convention, any event that does not end with the Init suffix is a candidate for firing in PartCommunicationMain. Listing 7-6 shows how a web part implementing ICellProvider sends its data by firing the CellReady event and passing the selected value from a ListBox control.

Listing 7-6. Sending Data

```
Public Overrides Sub PartCommunicationMain()

    Dim objReadyArgs As CellReadyEventArgs = New CellReadyEventArgs

    'Make sure we are connected and have a selected item in the list
    If intConnectionCount > 0 And lstCompanies.SelectedIndex <> -1 Then

        'Set the field value
        objReadyArgs.Cell = lstCompanies.SelectedItem.Text

        'Fire the CellReady event to send the data
        RaiseEvent CellReady(Me, objReadyArgs)

    End If

End Sub
```

The event fired in the provider part is implemented by the consumer part. Therefore, when the data is sent by the provider, the consumer part receives it and takes action. Listing 7-7 shows how a consumer might implement the CellReady event and use the passed data value to create a set of records from a database.

Listing 7-7. Receiving the Data

```
public void CellReady(object sender, CellReadyEventArgs cellReadyArgs)
{
    string strConn = "Password=" + password + ";Persist Security Info=True;
User ID=" + userName + ";Initial Catalog=" + database + ";
Data Source=" + sqlServer;

    //Build SQL statement
    string strSQL = "exec CustOrdersOrders '" + cellReadyArgs.Cell + "'";

    DataSet dataSet = new DataSet("orders");
```

```
//Run the query
try
{
    SqlConnection conn = new SqlConnection(strConn);
    SqlDataAdapter adapter = new SqlDataAdapter(strSQL,conn);
    adapter.Fill(dataSet,"orders");
}
catch(Exception x)
{
    lblMessage.Text += x.Message + "<br>";
}

//Bind to grid
try
{
    grdOrders.DataSource=dataSet;
    grdOrders.DataMember="orders";
    grdOrders.DataBind();
}
catch(Exception ex)
{
    lblMessage.Text += ex.Message + "<br>";
}
}
```

After the data is transferred, both web parts will draw their outputs through the `RenderWebPart` method. Whether or not the web part is involved in a connection does not make a difference as to how the output is rendered. In fact, you should remember that all of the methods that constitute the basic web part life cycle do not change. Therefore, everything you learned in Chapter 5 regarding initializing, loading, child controls, and rendering applies. When you design your web parts, you must combine the basic life cycle with the connection life cycle to achieve the behavior you want.

Using Transformers

Earlier in the chapter, I presented rules for interface compatibility. In that discussion, I said that certain interface pairs could be made compatible through the use of *transformers*. Transformers come into play in cases where a connected web part provides or consumes one of several different fields. In these scenarios, the end user must make a choice that maps the fields from the connected web parts. SPS always presents a visual tool for mapping fields when connected web parts require a transformer.

In order to provide the information necessary to map the fields, connected web parts that require a transformer must override the GetInitEventArgs method. In this method, a connected web part can tell the web part infrastructure what fields it supplies or consumes that are available for mapping. The web part infrastructure then uses this information to create the visual tool presented to the end user.

Each interface that requires a transformer supplies its field information through a class that inherits from InitEventArgs. Each event argument class accepts the appropriate metadata information necessary to describe the available fields—usually in the form of an array of Strings. This information is then returned from the GetInitEventArgs method to the web part infrastructure. Listing 7-8 shows an example of a web part providing field information through IFilterConsumer.

Listing 7-8. Returning Field Data

```
Public Overrides Function GetInitEventArgs _
(ByVal strInterfaceName As String) As InitEventArgs

    'Purpose: Provide a field list to pick from when connecting web parts.
    'This will be the field that consumes the filter.

    'Make sure we are being called on the IFilter interface
    If strInterfaceName = "FilterConsumer" Then

        'Create an object to hold the field list
        Dim objFilterConsumerInitEventArgs As New FilterConsumerInitEventArgs

        'The field list is created as an array of Strings
        Dim strFieldNames(2) As String
        Dim strFieldTitles(2) As String
        strFieldNames(0) = "comp"
        strFieldNames(1) = "cust"
        strFieldNames(2) = "ord"
        strFieldTitles(0) = "Company"
        strFieldTitles(1) = "Customer"
        strFieldTitles(2) = "Order"

        'Put the data in the event argument
        objFilterConsumerInitEventArgs.FieldList = strFieldNames
        objFilterConsumerInitEventArgs.FieldDisplayList = strFieldTitles

        'Pass the object back
        Return objFilterConsumerInitEventArgs
```

```
        Else
            Return Nothing
        End If

    End Function
```

Custom Tool Parts

Throughout your investigation of web parts, you have used properties to configure the parts within SPS. The web parts you have created have supported fundamental types such as `String` and `Boolean`. The tool pane in SPS automatically creates the appropriate user interface element—called a *tool part*—for these basic properties in the tool pane. For example, the tool pane uses a text box tool part for `String` properties and a checkbox tool part for `Boolean` properties.

There may be times, however, when you may want to create more complex properties. In these cases, you may need to create your own custom tool parts to allow the end user to set the properties of your web part. These custom tool parts allow you significant control over how your web parts are configured.

Default Tool Parts

As we have seen, every web part uses tool parts. By default, the web part infrastructure defines two types of tool parts that are associated with every web part: the `WebPartToolPart` object and the `CustomPropertyToolPart` object.

The `WebPartToolPart` object renders all of the properties associated with the `WebPart` base class. The `WebPart` base class includes fundamental properties such as `Title` and `Name`. This functionality is handled automatically by the base class and the web part infrastructure.

Whenever you create a custom property based on supported types such as `String`, `Integer`, and `Boolean`, the web part infrastructure creates the tool parts for these properties using the `CustomPropertyToolPart` object. As with the base class properties, the functionality to implement these tool parts is handled automatically by the web part infrastructure. Up to this point, these interactions have been invisible to your web parts.

The `WebPart` base class is responsible for providing a `WebPartToolPart` and `CustomPropertyToolPart` to the web part infrastructure. The `WebPart` base class creates these objects and sends them to the web part infrastructure when the `GetToolParts` method is called. Although previously you have never had to write this code, Listing 7-9 shows what the code would look like if you did have to write it.

Listing 7-9. The Default Implementation of GetToolParts

```
Public Overrides Function GetToolParts() As ToolPart()

    Dim toolParts(1) As ToolPart
    Dim objWebToolPart As WebPartToolPart = New WebPartToolPart
    Dim objCustomProperty As CustomPropertyToolPart = New CustomPropertyToolPart
    toolParts(0) = objWebToolPart
    toolParts(1) = objCustomProperty
    Return toolParts
End Function
```

In order to create a custom tool part, you must override the default implementation of GetToolParts and add your own part to the set of tool parts passed to the web part infrastructure. When you create your own tool part, you create a new class that inherits from the ToolPart class. Inheriting from the ToolPart class allows you to add the new tool part to the set. Listing 7-10 shows how the GetToolParts method would appear if you added a new tool part based on a custom class named Tool.

Listing 7-10. Overriding the GetToolParts Method

```
Public Overrides Function GetToolParts() As ToolPart()

    Dim toolParts(2) As ToolPart
    Dim objWebToolPart As WebPartToolPart = New WebPartToolPart
    Dim objCustomProperty As CustomPropertyToolPart = New CustomPropertyToolPart
    toolParts(0) = objWebToolPart
    toolParts(1) = objCustomProperty

    'This is where we add our tool part
    toolParts(2) = New Tool

    Return toolParts
End Function
```

Creating a Tool Part

As I said earlier, to create a custom tool part, you need to build a new class that inherits from the ToolPart class. Because a tool part is essentially a specialized web part that runs in the tool pane of SPS, you will find that you use many of the same skills to build a tool part that you used previously to build web parts. You can begin your tool part with a simple class definition shown in the following code.

```
Imports System.Web.UI
Imports System.Web.UI.WebControls
Imports Microsoft.SharePoint.Utilities
Imports Microsoft.SharePoint.WebPartPages

Public Class Tool
    Inherits ToolPart
End Class
```

Just like a standard web part, tool parts must override the CreateChildControls method to build a user interface. You draw the user interface by overriding the RenderToolPart method in the same way you would for a web part. When the user interface is drawn, the child controls show up in the property pane underneath the category you designate for the tool part.

What makes a tool part different from a standard web part is that it has methods that allow it to receive events from the property pane in SPS. These events are primarily fired whenever a user clicks Apply, OK, or Cancel in the tool pane. The ToolPart class allows your custom tool part to receive these events through the ApplyChanges, CancelChanges, and SyncChanges methods.

The ApplyChanges method is called by the web part infrastructure whenever a user clicks Apply or OK. In this method, you retrieve the new value of the property as it was entered into the property pane by the end user. You must in turn pass the property to the web part so that it can update its own display. In order to pass a value from the property pane to the web part, you must retrieve a reference to the web part using the SelectedWebPart property. The following code shows a simple example.

```
Public Overrides Sub ApplyChanges()
    'Move value from tool pane to web part
    Dim objWebPart As Part = DirectCast(Me.ParentToolPane.SelectedWebPart, Part)
    objWebPart.Text = txtProperty.Text
End Sub
```

After any changes are made in the property pane, the web part infrastructure calls the SyncChanges method. This method is used to pass changes back from the web part to the property pane. This is necessary because the web part and the property pane can be out of sync if the user cancels an action or if there is a validation error you need to report to the user. The following code shows a simple example.

```
Public Overrides Sub SyncChanges()
    Dim objWebPart As Part = DirectCast(Me.ParentToolPane.SelectedWebPart, Part)
    txtProperty.Text = objWebPart.Text
End Sub
```

The `CancelChanges` method is called by the web part infrastructure whenever a user clicks Cancel. In this method, you can take action to undo any changes that were made to the web part previously. You can also expect the `SyncChanges` method to be called after the `CancelChanges` method completes. The following code shows a simple example.

```
Public Overrides Sub CancelChanges()
    Dim objWebPart As Part = DirectCast(Me.ParentToolPane.SelectedWebPart, Part)
    objWebPart.Text = ""
End Sub
```

Exercise 7-1: Using Terminal Services

Integrating Microsoft Terminal Services with SPS provides a good mechanism for accessing legacy applications directly from the portal. Such a solution could mean a significant reduction in client-side installations and maintenance for older applications. In this exercise, you will set up Terminal Services and create a web part to access an application.

Setting Up Terminal Services

Before you can set up Terminal Services, you need to provide a separate server. Do not attempt to install Terminal Services on SPSPortal or SPSController because the installation can interfere with other projects in the book. I have solved this problem by creating a VMWare session named TS2K3. If you are not using a server consolidation product like VMWare, however, you will need a server capable of running Windows 2003.

Installing Terminal Services

Terminal Services should always be installed on the server as the first order of business after the operating system is installed. This is because applications that you want to access from Terminal Services must be installed after the server is configured or they will not be available. The rest of the exercise assumes that you have properly installed and configured Windows Server 2003, Enterprise Edition and joined it to the sps.local domain.

1. Select Start ➤ Manage Your Server to open the Manage Your Server page.

2. On the Manage Your Server page, click "Add or remove a role" to run the Configure Your Server wizard.

3. In the Configure Your Server wizard, click Next.

4. In the Server Role list, select Terminal Server.

5. Click Next.

6. View the summary screen and click Next.

7. After the installation is complete and the server reboots, click Finish.

Installing the Web Client

In order to access Terminal Services through the portal, you will use the web-based client control that ships with Windows 2003. Web-based access to Terminal Services is not configured by default. It must be installed separately along with Internet Information Server (IIS).

1. Select Start ➤ Control Panel ➤ Add or Remove Programs.

2. In the Add or Remove Programs dialog, click Add/Remove Windows Components.

3. In the Windows Components wizard, click Application Server and then the Details button.

4. In the Application Server dialog, click Internet Information Services and then the Details button.

5. In the Internet Information Services dialog, click World Wide Web Service and then the Details button.

6. In the World Wide Web Service dialog, check Remote Desktop Web Connection.

7. Click OK.

8. In the Internet Information Service dialog, click OK.

9. In the Application Server dialog, check ASP.NET and then click OK.

10. In the Windows Components wizard, click Next.

11. When installation is complete, click Finish.

Testing the Web Client

Once you have installed the web-based Terminal Services client, you can test it from any browser. The web client installation comes with a default web page that can be used immediately to access a terminal server. The actual functionality is provided by an ActiveX control that is automatically downloaded when the page is accessed.

1. Log in to SPSClient.

2. Open an instance of Internet Explorer.

3. Navigate the browser to http://ts2k3/tsweb/default.htm to view the Remote Desktop Web Connection page.

4. In the Remote Desktop Web Connection page, type **TS2K3** into the Server box.

5. In the Size drop-down box select 800 by 600.

6. Click Connect.

7. Use your administrator credentials to log in to TS2K3.

8. Log off of TS2K3.

9. Close Internet Explorer.

Configuring Terminal Services

Once you have verified that the web client is working correctly, you will need to configure Terminal Services for this exercise. By default, Terminal Services always logs remote users into a desktop session. Additionally, the default configuration always requires the user to enter a user name and password. In this example, you will configure Terminal Services to provide access to a single application through a common set of credentials. This will allow you to provide access to the application through the portal.

1. Select Start ➤ Administrative Tools ➤ Terminal Services Configuration.

2. In the configuration dialog, open the Connections folder.

3. Right-click the RDP-Tcp connection and select Properties from the pop-up menu.

4. On the Environment tab, check the "Override settings from user profile and Remote Desktop Connection or Terminal Services client" box.

5. In the "Program path and file name" text box, type `c:\windows\notepad.exe` to make Notepad the application that runs when a user connects to Terminal Services.

6. On the Logon Settings tab, select the "Always use the following logon information" option.

7. Enter a user name and password with permission to log on to the server and run the application.

8. Click OK.

 NOTE *Configuring Terminal Services to run a single application is best done by creating a policy in Active Directory. You are configuring the server directly to simplify the exercise. Consult the help documentation for Terminal Services for best practices.*

Creating the New Web Page

Although you can use the default web page that installs with the remote desktop connection components, typically you will want to modify the page. In this exercise, you will create your own simple ASP.NET page that accepts query string parameters as input. When the parameters are received, you will use ASP.NET to write a client-side script that will use the Terminal Services ActiveX control.

1. Log on to SPSPortal as the domain administrator.

2. Start Visual Studio .NET.

3. Select File ➤ New Project from the menu.

4. In the Add New Project dialog, open the Visual Basic Projects folder.

5. Select to create a new ASP.NET web application.

6. In the Location text box, type **http://ts2k3/SPSTSWeb**.

 NOTE *Ensure that the* wwwroot *directory is shared on TS2K3 or Visual Studio will not be able to create the project.*

---

7. Click OK.

8. In the Solution Explorer, rename WebForm1.aspx to **Default.aspx**.

9. In the Solution Explorer, open the code view for the page Default.aspx.

10. Modify the Page_Load event to generate the client-side HTML and script as shown in Listing 7-11.

11. Once the web page is correctly modified, select Build ➤ Build SPSTSWeb from the menu.

Listing 7-11. Creating the HTML and Script

```
Private Sub Page_Load(ByVal sender As System.Object, _
ByVal e As System.EventArgs) Handles MyBase.Load
```

```
With Response
 .Write(vbCrLf)
 .Write("<script language=""VBScript"">" + vbCrLf)
 .Write("<!-" + vbCrLf)
 .Write("Sub StateChange" + vbCrLf)
 .Write("  set RDP = Document.getElementById(""MsRdpClient"")" + vbCrLf)
 .Write("  If RDP.ReadyState = 4 Then" + vbCrLf)
 .Write("    RDP.Server = """ + Request.QueryString("Server") + """" + vbCrLf)
 .Write("    RDP.FullScreen = " + Request.QueryString("FullScreen") + vbCrLf)
 .Write("    RDP.DesktopWidth = """ + Request.QueryString("DesktopWidth") _
 + """" + vbCrLf)
 .Write("    RDP.DesktopHeight = """ + Request.QueryString("DesktopHeight") _
 + """" + vbCrLf)
 .Write("    RDP.AdvancedSettings2.RedirectDrives = " _
 + Request.QueryString("RedirectDrives") + vbCrLf)
 .Write("    RDP.AdvancedSettings2.RedirectPrinters = " _
 + Request.QueryString("RedirectPrinters") + vbCrLf)
 .Write("    RDP.FullScreenTitle = """ + Request.QueryString("Title") + _
 """" + vbCrLf)
 .Write("    RDP.Connect" + vbCrLf)
 .Write("  End If" + vbCrLf)
 .Write("End Sub" + vbCrLf)
 .Write("->" + vbCrLf)
 .Write("</script>" + vbCrLf)
 .Write(vbCrLf)

 .Write("<OBJECT ID=""MsRdpClient"" Language=""VBScript""" + vbCrLf)
 .Write("CLASSID=""CLSID:7584c670-2274-4efb-b00b-d6aaba6d3850""" + vbCrLf)
 .Write("CODEBASE=""msrdp.cab#version=5,2,3790,0""" + vbCrLf)
 .Write("OnReadyStateChange=""StateChange""" + vbCrLf)
 .Write("WIDTH=""" + Request.QueryString("DisplayWidth") + """" + vbCrLf)
 .Write("HEIGHT=""" + Request.QueryString("DisplayHeight") + """" + vbCrLf)
 .Write("</OBJECT>" + vbCrLf)
End With

End Sub
```

Creating the Web Part

The ASP.NET web application created in the previous steps could be called
directly from any browser to access Terminal Services using the web client.
However, you will want to integrate the functionality into SPS by creating a web

part that will dynamically build a hyperlink to call the page. The hyperlink will be created based on several properties of the web part. In this way, you will be able to configure access to Terminal Services using the properties of the web part.

Because you should be reasonably adept at creating the basic framework for a web part, I will not repeat the detailed instructions here. Simply open Visual Studio and create a new web part project using VB.NET. Name the new project **SPSTerminal** and name the class **Client**.

Defining the Properties

Your web part is limited to creating a simple hyperlink based on the properties necessary to access the Terminal Services web client. Although there are several properties, each of them corresponds to a value required by the Terminal Services web client. Add code to your web part to define the properties in Table 7-5.

Table 7-5. Web Part Properties

NAME	TYPE	DEFAULT VALUE	DESCRIPTION
URL	String	—	The URL where the web client ASP.NET page is located
Server	String	—	The name of the Terminal Services server
FullScreen	Boolean	False	Determines if the Terminal Services session runs in full screen mode
DisplayWidth	String	100%	Specifies the relative width of the session viewer
DisplayHeight	String	100%	Specifies the relative height of the session viewer
DesktopWidth	Integer	800	Specifies the width of the Terminal Services desktop
DesktopHeight	Integer	600	Specifies the height of the Terminal Services desktop
RedirectDrives	Boolean	False	Determines if the client drives are mapped to the Terminal Services session
RedirectPrinters	Boolean	True	Determines if the client printers are mapped to the Terminal Services session

Rendering the Web Part

Because you are simply creating a hyperlink as the sole interface element of the web part, no child controls are required. All you have to do is create the hyperlink in the RenderWebPart method. Add the code in Listing 7-12 to create the hyperlink for the web part.

Listing 7-12. Creating the Hyperlink

```
Protected Overrides Sub RenderWebPart( _
ByVal output As System.Web.UI.HtmlTextWriter)

    With output

        Dim strConnectURL As String = ""
        strConnectURL += URL
        strConnectURL += "?Server=" + Server
        strConnectURL += "&FullScreen=" + FullScreen.ToString
        strConnectURL += "&DeskTopWidth=" + DesktopWidth.ToString
        strConnectURL += "&DeskTopHeight=" + DesktopHeight.ToString
        strConnectURL += "&DisplayWidth=" + DisplayWidth
        strConnectURL += "&DisplayHeight=" + DisplayHeight
        strConnectURL += "&RedirectDrives=" + RedirectDrives.ToString
        strConnectURL += "&RedirectPrinters=" + RedirectPrinters.ToString
        strConnectURL += "&Title=" + Title

        .Write("<a href=""" + strConnectURL + """ Target=""_blank"">" & _
            "Connect to " + Server + "</a><br>" + vbCrLf)
    End With

End Sub
```

Deploying the Web Part

Deploying the Terminal Services web part is no different than deploying any basic web part. No special permissions are required for the part to run, so you should modify the web part description file appropriately, generate a strong name, build the part, and mark it as safe. You have already performed these steps several times in various exercises, so I will not repeat the steps here.

Using the Web Part

Once the web part is properly compiled, you should be able to add it to a site in SPS. The web part itself is an unassuming hyperlink; however, it should access the Terminal Services client when properly configured. Set the properties for the web part as listed in Table 7-6. Then click the hyperlink and verify that Notepad starts in a Terminal Services session.

NOTE   *The Remote Desktop ActiveX control must be installed on the client accessing Terminal Services.*

Table 7-6. Property Settings for the Web Part

NAME	VALUE
URL	http://ts2k3/SPSTSWeb/Default.aspx
Server	ts2k3
FullScreen	False
DisplayWidth	100%
DisplayHeight	100%
DesktopWidth	800
DesktopHeight	600
RedirectDrives	False
RedirectPrinters	True

Exercise 7-2: Connectable Web Parts

Connectable web parts are good for allowing end users to create more personalized views of data without additional programming assistance. Of course, someone still has to create the original web parts. In this exercise, you will create a web part that supports two different interfaces. These interfaces will allow you to connect the web part to custom lists you create in SPS.

Creating the Project

You will be building your web part in C#. Therefore, you should start a new web part library project in Visual Studio and name it **SPSMultiFace**. The web part itself will be named Detail. Once the project is created, take care to modify the web part description file and template code with the new names.

In order to code the project, you will also need to set several references. Your web part will need access to the appropriate namespaces for Single Sign-On (SSO), SQL Server database access, and web part connections. Listing 7-13 shows what your project should look like before you begin to add code.

Listing 7-13. Starting the Web Part

```csharp
using System;
using System.Web.UI;
using System.Web.UI.WebControls;
using System.ComponentModel;
using System.Xml.Serialization;
using System.Security;
using System.Security.Permissions;
using Microsoft.SharePoint;
using Microsoft.SharePoint.Utilities;
using Microsoft.SharePoint.WebPartPages;
using Microsoft.SharePoint.WebPartPages.Communication;
using Microsoft.SharePoint.Portal;
using Microsoft.SharePoint.Portal.SingleSignon;
using System.Data;
using System.Data.SqlClient;

namespace SPSMultiFace
{
    [DefaultProperty(""),
    ToolboxData("<{0}:Detail runat=server></{0}:Detail>"),
    XmlRoot(Namespace="SPSMultiFace")]

    public class Detail : Microsoft.SharePoint.WebPartPages.WebPart

    {
    }
}
```

Implementing the Interfaces

Your web part is designed to consume a cell as well as provide a row. Therefore your Detail class will have to implement ICellConsumer and IRowProvider. You can implement these interfaces by adding them to the class declaration. When you add the interfaces, Visual Studio should automatically offer to add the interface stubs. These stubs will define the events that the interface supports. Listing 7-14 shows how the code should appear with the stubs defined.

Listing 7-14. Adding the Event Stubs

```
//Inherits WebPart and implements ICellConsumer
public class Detail : Microsoft.SharePoint.WebPartPages.WebPart,
ICellConsumer, IRowProvider

{

public event CellConsumerInitEventHandler CellConsumerInit;

public event RowReadyEventHandler RowReady;
public event RowProviderInitEventHandler RowProviderInit;
}
```

Defining the Properties

Your web part will only use four properties. These properties will not be visible in the property pane and are used only to hold the connection information for the database. Because you have implemented properties many times in many web parts, the detailed code will not be repeated here. Instead, create the properties using the information in Table 7-7.

Table 7-7. Property Information

PROPERTY	TYPE	BROWSABLE	DESCRIPTION
sqlServer	string	false	The server name where SQL Server is located
database	string	false	The name of the database (e.g., pubs)
userName	string	false	The user name to access the database
password	string	false	The password for the database

Creating the Child Controls

Your web part uses a DataGrid to display book records from the pubs database. The records you display will be based on a search parameter received through the ICellConsumer interface. Once the records are displayed, the grid may in turn provide a row to another web part. Therefore, you have to construct our DataGrid to support row-level selection. Listing 7-15 shows how to code the CreateChildControls method to create the DataGrid and a Label for messages.

Listing 7-15. Creating Child Controls

```
//Child Controls
protected DataGrid grdBooks;
protected Label lblMessage;

protected override void CreateChildControls()
{

    //Purpose: draw the user interface
    grdBooks = new DataGrid();
    grdBooks.AutoGenerateColumns=false;
    grdBooks.Width=Unit.Percentage(100);
    grdBooks.HeaderStyle.Font.Name = "arial";
    grdBooks.HeaderStyle.Font.Name = "arial";
    grdBooks.HeaderStyle.Font.Bold = true;
    grdBooks.HeaderStyle.ForeColor = System.Drawing.Color.Wheat;
    grdBooks.HeaderStyle.BackColor = System.Drawing.Color.DarkBlue;
    grdBooks.AlternatingItemStyle.BackColor = System.Drawing.Color.LightCyan;
    grdBooks.SelectedItemStyle.BackColor=System.Drawing.Color.Blue;

    //Add a button to the grid for selection
    ButtonColumn objButtonColumn = new ButtonColumn();
    objButtonColumn.Text="Select";
    objButtonColumn.CommandName="Select";
    grdBooks.Columns.Add(objButtonColumn);

    //Add data columns
    BoundColumn objColumn = new BoundColumn();
    objColumn.DataField="title_id";
    objColumn.HeaderText="Title ID";
    grdBooks.Columns.Add(objColumn);

    objColumn = new BoundColumn();
    objColumn.DataField="title";
```

```
objColumn.HeaderText="Title";
grdBooks.Columns.Add(objColumn);

objColumn = new BoundColumn();
objColumn.DataField="price";
objColumn.HeaderText="Price";
grdBooks.Columns.Add(objColumn);

objColumn = new BoundColumn();
objColumn.DataField="ytd_sales";
objColumn.HeaderText="2003 Sales";
grdBooks.Columns.Add(objColumn);

objColumn = new BoundColumn();
objColumn.DataField="pubdate";
objColumn.HeaderText="Published";
grdBooks.Columns.Add(objColumn);

Controls.Add(grdBooks);

lblMessage = new Label();
lblMessage.Width = Unit.Percentage(100);
lblMessage.Font.Name = "arial";
lblMessage.Text = "";
Controls.Add(lblMessage);

}
```

Coding the Web Part Life Cycle

Once the child controls are defined, you are ready to code each step in the life cycle of the web part. Remember that a connectable web part not only goes through the normal steps such as OnLoad and RenderWebPart, but it must also properly register its interfaces and respond to connection events. In this section, you will code the life cycle methods in roughly the order they are called by the web part infrastructure.

 NOTE *You may want to refer back to Figure 7-2 during this exercise as an aid in understanding the life cycle.*

Registering Interfaces

The first thing your web part will do is register its interfaces with the web part infrastructure when the EnsureInterfaces method is called. Because you implement two interfaces, you will have to make two separate calls to the RegisterInterface method. Listing 7-16 shows how to code the EnsureInterfaces method.

Listing 7-16. Registering Interfaces

```
//Private member variables
private int m_rowConsumers = 0;
private int m_cellProviders=0;

public override void EnsureInterfaces()
{
    //Tell the connection infrastructure what interfaces the web part supports
    try
    {
        RegisterInterface("PublisherConsumer_WPQ_",
            "ICellConsumer",
            WebPart.LimitOneConnection,
            ConnectionRunAt.Server,
            this,
            "",
            "Get a publisher name from...",
            "Receives a publisher name.");

        RegisterInterface("BookProvider_WPQ_",
            "IRowProvider",
            WebPart.UnlimitedConnections,
            ConnectionRunAt.Server,
            this,
            "",
            "Provide a row to...",
            "Provides book information as a row of data.");

    }
    catch(SecurityException e)
    {
        //Use "WSS_Minimal" or "WSS_Medium" to utilize connections
        lblMessage.Text+=e.Message+ "<br>";
    }
}
```

Run Location

The web part infrastructure will query your web part to find out where it runs. All of your code executes on the server. Therefore, add the following simple code to tell the web part infrastructure that your part only runs on the server.

```
public override ConnectionRunAt CanRunAt()
{
    //This Web Part runs on the server
    return ConnectionRunAt.Server;
}
```

Connection Notification

An end user will connect your web part with another using the drop-down menu in SPS. When your part is connected, it will receive notification when the PartCommunicationConnect method is called. In this method, you will track the number of web parts that are connected based on the interface that is connecting. Add the code from Listing 7-17 to the web part.

Listing 7-17. The PartCommunicationConnect Method

```
public override void PartCommunicationConnect(string interfaceName,
WebPart connectedPart,string connectedInterfaceName,ConnectionRunAt runAt)
{
    //Make sure this is a server-side connection
    if (runAt==ConnectionRunAt.Server)
    {
        //Draw the controls for the web part
        EnsureChildControls();

        //Check if this is my particular cell interface
        if (interfaceName == "PublisherConsumer_WPQ_")
        {
            //Keep a count of the connections
            m_cellProviders++;
        }

        if (interfaceName == "BookProvider_WPQ_")
        {
```

```
                    //Keep a count of the connections
                    m_rowConsumers++;
            }
        }
    }
```

Implementing the Transformers

Both ICellConsumer and IRowProvider are compatible with several different
interfaces. Because of this, the web part infrastructure needs to implement a
transformer that allows the end user to map fields in the connected web parts.
Therefore, your web part must tell the web part infrastructure what fields are
available for mapping. Add the code from Listing 7-18 for the GetInitEventArgs
method, which is called by the web part infrastructure.

Listing 7-18. Providing Transformer Metadata

```
public override InitEventArgs GetInitEventArgs(string interfaceName)
{

    //Purpose: provide data for a transformer

    if (interfaceName == "PublisherConsumer_WPQ_")
    {
        EnsureChildControls();

        CellConsumerInitEventArgs initCellArgs = new CellConsumerInitEventArgs();

        //Field name metadata
        initCellArgs.FieldName = "pub_name";
        initCellArgs.FieldDisplayName = "Publisher name";

        //return the metadata
        return(initCellArgs);
    }

    else if (interfaceName == "BookProvider_WPQ_")
    {
        EnsureChildControls();

        RowProviderInitEventArgs initRowArgs = new RowProviderInitEventArgs();
```

```
        //Field names metadata
        char [] splitter =";".ToCharArray();
        string [] fieldNames =
"title_id;title;price;ytd_sales;pubdate".Split(splitter);
        string [] fieldTitles =
"Title ID;Title;Price;Sales;Date".Split(splitter);

        initRowArgs.FieldList = fieldNames;
        initRowArgs.FieldDisplayList=fieldTitles;

        //return the metadata
        return(initRowArgs);
    }

    else
    {
        return null;
    }
}
```

Communicating Schema Information

Before any data can be transferred between web parts, the connected parts must exchange schema information so that they will know what to expect. This schema exchange is accomplished when the PartCommunicationInit method is called by the web part infrastructure. In this method, your web part fires its init methods to transfer the schema information to the connected parts. Add the code from Listing 7-19 to transfer the schema information.

Listing 7-19. Sending Schema Information

```
public override void PartCommunicationInit()
{
    if(m_cellProviders > 0)
    {

        CellConsumerInitEventArgs initCellArgs = new CellConsumerInitEventArgs();

        //Field name metadata
        initCellArgs.FieldName = "pub_name";
        initCellArgs.FieldDisplayName = "Publisher name";
```

```
        //Fire the event to broadcast what field the web part can consume
        CellConsumerInit(this, initCellArgs);
    }


    if(m_rowConsumers>0)
    {
        RowProviderInitEventArgs initRowArgs = new RowProviderInitEventArgs();

        //Field names metadata
        char [] splitter =";".ToCharArray();
        string [] fieldNames =
"title_id;title;price;ytd_sales;pubdate".Split(splitter);
        string [] fieldTitles =
"Title ID;Title;Price;Sales;Date".Split(splitter);

        initRowArgs.FieldList = fieldNames;
        initRowArgs.FieldDisplayList=fieldTitles;

        //Fire event to broadcast what fields the web part can provide
        RowProviderInit(this,initRowArgs);


    }
}
```

Sending Data

The actual data is transferred between connected parts when the web part infrastructure calls the PartCommunicationMain method. We only have to code this method for the IRowProvider interface because it must initiate the transfer by firing the RowReady event. This event expects to send a row of information to a connected part based on a selection made in the DataGrid. If no selection is made, then a null row is transferred. Add the code from Listing 7-20 to fire the RowReady event.

Listing 7-20. Sending a Row of Data

```
public override void PartCommunicationMain()
{
    if (m_rowConsumers>0)
    {
        string status = string.Empty;
        DataRow[] dataRows = new DataRow[1];
```

```
if(grdBooks.SelectedIndex > -1)
{
    //Send selected row
    DataSet dataSet = (DataSet)grdBooks.DataSource;
    DataTable objTable = dataSet.Tables["books"];
    dataRows[0] = objTable.Rows[grdBooks.SelectedIndex];
    status = "Standard";
}
else
{
    //Send a null row
    dataRows[0] = null;
    status = "None";
}

//Fire the event
RowReadyEventArgs rowReadyArgs = new RowReadyEventArgs();
rowReadyArgs.Rows=dataRows;
rowReadyArgs.SelectionStatus=status;
RowReady(this,rowReadyArgs);

    }
}
```

Receiving Data

When your web part receives data from a cell provider, the CellReady event will fire. Your web part is designed to only run a query when a valid cell is provided by a connected web part. Therefore, all of the database code will be run in this event. Also note that you must implement the CellProviderInit method because it is part of the ICellConsumer interface, but your web part has nothing to do for this event. Add the code from Listing 7-21 to receive the cell data, run the query, and populate the grid.

 NOTE *For simplicity, I have hard-coded some database credentials into the code. Be sure to change these credentials to suit your environment. Also, you can get some "extra credit" by modifying the code to use the Microsoft SSO service.*

Listing 7-21. Returning Book Information

```
public void CellProviderInit(object sender,
CellProviderInitEventArgs cellProviderInitArgs)
{
//Since we can only consume one kind of cell, nothing can be done here
}

public void CellReady(object sender, CellReadyEventArgs cellReadyArgs)
{

    //Purpose: Run the query whenever a new cell value is provided
    EnsureChildControls();

    //Get Credentials (from SSO in production environment)
    userName="sa";
    password="";
    database="pubs";
    sqlServer="(local)";
    string strConn = "Password=" + password + ";Persist Security Info=True " +
    ";User ID=" + userName + ";Initial Catalog=" + database + ";Data Source=" +
    sqlServer;

    //Build SQL statement
    string strSQL;
    DataSet dataSet = new DataSet("books");

    try
    {
        strSQL = "SELECT title_id, title, price, ytd_sales, pubdate ";
        strSQL += "FROM publishers INNER JOIN titles ";
        strSQL += "ON publishers.pub_id = titles.pub_id ";
        strSQL += "WHERE (pub_name = '" + cellReadyArgs.Cell.ToString() + " ')";
    }
    catch
    {
        lblMessage.Text="Select a value from a connected web part.";
        return;
    }

    //Run the query
    try
    {
```

```
        SqlConnection conn = new SqlConnection(strConn);
        SqlDataAdapter adapter = new SqlDataAdapter(strSQL,conn);
        adapter.Fill(dataSet,"books");
    }
    catch(Exception x)
    {
        lblMessage.Text += x.Message + "<br>";
    }


    //Bind to grid
    try
    {
        grdBooks.DataSource=dataSet;
        grdBooks.DataMember="books";
        grdBooks.DataBind();
    }
    catch(Exception ex)
    {
        lblMessage.Text += ex.Message + "<br>";
    }


}
```

Rendering the Web Part

Once all of the data is retrieved from the database, you can render the grid.
Because you added a `ButtonColumn` to the `DataGrid`, the rows in the grid will be
selectable through a hyperlink. If you connect another web part as a row consumer, selecting a row will result in a data transfer. Add the code from Listing 7-22
to render the web part.

Listing 7-22. Rendering the Web Part

```
protected override void RenderWebPart(HtmlTextWriter output)
{

    //Draw the control
    grdBooks.RenderControl(output);
    output.Write("<br>");
    lblMessage.RenderControl(output);
}
```

Using the Web Part

Once the web part is coded, you may compile it and use it in SPS. Before compiling, be sure that you have provided a strong name for the web part and marked it as safe in the web.config file. Also note that connecting web parts is affected by the current code access security policy. In order to connect web parts, you should be sure that you have implemented WSS_Minimal or WSS_Medium as the policy. Also, don't forget to restart IIS if you make any changes to web.config.

Creating the Publishers List

Before you import the web part into SPS, you will create a list of publishers that you can use to provide the search parameter to your web part. You will create this list from scratch inside the portal. Once the list is created, you will add some items for the search.

To create the publishers list, follow these steps:

1. Log in to SPSPortal as a member of the Administrators site group.

2. Navigate to any site you created earlier.

3. In the site, click the Create link to open the Create page.

4. On the Create page, select Custom Lists ➤ Custom List.

5. Name the new list **Publishers** and click Create.

6. Once the list is created, click "Modify settings and columns" in the Actions list.

7. On the Customize Publishers page, select Columns ➤ Title to modify the one existing column.

8. On the Change Column page, change the column name to **Publisher**.

9. Click OK.

10. Click the Home link to return to the site home page.

11. On the home page, select Modify Shared Page ➤ Add Web Parts ➤ Browse.

12. In the Add Web Parts pane, locate the Publishers list and drag it to a zone on the page.

13. Close the Add Web Parts pane.

14. Add the following Publisher items to the Publishers list:

    • New Moon Books

    • Binnet & Hardley

    • Algodata Infosystems

    • Five Lakes Publishing

    • Ramona Publishers

    • GGG&G

    • Scootney Books

    • Lucerne Publishing

Importing the Web Part

Once the Publishers list is set up, you can import the new web part and connect it. The web part will fill the grid based on selections made in the Publishers list.
    To import the new web part, follow these steps:

1. On the home page, select Modify Shared Page ➤ Add Web Parts ➤ Import.

2. In the Add Web Parts pane, click Browse.

3. Locate the web part description file for SPSMultiFace and click Open.

4. Click Upload.

5. Drag the new web part from the Add Web Parts pane onto any zone.

6. Using the drop-down list for SPSMultiFace, select Connections ➤ Get a Publisher Name From ➤ Publishers.

7. In the Edit Connection dialog, select Publisher as the column name to provide.

8. Click Finish.

9. Close the Add Web Parts pane.

10. Select a publisher name from the list and verify that the grid fills with book information. Figure 7-3 shows the final site.

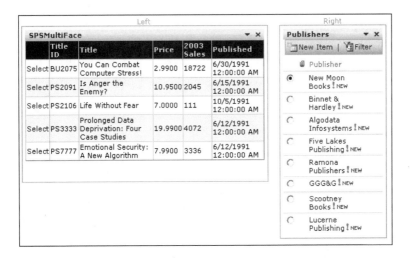

Figure 7-3. Connecting the new web part

Creating the Authors List

The Publishers list uses the ICellConsumer interface. In order to test out the IRowProvider interface, you will need to create a second list. This list will contain authors associated with titles.

To create the Authors list, take these steps:

1. In the site, click the Create link to open the Create page.

2. On the Create page, select Custom Lists ➤ Custom List.

3. Name the new list **Authors** and then click Create.

4. Once the list is created, click "Modify settings and columns" in the Actions list.

5. On the Customize Authors page, select Columns ➤ Add a New Column.

6. Name the new column **Author** and then click OK.

7. Click the Home link to return to the site home page.

8. On the home page, select Modify Shared Page ➤ Add Web Parts ➤ Browse.

9. In the Add Web Parts pane, locate the Authors list and drag it to a zone on the page.

10. Close the Add Web Parts pane.

11. Add the following items to the Authors list:

    - Title: *The Busy Executive's Database Guide*; Author: Bennet

    - Title: *Fifty Years in Buckingham Palace Kitchens*; Author: Blotchet-Halls

    - Title: *But Is It User Friendly?*; Author: Carson

    - Title: *The Gourmet Microwave*; Author: Deface

    - Title: *Silicon Valley Gastronomic Treats*; Author: del Castillo

    - Title: *Secrets of Silicon Valley*, Author; Dull

    - Title: *The Busy Executive's Database Guide*; Author: Green

    - Title: *You Can Combat Computer Stress!*; Author: Green

12. Using the drop-down menu associated with the Authors list, select Modify Shared Web Part.

13. Using the drop-down menu associated with the Authors list, select Connections ➤ Get Sort/Filter From ➤ SPSMultiFace.

14. In the Edit Connection dialog, select Title as the SPSMultiFace column to use when connecting.

15. Click Next.

16. In the Edit Connection dialog, select Title as the Authors list column to use when connecting.

17. Click Finish.

18. Close the Authors properties pane.

19. In the Publishers list, click Algodata Infosystems and verify the grid data appears.

20. In the grid of books, click the Select link associated with the title *The Busy Executive's Database Guide*. Verify that the Authors list is filtered. Figure 7-4 shows the final project.

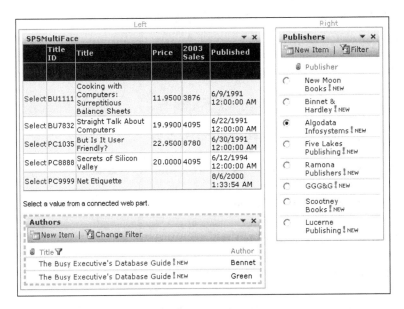

Figure 7-4. The completed project

Exercise 7-3: Custom Tool Parts

Custom tool parts allow you to create specialized user interfaces within the property pane. These tool parts lend support to properties that go beyond the fundamental data types. In this exercise, you will create a web part with a text property designed to only accept a properly formatted phone number as a value.

Building the Basic Web Part

Start this project by creating a new web part library in Visual Studio using VB.NET. As always, clean up the template code and modify the web part description file. Name the project **SPSMaskTool** and name the class **Part**. Additionally, define a text property for the web part and render that text as HTML. Listing 7-23 shows what the web part should look like to get started.

Listing 7-23. The Simple Web Part

```
Imports System
Imports System.ComponentModel
Imports System.Web.UI
Imports System.Web.UI.WebControls
Imports System.Xml.Serialization
Imports Microsoft.SharePoint
Imports Microsoft.SharePoint.Utilities
Imports Microsoft.SharePoint.WebPartPages

<DefaultProperty("Text"), ToolboxData("<{0}:Part runat=server></{0}:Part>"),
XmlRoot(Namespace:="SPSMaskTool")> _
 Public Class Part
     Inherits Microsoft.SharePoint.WebPartPages.WebPart

     Dim m_text As String = ""

     'Browsable must be False to hide the normal custom property tool part
     <Browsable(False), Category("Miscellaneous"), DefaultValue(""),
WebPartStorage(Storage.Personal), FriendlyName("Text"),
Description("Text Property")> _
     Property [Text]() As String
         Get
             Return m_text
         End Get

         Set(ByVal Value As String)
             m_text = Value
         End Set
     End Property

     Protected Overrides Sub RenderWebPart(ByVal output As _
System.Web.UI.HtmlTextWriter)
```

```
            output.Write(SPEncode.HtmlEncode([Text]))
        End Sub

End Class
```

The Custom Tool Part

Your custom tool part will be built as a separate class that inherits from the
ToolPart class. In this class, you will code the methods to handle events from the
Apply, OK, and Cancel buttons. When the tool part is complete, you will add it to
the property pane.

Creating the New Class

Because your custom tool part is defined in a new class, you must add a class
to the project. Fortunately, the web part templates provide a template for the
custom tool part as well. You can add this template to your project directly from
the menu.

Here is what you need to do to add the new tool part:

1. From the Visual Studio menu, select Project ➤ Add New Item.

2. In the Add New Item dialog, click the Tool Part template.

3. Change the name of the new file to **Tool.vb**.

4. Click Open.

5. From the Solution Explorer, open Tool.vb.

6. Modify the code in Tool.vb to appear as follows:

```
Imports System.Web.UI
Imports System.Web.UI.WebControls
Imports Microsoft.SharePoint.Utilities
Imports Microsoft.SharePoint.WebPartPages
Imports System.Text.RegularExpressions

Public Class Tool
    Inherits ToolPart
End Class
```

Creating the Child Controls

Just like a web part, a tool part must create child controls to render in the user interface. In fact, the code is identical to the code you have created several times in past exercises. In the custom tool part, you will use a TextBox to accept the user input and a Label to present error messages if the input is not a valid phone number. Add the code from Listing 7-24 to the tool part to create these controls.

Listing 7-24. Creating the Child Controls

```
'Controls to appear in the tool part
Protected WithEvents txtProperty As TextBox
Protected WithEvents lblMessage As Label

Protected Overrides Sub CreateChildControls()

    'Purpose: Add the child controls to the web part

    'Label for the errors
    lblMessage = New Label
    With lblMessage
        .Width = Unit.Percentage(100)
    End With
    Controls.Add(lblMessage)

    'Text Box for input
    txtProperty = New TextBox
    With txtProperty
        .Width = Unit.Percentage(100)
    End With
    Controls.Add(txtProperty)

End Sub
```

Coding the Property Pane Events

When the user clicks any of the buttons in the property pane, events are fired in your tool part. This allows you to use a regular expression to validate the input and modify the web part based on the results. Add the code from Listing 7-25 to implement the event handling for the buttons.

Listing 7-25. Coding the Button Events

```
Public Overrides Sub ApplyChanges ()
    'User pushes "OK" or "Apply"

    Try
        'Test the input value against the regular expression
        Dim objRegEx As New Regex("\b\d{3}-\d{3}-\d{4}\b ")
        Dim objMatch As Match = objRegEx.Match(txtProperty.Text)
        If objMatch.Success Then
            'Move value from tool pane to web part
            Dim objWebPart As Part = _
DirectCast(Me.ParentToolPane.SelectedWebPart, Part)
            objWebPart.Text = txtProperty.Text
            lblMessage.Text = ""
        Else
            lblMessage.Text = "Invalid phone number."
            txtProperty.Text = "###-###-####"
        End If
    Catch x As ArgumentException
    End Try
End Sub


Public Overrides Sub SyncChanges ()
    'This is called after ApplyChanges to sync tool pane with web part
    Try
        'Test the input value against the regular expression
        Dim objRegEx As New Regex("\b\d{3}-\d{3}-\d{4}\b")
        Dim objMatch As Match = objRegEx.Match(txtProperty.Text)
        If objMatch.Success Then
            'Move value from web part to tool pane
            Dim objWebPart As Part = _
DirectCast(Me.ParentToolPane.SelectedWebPart, Part)
            txtProperty.Text = objWebPart.Text
            lblMessage.Text = ""
        Else
            lblMessage.Text = "Invalid phone number."
            txtProperty.Text = "###-###-####"
        End If
    Catch x As ArgumentException
    End Try
End Sub
```

```
Public Overrides Sub CancelChanges()
    'User pushes "Cancel"
    Dim objWebPart As Part = DirectCast(Me.ParentToolPane.SelectedWebPart, Part)
    objWebPart.Text = ""
    txtProperty.Text = "###-###-####"
    lblMessage.Text = ""
End Sub
```

Rendering the Tool Part

Just like a web part, a tool part must be rendered. In this case, the tool part
overrides the RenderToolPart method. Other than the name change, the code is
identical. Add the following code to the tool part to render the user interface in
the property pane.

```
Protected Overrides Sub RenderToolPart(ByVal output As HtmlTextWriter)
    'Display the existing property
    Dim objWebPart As Part = DirectCast(Me.ParentToolPane.SelectedWebPart, Part)
    txtProperty.Text = objWebPart.Text

    'Draw the tool part
    lblMessage.RenderControl(output)
    output.Write("<br>")
    txtProperty.RenderControl(output)
End Sub
```

Adding the Custom Tool Part

Once the tool part is coded, you can add it to the tool pane. The custom tool part
is added by overriding the GetToolParts method. This method is part of the web
part class, so you will have to open SPSMaskTool.Part for editing. Once you have
this open, add the code from Listing 7-26 to override the method.

Listing 7-26. Adding the Tool Part to the Property Pane

```
Public Overrides Function GetToolParts() As ToolPart()

    'This code is required because it was contained in the
    'method we are overriding.  We cannot simply call the base class
    'because we can only return a single array, so we have to rebuild it.
```

```
    Dim toolParts(3) As ToolPart
    Dim objWebToolPart As WebPartToolPart = New WebPartToolPart
    Dim objCustomProperty As CustomPropertyToolPart = New CustomPropertyToolPart
    toolParts(0) = objWebToolPart
    toolParts(1) = objCustomProperty

    'This is where we add our tool part
    toolParts(2) = New Tool

    Return toolParts
End Function
```

Using the Tool Part

Once the web part and tool part are coded, you may compile and use them. Be sure to give the web part a strong name, modify the web part description file, and mark the web part as safe in the web.config file. After you have properly deployed the web part to the \inetpub\wwwroot\bin directory, import it into a web site and try the functionality. Figure 7-5 shows the tool part after an incorrectly formatted property was entered.

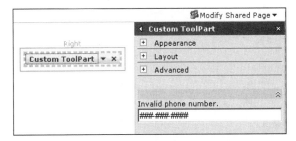

Figure 7-5. The custom tool part

CHAPTER 8

The Microsoft Office System

ALONG WITH UPGRADES TO THE WINDOWS operating systems, upgrades to the Office suite form the financial backbone of Microsoft. To support this business model, Microsoft has traditionally focused on improving the feature set of the Office suite. Customers were asked to upgrade based on new fonts, new toolbars, new editing capabilities, and the like. With Office 2003, Microsoft has changed its focus from features to collaboration. Everything in the Office suite is designed to allow teams to work together more effectively, and SharePoint Services forms the foundation for the collaboration. When referring to the combined capabilities of Office 2003, SharePoint Services, and SharePoint Portal Server (SPS), Microsoft uses the term *Office System*.

Office Integration

As we all know, the Microsoft Office suite is primarily concerned with creating documents. We also know from our discussions throughout the book that SharePoint Services is primarily concerned with managing documents. Although much of their value comes from complementary functionality centered on document creation and management, both Microsoft Office and SPS have non-document capabilities. In this section, I'll show you the document-centric integration between Office and SharePoint Services and follow it with an overview of additional integration points.

Document Management

The cornerstone of document management within the Office 2003 system is the document library. Document libraries are fully integrated with Office 2003. Fundamental document management features like check-in, check-out, and versioning are available directly from the File menu in most products. Additionally, you can access any document library directly from the Open dialog.

Once SPS is set up with an area taxonomy and document libraries, you can access documents by selecting File ➤ Open from the main menu of most Office products. However, the integration with SharePoint Services is not immediately obvious in the Open dialog because no special icons or options suggest that the document libraries are available. Instead, you can simply type the URL of the portal site into the dialog to reveal the same area taxonomy that is present in SPS. Figure 8-1 shows the Open dialog with the area taxonomy displayed.

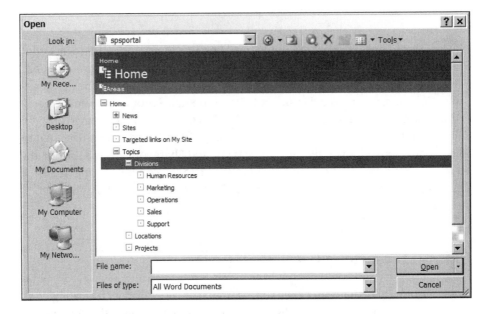

Figure 8-1. Viewing the area taxonomy

Because the area taxonomy provides a critical and familiar way to find documents, you may want to make it more easily accessible to end users. You can do this by adding it to the Look In list that appears in the Open dialog. Once you add it, end users can just click the icon to gain immediate access to the area taxonomy.

To add the area taxonomy, follow these steps:

1. From an Office product select File ➤ Open.

2. In the Open dialog, type **http://spsportal** into the File Name text box and click Open.

3. When the area taxonomy is displayed, select Tools ➤ Add to My Places from the menu in the dialog box.

4. Locate the reference to the portal in the Look In list.

5. Right-click the icon and select Move Up from the pop-up menu until the icon is at the top of the list.

6. When it is positioned correctly, right-click the icon again and select Rename from the pop-up menu.

7. Name the icon **SharePoint Portal**.

Using the area taxonomy, you can access any of the libraries that are immediately associated with an area, but you cannot easily navigate the site structure of the portal. Instead, document libraries associated with sites are treated as web folders. This means you can access them directly, if you know the URL. However, you will not find an easy way to manage URLs associated with sites. The only way to use them with a team is to e-mail them to others, but this is no better than e-mailing a link to a document on a file server.

When it comes to accessing document libraries associated with sites, users will have an easier time using SPS to locate the library. From the library, users can then create new documents or open existing ones. These actions will in turn start the appropriate Office product to view and edit the document. Later, when the user wants to save the document, Office will automatically open the correct document library. This approach ensures that users never have to know complicated URL addresses to access a document.

Document Workspaces

Regardless of how the document is accessed, when it is ultimately opened in a Microsoft Office product, it will be associated with a *document workspace*. Document workspaces are SharePoint Services sites that contain a document library, tasks, links, and other information. Document workspaces may exist because they were created directly in SPS as a new site, or they may be created ad-hoc from within an Office product. Because document workspaces provide many of the capabilities associated with SharePoint Services directly in the Office product, end users can collaborate without having SPS open alongside Office. This is significant not only because SharePoint Services capabilities are integrated, but also simply because it requires less screen real estate.

A good way to create general ad-hoc sites is to create a new site collection in SPS called "adhoc" under which all ad-hoc sites will be created. Then you can assign users to the Administrators site group for this master site. Additionally, users may choose to build personal workspaces beneath My Site. In fact the first time a user visits My Site, Office will prompt the user to designate My Site as the default collection for the user's personal workspaces.

To create a document workspace from Microsoft Word, perform these steps:

1. Log in to SPSClient as a member of the Administrators site group for the site where the new workspace will be created.

2. Start Microsoft Word 2003.

3. Select File ➤ New from the menu.

4. In the New Document pane, select Templates ➤ On My Computer.

5. In the Templates dialog, click the Memos tab.

6. On the Memos tab, select the Professional Memo template.

7. Click OK.

8. From the main menu, select Tools ➤ Shared Workspace.

9. In the Shared Workspace pane, click the Members tab.

10. In the Document Workspace Name box, type **Meeting memo**.

11. In the Location for New Workspace box, type the address of a site that you have created already (e.g., http://spsportal/sites/adhoc).

12. Click Create.

The center of document collaboration within Office 2003 is the *workspace pane*. A workspace pane is directly associated with a document workspace and will appear whenever a document is opened from an existing workspace or a new workspace is created. The workspace pane consists of tabs for the document status, workspace membership, tasks, a list of documents in the workspace, links, and the document profile. Figure 8-2 shows a typical workspace pane.

Figure 8-2. The workspace pane

The Membership Tab

Once a new workspace is created, portal users can be invited to join the workspace. It is important to note that document workspaces created in Office 2003 do not inherit permissions from the site collection in which they reside. This means that users must be invited to the document workspace in order to participate. The user who initially creates the workspace typically does this.

These are the steps you would take to invite portal users:

1. In the Shared Workspace pane, click the Members tab.

2. On the Members tab, click the Add New Members link to open the Add New Members dialog.

3. In the Add New Members dialog, type the e-mail addresses or user names for the portal users you want to invite.

4. Assign the members to a site group for the workspace. Most members will belong to the Contributors site group.

5. Click Next.

6. Verify the user information is correct and click the Finish button.

7. When you are invited to send an e-mail to the new members, click OK to start Microsoft Outlook.

8. Edit the invitation message to your liking and click Send.

The Status Tab

The Status tab in the workspace displays information regarding the status of the current document. Status changes can occur, for example, because edits were made to the document that have not been reflected in the document workspace. When this happens, the Status tab will notify members of the workspace that there is a difference between the two versions. It will also present a link to allow the document library version to be updated. Additionally, if a portal user updates the document directly in the library, members of the workspace will be given a link to get the latest copy.

Of course with this level of flexibility, conflicts are bound to occur. If users make changes to the same documents that are in conflict with each other, then the Status tab displays a message noting the conflict. In this case, you are presented with a set of options for resolving the conflict. Figure 8-3 shows the available options.

The first option is to merge the changes. In this case, you may view all of the changes and accept or reject them individually or all at once. The second option is to open both documents simultaneously and resolve the conflicts by hand. The final option is to simply override one copy of the document with the other. Once the document conflicts have been resolved, you can save the document back to the workspace.

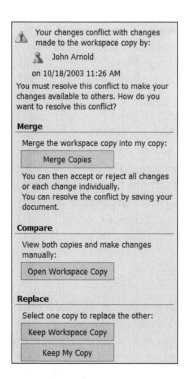

Figure 8-3. Conflict resolution options

The Tasks Tab

The Tasks tab in the workspace is used to assign and track tasks associated with the document. This is especially useful if several people are going to work on preparing a document. In such a case, you might assign certain sections of the document to a user. Each user can add their section to the document and track the progress through the task list.

The Documents Tab

The Documents tab in the workspace is used to see all of the documents that are available in the document library. This is useful when a document is being prepared from a set of subdocuments. For example, a sales proposal might consist of a product description copied from a catalog. This description could be excerpted by a member and placed in the library as a separate document. The team leader could then open the excerpt and add it into the master document later.

The Links Tab

From the Links tab in the workspace, you can add links for resources associated with the document preparation. This is useful when some of the information for the document will come from other web sites—for example, background information on a customer's organization. This way, the document preparation team can lift the text from the site and paste it into the final document.

The Document Information Tab

The Document Information tab contains metadata about the current document. This includes basic information such as who created the document or who modified it. It also allows you access to the different versions that exist in the document library and a quick link for checking in/checking out functionality. You can also configure an e-mail alert from this tab to notify you when the document has changed.

Meeting Workspaces

Although organizations often collaborate around documents, not every meeting results in a document. Instead, the organization may have a meeting to make a decision, update a project's status, or review a sales report. In these cases, people need a different set of tools to facilitate the meeting.

The Microsoft Office System provides a location specifically designed to track meeting participants, agendas, and a set of tasks called a *meeting workspace*. A meeting workspace is a specialized SharePoint Services site. It can be created directly in SPS or in Microsoft Outlook as part of a meeting request. Figure 8-4 shows a meeting workspace in SPS.

Although meeting workspaces offer a set of tools for managing information associated with a meeting, it is important to realize that they are not intended to actually host a meeting. This means that meeting workspaces should never be confused with the functionality found in Microsoft Live Meeting or similar competing services like WebEx. In a typical scenario, you could use Microsoft Live Meeting to host a meeting while tracking the agenda and action items on the meeting workspace. This way, a complete record is available to the participants after the meeting is completed.

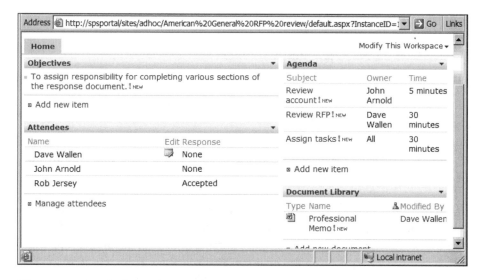

Figure 8-4. A typical meeting workspace

When preparing SPS to allow meeting workspaces, follow the same approach you used for document workspaces. Allow users to create these workspaces under a site collection. This way, all portal users can create meeting workspaces as they are needed whenever a meeting is scheduled in Outlook.

Here are the steps to create a meeting workspace:

1. Log in to SPSClient as a user with permissions to create a new workspace.

2. Open Microsoft Outlook.

3. In Microsoft Outlook, click the Calendar icon.

4. On the calendar, right-click a time slot and select New Meeting Request from the pop-up menu.

5. Give the new meeting a subject and location.

6. Click the Scheduling tab.

7. Select Add Others ➤ Add from Address Book.

8. In the Select Attendees and Resources dialog, add several users to the meeting request by double-clicking their names.

9. Click OK when you are done.

10. Click the Appointment tab.

11. Click the Meeting Workspace button.

12. Select to create the workspace in an appropriate location.

13. Click Create.

14. When the new workspace is created, click the Send button to notify the attendees.

When a new meeting workspace is created from Outlook, attendees will receive the traditional message inviting them to the meeting. The body of the meeting invitation will contain a link to the meeting workspace so that they can visit it before, during, or after the meeting. This will allow attendees to upload important documents before the meeting takes place and review action items after the meeting ends.

Contacts and Calendars

Contacts and calendars in Outlook are fully integrated with SPS. Whenever you encounter a contact list in SPS, you can import or export contacts with your personal Outlook. Anywhere you find an event in SPS, you can also export it to your local Outlook calendar. Additionally, you can link an entire event list as a calendar in your Outlook; you will be able to access it as a separate folder under the Calendars icon.

Linked Lists

For all of the line-of-business applications that have been created by independent software vendors (ISVs), Microsoft Excel remains a significant tool for creating and analyzing data. The use of Excel seems to be a testament to the way most people work. They simply want to grab a blank piece of paper, write down what they need, analyze it, and make a decision. Often it appears that line-of-business systems try to make the user conform to the process embodied in the software instead of the other way around.

It is for this reason that end users should find the list integration capability between Excel and SPS truly worthwhile. Instead of fighting the way many people work, Excel now lets end users create a list and then link it to a SharePoint Services site. This link is a simple idea, but it allows Excel users to continue editing the list directly while the data is available to all portal users through a public site.

To create and link a list, follow these steps:

1. Log in to SPSClient.

2. Open Microsoft Excel.

3. In Microsoft Excel, set up a simple list with the column headers and data as detailed here:

   - Column headers: Sales Rep, Quarterly Sales

   - Row 1 data: Bellotti, 500

   - Row 2 data: Mineweaser, 400

   - Row 3 data: Hillier, 475

4. Select the entire list you just created.

5. From the menu, select Format ➤ AutoFormat.

6. In the AutoFormat dialog, select the Accounting 1 layout and click OK.

7. Select any cell in the list you just created.

8. From the menu, select Data ➤ List ➤ Create List.

9. When prompted by the Create List dialog, click OK.

10. When the new list is created, the List toolbar should appear. Click the Toggle Total Row button on the List toolbar.

11. From the List toolbar, select List ➤ Publish List to start the Publish List wizard.

12. In the Publish List wizard, type the URL of a site that you have already created in SPS where you have permission to add content.

13. Check the "Link to the new SharePoint list" box.

14. In the Name text box, type **Sales Performance**.

15. Click Next.

16. Verify the data types in your list and click Finish.

17. If you do not have appropriate permissions, you will be prompted with a logon box. Provide credentials, if necessary, to publish the list.

When the list is published to the site, it will not be immediately visible. Instead, it will be available under the Lists link on the site. If you want to make it visible on the home page, you must edit the page. The published list can be dragged onto the page from a web part gallery just like any other list.

Whenever you update the list, the changes will be reflected on the SharePoint site if you click the Synchronize button on the List toolbar. Just like documents, however, the synchronization process can result in conflicts when the data is updated in both Excel and SPS. In these cases, clicking Synchronize displays a conflict resolution dialog. In this dialog, you can discard your changes, force your changes, or unlink the list. Figure 8-5 shows a typical conflict resolution dialog.

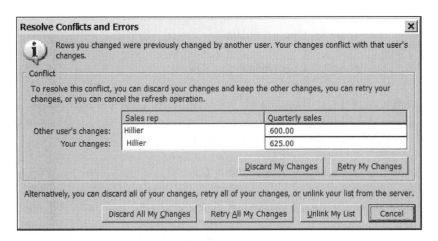

Figure 8-5. Resolving list update conflicts

Developing Office Solutions

Although the Office 2003 System offers several collaboration features for end users that do not require any separate development, in order to create more complicated solutions, you will need to roll up your sleeves and write some code. Office 2003 development is a broad and deep topic, and complete coverage is beyond the scope of this book. In this section, however, we'll investigate several key topics that can be integrated with an organizational solution based on SharePoint products and technologies.

XML Support

One of the greatest challenges in creating business solutions based on documents has always been navigating the document structure. In the past, developers have been limited to using bookmarks and the clumsy Range object to locate key portions of a document through code. Microsoft has attempted to address this problem by providing XML structural support in the Office system. This support includes both native XML structures and the ability to use external schemas to define document structure. Imposing an XML schema on a document causes it to be well formed and therefore much easier to manipulate through code.

Both Microsoft Word and Excel have the ability to save documents in XML format directly from the product menu. In Microsoft Word, however, this ability is taken even further through the use of a native XML structure called *WordML*. WordML is a detailed XML format that preserves all native Word document formatting. In this way, you can utilize well-formed XML within Word documents to easily locate document sections with standard XML processing tools.

In addition to the built-in structure of WordML, you can define your own XML schemas and impose those schemas upon a Word document. The value of this approach is that you can make the schema as simple or as complex as you need, and you do not have to impose the schema upon the entire document. Instead, you can select parts of the document and insert nodes that will enforce document structure.

Before you can insert nodes into a document, you must define an XML schema and attach it to a document. Your custom XML schema is defined in an XML Schema Document (XSD) document according to the schema definition expected by Word. A discussion of the complete schema definition is beyond the scope of this book, but you can reference it by downloading the Word developer SDK from msdn.microsoft.com. Nonetheless, creating a basic schema can be straightforward and requires little more than the definition of a set of nodes. Listing 8-1 shows a simple schema definition for an address label.

Listing 8-1. A Simple Schema

```
<?xml version="1.0" encoding="utf-8" ?>
<xsd:schema xmlns:xsd="http://www.w3.org/2001/XMLSchema"
    xmlns="urn:schemas-microsoft-com.DataLan.Address"
    targetNamespace="urn:schemas-microsoft-com.DataLan.Address"
    elementFormDefault="qualified"
    attributeFormDefault="unqualified"
    id="AddressInfo">
    <xsd:element name="Address1" type="xsd:string"/>
    <xsd:element name="Address2" type="xsd:string"/>
```

```
    <xsd:element name="City" type="xsd:string"/>
    <xsd:element name="State" type="xsd:string"/>
    <xsd:element name="Zip" type="xsd:string"/>
</xsd:schema>
```

Notice that the schema defines a set of fields for the address label and the data type for each field. In this case, I have defined a string for each field, but you can also use types such as integer and boolean. These types are used by Word to validate the structure of the document after the schema is attached. The designer can attach schemas to documents directly from the Word menu.

Here is how to attach a schema:

1. From the menu in Microsoft Word, select Tools ➤ Templates and Add-Ins.

2. In the Templates and Add-Ins dialog, select the XML Schema tab.

3. On the XML Schema tab, click the Add Schema button.

4. Navigate to the XSD file containing the schema you want to load and click Open.

Once the schema is attached to a document, you can insert nodes from the task pane. The top of the task pane has a drop-down menu that allows you to access the XML structure of the document. In this view, you are shown the available node definitions and can select to insert them. You can also choose to make the XML structure visible in the document or hide the nodes. Figure 8-6 shows a mailing label in Microsoft Word built using the schema from Listing 8-1.

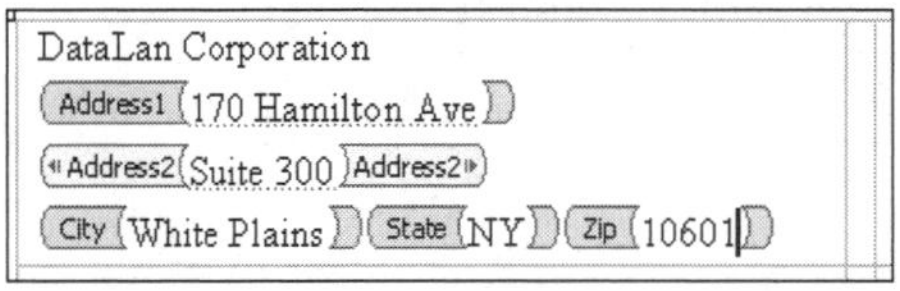

Figure 8-6. XML schema visible in Word

A schema can be immediately helpful to an end user. For example, when you are collaborating to create a document, you can easily use the node definitions to assign tasks to others. Additionally, an attached schema will be used to validate the document structure. Whenever the entered data violates the schema definition, an error will appear in the document as well as in the task pane. Figure 8-7 shows an error when a user enters the wrong data type in a field.

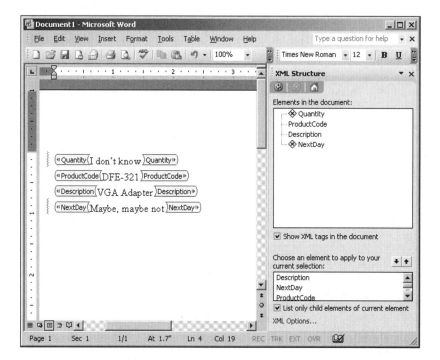

Figure 8-7. Displaying schema errors

Along with providing structure and validation, an XML schema makes it much easier to write programs that manipulate document sections. Developers can access the document sections through the node definitions to create workflow applications or automate processing. This even includes documents that can fill in their own information.

Smart Documents

With the release of Office 2003, Microsoft has tried to make document-centric development more attractive by enhancing the Smart Document capability originally introduced in Office XP. *Smart documents* are documents that have a level of situational and contextual awareness. This means, for example, that a document table with a list of products knows that it is associated with a product catalog. Furthermore, the information contained in the table is accessible to programmers in a standardized schema embodied in XML.

The primary characteristic of smart documents is that they present a set of controls to a user based on the XML node that is currently active. These controls typically appear in the task pane and offer information necessary to complete the active section of the document. Figure 8-8 shows a typical smart document with controls visible in the task pane.

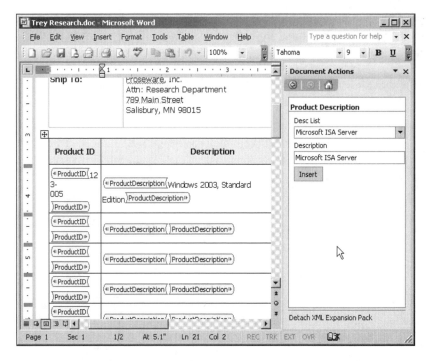

Figure 8-8. Accessing smart document controls

Smart documents are a combination of an XML schema and programming code developed in C# or VB.NET. They are deployed to end users through an XML expansion pack, which is a combination of a manifest, an assembly, and a schema. The manifest is an XML file that tells the Office product what files make up the smart document solution. The assembly is the encapsulation of the smart document functionality. The schema is the same type of schema discussed earlier. Creating smart documents is about as difficult as creating a basic web part. Not only must you create the functionality and XML files, you must also deal with code access security issues.

Preparing the Environment

Before you can begin to create smart documents, you must create a development environment. Although you should already have Visual Studio installed, you must also install the primary Interop assemblies (PIA) for the target Office product and Smart Tags. Developing smart documents requires the PIAs because Office is still a Component Object Model (COM)–based product. As a result, you must install the PIAs in order to use the .NET environment with the Office suite.

To install required programmability support, you will need to take these steps:

1. Log in to SPSPortal as a local administrator.

2. Place the Microsoft Office 2003 setup disc in the drive.

3. When prompted by the setup routine, choose to perform a Custom Install.

4. Click Next.

5. On the Custom Setup screen, check the "Choose advanced customization of applications" box.

6. Click Next.

7. On the Advance Customization screen, expand the tree and choose to install .NET Programmability Support for each Office product.

8. Expand the tree for Office Tools and choose to install Microsoft Forms 2.0 .NET Programmability Support and Smart Tag .NET Programmability Support. Figure 8-9 shows the selections.

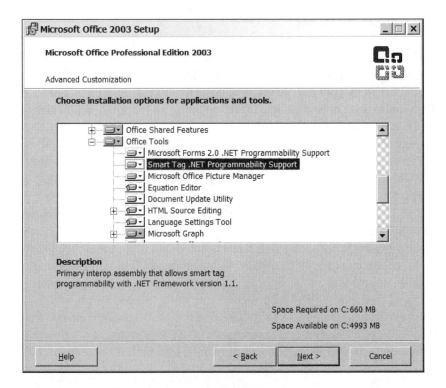

Figure 8-9. Installing programmability support

9. Click Next.

10. Review the installation options and click the Install button.

Along with the PIAs, you should also install the Office 2003 Smart Document SDK. This SDK not only contains valuable documentation, but also several tools that you will need to successfully build smart documents. In particular, smart documents run as partially trusted code, so you will have to modify configuration files on the client to trust them. The Office 2003 Smart Document SDK contains a graphical tool that makes it much easier to modify the .NET configuration for a client.

NOTE *Do not confuse the client configuration required for smart documents with the server configuration you performed for SPS. Although both client and server use .NET security, the client configuration affects how local code runs and is not related to the code access security configuration of the server where SPS runs.*

Relating Schema and Functionality

Once you have set up the development environment, you can begin a new smart document project. The functionality of smart documents is created as a .NET assembly that implements an interface to allow interaction between the assembly and the associated Office product. Therefore, every smart document begins as a class library project in Visual Studio.

In order to participate in the smart document life cycle, a class library must implement the ISmartDocument interface. This interface is contained in the primary Interop assembly for Smart Tags in the namespace Microsoft.Office. Interop.SmartTag. Therefore, you need to set a reference to the Microsoft Smart Tags 2.0 Type Library, which is located under the COM tab in the Add Reference dialog in Visual Studio.

The functionality of the smart document is embodied in the assembly, but it is related to the document itself through the XML schema. The smart document examines the document schema first and then associates the assembly functionality with the nodes according to the design of your code. As an example, suppose you wanted to create an address label using a smart document that connected to a Microsoft Customer Relationship Management (MSCRM) system on the back end. Your smart document would exist in Word with functionality to search for a company name and then fill in the rest of the label. Listing 8-2 shows a schema that defines just the company name and a single address field for simplicity.

Listing 8-2. A Schema for Address Labels

```
<?xml version="1.0" encoding="utf-8" ?>
<xsd:schema xmlns:xsd="http://www.w3.org/2001/XMLSchema"
    xmlns="urn:schemas-microsoft-com.DataLan.SmartLabelSD"
    targetNamespace="urn:schemas-microsoft-com.DataLan.SmartLabelSD"
    elementFormDefault="qualified"
    attributeFormDefault="unqualified"
    id="CompanyName">
    <xsd:element name="CompanyName" type="xsd:string"/>
    <xsd:element name="AddressBody" type="xsd:string"/>
</xsd:schema>
```

When coupling the assembly functionality to the document, Word calls into the assembly through the ISmartDocument interface using information from the schema. This process begins through a call to SmartDocInitialize, which is the initializing routine for the document. In this method, you can perform any functions that are required before any other processing.

Building Control Sets

Once the document is initialized, most of the subsequent calls to the assembly are used to construct the control set that will appear in the task pane of Word. Frankly, the process is ugly, but it is effective. Essentially the entire user interface is built through late binding with your assembly, providing all the required information Word needs to populate the task pane. This process begins when Word calls SmartDocXmlTypeCount, from which you simply return the number of nodes contained in the XML schema that have controls associated with them. In this example, you will perform a lookup for the company name and return two address lines, which may be pasted into a document. Therefore you return the integer value of 2.

After Word has determined how many nodes it must deal with, it calls the assembly again to determine which nodes will have controls associated with them. This is accomplished by successive calls to the SmartDocXmlTypeName property. Word will call this function the same number of times as the value returned from SmartDocXmlTypeCount. Your job is to return the fully qualified reference to the nodes that will have controls associated with them. The order of the nodes is unimportant in this method; just return one reference for each call as shown in the following code.

```
public string get_SmartDocXmlTypeName(int XMLTypeID)
{
    if (XMLTypeID ==1)
    {return "urn:schemas-microsoft-com.DataLan.SmartLabelSD#CompanyName";}
    if (XMLTypeID ==2)
    {return "urn:schemas-microsoft-com.DataLan.SmartLabelSD#AddressBody";}
    else {return null;}
}
```

Once the node references are passed, Word requests a friendly caption for each control set. This is accomplished by successive calls to the SmartDocXmlTypeCaption property. Because the node references have been given to Word, the subsequent call order is now important. This is because the smart document infrastructure has established a list of nodes for which it will build controls sets. In this example, you will always provide information about the CompanyName node first. The following code shows how to return friendly captions for each control set.

```
public string get_SmartDocXmlTypeCaption(int XMLTypeID, int LocaleID)
{
    if (XMLTypeID ==1){return "Company Name";}
    if (XMLTypeID ==2){return "Company Address";}
    else {return null;}
}
```

After the control set is given a caption, the smart document infrastructure queries to find out how many individual controls are associated with each control set. This is done through a call to the ControlCount property. The infrastructure sends in the fully qualified node and expects to receive a number in return. The following code shows an example.

```
public int get_ControlCount(string XMLTypeName)
{
    if(XMLTypeName=="urn:schemas-microsoft-com.DataLan.SmartLabelSD#CompanyName")
    {return 3;}
    if(XMLTypeName=="urn:schemas-microsoft-com.DataLan.SmartLabelSD#AddressBody")
    {return 2;}
    else {return 0;}
}
```

Before the actual control set can be built, the smart document infrastructure needs to assign each individual control a unique identifier across all control sets. This is accomplished by repeated calls to the `ControlID` property. This property is called for each control that will be part of the smart document. The calls are made by passing in the fully qualified node reference and an index number. The index is simply the count order for a control set and is not unique, so you must create a unique number for it.

In this example, the Company Name control set has three controls and the Company Address control set has two controls. When these control sets are built, the smart document infrastructure calls the `ControlID` and passes in the `ControlIndex` and `XMLTypeName`. Your code must respond with a unique `ControlID`. Table 8-1 details the unique `ControlID` returned for each possible combination of arguments.

Table 8-1. ControlID Return Values

CONTROL INDEX	XMLTYPENAME	CONTROLID RETURNED
1	urn:schemas-microsoft-com. DataLan.SmartLabelSD#CompanyName	10
2	urn:schemas-microsoft-com. DataLan.SmartLabelSD#CompanyName	20
3	urn:schemas-microsoft-com. DataLan.SmartLabelSD#CompanyName	30
1	urn:schemas-microsoft-com. DataLan.SmartLabelSD#AddressBody	100
2	urn:schemas-microsoft-com. DataLan.SmartLabelSD#AddressBody	200

Generating the unique values is a simple process of operating a mathematical function on the index. In this case, you are simply multiplying the index by 10 for the first control set and 100 for the second. The following code shows how it is done.

```
public int get_ControlID(string XMLTypeName, int ControlIndex)
{
    if(XMLTypeName=="urn:schemas-microsoft-com.DataLan.SmartLabelSD#CompanyName")
    {return 10*ControlIndex;}
    if(XMLTypeName=="urn:schemas-microsoft-com.DataLan.SmartLabelSD#AddressBody")
    {return 100*ControlIndex;}
    else {return 0;}
}
```

Along with a unique identifier, the controls are also given unique names that can be associated with the document schema. For each `ControlID` created in the previous step, a name is requested through a call to the `ControlNameFromID` property. In this example, you simply append the `ControlID` to the base URI of the schema. The following code shows how it is done.

```
public string get_ControlNameFromID(int ControlID)
{
    return "urn:schemas-microsoft-com.DataLan.SmartLabelSD"
+ ControlID.ToString();
}
```

The next step in building the control sets is to provide a caption for each individual control. These are generated by your code when the `ControlCaptionFromID` property is called. The smart document infrastructure calls this property for each unique `ControlID` you defined earlier. Your code then responds with a friendly caption for each control. At this point, you have to decide which `ControlID` will be for what control. You need to remember this throughout the rest of the project to ensure that the correct control type is rendered with the caption when you create the controls later. The following code shows how to generate the captions.

```
public string get_ControlCaptionFromID(int ControlID, string ApplicationName,
int LocaleID, string Text, string Xml, object Target)
{
    if(ControlID==10){return "Search Text";}      //TextBox
    if(ControlID==20){return "Search";}           //Button
    if(ControlID==30){return "Companies";}        //List
    if(ControlID==100){return "Addresses";}       //List
    if(ControlID==200){return "Insert";}          //Button
    else {return null;}
}
```

Now that the captions are generated, you have to define the actual control type for each `ControlID`. This is accomplished by repeated calls to the `ControlTypeFromID` property. The process is similar to defining captions, except you return an enumerated type of `Microsoft.Office.Interop.SmartTag.C_TYPE` that defines each control type. Using this enumeration, you can define any basic control you might need. The following code shows how to define the controls.

```
public C_TYPE get_ControlTypeFromID(int ControlID,
string ApplicationName, int LocaleID)
```

```
{
    if(ControlID==10){return C_TYPE.C_TYPE_TEXTBOX;}
    if(ControlID==20){return C_TYPE.C_TYPE_BUTTON;}
    if(ControlID==30){return C_TYPE.C_TYPE_LISTBOX;}
    if(ControlID==100){return C_TYPE.C_TYPE_TEXTBOX;}
    if(ControlID==200){return C_TYPE.C_TYPE_BUTTON;}
    else {return 0;}
}
```

Working with Control Sets

Once the control sets are defined, you may want to populate them with some initial values. These values are the ones that will appear in the controls whenever their related schema section becomes active in the document. At the very least, you will want to assign button captions through the PopulateOther method, but other methods exist in the interface for each type of possible control.

All of the population methods work in essentially the same way. The ControlID is passed in along with several arguments that can be set to populate the appropriate control. For example, C_TYPE_BUTTON controls and C_TYPE_TEXTBOX controls can have a Text argument passed in. For C_TYPE_LISTBOX controls and C_TYPE_COMBO controls, you set the value of a list item by using a 1-based array named List. The following code shows a simple example of setting button captions and list items.

```
if(ControlID==20){Text="Lookup";}
if(ControlID==100){Text=addressBody;}
if(ControlID==200)
    {
        List[1] = "Item 1";
        List[2] = "Item 2";
        List[3] = "Item 3";
    }
```

When the user interacts with controls in the set, they cause events that are handled by methods in the ISmartDocument interface. In keeping with the programming model you have seen throughout this discussion, events are handled in a common location for all controls of the same type. In order to distinguish which control actually caused the event, the event methods receive the ControlID of the firing control. Using conditional programming, you can take action based on the ControlID and the event fired.

Deploying Smart Documents

Smart documents are deployed through the use of a manifest file that specifies every file contained in the solution. A manifest file is an XML document that contains information about the assembly, document schema, and other related documents, such as templates necessary to run your smart document. Office 2003 refers to this set of documents and assemblies as an *XML expansion pack*. Listing 8-3 shows a complete manifest file that defines an XML expansion pack.

Listing 8-3. A Manifest File

```xml
<?xml version="1.0" encoding="UTF-8" standalone="no"?>
<manifest xmlns="http://schemas.microsoft.com/office/xmlexpansionpacks/2003">
    <version>1.0</version>
    <updateFrequency>20160</updateFrequency>
    <uri>urn:schemas-microsoft-com.DataLan.SmartLabel</uri>
    <solution>
        <solutionID>{1F5E8807-262A-4992-A0D0-05033C41EFC0}</solutionID>
        <type>smartDocument</type>
        <alias lcid="1033">Smart Label</alias>
        <documentSpecific>False</documentSpecific>
        <targetApplication>Word.Application.11</targetApplication>
        <file>
            <type>solutionActionHandler</type>
            <version>1.0</version>
            <filePath>Address.dll</filePath>
            <CLSNAME>Address.SmartLabel</CLSNAME>
            <managed/>
            <runFromServer>True</runFromServer>
        </file>
    </solution>
    <solution>
        <solutionID>schema</solutionID>
        <type>schema</type>
        <alias lcid="1033">Smart Label</alias>
        <file>
            <type>schema</type>
            <version>1.0</version>
            <filePath>SmartLabel.xsd</filePath>
        </file>
    </solution>
</manifest>
```

The manifest file consists of information that defines the XML expansion pack as a whole and each constituent of the pack. This information is loaded directly from Word and must be completely accurate for the solution to run. Unfortunately, the manifest file must be created by hand, so it is important to understand the various elements that make up the XML structure. Table 8-2 lists the key elements and a brief explanation of each.

Table 8-2. Elements of the Manifest File

ELEMENT	DESCRIPTION
`<version>`	The version of the solution.
`<updateFrequency>`	The interval for update checks in minutes.
`<uri>`	The schema associated with the solution.
`<solutionID>`	A Globally Unique Identifier (GUID) uniquely identifying the solution.
`<type>`	The type of solution or file.
`<alias>`	A friendly name that appears in Office referencing the solution.
`<documentSpecific>`	If true, this means that this solution is intimately associated with a particular document type and should never be allowed to attach to other documents.
`<targetApplication>`	The target for the solution.
`<filePath>`	The complete path to the solution.
`<CLSNAME>`	The fully qualified name of the assembly.
`<managed>`	This indicates this smart document solution is .NET based.
`<runFromServer>`	This determines if a solution is downloaded to the client or run in place on the server.

* A complete listing of every possible element is available in the Office 2003 Smart Document SDK.

Once a proper manifest file is created, you can deploy the contents of the file to a central location. Users may then load the XML expansion pack by selecting Tools ➤ Templates and Add-Ins from the Word menu. In the Templates and Add-Ins dialog, the XML Expansion Packs tab allows new packs to be added.

Security Considerations

Even though you correctly create a manifest, schema, and assembly for your
XML expansion pack, the solution will not run on a client machine unless it is
trusted. Office 2003 has a special security component for managed add-ins
called the Visual Studio Tools for Office loader. This loader handles the security
for partially trusted code that runs as part of an Office product. The loader works
with the .NET security classes to verify the evidence of an assembly before it is
allowed to run.

Configuring the client to trust your smart document is similar to configuring SPS to trust a web part, but client configuration poses a separate set of
challenges. When you configured code access security on the server, the configuration could be done once centrally for all portal users. Smart documents
require the configuration of each client machine that will use the solution. The
simplest way to set up configuration for each user to trust your smart documents is to use a strong name for your assembly and digitally sign both the
assembly and the manifest.

Generating a strong name for the assembly is identical to generating one for
a web part. Digitally signing the assembly, however, requires that you have a digital certificate installed specifically for signing code. If the certificate is installed,
you can use the SignCode.exe utility to apply the certificate to your assembly. You
should use the same certificate to sign the manifest as well. The Office 2003
Smart Document SDK ships with a tool that allows you to sign the manifest.

If you do not have a digital certificate suitable for signing code, you still have
a couple of options with which to configure security. Your first option is to create
your own test certificate for signing using the MakeCert.exe tool that ships with
Visual Studio. The second option—and the one I will use in the examples—
involves modifying the security settings to trust your smart documents based
on their file location and disabling the XML signature check.

Disabling the signature check for manifest files is a matter of altering a registry key; however, if you have the Office 2003 Smart Document SDK installed,
you may use the utility available on the program menu. Configuring trust for the
smart documents is accomplished by running one of several wizards also provided by the Office 2003 Smart Document SDK. These wizards allow you to
adjust security for the machine as a whole or just for a particular assembly by
selecting Start ➤ Administrative Tools ➤ Microsoft .NET Framework 1.1 Wizards.

Research Library

Using document workspaces through SharePoint Services helps end users assign
tasks and assemble documents more easily when those documents are primarily

built by teams. However, these collaboration features do not help the individual locate the actual *information* required to create the document. Smart documents certainly help in this area, but smart documents provide only specific information associated with a document field or section. What is missing from the solution is a general tool that can bring back various types of information. This is where the *Research Library* comes into play. The Research Library is a general-purpose search tool that can search for information in reference books, line-of-business systems, the Internet, and even SPS. Out of the box, the Research Library provides access to several sources of information like a dictionary and thesaurus.

The Research Library is available in most of the Office 2003 products and is accessible by selecting Tools ➤ Research from the menu. Using the Research Library is straightforward regardless of the source you want to search. The end user simply selects a service and types a search string into the task pane. The Research Library then searches the selected service for responses to the search string. The responses vary depending upon the service. The Research Library might display definitions, alternative word choices, Internet hyperlinks, or any other kind of appropriate information. In many cases, you can then insert the information directly into your document. Figure 8-10 shows the Research Library after a typical search.

Figure 8-10. The Research Library

The initial set of services that ship with Office 2003 are only moderately interesting, but the true value of the Research Library lies in the fact that you can extend the library to include SharePoint Services sites or even your own custom services. This is possible because the Research Library architecture is based on web services. The web services communicate with the Research Library through a set of XML documents. As long as the correct documents are exchanged, you can integrate any system with the library. In fact, SPS supports the required XML schemas so that it can be searched using the library.

To search a SharePoint Services site, follow these steps:

1. Open the Research Library in Microsoft Word by selecting Tools ➤ Research from the menu.

2. At the bottom of the research pane, click the Research Options link.

3. In the Research Options dialog, click the Add Services button.

4. In the Address box, type the URL `http://spsportal/_vti_bin/search.asmx`.

5. Click Add.

6. Close the Research Options dialog.

7. In the research pane, select the SPS source from under the All Intranet Sites and Portals section.

8. Type a search string into the Search For box and click the green arrow.

Building a Research Service

Building your own research service allows you to integrate systems directly with the Research Library. To construct a research service, you must build a web service to support registering the service with the library and responding to queries from the library. Both of these activities are accomplished by passing request/ response XML documents between the library and the service.

The request/response paradigm allows you to treat the research pane like a web browser. The difference is that the information is passed as a payload in an XML stream. The schemas defining these streams are all documented in the Research Library SDK. The SDK itself is not required to create or deploy a research service, but the schema references are critical to creating the exact presentation and behavior you want.

Registering a Service

When an end user wants to add a new source to the Research Library, they must provide a URL that refers to a web service capable of registering the source with the library. The Research Library expects the web service to expose a function named Registration. This function must accept a single String argument and return a String result. The registration request is made when the library passes an XML stream to the Registration method. The method then responds with a properly formatted XML stream that defines the new research service. Listing 8-4 shows a typical response from a research service.

Listing 8-4. Registration Response XML Stream

```xml
<?xml version="1.0" encoding="utf-8" ?>
<ProviderUpdate xmlns="urn:Microsoft.Search.Registration.Response">
<Status>SUCCESS</Status>
<Providers>
<Provider>
     <Message>This is a research library for the CRM system</Message>
     <Id>{BC907F3F-D894-42ef-BBC6-C9EE5C0AE46D}</Id>
     <Name>CRM</Name>
     <QueryPath>http://spsportal/myService/query.asmx</QueryPath>
     <RegistrationPath> http://spsportal/myService/registration.asmx
     </RegistrationPath>
     <AboutPath> http://spsportal/myService/about.asmx </AboutPath>
     <Type>SOAP</Type>
     <Services>
         <Service>
             <Id>{351B0D21-9767-4677-9880-361AA722EA1A}</Id>
             <Name>Company Lookup</Name>
             <Description>Returns address information</Description>
             <Copyright></Copyright>
             <Display>On</Display>
             <Category>BUSINESS_BUSINESS</Category>
         </Service>
     </Services>
</Provider>
</Providers>
</ProviderUpdate>
```

The XML response to the Registration method could be completely hard-coded in a single XML document because none of the values in the stream needs to be calculated. In practical applications, the location of the web service is likely to change when moving from development to production, so you typically have to modify the stream at runtime. In most cases, this means changing the path associated with the `<QueryPath>`, `<RegistrationPath>`, and `<AboutPath>` elements. The rest of the elements are generally fixed. Table 8-3 lists the key elements in the registration response stream with a brief description.

Table 8-3. Elements in the Registration Response Stream

ELEMENT	DESCRIPTION
`<ProviderUpdate>`	The outer envelope of the response. Must refer to the `urn:Microsoft.Search.Registration.Response` namespace.
`<Status>`	The result of the registration. May be SUCCESS, ERROR, or ERROR_NOT_COMPATIBLE.
`<Providers>`	Contains multiple provider registrations.
`<Provider>`	Contains the detailed registration information for a provider.
`<Message>`	A message that will appear when the service is registered.
`<Id>`	A GUID uniquely identifying a provider or service.
`<Name>`	The name of a provider or service.
`<RegistrationPath>`	The complete URL to a web service with a Registration method.
`<QueryPath>`	The complete URL to a web service with a Query method.
`<AboutPath>`	The complete URL to "about" information.
`<Type>`	The communication protocol. Always set to SOAP.
`<Services>`	Contains multiple service descriptions.
`<Service>`	Contains detailed information about a service.
`<Description>`	A description of the service.
`<Copyright>`	A copyright message.
`<Display>`	Determines if service is visible. May be ON, OFF, or HIDDEN.
`<Category>`	The category under which the service will be listed.

* A complete listing of every possible element is available in the Research SDK.

Responding to Queries

The registration response stream must specify a complete URL to a web service that contains a Query method. Just like the Registration method, the Query method accepts an XML stream as a `String` argument and returns an XML stream as a `String`. The Research Library packages the query in the XML stream along with metadata about the request. When you write the code for the `Query` method, you extract the query text from the `<QueryText>` element of the XML stream and use it to process the search request.

The basic approach to processing the incoming XML query stream is to load it into an `XmlDocument` object. Once the query stream is loaded, you can use the object to select out the nodes that you need to process the query. Listing 8-5 is a partial listing focused on how to access the `<QueryText>` node using VB.NET.

Listing 8-5. Processing the XML Query Stream

```
<WebMethod()>Public Function Query(ByVal queryXml As String) As String

    'Load query into new document
    Dim objXMLRequest As New XmlDocument
    objXMLRequest.LoadXml(queryXml)

    'Prepare for parsing
    Dim objRequestManager As New XmlNamespaceManager(objXMLRequest.NameTable)
    objRequestManager.AddNamespace("ns", "urn:Microsoft.Search.Query")

    'Get query string
    Dim strQuery = _
    objXMLRequest.SelectSingleNode("//ns:QueryText",objRequestManager).InnerText

End Function
```

Depending upon how you design your service, you may be interested in several other nodes available in the query stream. The `<Name>` element contains the name of the application making the request. This is important if you must customize your response to different Office products. The `<StartAt>` element specifies which record to begin with in the result set, and the `<Count>` element specifies how many records to return with the result set. These are important if you are paging your results through multiple responses.

Once you have completed your processing, you must return a result stream to the client in accordance with the expected XML schema. The Research Library recognizes a general schema that forms an envelope for the result set and specific schemas to define the query results. The following code shows a typical envelope for results.

```
<?xml version="1.0" encoding="utf-8" ?>
<ResponsePacket revision="1" xmlns="urn:Microsoft.Search.Response">
    <Response domain="{351B0D21-9767-4677-9880-361AA722EA1A}">
```

```
        <Range>
        </Range>
        <Status>SUCCESS</Status>
    </Response>
</ResponsePacket>
```

The response envelope contains the metadata information the Research Library needs to properly handle the returned results. Most importantly, the `<Response>` element must contain a `domain` attribute that is identical to the `<Id>` of the service that was originally registered. The actual query results are then built between the `<Range>` and `</Range>` tags.

When the results are written into the stream, the format must be in compliance with the `urn:Microsoft.Search.Response.Content` schema. Generally, the process involves creating a new `XmlTextWriter` object and painstakingly creating the results one element at a time. The schema, however, is reasonably flexible and allows you to include things such as images, hyperlinks, and Text, Copy, and Insert buttons. Listing 8-6 shows a typical result stream returning a single record.

Listing 8-6. A Query Response Stream

```
<?xml version="1.0" encoding="utf-8"?>
<ResponsePacket revision="1" xmlns="urn:Microsoft.Search.Response">
<Response domain="{351B0D21-9767-4677-9880-361AA722EA1A}">
<Range>
    <StartAt>1</StartAt>
    <Count>1</Count>
    <TotalAvailable>1</TotalAvailable>
    <Results>
        <Content xmlns="urn:Microsoft.Search.Response.Content">
        <Heading collapsible="true" collapsed="true">
            <Text>DataLan Corporation</Text>
            <P>
            <Char>170 Hamilton Avenue</Char>
            <Actions><Insert/><Copy/></Actions>
            </P>
            <P>
            <Char>White Plains, NY 10601</Char>
            <Actions><Insert/><Copy/></Actions>
            </P>
        </Heading>
        </Content>
    </Results>
</Range>
<Status>SUCCESS</Status>
```

```
</Response>
</ResponsePacket>
```

Exercise 8-1: Building a Smart Document

Smart documents can bring significant value to end users. Typically when users create a document, they start with a template and little else. Generally the information required by the template is locked in line-of-business systems and is not easily retrieved. In most cases, end users complete documents by cutting and pasting from line-of-business systems into Microsoft Word. In this exercise, you will create an invoice using the Northwind database. Figure 8-11 shows the task pane from the final document with a product name ready to insert into the invoice.

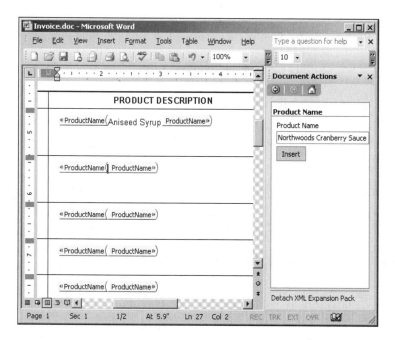

Figure 8-11. The task pane for the exercise

Prerequisites

Before you begin this project, make sure that you have installed the primary Interop assemblies for Microsoft Word and Smart Tags 2.0. If you are using the standard configuration described in this book, then you should install the PIAs on both SPSPortal and SPSClient. The PIAs are required on SPSClient because this is where you run the completed smart document. The PIAs are required on SPSPortal because this is where you originally installed Visual Studio. You could optionally install the entire Office suite on SPSPortal to make your exercise easier. Along with the PIAs, be sure to download and install the Office 2003 Smart Document SDK from msdn.microsoft.com. Finally, you may want to download an appropriate template for your smart document. I found a simple invoice template to use, but it is not required. Even a blank document will do for the exercise.

Setting Up the Project

Your smart document begins by creating a new project in Visual Studio where you can build the XML expansion pack. In this project, you will build the assembly, create the schema, and write the manifest. For this exercise, you will write the assembly in VB.NET.

To set up the project, follow these steps:

1. Start Visual Studio and select File ➤ New ➤ Project from the menu.

2. In the Add New Project dialog, click the Visual Basic Projects folder.

3. Create a new Class Library project and name the new project **SmartInvoice**.

4. In the Solution Explorer, rename the Class1.vb file to **Northwind.vb**.

5. Select Project ➤ Add Reference from the Visual Studio menu.

6. In the Add Reference dialog, click the COM tab.

7. Select to add references to the Microsoft Smart Tags 2.0 Type Library and Microsoft Word 11.0 Object Library.

8. Click OK.

9. Open the Northwind.vb file. Change the class name and add the import statements as shown in Listing 8-7.

Listing 8-7. The Initial Code

```
Imports System
Imports System.Data
```

```
Imports System.Data.SqlClient
Imports Microsoft.Office.Interop.SmartTag
Imports Word = Microsoft.Office.Interop.Word


Public Class Northwind

End Class
```

Creating the XML Schema

Before you code the assembly, you must create the XML schema that you will use to map the assembly functionality to the smart document. In this exercise, you are going to map the product catalog from the Northwind database to the smart document. This will include not only product description information, but prices as well. This will allow you to use some different types of data in the document.

To create the XML schema, follow these steps:

1. In Visual Studio, select Project ➤ Add New Item.

2. In the Add New Item dialog, select XML Schema and name the file **SmartInvoice.xsd**.

3. Modify the schema file to appear exactly as shown in Listing 8-8.

Listing 8-8. The Schema for the Smart Invoice

```
<?xml version="1.0" encoding="utf-8" ?>
<xsd:schema xmlns:xsd="http://www.w3.org/2001/XMLSchema"
    xmlns="urn:schemas-microsoft-com.DataLan.SmartInvoice"
    targetNamespace="urn:schemas-microsoft-com.DataLan.SmartInvoice"
    elementFormDefault="qualified"
    attributeFormDefault="unqualified"
    id="ProductInfo">
    <xsd:element name="ProductID" type="xsd:string"/>
    <xsd:element name="ProductName" type="xsd:string"/>
    <xsd:element name="QuantityPerUnit" type="xsd:string"/>
    <xsd:element name="UnitPrice" type="xsd:double"/>
</xsd:schema>
```

Creating the Control Sets

Once the schema is created, you can create the control sets associated with each of the XML nodes in your schema. This process follows the steps outlined earlier in the chapter. You must first implement the ISmartDocument interface and then code each required property and method. You will not use every method in the interface, just the ones needed for your specific functionality.

In order to implement the ISmartDocument interface, you should open Northwind.vb in Visual Studio. On the line directly below the class definition, type **Implements ISmartDocument** and hit the Enter key. This should automatically place all of the interface stubs in your code.

Building the User Interface

Building the user interface follows the same life cycle steps that we discussed earlier in the chapter. In most cases, the code is fairly straightforward. You simply respond to each request for information made by the smart document infrastructure. Initially, you'll create some constants to make it easier to handle the node references in the XML schema. The following code shows the constants to add.

```
'Variables
Public Const URI As String = "urn:schemas-microsoft-com.DataLan.SmartInvoice"
Public Const PRODUCTID As String = URI & "#ProductID"
Public Const PRODUCTNAME As String = URI & "#ProductName"
Public Const QUANTITYPERUNIT As String = URI & "#QuantityPerUnit"
Public Const UNITPRICE As String = URI & "#UnitPrice"
Dim intSelectedIndex As Integer = 0
Dim objDataSet As DataSet
```

Specifying the Number of Control Sets

The first piece of information is to specify how many nodes in your schema will have a control set. In this exercise, all the nodes will have a control set. Therefore, you simply return a fixed value from the SmartDocXmlTypeCount property. Code the property as follows:

```
Public ReadOnly Property SmartDocXmlTypeCount() As Integer Implements _
Microsoft.Office.Interop.SmartTag.ISmartDocument.SmartDocXmlTypeCount
    Get
        Return 4
    End Get
End Property
```

Specifying Which Nodes Have Control Sets

Once the smart document infrastructure knows how many control sets to create, it needs to know which nodes will have the control sets. It determines this by calling the SmartDocXmlTypeName property once for each control set. An element name is subsequently returned for each call. Code the SmartDocXmlTypeName property as shown in Listing 8-9.

Listing 8-9. The SmartDocXmlTypeName Property

```
Public ReadOnly Property SmartDocXmlTypeName _
(ByVal XMLTypeID As Integer) As String _
Implements Microsoft.Office.Interop.SmartTag.ISmartDocument.SmartDocXmlTypeName
    'Returns the the element name
    'Order is not important
    Get
        Select Case XMLTypeID
            Case 1
                Return PRODUCTID
            Case 2
                Return PRODUCTNAME
            Case 3
                Return QUANTITYPERUNIT
            Case 4
                Return UNITPRICE
        End Select
    End Get
End Property
```

Specifying Control Set Captions

For each control set, a caption is assigned by the smart document infrastructure. It does this by calling the SmartDocXmlTypeCaption property for each control set. A text caption is subsequently returned for each call. Code the SmartDocXmlTypeCaption property as shown in Listing 8-10.

Listing 8-10. The SmartDocXmlTypeCaption Property

```
Public ReadOnly Property SmartDocXmlTypeCaption(ByVal XMLTypeID As Integer, _
ByVal LocaleID As Integer) As String Implements
Microsoft.Office.Interop.SmartTag.ISmartDocument.SmartDocXmlTypeCaption
    'Order must be the same as in Step 2
    Get
```

```
        Select Case XMLTypeID
            Case 1
                Return "Product ID"
            Case 2
                Return "Product Name"
            Case 3
                Return "Quantity per Unit"
            Case 4
                Return "Unit Price"
        End Select
    End Get
End Property
```

Specifying How Many Controls Are in Each Set

The smart document infrastructure next needs to know how many controls are in each set. It determines this by calling the ControlCount property. The control count is subsequently returned for each call. Code the ControlCount property as shown in Listing 8-11.

Listing 8-11. The ControlCount Property

```
Public ReadOnly Property ControlCount(ByVal XMLTypeName As String) As Integer _
Implements Microsoft.Office.Interop.SmartTag.ISmartDocument.ControlCount
    Get
        Select Case XMLTypeName
            Case PRODUCTID
                Return 2
            Case PRODUCTNAME
                Return 2
            Case QUANTITYPERUNIT
                Return 2
            Case UNITPRICE
                Return 2
        End Select
    End Get
End Property
```

Specifying Unique IDs for Each Control

In order to track the controls in each set internally, the smart document infra-structure needs to assign them unique identifiers. It does this by calling the ControlID property. An identifier is returned for each call made. Code the ControlID property as shown in Listing 8-12.

Listing 8-12. The ControlID Property

```
Public ReadOnly Property ControlID(ByVal XMLTypeName As String, _
ByVal ControlIndex As Integer) _
As Integer Implements Microsoft.Office.Interop.SmartTag.ISmartDocument.ControlID
    'ControlIndex is just the index for each set 1,2,3...
    'Therefore, we add an arbitrary number to guarantee uniqueness
    Get
        Select Case XMLTypeName
            Case PRODUCTID
                Return ControlIndex
            Case PRODUCTNAME
                Return ControlIndex + 100
            Case QUANTITYPERUNIT
                Return ControlIndex + 200
            Case UNITPRICE
                Return ControlIndex + 300
        End Select
    End Get
End Property
```

Adding the Controls to the Schema

The smart document infrastructure adds the controls to the schema so that they can be used with the document. It does this by creating a unique node name for each control through calls to the ControlNameFromID property. A node name is returned for each call. You can code the ControlNameFromID property as shown here:

```
Public ReadOnly Property ControlNameFromID(ByVal ControlID As Integer) As String
_
Implements Microsoft.Office.Interop.SmartTag.ISmartDocument.ControlNameFromID
    Get
        Return URI & ControlID.ToString
    End Get
End Property
```

Specifying Individual Control Captions

The smart document infrastructure assigns individual captions to each control in the set. It does this by calling the ControlCaptionFromID property. Then a caption is returned for each call. You can code the ControlCaptionFromID property as shown in Listing 8-13.

Listing 8-13. The ControlCaptionFromID Property

```
Public ReadOnly Property ControlCaptionFromID(ByVal ControlID As Integer, _
ByVal ApplicationName As String, ByVal LocaleID As Integer, _
ByVal Text As String, ByVal Xml As String, ByVal Target As Object) _
As String _
Implements Microsoft.Office.Interop.SmartTag.ISmartDocument.ControlCaptionFromID
    Get
        Select Case ControlID
            Case 1
                Return "Product ID"
            Case 2, 102, 202, 302
                Return "Insert"
            Case 101
                Return "Product Name"
            Case 201
                Return "Quantity Per Unit"
            Case 301
                Return "Unit Price"
        End Select
    End Get
End Property
```

Specifying the Type for Each Control

The smart document infrastructure needs to determine what types of controls make up each set. It uses the ControlTypeFromID property to determine this. A control class is returned for each call. You can code the ControlTypeFromID property as shown in Listing 8-14.

Listing 8-14. The ControlTypeFromID Property

```
Public ReadOnly Property ControlTypeFromID(ByVal ControlID As Integer, _
ByVal ApplicationName As String, ByVal LocaleID As Integer) _
As Microsoft.Office.Interop.SmartTag.C_TYPE Implements _
Microsoft.Office.Interop.SmartTag.ISmartDocument.ControlTypeFromID
    Get
```

```
        Select Case ControlID
            Case 1
                Return C_TYPE.C_TYPE_COMBO
            Case 2, 102, 202, 302
                Return C_TYPE.C_TYPE_BUTTON
            Case 101, 201, 301
                Return C_TYPE.C_TYPE_TEXTBOX
        End Select
    End Get
End Property
```

Handling the Controls

Once the control sets are created, you can fill them with the initial values that will appear in the task pane. For buttons, this is a simple matter of setting the caption text, but for your lists and text boxes, you want to extract information from the Northwind database. Start by coding the PopulateOther method to place captions on the button as shown in Listing 8-15.

Listing 8-15. Setting Button Captions

```
Public Sub PopulateOther(ByVal ControlID As Integer, _
ByVal ApplicationName As String, _
ByVal LocaleID As Integer, ByVal Text As String, _
ByVal Xml As String, ByVal Target As Object, _
ByVal Props As Microsoft.Office.Interop.SmartTag.ISmartDocProperties) _
Implements Microsoft.Office.Interop.SmartTag.ISmartDocument.PopulateOther
    'Set control values
    Select Case ControlID
        Case 2, 102, 202, 302
            Text = "Insert"
    End Select
End Sub
```

Filling the List

In this exercise, you provide a list of Product IDs to begin. A user can select one of these entries to start filling in the invoice. However, this assumes that you are dealing with users who know the Product IDs well and prefer to work that way. In other applications, you might choose to use a product name as the starting point.

You can access the Northwind database in the PopulateListOrComboContent method. Most of the code here is standard data access code. Note, however, that you populate the list by referencing the List argument. You also tell the list how many items it contains by using the Count argument. Finally, you indicate that the first item in the list is selected through the InitialSelected argument. Add the code from Listing 8-16 to code this method.

Listing 8-16. Populating the List

```
Public Sub PopulateListOrComboContent(ByVal ControlID As Integer, _
ByVal ApplicationName As String, ByVal LocaleID As Integer, _
ByVal Text As String, ByVal Xml As String, ByVal Target As Object, _
ByVal Props As Microsoft.Office.Interop.SmartTag.ISmartDocProperties, _
ByRef List As System.Array, ByRef Count As Integer, _
ByRef InitialSelected As Integer) _
Implements _
Microsoft.Office.Interop.SmartTag.ISmartDocument.PopulateListOrComboContent

    Select Case ControlID
        Case 1
            'Set up connection string from custom properties
            Dim strPassword As String = ""
            Dim strUserName As String = "sa"
            Dim strDatabase As String = "Northwind"
            Dim strSQLServer = "SPSPortal"

            Dim strConnection As String = "Password=" & strPassword
            strConnection += ";Persist Security Info=True;User ID=" + strUserName
            strConnection += ";Initial Catalog=" + strDatabase
            strConnection += ";Data Source=" + strSQLServer

            'Create SQL String
            Dim strSQL As String = "SELECT ProductID, ProductName, " & _
"QuantityPerUnit, UnitPrice FROM Products"

            'Try to run the query
            With New SqlDataAdapter
                objDataSet = New DataSet("root")
                .SelectCommand = New SqlCommand _
                  (strSQL, New SqlConnection(strConnection))
                .Fill(objDataSet, "Products")
            End With
```

```
         'Fill List
         Dim index As Integer = 0
         Dim objTable As DataTable = objDataSet.Tables("Products")
         Dim objRows As DataRowCollection = objTable.Rows
         Dim objRow As DataRow

         'Set the number of items in the list
         Count = objTable.Rows.Count
         For Each objRow In objRows
             index += 1
             List(index) = objRow.Item("ProductID")
         Next
         'Select the first item
         InitialSelected = 1
     End Select

End Sub
```

Populating the Text Boxes

After a Product ID is selected, the remaining control sets are populated based
on the value selected in the list. This allows the user to review the value before
inserting it into the document. The text boxes are populated through calls to the
PopulateTextboxContent method. Add the code in Listing 8-17 to retrieve the values
from the DataSet and place them in the appropriate text boxes.

Listing 8-17. Populating the Text Boxes

```
Public Sub PopulateTextboxContent(ByVal ControlID As Integer, _
ByVal ApplicationName As String, ByVal LocaleID As Integer, _
ByVal Text As String, _
ByVal Xml As String, ByVal Target As Object, _
ByVal Props As Microsoft.Office.Interop.SmartTag.ISmartDocProperties, _
ByRef Value As String) Implements _
Microsoft.Office.Interop.SmartTag.ISmartDocument.PopulateTextboxContent

    'Variables for insert text
    Dim txtProductName As String
    Dim txtQuantityPerUnit As String
    Dim txtUnitPrice As String
```

```
    'Get values based on Product ID selection
    If objDataSet.Tables.Count > 0 Then
        txtProductName = _
objDataSet.Tables("Products").Rows.Item(intSelectedIndex) _
.Item("ProductName").ToString
        txtQuantityPerUnit = _
objDataSet.Tables("Products").Rows.Item(intSelectedIndex). _
Item("QuantityPerUnit").ToString
        txtUnitPrice = _
objDataSet.Tables("Products").Rows.Item(intSelectedIndex). _
Item("UnitPrice").ToString
    End If

    'Set control values
    Select Case ControlID
        Case 101
            Value = txtProductName
        Case 201
            Value = txtQuantityPerUnit
        Case 301
            Value = txtUnitPrice
    End Select

End Sub
```

Handling Events

Your smart document needs to react when a new product ID is selected or when text is inserted in the document. You can code events for both the buttons and the list to capture user actions. When the buttons are pushed, you insert text into the document. When the list selection changes, you trap the index so that you can use it to fill the other controls with appropriate information. Add the code from Listing 8-18 to handle the events.

Listing 8-18. Handling Events

```
'List
Public Sub OnListOrComboSelectChange(ByVal ControlID As Integer, _
ByVal Target As Object, _
ByVal Selected As Integer, ByVal Value As String) Implements _
Microsoft.Office.Interop.SmartTag.ISmartDocument.OnListOrComboSelectChange
    intSelectedIndex = Selected - 1
End Sub
```

```
'Buttons
Public Sub InvokeControl(ByVal ControlID As Integer, _
ByVal ApplicationName As String, _
ByVal Target As Object, ByVal Text As String, _
ByVal Xml As String, ByVal LocaleID As _
Integer) Implements
Microsoft.Office.Interop.SmartTag.ISmartDocument.InvokeControl

    Dim objRange As Word.Range
    objRange = CType(Target, Word.Range)

    'Create insert text from a text control based on which button is pushed
    Select Case ControlID
        Case 2
            Dim intIndex As Integer = _
objRange.XMLNodes(1).SmartTag.SmartTagActions(1).ListSelection
            objRange.XMLNodes(1).Text = "Product " & _
objDataSet.Tables("Products").Rows.Item(intSelectedIndex).Item("ProductID")
        Case 102, 202, 302
            objRange.XMLNodes(1).Text = _
objRange.XMLNodes(1).SmartTag.SmartTagActions(1).TextboxText
        Case 203

    End Select

End Sub
```

Deploying the Smart Document

In order to deploy your smart document solution, you must create a manifest file and configure security. In this exercise, you will keep things simple by deploying directly from the \bin directory where you compile the assembly. You will create a manifest that will be placed in the same directory, and set up your machine to trust the file location.

Creating the Manifest

As we discussed earlier in the chapter, the manifest file contains the details regarding the contents of the XML expansion pack. Using Visual Studio, add a new XML file named manifest.xml to the project. Modify the file to appear exactly as shown in Listing 8-19.

Listing 8-19. The Manifest File

```xml
<?xml version="1.0" encoding="UTF-8" standalone="no"?>
<manifest xmlns="http://schemas.microsoft.com/office/xmlexpansionpacks/2003">
    <version>1.0</version>
    <updateFrequency>20160</updateFrequency>
    <uri>urn:schemas-microsoft-com.DataLan.SmartInvoice</uri>
    <solution>
        <solutionID>{BDE88D2F-FA67-4890-A674-A2BEE936A1A4}</solutionID>
        <type>smartDocument</type>
        <alias lcid="1033">Smart Invoice</alias>
        <documentSpecific>False</documentSpecific>
        <targetApplication>Word.Application.11</targetApplication>
        <file>
            <type>solutionActionHandler</type>
            <version>1.0</version>
            <filePath>SmartInvoice.dll</filePath>
            <CLSNAME>SmartInvoice.Northwind</CLSNAME>
            <managed/>
            <runFromServer>True</runFromServer>
        </file>
    </solution>
    <solution>
        <solutionID>schema</solutionID>
        <type>schema</type>
        <alias lcid="1033">Smart Invoice</alias>
        <file>
            <type>schema</type>
            <version>1.0</version>
            <filePath>SmartInvoice.xsd</filePath>
        </file>
    </solution>
</manifest>
```

Configuring Security

Normally when you distribute an XML expansion pack, you need to digitally sign the manifest file and the assembly. For this exercise, however, you will disable the signature check for the manifest and the assembly. Disabling the manifest check is simple if you have installed the Office 2003 Smart Document SDK. A tool is available directly from Start ➤ All Programs ➤ Microsoft Office 2003

Developer Resources ➤ Microsoft Office 2003 Smart Document SDK ➤ Tools ➤ Disable XML Expansion Pack Manifest Security. This tool should be run on SPSClient. In order to trust the assembly, you must configure the .NET security for the SPSClient. Once again, you will rely on tools available in the SDK.

To trust the assembly, follow these steps:

1. Copy the assembly named SmartInvoice.dll and the manifest file into a directory on SPSClient.

2. From SPSClient, select Start ➤ Administrative Tools ➤ Microsoft .NET Framework 1.1 Wizards.

3. In the .NET Wizards window, click Trust an Assembly.

4. In the Trust an Assembly wizard, select "Make changes to this computer" and click the Next button.

5. Browse to the directory where you copied the project files, locate the assembly named SmartInvoice.dll, and click Next.

6. Move the slider up to Full Trust and then click Next.

7. Verify the settings and click Finish.

NOTE *By default, the version number of your assembly is incremented each time you compile it. As a result, you have to repeat these steps each time the assembly is rebuilt. You can remedy this behavior by replacing the wildcard characters in the version number found in the* AssemblyInfo *file.*

Loading the XML Expansion Pack

Once the security configuration is complete, you are ready to load the XML expansion pack into Word. Because you intend to run the pack from the \bin directory, copy the schema and manifest file into the \bin directory with the assembly file. Once the three files are together in the same directory, you can use the XML expansion pack. If you have selected a template to use with the XML expansion pack, you can open it now in Word. Otherwise, just open a blank document.

To load the XML expansion pack, follow these steps:

1. From Word, select Tools ➤ Templates and Add-Ins.

2. In the Templates and Add-Ins dialog, click the XML Expansion Packs tab.

3. On the XML Expansion Packs tab, click Add.

4. Navigate to the directory where you copied the project files and locate the manifest file you created earlier.

5. Click Open.

6. When you receive a security warning about the unsigned manifest, click No.

7. In the Templates and Add-Ins dialog, click OK to finish loading the schema and then open the task pane.

8. In the task pane, drop down the menu and select XML Structure.

9. Using the list of available nodes, add a single node of each type to the document.

10. Once you have added nodes, select Document Actions from the drop-down menu in the task pane.

11. Place the document cursor in the ProductID node. You should see a list of product codes in the task pane.

12. Select a ProductID and click Insert.

13. Now place the document cursor in the ProductName node. The text box should automatically fill with the associated product name.

14. Click Insert to add the product name to the document.

Exercise 8-2: Building a Research Service

Building a custom research service allows you to integrate information from line-of-business systems with the task pane of Office 2003 products. This integration has the potential to improve end-user productivity by placing key information about products, customers, and so on in close proximity with the documents that are being created. In this exercise, you will create a custom research service that displays publisher names and addresses from the pubs database.

Prerequisites

When SPS is installed, it prevents Visual Studio from accessing the site for development. Additionally, the security restrictions that SharePoint Services places on the site can prevent web applications and web services from running normally. Therefore, your best bet is to use a completely separate server running Internet Information Server (IIS) for all of your web services. For this exercise, however, you will create a new site on SPSPortal for the research service.

To create this new web site, you will need to perform these steps:

1. Log in to SPSPortal as the local administrator.

2. Select Start ➤ Administrative Tools ➤ Internet Information Services (IIS) Manager.

3. In the IIS Manager, expand the tree until the Web Sites folder is visible.

4. Right-click the Web Sites folder and select New ➤ Web Site. This will start the web site wizard.

5. In the Description text box, type **Research** and then click Next.

6. In the "TCP port this web site should use (Default 80)" text box, type **8888** and then click Next.

7. Click Browse to search for a new directory.

8. In the Browse for Folder dialog, select the root of the C: drive and click the Make New Folder button.

9. Name the new folder **ResearchWeb** and click OK.

10. Finish the rest of the wizard to create the new web site.

11. Close the IIS Manager.

Starting the Project

Custom research services are built on top of web services. The fundamental structure of a service requires a Registration and a Query web method. The bulk of the programming work is parsing the incoming request stream and providing an appropriate response stream.

Here is what you need to do to begin the project:

1. Select File ➤ New ➤ Project from the Visual Studio menu.

2. In the New Project dialog, click the Visual C# Projects folder.

3. In the Templates window, select ASP.NET Web Service.

4. Make sure the web service is designated to be built on the correct web site, name the new project **ResearchPubs**, and click OK.

5. When the project is created, open Service1.asmx.

6. The web service must reference the urn:Microsoft.Search namespace and needs several using statements so that it can access the database and parse XML. The code in Listing 8-20 shows how the beginning of your class file should appear.

Listing 8-20. Starting the Project

```
using System;
using System.Collections;
using System.ComponentModel;
using System.Data;
using System.Data.SqlClient;
using System.Diagnostics;
using System.Web;
using System.Web.Services;
using System.Configuration;
using System.IO;
using System.Xml;

namespace ResearchPubs
{
    [WebService(Namespace="urn:Microsoft.Search")]
    public class Service1 : System.Web.Services.WebService
    {
```

Creating the Registration Response

When the research service is registered, it must respond with an appropriate XML stream. Because much of the response is boilerplate, you use an XML document as a template for the response. Before you begin to code the Registration method, you need to create the template. Add a new XML file to your project named RegistrationResponse.xml. Modify the template to appear as shown in Listing 8-21.

Listing 8-21. The Response Template

```xml
<?xml version="1.0" encoding="utf-8" ?>
<ProviderUpdate xmlns="urn:Microsoft.Search.Registration.Response">
<Status>SUCCESS</Status>
<Providers>
<Provider>
    <Message>This is a research service for publisher information</Message>
    <Id>{DEA2797E-DEDC-4a7d-AEB5-DD8DF82F753F}</Id>
    <Name>Publishers</Name>
    <QueryPath/>
    <RegistrationPath/>
    <AboutPath/>
    <Type>SOAP</Type>
    <Services>
        <Service>
            <Id>{3C927E62-566D-4193-AF40-B0CA3E4F3E00}</Id>
            <Name>Publisher Lookup</Name>
            <Description>Returns address information for a publisher</Description>
            <Copyright></Copyright>
            <Display>On</Display>
            <Category>BUSINESS_BUSINESS</Category>
        </Service>
    </Services>
</Provider>
</Providers>
</ProviderUpdate>
```

Once the template is written, you are ready to code the Registration method. This method loads the template and then modifies the <RegistrationPath/>, <QueryPath/>, and <AboutPath/> elements to reflect the true location of the service. When you create a research service for distribution, you will probably want to make this code more portable. In this exercise, you have hard-coded some path information. Add the code in Listing 8-22 to complete the Registration method.

CAUTION *The input argument of the* Registration *method must be named* registrationxml *or the XML data sent from Office will not reach the method. Office 2003 expects this exact name for the argument.*

Listing 8-22. The Registration Method

```
[WebMethod()]public string Registration(string registrationxml)
{
    //Key path information
    string templatePath =
    HttpContext.Current.Server.MapPath(".").ToString()
        + "\\RegistrationResponse.xml";
    string servicePath = "http://spsportal:8888/ResearchPubs/Service1.asmx";

    //Load template
    XmlDocument outXML = new XmlDocument();
    outXML.Load(templatePath);

    //Prepare to modify template
    XmlNamespaceManager manager =
        new XmlNamespaceManager(outXML.NameTable);
    manager.AddNamespace("ns", "urn:Microsoft.Search.Registration.Response");

    //Modify XML
    outXML.SelectSingleNode("//ns:QueryPath", manager).InnerText = servicePath;
    outXML.SelectSingleNode("//ns:RegistrationPath", manager).InnerText _
        = servicePath;
    outXML.SelectSingleNode("//ns:AboutPath", manager).InnerText = servicePath;

    return outXML.InnerXml.ToString();

}
```

Creating the Query Response

After the service is registered with the Research Library, new queries will be made by calls to the Query method. The response you formulate will be based on a search of the pubs database using the <QueryText> element passed in by the Research Library. The stream is contained in an XML envelope that you will create as a template. Although the envelope is fairly simple, you must ensure that the domain attribute of the <Response> element is identical to the <Id> element for the <Service> defined in the registration response template. Add a new XML file to your project named QueryResponse.xml and modify it to appear as shown in Listing 8-23.

Listing 8-23. The Query Response Envelope

```
<?xml version="1.0" encoding="utf-8" ?>
<ResponsePacket revision="1" xmlns="urn:Microsoft.Search.Response">
    <Response domain="{3C927E62-566D-4193-AF40-B0CA3E4F3E00}">
    <Range>
    </Range>
    <Status>SUCCESS</Status>
    </Response>
</ResponsePacket>
```

Coding the Query Method

Your Query method will be responsible for parsing the <QueryText> element and packaging the results for return to the Research Library. The actual database query will be handled by a separate function. The basics of the Query method are similar to those in the Registration method. You parse the incoming XML and build the outgoing XML based on a template. Add the code from Listing 8-24 to create the Query method.

 CAUTION *The input argument of the Query method must be named* queryXml *or the XML data sent from Office will not reach the method. Office 2003 expects this exact name for the argument.*

Listing 8-24. The Query Method

```
[WebMethod()]public string Query(string queryXml)
{
    //The query text from the Research Library
    string queryText="";
```

```
//Key path information
string templatePath =
    HttpContext.Current.Server.MapPath(".").ToString()
    + "\\QueryResponse.xml";

//Load incoming XML into a document
XmlDocument inXMLDoc = new XmlDocument();

try
{
    if (queryXml.Length > 0)
    {
        inXMLDoc.LoadXml(queryXml.ToString());

        //Prepare to parse incoming XML
        XmlNamespaceManager inManager =
            new XmlNamespaceManager(inXMLDoc.NameTable);
        inManager.AddNamespace("ns", "urn:Microsoft.Search.Query");
        inManager.AddNamespace _
          ("oc", "urn:Microsoft.Search.Query.Office.Context");

        //Parse out query text
        queryText = inXMLDoc.SelectSingleNode _
          ("//ns:QueryText", inManager).InnerText;
    }
}
catch{queryText="";}

//Load response template
XmlDocument outXML = new XmlDocument();
outXML.Load(templatePath);

//Prepare to modify template
XmlNamespaceManager outManager =
    new XmlNamespaceManager(outXML.NameTable);
outManager.AddNamespace("ns", "urn:Microsoft.Search.Response");

//Add results
outXML.SelectSingleNode("//ns:Range",outManager). _
 InnerXml = getResults(queryText);

//Return XML stream
return outXML.InnerXml.ToString();
}
```

Packaging the Results

The actual result set that your service returns to the Research Library must be contained inside of an XML stream that complies with the expected schema. Therefore, you must loop through every record returned from the query and write out the XML elements to contain them. This is mostly a matter of carefully coding the XML construction. Add the code from Listing 8-25 to build the results.

Listing 8-25. Packaging the Result Set

```
public string getResults(string queryText)
{

    //Credentials
    string userName="sa";
    string password="";
    string database="pubs";
    string sqlServer="(local)";

    //Build connection string
    string strConn = "Password=" + password +
        ";Persist Security Info=True;User ID=" + userName +
        ";Initial Catalog=" + database + ";Data Source=" + sqlServer;

    //Build SQL statement
    string strSQL = "SELECT pub_name, city, state FROM Publishers " +
        "WHERE pub_name LIKE '" + queryText + "%'";

    DataSet dataSet = new DataSet("publishers");

    //Run the query
    SqlConnection conn = new SqlConnection(strConn);
    SqlDataAdapter adapter = new SqlDataAdapter(strSQL,conn);
    adapter.Fill(dataSet,"publishers");

    //Build the results
    StringWriter stringWriter = new StringWriter();
    XmlTextWriter textWriter = new XmlTextWriter(stringWriter);
    DataTable dataTable = dataSet.Tables["publishers"];
    DataRowCollection dataRows = dataTable.Rows;

    textWriter.WriteElementString("StartAt", "1");
    textWriter.WriteElementString("Count", dataRows.Count.ToString());
```

```
textWriter.WriteElementString("TotalAvailable", dataRows.Count.ToString());
textWriter.WriteStartElement("Results");
textWriter.WriteStartElement _
 ("Content", "urn:Microsoft.Search.Response.Content");

foreach(DataRow dataRow in dataRows)
{
    ///Heading
    textWriter.WriteStartElement("Heading");
    textWriter.WriteAttributeString("collapsible", "true");
    textWriter.WriteAttributeString("collapsed", "true");
    textWriter.WriteElementString("Text", dataRow["pub_name"].ToString());

    //City
    textWriter.WriteStartElement("P");
    textWriter.WriteElementString("Char", dataRow["city"].ToString());
    textWriter.WriteStartElement("Actions");
    textWriter.WriteElementString("Insert", "");
    textWriter.WriteElementString("Copy", "");
    textWriter.WriteEndElement();
    textWriter.WriteEndElement();

    //State
    textWriter.WriteStartElement("P");
    textWriter.WriteElementString("Char", dataRow["state"].ToString());
    textWriter.WriteStartElement("Actions");
    textWriter.WriteElementString("Insert", "");
    textWriter.WriteElementString("Copy", "");
    textWriter.WriteEndElement();
    textWriter.WriteEndElement();

    textWriter.WriteEndElement();
}

textWriter.WriteEndElement();
textWriter.WriteEndElement();
textWriter.Close();

return stringWriter.ToString();


}
```

Using the Custom Service

Using the service is a matter of registering the service and sending a query. Registering always requires you to know the URL of the web service. Once registered, the service will be available in the research pane.

To use the new service, take these steps:

1. Open the Research Library in Microsoft Word by selecting Tools ➤ Research from the menu.

2. At the bottom of the research pane, click the Research Options link.

3. In the Research options dialog, click Add Services.

4. In the Address box, type the URL `http://spsportal:8888/ResearchPubs/Service1.asmx`.

5. Click Add and accept any additional prompts.

6. Close the Research Options dialog.

7. In the research pane, select the service source from under the All Business and Financial Sites section.

8. Type a search string into the Search For box and click the green arrow. Figure 8-12 shows the final project.

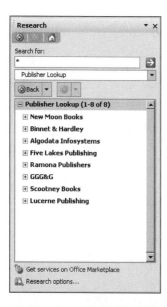

Figure 8-12. The final project

CHAPTER 9

Programming SharePoint Services

THROUGHOUT OUR INVESTIGATION OF SHAREPOINT SERVICES, we have found many
different ways to use the built-in features to solve business problems; however,
Microsoft has not provided all of the capabilities you are likely to need. As soon
as you roll out SharePoint Portal Server (SPS), your end users will begin to point
out the weaknesses in the product. Some of the more obvious weaknesses include
lack of support for workflow, difficulty in navigating site collections, and cum-
bersome task management.

The solution to these missing pieces is to extend the capabilities of SharePoint
Services. Fortunately, Microsoft has spent a significant amount of time developing
.NET namespaces and web services for SharePoint Services. This comprehensive
set of namespaces allows you programmatic access to a significant portion of
SharePoint Services.

The SharePoint Services object model is extensive, to say the least. There are
18 namespaces within the object model and dozens of classes covering most of
the features of SharePoint Services. The depth and breadth of the architecture
makes it impractical to study the object model directly. Instead, it is better to use
the object model to solve specific problems. In this chapter, you will get started
using these namespaces by creating solutions to some of the fundamental weaknesses in SharePoint Services.

Document Workflow

Workflow is truly a necessity for a system like Office 2003, and its absence from
SharePoint Services is significant. What makes the situation worse is the fact
that SharePoint Portal Server 2001 (SPS2001) had a workflow engine—albeit a
simple one. This means that users of SPS2001 may see the lack of workflow as
an indication that SPS2003 is a lesser product.

On the positive side, you can reproduce the workflows that were available
in SPS2001 using the SharePoint Services object model. This object model will
allow you to capture events associated with a document library and respond to
those events by moving documents, sending mail, or other actions.

NOTE *If you want to move beyond basic workflow to automate more complex processes, you may find that SharePoint Services does not offer enough functionality. In these cases, you will want to investigate the use of third-party workflow engines. My favorite engine is K2.net 2003 available at* www.k2workflow.com.

Capturing Events

You begin developing document workflow by trapping events that occur in a document library. To capture events, you must perform a series of configuration and programming tasks. These tasks include enabling event handlers, creating the event-handling class, and connecting the class to a target document library.

Enabling Event Handlers

Before you begin to receive the events, however, you have to enable document events for libraries associated with your SharePoint installation.

To enable document library events, follow these steps:

1. Log on to SPSPortal as the local administrator.

2. Select Start ➤ All Programs ➤ SharePoint Portal Server ➤ SharePoint Central Administration.

3. On the SharePoint Portal Server Central Administration page, select Portal Site and Virtual Server Configuration ➤ Configure Virtual Server Settings from the Virtual Server List.

4. On the Virtual Server List page, select the link for the site where you have installed SharePoint Services (typically Default Web Site).

5. On the Virtual Server Settings page, select Virtual Server Management ➤ Virtual Server General Settings.

6. On the Virtual Server General Settings page, in the Event Handlers section, select to turn on event handlers.

7. Click OK.

Creating the Event Handler

Once event handlers are enabled for document libraries, you may trap them by creating a custom class library that implements the `Microsoft.SharePoint.IListEventSink` interface. This interface has only one member, the `OnEvent` method. This method is called whenever a trappable event occurs in a targeted document library and receives an `SPListEvent` object that describes the event through the `SPListEventType` enumeration. Table 9-1 lists the events that are trapped by the `OnEvent` method.

Table 9-1. Document Library Events

EVENT	DESCRIPTION
SPListEventType.CheckIn	Fires when a document is checked into the library
SPListEventType.CheckOut	Fires when a document is checked out of the library
SPListEventType.Copy	Fires when a document is copied
SPListEventType.Delete	Fires when a document is deleted
SPListEventType.Insert	Fires when a new document is added to the library
SPListEventType.Move	Fires when a document is moved to another library
SPListEventType.UncheckOut	Fires when a checkout is overridden by an administrator
SPListEventType.Update	Fires when a document is edited or the status changes

Typically, when you code the `OnEvent` method, you use conditional programming to trap the event of interest. In the branch logic, you can then take appropriate action to respond to the event. Listing 9-1 shows a simple `Select-Case` structure that allows a class to trap any event fired by a document library.

Listing 9-1. Trapping Library Events

```
Public Sub OnEvent(ByVal listEvent As Microsoft.SharePoint.SPListEvent) _
Implements Microsoft.SharePoint.IListEventSink.OnEvent

    Dim objWriter As StreamWriter
    objWriter = New StreamWriter("c:\events.txt", False)

    Select Case listEvent.Type
        Case SPListEventType.CheckIn
            objWriter.WriteLine("CheckIn")
```

```
        Case SPListEventType.CheckOut
            objWriter.WriteLine("CheckOut")
        Case SPListEventType.Copy
            objWriter.WriteLine("Copy")
        Case SPListEventType.Delete
            objWriter.WriteLine("Delete")
        Case SPListEventType.Insert
            objWriter.WriteLine("Insert")
        Case SPListEventType.Invalid 'Not used
        Case SPListEventType.Move
            objWriter.WriteLine("Move")
        Case SPListEventType.UncheckOut
            objWriter.WriteLine("UncheckOut")
        Case SPListEventType.Update
            objWriter.WriteLine("Update")
    End Select

    objWriter.Close()
End Sub
```

Although the basics of coding the class are simple, there is one wrinkle when implementing it in production. Event handling classes run in the context of the Internet Information Server (IIS) Application Pool Identity. This identity typically has little permission and cannot access objects in SharePoint Services. You can find out what account is running the application pool using the IIS Manager.

Here are the steps to follow to view the Application Pool Identity:

1. Log on to SPSPortal as the local administrator.

2. Select Start ➤ Administrative Tools ➤ Internet Information Services (IIS) Manager.

3. In the Internet Information Services (IIS) Manager dialog, expand the tree and open the Application Pools folder.

4. Right-click the MSSharePointPortalAppPool node and select Properties from the pop-up menu.

5. Click the Identity tab.

NOTE *If you have set up your test environment in accordance with this book, your Application Pool Identity will be the local administrator for* SPSPortal. *Although this is fine for the test environment, you may want to consider changing it for production systems. You can change the identity in the SPS Central Administration pages in the same way you initially did during setup.*

Because the Application Pool Identity does not generally have permission to access the SharePoint Services namespaces necessary to manage the document workflow, you need to change the identity under which the event handler runs. You can do this by retrieving a new Windows token for an account that has the appropriate permissions and creating a new System.Security.Principal.WindowsIdentity object. A WindowsImpersonationContext object is then created to build a context under which the handler can run. Listing 9-2 shows how to create the new context in VB.NET using the Windows API Function LogonUser.

Listing 9-2. Changing the Identity Context

```
Dim objContext As WindowsImpersonationContext
Dim objToken As New IntPtr(0)
Dim ID As WindowsIdentity
Const LOGON32_PROVIDER_DEFAULT As Integer = 0
Const LOGON32_LOGON_NETWORK As Integer = 3

'Logon using the new credentials
objToken = IntPtr.Zero
Dim blnReturn As Boolean = _
    LogonUser ("administrator", "sps", "password", _
        LOGON32_LOGON_NETWORK, _
        LOGON32_PROVIDER_DEFAULT, objToken)

'Create the new identity context
ID = New WindowsIdentity(objToken)
objContext =ID.Impersonate

'Handle library events here

'Tear down context
objContext.Undo
```

Once the class is written, you are ready to build it and connect it to a target library. Event handling classes must be placed in the Global Assembly Cache (GAC) to function correctly, and assemblies in the GAC require strong names. Therefore, you need to create a key pair for the class and reference the key pair in the `AssemblyInfo` file. These steps will not be repeated here because you have performed them several times when you were building web parts in the earlier chapters.

After you have given the assembly a strong name and compiled it, you may place it in the GAC. Although a special utility called `gacutil.exe` is available for adding assemblies to the GAC, all you really need to do is drag the assembly to `C:\Windows\assembly` and drop it. This directory contains the GAC and is outfitted with a special shell extension that will automatically add your assembly to the GAC.

Connecting to the Target Library

Once the assembly is properly installed in the GAC, you can connect it to a target document library. Connecting the event handler to a library is accomplished from within SPS itself. You must navigate to the target library and select to change the advanced settings. The connection is made by specifying the full strong name for the assembly in the form `Assembly,Version,Culture,PublicKeyToken`.

The required format is identical to the format you have already used to mark web parts as safe in the `web.config` file. However, you must be very careful to type in the string correctly and observe case-sensitivity with the assembly and class name. Any mistake in the string will cause SharePoint Services to throw an error.

Here is what you need to do to connect the event handler to a library:

1. Log in to SPS as a member of the Administrator site group.

2. Navigate to a document library from which you want to receive events.

3. Click the Modify Settings and Columns link in the Actions list.

4. On the Customize Library page, select General Settings ➤ Change Advanced Settings.

5. On the Document Library Advanced Settings page, locate the Event Handler section.

6. In the Assembly Name text box, type the full, case-sensitive strong name of the assembly. The following code shows an example:

```
LibraryEvents,Version=1.0.0.0,Culture=Neutral,
PublicKeyToken=b2bb66c9e13ee2f9
```

7. In the Class Name text box, type the full, case-sensitive name of the handling class. The following code shows an example:

```
LibraryEvents.Handler
```

NOTE *The Properties field is optional and may contain any text. This value is available in the event handler from the* SinkData *property of the* SPListEvent *object, which is discussed momentarily.*

8. Click OK.

9. Restart IIS.

Manipulating Documents

After you have trapped the document library events, you will want to respond by taking programmatic action on the targeted document. The SharePoint Services namespace contains classes that allow you access to library structures, document properties, and document actions. Using these classes, you can detect a wide variety of user actions, from document changes to approvals and rejections. Your event handler can then complete the workflow by moving or copying files based on these user actions.

Referencing Event Information

Once an event is received by your handling class, you will immediately want to know key information about the event such as what document caused it to fire. The OnEvent method receives an SPListEvent object that contains references to many of the objects that you will need to respond to user-generated events. Table 9-2 lists each property of the SPListEvent class with a brief explanation.

Table 9-2. Properties of the SPListEvent Class

PROPERTY	TYPE	DESCRIPTION
Type	Microsoft.SharePoint. SPListEventType	Returns the type of event that was trapped.
ListID	System.Guid	Returns the Globally Unique Identifier (GUID) of the document library where the event occurred.
Site	Microsoft.SharePoint. SPSite	Returns the parent site object containing the document library that caused the event. This is useful if the same handler is connected to multiple libraries.
WebUrl	String	Returns the absolute URL of the site where the event occurred.
SinkData	String	The value of the user-defined text entered in the Properties text box when the event handler is initially connected to the document library. This is useful if the same handler is connected to multiple libraries.
Title	String	The title of the document library that raised the event.
PropertiesBefore	System.Collections. Hashtable	Returns a set of key-value pairs that represents the state of the document before the event was fired.
PropertiesAfter	System.Collections. Hashtable	Returns a set of key-value pairs that represents the state of the document after the event is fired.
UrlAfter	String	Returns the site-relative URL of the document after the event is fired. The document URL can change based on user actions such as document rejection.
UrlBefore	String	Returns the site-relative URL of the document before the event was fired.
UserDisplayName	String	Returns the display name of the user whose actions fired the event.

PROPERTY	TYPE	DESCRIPTION
UserID	Int32	Returns the ID of the user whose actions fired the event.
UserLoginName	String	Returns the user name of the user whose actions fired the event.

If you examine the properties returned by the SPListEvent object, you will notice that it does not have a property to return the document that caused the event to fire. In workflow applications, however, you will almost always manipulate the document in response to an event. Retrieving a reference to the document itself is actually accomplished through the SPWeb object in conjunction with the SPListEvent object. The following code shows how to return a reference to the document that caused the event to fire.

```
Dim objSite As SPWeb = listEvent.Site.OpenWeb
Dim objFile As SPFile = objSite.GetFile(listEvent.UrlAfter)
```

Accessing Document Properties

Once you have retrieved a reference to the SPFile object, you can use it to access a multitude of properties for the target document. These properties may subsequently be the target of changes generated by an event-handling class. You may choose, for example, to change the Approval Status property based on some user action.

File properties come in three main categories that are each accessed in a different way. Some document properties like Name, Author, and Title are accessible directly as properties of the SPFile object. Other properties that represent document metadata are available only through a Hashtable object. Still other properties, such as Approval Status, are available only by accessing the SPListItem object that contains the file data in the library list. Accessing the properties that are available directly from the SPFile object is simple. The properties are available immediately upon retrieving a reference to the target document. The other categories of properties, however, take a little more effort.

The Properties collection of the SPFile object contains a set of key-value pairs that represent document metadata. Most of the metadata is of limited use, but you can access the values of custom columns in the document library using this collection. In order to access this set of properties, you must use a Hashtable object. Listing 9-3 shows the code required to print out the metadata values to a file.

Listing 9-3. Writing Out Metadata Values

```
objWriter = New StreamWriter("c:\events.txt", False)

'Get document associated with this event
Dim objSite As SPWeb = listEvent.Site.OpenWeb
Dim objFile As SPFile = objSite.GetFile(listEvent.UrlAfter)

'List the metadata
Dim objHashTable As System.Collections.Hashtable = objFile.Properties
Dim objKeys As System.Collections.ICollection = objHashTable.Keys
Dim objKey As Object

For Each objKey In objKeys
    objWriter.WriteLine(objKey.ToString & ": " & _
        objFile.Properties(objKey.ToString).ToString)
Next
```

Metadata properties contain many values associated with the document as it relates to the web site along with any custom columns you have defined in the library. Although you are focused on using the SPFile object for documents in libraries, this metadata can also be retrieved for web pages on a site. Listing 9-4 shows a typical set of key-value pairs for a Microsoft Word document stored in a document library. Take special note of the Status property, which is a custom property defined just for this particular document library.

Listing 9-4. Typical Metadata Values for a Word Document

```
vti_categories:
vti_author: SPS\administrator
Status: Editor Reviewed
vti_modifiedby: SPS\administrator
vti_nexttolasttimemodified: 11/1/2003 7:27:18 AM
vti_filesize: 20480
vti_approvallevel:
vti_cachedtitle:
vti_timelastmodified: 11/1/2003 8:52:10 AM
vti_title:
vti_docstoreversion: 2
vti_sourcecontrolcookie: fp_internal
vti_sourcecontrolversion: V2
vti_timecreated: 11/1/2003 7:27:18 AM
vti_cachedcustomprops: vti_approvallevel
```

```
vti_categories vti_assignedto vti_title Status
vti_assignedto:
vti_docstoretype: 0
```

Some of the document properties that are of value to us in designing workflow can only be accessed through the SPListItem object that contains the document. The SPListItem class represents a single row in the document library. Using this object, you can access the values of all of the columns in the document library. Listing 9-5 shows how to write these values out to a file.

Listing 9-5. Accessing SPListItem Fields

```
Dim objListItem As SPListItem = objFile.Item
Dim objFields As SPFieldCollection = objListItem.Fields
Dim objField As SPField

For Each objField In objFields
    objWriter.WriteLine(objField.Title & ": " & _
        objListItem.Item(objField.Title).ToString)
Next
```

Probably the most significant field in the SPListItem object is the Approval Status field. This field can have a value of 0, 1, or 2 to represent status values of Approved, Rejected, or Pending respectively. This field will be the foundation of many workflow processes that rely upon document approval by multiple people in an organization. Along with this field you can access several other valuable properties including the same custom fields that we accessed using the Hashtable approach. Listing 9-6 shows a typical set of properties and values retrieved from an SPListItem object. Take special note of the Approval Status property and the custom Status property.

Listing 9-6. Typical SPListItem Fields and Values

```
ID: 9
Created Date: 11/1/2003 2:27:17 AM
Created By: 1;#SPS\administrator
Last Modified: 11/1/2003 3:52:09 AM
Modified By: 1;#SPS\administrator
Approval Status: 0
URL Path: /sites/showroom/Events Library/Doc3.doc
URL Dir Name: 9;#sites/showroom/Events Library
Modified: 11/1/2003 3:52:09 AM
Created: 11/1/2003 2:27:17 AM
```

```
File Size: 20480
File System Object Type: 0
ID of the User who has the item Checked Out: 9;#
Name: Doc3.doc
Virus Status: 9;#20480
Checked Out To: 9;#
Checked Out To: 9;#
Document Modified By: SPS\administrator
Document Created By: SPS\administrator
owshiddenversion: 2
File Type: doc
Name: Doc3.doc
Name: Doc3.doc
Select: 9
Select: 9
Edit:
Type: doc
Server Relative URL: /sites/showroom/Events Library/Doc3.doc
Encoded Absolute URL: http://spsportal/sites/showroom/Events%20Library/Doc3.doc
Name: Doc3.doc
File Size: 20480
Order: 900
Status: Editor Reviewed
```

Beyond reading and writing values, accessing document properties in a workflow application is significant because it allows your event handler to respond to situations that go beyond the events defined by the SPListEventType object. The SharePoint Services event model allows you to trap most user actions directly; events such as document deletion are unambiguous and you can typically respond to them directly. However, when an SPListEventType.Update event is trapped, you cannot immediately determine what caused the event. This is because the SPListEventType.Update event can occur when the body of a document is changed, its approval status is changed, or its property profile is changed. The only way to determine the exact cause of the event is to examine properties of the document causing the event.

Acting on Documents

Once you have determined that an event of interest has occurred, you will want to take action on the target document. In most cases, this simply means moving or copying the document to another library. For example, when your handler receives the SPListEventType.Update event, you may check the Approval Status of the document. If this value is 0 (Approved), you may then move it to a library where it would await the next level of review and approval. This technique of using libraries as review and approval queues works well for automating workflow. Interested parties can simply set up alerts against the libraries of interest and await notification that a document has reached their particular review stage in the workflow. Listing 9-7 shows a simple example of using the MoveTo method to move a document based on its approval status.

Listing 9-7. Moving Documents

```
If listEvent.Type = SPListEventType.Update Then

    Dim objSite As SPWeb = listEvent.Site.OpenWeb
    Dim objFile As SPFile = objSite.GetFile(listEvent.UrlAfter)

    Select Case objFile.Item.Item("Approval Status")
        Case 0 'Approved
            objFile.MoveTo("http://spsportal/sites/showroom/Approved/" & _
                objFile.Name, False)
        Case 1 'Reject
            objFile.MoveTo("http://spsportal/sites/showroom/Rejected/" & _
                objFile.Name, False)
        Case 2 'Pending
            objFile.MoveTo("http://spsportal/sites/showroom/Pending/" & _
                objFile.Name, False)
    End Select
End If
```

Along with moving documents, the SPFile object also supports copying, deleting, and check in/out functions. Using these methods, you can build simple workflows that support business processes within the organization.

Accessing Portal Site and User Information

One of the major uses of the SharePoint Services object model is to access component parts of a SharePoint installation. Using the object model, you can access any site collection, site, or list on an extended virtual server. You can also identify the current user and access information about the user, associated groups, and assigned roles. Accessing the site and user components of the installation will allow you to create web parts that fill in some of the gaps in SharePoint Services that users will surely encounter.

Consider the scenario where an end user has navigated to the top-level site in a collection. With the top-level site open, the user has no simple way to discover what other sites are contained in the collection. If you could present a list of available sites in the current collection, users would be better able to find what they are interested in. The SharePoint Services object model allows you to provide this view to the user.

Accessing Site Collections

Accessing objects in the SharePoint Services model is accomplished in a manner similar to any hierarchical object model you may have worked with in the past. The key to navigating such a model is to find the starting point—or root—of the model. In SharePoint Services, you can access the navigation root in the hierarchy with one of the following lines of code.

```
//C#
SPSite thisSite = SPControl.GetContextSite(Context);
'VB.NET
Dim objSite As SPSite = SPControl.GetContextSite(Context)
```

The SPControl class is a member of the Microsoft.SharePoint.WebControls namespace and is the base class from which all other WebControls in the namespace are created. In order to use this namespace, you must set a reference to the Microsoft SharePoint Services library. You do not have to create an instance of this class to use it. Simply call the GetContextSite method and pass the Context variable. The Context variable is inherited from System.Web.UI.Page and is always available to web parts and web applications you create in Visual Studio. The GetContextSite method returns an SPSite object, which represents the site collection where the web part is currently running.

SPSite objects represent a site collection as an aggregate object. In order to access any particular site in the collection, you must return a collection of SPWeb objects. You may then access the individual web sites by enumerating them or accessing one directly through an index. The following code shows how to enumerate the sites in a collection using C#.

```
SPSite thisSite = SPControl.GetContextSite(Context);
SPWebCollection webs = thisSite.AllWebs;

foreach(SPWeb web in webs)
{
    //add code here
}
```

Accessing Lists and List Items

Along with site collections, you will access lists and list items frequently. A significant problem for end users of SPS is that they are typically assigned tasks associated with many different sites. This rapidly results in a situation where end users cannot manage all of the tasks they are assigned and frequently are not even aware that a task exists. Of course, alerts are helpful, but alerts must be created by the end user. You have seen many cases where someone creates a team site and enters tasks on a list, but no one visits the site to create an alert. Therefore, building web parts that help manage task lists is critical to the success of an SPS implementation.

Once a web site is opened, you may access all of the lists it contains through the SPListCollection object. The collection contains an SPList object for every list on the web site. The following code shows how to enumerate the lists for the current web site from which a web part is running.

```
SPWeb thisWeb = SPControl.GetContextWeb(Context);
SPListCollection spsLists= thisWeb.Lists;

foreach(SPList spsList in spsLists)
{
    //add code here
}
```

It is important to understand that SharePoint Services considers almost everything to be a list. This includes not only obvious components such as task lists, but more subtle components like document libraries and discussion forums. Therefore, you will find it useful to be able to differentiate between various lists that are returned in code. Each SPList object has a BaseType property that returns an SPBaseType enumeration specifying what kind of list is represented. Here is a list of the members of the SPBaseType enumeration:

- SPBaseType.DiscussionBoard

- SPBaseType.DocumentLibrary

- SPBaseType.GenericList

- SPBaseType.Issue

- SPBaseType.Survey

- SPBaseType.UnspecifiedBaseType

Once you have accessed a list of interest, you may subsequently access the items in the list. Each item in the list is represented by an SPListItem object contained in an SPListItemCollection object. Enumerating these list items follows the same pattern as you have already seen.

Regardless of whether you are accessing sites, lists, or items, each object has a set of properties and methods that are meaningful. Typically, this means returning the Name, Title, or URL associated with an object. Additionally, each object has some special properties and methods designed to return useful collections. For example, you can return just the webs associated with the current user by utilizing the GetSubwebsForCurrentUser method of the SPWeb class. All of these classes, and others, are fully documented in the SharePoint Services SDK available at msdn.microsoft.com.

Accessing User Information

When iterating through sites and lists, you quite often want to know how they apply to the current user. You may be interested in knowing what role the current user has on a site or what items in a list are assigned to the current user. You can access this information using an SPUser object. The following code shows how to return the SPUser object that represents the current user.

```
SPSite site = SPControl.GetContextSite(Context);
SPWeb web = site.OpenWeb();
SPUser user = web.CurrentUser;
```

Once the SPUser object is returned, you can retrieve the logon name of the user through the LoginName property. You can also retrieve the display name for the user through the Name property. Because list assignments are made using these values, you can often determine which items in a list belong to the current user by comparing the Assign To field of a list item to these values. Listing 9-8 shows how to look through a collection of lists and identify tasks assigned to the current user.

Listing 9-8. Determining List Item Ownership

```
Dim objSite As SPSite = SPControl.GetContextSite(Context)
Dim objWeb As SPWeb = objSite.OpenWeb()
Dim objUser As SPUser = objWeb.CurrentUser
Dim objLists As SPListCollection = objWeb.Lists
Dim objList As SPList

    'Walk every list on a site
```

```
For Each objList In objLists

    If objList.BaseType = SPBaseType.GenericList _
    OrElse objList.BaseType = SPBaseType.Issue Then

        For i As Integer = 0 To objList.ItemCount - 1
            Try
                Dim objItem As SPListItem = objList.Items(i)

                'Check to see if this task is assigned to the user
                Dim strAssignedTo As String = _
                 UCase(objItem.Item("Assigned To").ToString)

                If strAssignedTo.IndexOf(UCase(objUser.LoginName)) > -1 _
                OrElse strAssignedTo.IndexOf(UCase(objUser.Name)) > -1 Then

                    'Add code here
                End If

            Catch
            End Try

        Next
    End If
Next

objWeb.Close()
objSite.Close()
```

Using SharePoint Web Services

In addition to the object model, you can also access SharePoint Services information using web services. SharePoint Services exposes web services for remote management of nearly every aspect of SharePoint Services. Using these services, you can integrate the information in SharePoint Services with other line-of-business systems.

To use a web service in Visual Studio, follow these steps:

1. In Visual Studio, select File ➤ New ➤ Project.

2. In the New Project dialog, click Visual C# Projects, and then select Windows Application.

3. Name the project and then click OK.

4. In the Solution Explorer, right-click Web References and select Add Web Reference from the pop-up menu.

5. In the Add Web Reference dialog box, enter **http://spsportal/_vti_bin/ lists.asmx** to reference the list web service.

 NOTE *Each web service requires a different reference.*

6. Click Go to see the web service definition.

7. Click Add Reference to make the service available to your project.

Once the web service is referenced, you can use it in your project just like any other namespace. Values returned from the web service vary depending upon which service is called, but the calling technique is largely the same. Before calling the web service, you must authenticate the current user with the service. After authentication, you can make calls to the methods of the service. The following code shows how to authenticate the current user with the service and return a set of lists.

```
spsportal.Lists service = new spsportal.Lists();
service.Credentials=System.Net.CredentialCache.DefaultCredentials;
System.Xml.XmlNode node = service.GetListCollection();
textBox1.Text=node.OuterXml;
```

You can also use the web services to create and manage your own document and meeting workspaces. This is perhaps the most compelling use of the available web services because it allows you to create functionality similar to the workspace pane found in Microsoft Office. You can reference the document workspace web service at spsportal/_vti_bin/Dws.asmx and the meeting workspace web service at spsportal/_vti_bin/Meetings.asmx. Creating a document or meeting workspace uses essentially the same approach with differences primarily in the arguments and return values.

Creating a document workspace is done by calling the CreateDws method of the web service. This method can be used to create the workspace, add users, and associate documents. It expects the user and document data to be in a designated XML format. It also needs the user to specify a name and a title for the new workspace. Listing 9-9 shows an example of creating a document workspace and adding users.

Listing 9-9. Creating a Document Workspace

```
spsportaldws.Dws dwsService = new spsportaldws.Dws();
dwsService.Credentials = System.Net.CredentialCache.DefaultCredentials;

string users =   "<UserInfo>"
+ "<item Email='" + txtMail1.Text + "' Name='" + txtName1.Text + "'/>"
+ "<item Email='" + txtMail2.Text + "' Name='" + txtName2.Text + "'/>"
+ "<item Email='" + txtMail3.Text + "' Name='" + txtName3.Text + "'/>"
+ "</UserInfo>";
txtResponse.Text= dwsService.CreateDws(txtName.Text,users,txtTitle.Text,"");
```

When the workspace is created, the service responds with an XML payload that states the results of the call. If a workspace already exists, for example, an error code will return. If the creation process was successful but errors occurred when adding users or documents, that information is also provided. Listing 9-10 shows a typical response to site creation.

Listing 9-10. Workspace Creation Response

```
<Results>
<Url>http://spsportal/Workspace</Url>
<DoclibUrl>Shared Documents</DoclibUrl>
<ParentWeb>DataLan Corporation</ParentWeb>
<FailedUsers>
    <User Email="JohnArnold@sps.local" />
</FailedUsers>
<AddUsersUrl>http://spsportal/Workspace/_layouts/1033/aclinv.aspx</AddUsersUrl>
<AddUsersRole>Contributor</AddUsersRole>
</Results>
```

Once the workspace is created, you may use other methods of the services to manage users, documents, tasks, and alerts. In this way, you can create a fully functional document or meeting workspace for any application.

Exercise 9-1: Creating a Workflow Engine

Because SPS lacks any kind of workflow designer and engine, implementing even simple business processes requires writing code. If you custom-code each process, then you will rapidly find that performing maintenance on the code will become time consuming. Therefore, you will want to create some kind of engine that is more generic. In this exercise, you will create a simple workflow engine for approval routing that is programmable using an XML document.

Prerequisites

Before you begin to create the engine, you must perform several operations to prepare the environment. The first thing to do is enable event handling on your virtual server using the steps outlined earlier in the chapter. No document library events are trapped unless they are specifically enabled. After the document library events are enabled, you will need to create a new site with three libraries you can use to simulate routing the document. Your engine will be designed to move a document from a Submit library to a Review library to an Approve library.

Here are the steps to set up the libraries:

1. Log in to SPS as a member of the Administrator site group.

2. Navigate to the Site Directory by clicking the Sites link.

3. In the Site Directory, click the Create Site link under the Actions list.

4. Create a new blank site named **Workflow**.

5. When the new site is created, click the Create link.

6. On the Create page, select to create a new document library named **Submit**.

7. Repeat this to create a second document library named **Review** and a third named **Approve**.

The last thing to do before you start writing the engine is configure the Microsoft Single Sign-On (SSO) service with a set of impersonation credentials you can use to run the event handler. You will retrieve these credentials within the event handler. This section assumes that you have already set up SSO in accordance with Chapter 6.

To configure SSO credentials, take these steps:

1. Log in to SPSPortal as a member of the MSSSOAdmins group.

2. Select Start ➤ All Programs ➤ SharePoint Portal Server ➤ SharePoint Portal Server Single Sign-On Administration.

3. On the Manage Settings page select Enterprise Application Definition Settings ➤ Manage Settings for Enterprise Application Definitions.

4. On the Manage Enterprise Application Definitions page, click the New Item link.

5. On the Create Enterprise Application Definition page, enter **Workflow Engine** in the Display Name box.

6. Enter **Workflow** in the Application Name box.

7. Enter **administrator@sps.local** in the Contact E-mail Address box.

8. Enter **UserName** in the Field 1: Display Name box.

9. Enter **Domain** in the Field 2: Display Name box.

10. Enter **Password** in the Field 3: Display Name box.

11. Select Yes for the Mask option associated with Field 3.

12. Click OK.

13. Return to the Manage Settings page and select Enterprise Application Definition Settings ➤ Manage Account Information for Enterprise Application Definitions.

14. In the Account Information section, choose Workflow Engine from the drop-down list.

15. Type **sps\Domain Users** in the Group Account Name box.

16. Click OK.

17. On the "Provide workflow engine account information" page, type **administrator** in the UserName box.

18. Type **sps** in the Domain box.

19. Type the administrator password in the Password box.

20. Click OK.

Building the Workflow Engine

Document library event handlers are built as class library assemblies. For your workflow engine, you will build a class library in C# and implement the IListEventSink interface. This interface traps document approval events for the Submit and Review libraries and routes the document to the next library when it is approved. The routing details will be managed through an XML document.

Here is what to do to start the project:

1. Log in to SPSPortal as a local administrator.

2. Start Visual Studio and choose File ➤ New ➤ Project from the menu.

3. In the New Project dialog, click the Visual C# Projects folder.

4. In the Templates window, click Class Library.

5. Name the new project **Workflow** and click OK.

6. When the new project is created, select Project ➤ Add Reference from the menu.

7. In the Add Reference dialog, select to add references to Microsoft.SharePoint.Portal.SingleSignon.dll, System.Windows.Forms.dll, System.Xml.dll, and Windows SharePoint Services.

8. Click OK.

9. Rename the Class1.cs file as **Engine.cs**.

10. Open the Engine.cs file and rename the namespace to **WorkFlow** and the class to **Engine**.

11. Add code references to the imported assemblies so that your code appears exactly as shown in Listing 9-11.

Listing 9-11. The WorkFlow.Engine Class

```
using System;
using System.Windows.Forms;
using System.Xml;
```

```
using System.Security.Principal;
using System.Runtime.InteropServices;
using Microsoft.SharePoint;
using Microsoft.SharePoint.Portal.SingleSignon;
namespace WorkFlow
{
    public class Engine
    {
    }
}
```

Creating the New Identity Helper

Before you code the body of the event handler, you will construct a helper function to establish the identity under which the event handler will run. This helper function is essentially the same in every event-handling class you create. It makes a call to the Windows API to log the impersonation user on to the system. It then returns a WindowsIdentity object to the main code. Add the code in Listing 9-12 to the Engine class to get the impersonation identity.

Listing 9-12. Creating the Impersonation Identity

```
protected static WindowsIdentity CreateIdentity
(string userName, string domain, string password)
{

    IntPtr tokenHandle = new IntPtr(0);
    tokenHandle=IntPtr.Zero;

    const int LOGON32_PROVIDER_DEFAULT=0;
    const int LOGON32_LOGON_NETWORK=3;

    //Logon the new user
    bool returnValue = LogonUser(userName,domain,password,
        LOGON32_LOGON_NETWORK,LOGON32_PROVIDER_DEFAULT,
        ref tokenHandle);

    if(returnValue==false)
    {
        int returnError = Marshal.GetLastWin32Error();
        throw new Exception("Log on failed: " + returnError);
```

```
    }

    //return new identity
    WindowsIdentity id = new WindowsIdentity(tokenHandle);
    CloseHandle(tokenHandle);
    return id;

}

[DllImport("advapi32.dll", SetLastError=true)]
private static extern bool LogonUser
(String lpszUsername, String lpszDomain, String lpszPassword,
int dwLogonType, int dwLogonProvider, ref IntPtr phToken);

[DllImport("kernel32.dll", CharSet=CharSet.Auto)]
private extern static bool CloseHandle(IntPtr handle);
```

Creating the XML Document

The last task to perform before you build the body of the event handler is to create the XML document that will contain the routing instructions. Your strategy is to use the SinkData property to identify which of the libraries has triggered the event and then route the document to the next library. To make your solution more flexible, you will build an XML file that contains elements based on the SinkData property and the addresses of the libraries.

To create the XML routing document, follow these steps:

1. In Visual Studio, select Project ➤ Add New Item from the menu.

2. In the Add New Item dialog, select to add an XML file.

3. Name the new file **Workflow.xml** and click Open.

4. Open Workflow.xml in Visual Studio and modify it to appear as follows:

   ```xml
   <?xml version="1.0" encoding="utf-8" ?>
   <Workflow xmlns="urn:DataLan.SharePoint.WorkFlow.Engine">
       <Submit></Submit>
       <Review></Review>
   </Workflow>
   ```

5. Open SPS in Internet Explorer and navigate to the Review library you created earlier.

6. From the document library page, copy the URL associated with the root of the library.

7. Copy this fragment between the `<Submit></Submit>` elements in the XML file so that approved documents from the Submit library will be moved to the address of the Review library.

8. Repeat this action to route approved documents in the Review library to the Approve library. The following code shows an example of how the final XML file might appear.

```
<?xml version="1.0" encoding="utf-8" ?>
<Workflow xmlns="urn:DataLan.SharePoint.WorkFlow.Engine">
    <Submit>http://spsportal/sites/workflow/Review</Submit>
    <Review>http://spsportal/sites/workflow/Approve</Review>
</Workflow>
```

9. Copy the XML file into the root of the C: drive.

Coding the IListEventSink Interface

Now that the supporting elements are prepared, you can code the main body of the event handler in the `IListEventSink` interface. Add this interface to your class by typing a colon after the class name followed by the interface name. You should then be able to press the Tab key and have Visual Studio automatically insert the interface stubs for you so the beginning of your class will appear as follows:

```
public class Engine:IListEventSink
    {

        public void OnEvent(SPListEvent listEvent)
        {
```

In the body of the `OnEvent` method, you will retrieve the credentials for the impersonation identity from SSO and create the new identity context. Then you will determine if an approval event has occurred in the connected library. If an approval event has occurred, then you will read the XML file to determine the destination of the approved file. Finally, you will move the file to the destination library. Add the code necessary to make your final implementation of the OnEvent method as shown in Listing 9-13.

Listing 9-13. The OnEvent Method

```
public void OnEvent(SPListEvent listEvent)
{
    //Call MSSSO
    string[] strCredentials=null;
    Credentials.GetCredentials
        (Convert.ToUInt32(1),"Workflow",ref strCredentials);
    string userName = strCredentials[0];
    string domain = strCredentials[1];
    string password = strCredentials[2];

    //Create new context
    WindowsImpersonationContext windowsContext =
        CreateIdentity(userName,domain,password).Impersonate();

    //Get event objects
    SPWeb eventSite = listEvent.Site.OpenWeb();
    SPFile eventFile = eventSite.GetFile(listEvent.UrlAfter);
    SPListItem eventItem = eventFile.Item;

    //Determine if an approval event fired
    if((listEvent.Type == SPListEventType.Update) &&
        ((string)eventItem["Approval Status"]=="0"))
    {

        //Load the XML document
        string xmlPath ="C:\\Workflow.xml";
        XmlDocument xmlDoc = new XmlDocument();
        xmlDoc.Load(xmlPath);

        //Prepare to parse XML
        XmlNamespaceManager manager = new XmlNamespaceManager(xmlDoc.NameTable);
manager.AddNamespace("ns","urn:DataLan.SharePoint.WorkFlow.Engine");

        //Find the target library for the move
        string targetPath = xmlDoc.SelectSingleNode
            ("//ns:" + listEvent.SinkData,manager).InnerText;
```

```
        //Move the document
        eventFile.MoveTo(targetPath + "/" + eventFile.Name,false);


    }


    //Tear down context
    windowsContext.Undo();
}
```

Compiling the Engine

Event-handling classes must be placed in the GAC in order to function. Assemblies placed in the GAC must have a strong name; therefore, you must create a strong name for your assembly before you compile it. Additionally, you must ensure that the version attribute of your assembly is fixed and not changed dynamically each time the assembly is compiled. Both of these changes are essential to properly deploying an assembly to the GAC.

Here is what you need to do to compile the assembly:

1. Open a command window by selecting Start ➤ All Programs ➤ Accessories ➤ Command Prompt.

2. In the command window, navigate to `\Program Files\Microsoft Visual Studio .NET 2003\SDK\v1.1\bin`.

3. In the command-line window, create a key file by executing the following line:

   ```
   sn.exe -k c:\workflow.snk
   ```

4. In Visual Studio .NET, open the `AssemblyInfo.cs` file.

5. In the `AssemblyInfo.cs` file, scroll to the bottom of the file and add a reference to the key file by editing the `AssemblyKeyFile` entry to read as follows:

   ```
   [assembly: AssemblyKeyFile("c:\\workflow.snk")]
   ```

6. Locate and modify the AssemblyVersion attribute to remove the wild cards and create a static version number as shown in the following code:

```
[assembly: AssemblyVersion("1.0.0.0")]
```

7. Save and close the AssemblyInfo.cs file.

8. Compile your assembly by selecting Build ➤ Build Workflow.

9. Once the assembly is compiled, drag it from your project directory into the folder c:\windows\assembly to add it to the GAC.

Connecting the Libraries

Your workflow engine is designed to react to approval events in the Submit and Review libraries. Therefore, you must connect your assembly to both of these libraries. Additionally, you must enable document approval on all three libraries to complete the process.

To connect the event handler, take these steps:

1. Log in to SPSPortal as the local administrator.

2. Open Windows Explorer and navigate to C:\Windows\Assembly.

3. Locate the Workflow assembly, right-click it, and select Properties from the pop-up menu.

4. Note the Version, Culture, and PublicKeyToken information for the assembly.

5. Log in to SPS as a member of the Administrator site group.

6. Navigate to the Submit library you created earlier.

7. Click the Modify Settings and Columns link under the Actions list.

8. On the Customize page, select General Settings ➤ Change Advanced Settings.

9. In the Assembly Name box, type the full strong name of the assembly. An example is shown here:

```
WorkFlow,Version=1.0.0.0,Culture=Neutral,
PublicKeyToken=5959aab8a976a104
```

10. In the Class Name box, type the fully qualified class name as shown here:

```
WorkFlow.Engine
```

11. In the Properties box, type **Submit**.

12. Click OK.

13. On the Customize page, select General Settings ➤ Change General Settings.

14. On the Document Library Settings page, select to require content approval for submitted items.

15. Click OK.

16. Navigate to the Review library you created earlier.

17. Click the Modify Settings and Columns link under the Actions list.

18. On the Customize page, select General Settings ➤ Change Advanced Settings.

19. In the Assembly Name box, type the full strong name of the assembly. Here is an example:

```
WorkFlow,Version=1.0.0.0,Culture=Neutral,
PublicKeyToken=5959aab8a976a104
```

20. In the Class Name box, type the fully qualified class name as shown here:

```
WorkFlow.Engine
```

21. In the Properties box, type **Review**.

22. Click OK.

23. On the Customize page, select General Settings ➤ Change General Settings.

24. On the Document Library Settings page, select to require content approval for submitted items.

25. Click OK.

26. Navigate to the Approve library you created earlier.

27. Click the Modify Settings and Columns link under the Actions list.

28. On the Customize page, select General Settings ➤ Change General settings.

29. On the Document Library Settings page, select to require content approval for submitted items.

30. Click OK.

31. Restart IIS to make your changes take effect.

If you have successfully created the solution, you should now be able to create a new document in the Submit library and approve it. Once you have approved the document, it should automatically move to the Review library. Once approved in the Review library, the document should automatically move to the Approve library.

Debugging the Solution

This project is moderately difficult, and chances are that you will not get it all correct the first time through. Therefore, you will likely have to debug the solution. Because the event handler is created as a class library, you can use standard debugging techniques to set breakpoints and walk through the code.

To debug the project, follow these steps:

1. In Visual Studio, change the solution configuration to **Debug**.

2. Rebuild the project by selecting Build ➤ Rebuild WorkFlow.

3. Open Windows Explorer and navigate to `C:\Windows\Assembly`.

4. Locate the WorkFlow assembly, right-click it, and select Delete from the pop-up menu.

5. Drag the debug version of your assembly into the GAC.

6. Restart IIS to unload the old version of the assembly from memory.

7. Open the SPS home page in Internet Explorer.

8. In Visual Studio, set breakpoints in your project code at the desired locations.

9. Select Debug ➤ Processes.

10. In the Processes dialog, select w3wp.exe from the list of Available Processes.

 NOTE   *The* w3wp.exe *process will not be visible until you open a portal web page in the browser. You should also be sure that the "Show processes in all sessions" box is checked on the Processes dialog.*

---

11. Click Attach.

12. In the Attach to Process dialog, check the Common Language Runtime box.

13. Click OK.

14. Return to Internet Explorer and navigate to the Submit library. When you approve a document, your code should break in Visual Studio.

Exercise 9-2: Building a Site Collection Web Part

As your SPS installation grows, you may find that the number of site collections, team sites, and workspaces grows to the point where it is difficult to navigate the hierarchy. With that in mind, this project creates a site collection web part that shows all of the subsites underneath a top-level site. This is useful because it allows end users to discover sites they may not have known. Additionally, the web part has the ability to show users sites to which they do not belong so that they can request access, if appropriate. Figure 9-1 shows a view of the final project.

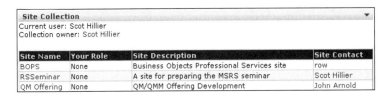

Figure 9-1. Listing sites in a collection

Prerequisites

Before beginning the project, you will need to define a new application for the Microsoft SSO service. The web part developed in this project will programmatically interact with several web sites, and it requires administrator permission to complete its function. Use the following steps to create the new application definition:

1. Log in to SPSPortal as a member of the MSSSOAdmins group.

2. Select Start ➤ All Programs ➤ SharePoint Portal Server ➤ SharePoint Portal Server Single Sign-On Administration.

3. On the Manage Settings page, select Enterprise Application Definition Settings ➤ Manage Settings for Enterprise Application Definitions.

4. On the Manage Enterprise Application Definitions page, click the New Item link.

5. On the Create Enterprise Application Definition page, enter **SubSiteList** in the Display Name box.

6. Enter **SubSiteList** in the Application Name box.

7. Enter **administrator@sps.local** in the Contact E-mail Address box.

8. Enter **UserName** in the Field 1: Display Name box.

9. Enter **Domain** in the Field 2: Display Name box.

10. Enter **Password** in the Field 3: Display Name box.

11. Select Yes for the Mask option associated with Field 3.

12. Click OK.

13. Return to the Manage Settings page and select Enterprise Application Definition Settings ➤ Manage Account Information for Enterprise Application Definitions.

14. In the Account Information section, choose SubSiteList from the drop-down list.

15. Type **sps\Domain Users** in the Group Account Name box.

16. Click OK.

17. On the "Provide workflow engine account information" page, type **administrator** in the UserName box.

18. Type **sps** in the Domain box.

19. Type the administrator password in the Password box.

20. Click OK.

Creating the Project

This web part project will be written in VB.NET. Therefore, you should open Visual Studio and create a new web part project in VB.NET named SPSSubSites. When the project is created, rename the class file and the web part description file as **SPSSubSites.dwp** and **SPSSubSites.vb** respectively. Then, open SPSSubSites.dwp from the Solution Explorer and change the file to appear as shown in Listing 9-14.

Listing 9-14. The Web Part Description File

```xml
<?xml version="1.0" encoding="utf-8"?>
<WebPart xmlns="http://schemas.microsoft.com/WebPart/v2" >
    <Title>Site Collection</Title>
    <Description>A web part to list sub sites</Description>
    <Assembly>SPSSubSites</Assembly>
    <TypeName>SPSSubSites.Lister</TypeName>
</WebPart>
```

Before you begin to modify the web part code, you must add a couple of references to the project. This web part will change identity, just as you did when you created document workflow to get permission to list web sites. Therefore, you need access to the SSO system. You also have to set a reference to the SharePoint Services namespace.

To set the references, follow these steps:

1. Select Project ➤ Add Reference from the Visual Studio menu.

2. In the Add References dialog, double-click
   `Microsoft.SharePoint.Portal.SingleSignon.dll` and `Windows SharePoint Services`.

3. Click OK.

Once the references are added, open the `SPSSubSites.vb` file for editing. You will add several `Imports` statements to the file and modify the class name. Change your web part to appear as shown in Listing 9-15.

Listing 9-15. Starting the Project

```
Option Strict On
Option Explicit On
Option Compare Text

Imports System
Imports System.ComponentModel
Imports System.Web.UI
Imports System.Web.UI.WebControls
Imports System.Xml.Serialization
Imports Microsoft.SharePoint
Imports Microsoft.SharePoint.Utilities
Imports Microsoft.SharePoint.WebPartPages
Imports Microsoft.SharePoint.WebControls
Imports System.Security.Principal
Imports System.Runtime.InteropServices
Imports Microsoft.SharePoint.Portal.SingleSignon

<DefaultProperty("ShowAllSites"), _
ToolboxData("<{0}:Lister runat=server></{0}:Lister>"), _
XmlRoot(Namespace:="SPSSubSites")> _
  Public Class Lister
    Inherits Microsoft.SharePoint.WebPartPages.WebPart
```

Defining the Properties

Your web part has only a single property defined named ShowAllSites. ShowAllSites is a Boolean value that determines if the web part lists sites to which the current user does not belong. Listing such sites allows the end user to discover sites and request access. If you want to hide sites in the collection, however, set this property to False. The property is simple to define. Just add the code from Listing 9-16.

Listing 9-16. The ShowAllSites Property

```
Protected blnShowAllSites As Boolean = False

<Browsable(True), Category("Behavior"), DefaultValue(False), _
WebPartStorage(Storage.Shared), FriendlyName("Show All Sites"), _
Description("Show sites to which the user does not belong.")> _
Property ShowAllSites() As Boolean
    Get
        Return blnShowAllSites
    End Get

    Set(ByVal Value As Boolean)
        blnShowAllSites = Value
    End Set
End Property
```

Creating the Child Controls

The child sites discovered by the web part are listed in a grid. The grid creates a hyperlink to the site—so a user can navigate directly—as well as an e-mail link to the site collection owner. Therefore, you have to create the HyperLinkColumns and BoundColumns by hand for your grid. You have used similar techniques several times in other web parts throughout the book. Add the code from Listing 9-17 to create the grid for the web part.

Listing 9-17. Creating the Child Controls

```
Protected WithEvents grdSites As DataGrid
Protected WithEvents lblMessage As Label

Protected Overrides Sub CreateChildControls()
```

```vbnet
'Grid to display results
grdSites = New DataGrid
With grdSites
    .AutoGenerateColumns = False
    .Width = Unit.Percentage(100)
    .HeaderStyle.Font.Name = "arial"
    .HeaderStyle.Font.Size = New FontUnit(FontSize.AsUnit).Point(10)
    .HeaderStyle.Font.Bold = True
    .HeaderStyle.ForeColor = System.Drawing.Color.Wheat
    .HeaderStyle.BackColor = System.Drawing.Color.DarkBlue
    .AlternatingItemStyle.BackColor = System.Drawing.Color.LightCyan
End With

Dim objBoundColumn As BoundColumn
Dim objHyperColumn As HyperLinkColumn

'Name Column
objHyperColumn = New HyperLinkColumn
With objHyperColumn
    .HeaderText = "Site Name"
    .DataTextField = "Name"
    .DataNavigateUrlField = "URL"
    grdSites.Columns.Add(objHyperColumn)
End With

'Membership Column
objBoundColumn = New BoundColumn
With objBoundColumn
    .HeaderText = "Your Role"
    .DataField = "Role"
    grdSites.Columns.Add(objBoundColumn)
End With

'Description Column
objBoundColumn = New BoundColumn
With objBoundColumn
    .HeaderText = "Site Description"
    .DataField = "Description"
    grdSites.Columns.Add(objBoundColumn)
End With

'Contact Column
objHyperColumn = New HyperLinkColumn
With objHyperColumn
```

```
        .HeaderText = "Site Contact"
        .DataTextField = "Author"
        .DataNavigateUrlField = "eMail"
        grdSites.Columns.Add(objHyperColumn)
    End With

    Controls.Add(grdSites)

    'Label for error messages
    lblMessage = New Label
    With lblMessage
        .Width = Unit.Percentage(100)
        .Font.Name = "arial"
        .Font.Size = New FontUnit(FontSize.AsUnit).Point(10)
        .Text = ""
    End With
    Controls.Add(lblMessage)

End Sub
```

Creating the Helper Functions

As I mentioned earlier, this web part needs to change its identity to access all the necessary site information. Therefore, you need to provide the same help function to create a new identity as you did for document workflow. This function is useful in many web parts and you will use it often. Add the code from Listing 9-18 to create the new identity.

Listing 9-18. Creating a New Identity

```
Protected Shared Function CreateIdentity(ByVal User As String, _
ByVal Domain As String, ByVal Password As String) As WindowsIdentity

    Dim objToken As New IntPtr(0)
    Dim ID As WindowsIdentity
    Const LOGON32_PROVIDER_DEFAULT As Integer = 0
    Const LOGON32_LOGON_NETWORK As Integer = 3

    'Initialize token object
    objToken = IntPtr.Zero
```

```
' Attempt to log on
Dim blnReturn As Boolean = LogonUser(User, Domain, Password, _
LOGON32_LOGON_NETWORK, LOGON32_PROVIDER_DEFAULT, objToken)

'Check for failure
If blnReturn = False Then
    Dim intCode As Integer = Marshal.GetLastWin32Error()
    Throw New Exception("Logon failed: " & intCode.ToString)
End If

'Return new token
ID = New WindowsIdentity(objToken)
CloseHandle(objToken)
Return ID

End Function

<DllImport("advapi32.dll", SetLastError:=True)> _
    Private Shared Function LogonUser(ByVal lpszUsername As String, _
ByVal lpszDomain As String, _
ByVal lpszPassword As String, ByVal dwLogonType As Integer, _
ByVal dwLogonProvider As Integer, _
        ByRef phToken As IntPtr) As Boolean
End Function

<DllImport("kernel32.dll", CharSet:=CharSet.Auto)> _
    Private Shared Function CloseHandle(ByVal handle As IntPtr) As Boolean
End Function
```

Rendering the Web Part

Once the helper functions are defined, you can begin to code the main body of
the web part. You will write this code directly in the RenderWebPart method. We
will discuss each part of the code so that you can follow how it works. Essentially,
your strategy will be to enumerate the sites in the collection, add them to a
DataSet, and bind the DataSet to the grid for display. Begin by adding the code
from Listing 9-19 to the RenderWebPart method.

Listing 9-19. Declaring Initial Objects

```
Protected Overrides Sub RenderWebPart( _
ByVal output As System.Web.UI.HtmlTextWriter)
```

```
'Get the site collection
Dim objSite As SPSite = SPControl.GetContextSite(Context)
Dim objMainSite As SPWeb = objSite.OpenWeb
Dim objAllSites As SPWebCollection = objSite.AllWebs
Dim objMemberSites As SPWebCollection = objMainSite.GetSubwebsForCurrentUser
Dim objSubSite As SPWeb

'Get the user identity
Dim strUsername As String = objMainSite.CurrentUser.LoginName

'Create a DataSet and DataTable for the site collection
Dim objDataset As DataSet = New DataSet("root")
Dim objTable As DataTable = objDataset.Tables.Add("Sites")

'Context for the new identity
Dim objContext As WindowsImpersonationContext
Dim arrCredentials() As String
Dim strUID As String
Dim strDomain As String
Dim strPassword As String
```

Once you have retrieved the basic information for the site collection and the user, you are ready to change the identity of the web part so that it can enumerate the subsites in the collection. To accomplish this, you will retrieve credentials from the SSO system. Add the code from Listing 9-20 to the RenderWebPart method to change the identity.

 NOTE *After you change the identity of the web part, the identity of the current user is no longer available; therefore, you should always retrieve the identity of the current user before changing the identity of the web part.*

Listing 9-20. Changing the Web Part Identity

```
Try

    'Try to get credentials
    Credentials.GetCredentials( _
    Convert.ToUInt32("0"), "SubSiteList", arrCredentials)
    strUID = arrCredentials(0)
    strDomain = arrCredentials(1)
    strPassword = arrCredentials(2)
```

```
                'Change the context
            Dim objIdentity As WindowsIdentity
            objIdentity = CreateIdentity(strUID, strDomain, strPassword)
            objContext = objIdentity.Impersonate

    Catch x As SingleSignonException
            lblMessage.Text += "No credentials available." + vbCrLf
    Catch x As Exception
            lblMessage.Text += x.Message + vbCrLf
    End Try
```

After the new identity is created, the web part can enumerate the child sites and add them to the DataSet. Which sites are enumerated is determined by the value of the ShowAllSites property. Along the way, the web part builds the appropriate site and e-mail links for the end user. Add the code from Listing 9-21 to enumerate the child sites.

Listing 9-21. Enumerating Child Sites

```
Try
    'Design Table
    With objTable.Columns
        .Add("Role", Type.GetType("System.String"))
        .Add("Name", Type.GetType("System.String"))
        .Add("Description", Type.GetType("System.String"))
        .Add("URL", Type.GetType("System.String"))
        .Add("Author", Type.GetType("System.String"))
        .Add("eMail", Type.GetType("System.String"))
    End With

    'Fill the Table with Member Sites
    For Each objSubSite In objMemberSites
        Dim objRow As DataRow = objTable.NewRow()
        With objRow
            Try
                .Item("Role") = objSubSite.Users(strUsername).Roles(0).Name
            Catch
                .Item("Role") = "None"
            End Try
            .Item("Name") = objSubSite.Name
            .Item("Description") = objSubSite.Description
            .Item("URL") = objSubSite.Url
            .Item("Author") = objSubSite.Author.Name
            .Item("eMail") = "mailto:" + objSubSite.Author.Email
```

```
            End With
            objTable.Rows.Add(objRow)
        Next
Catch x As Exception
    lblMessage.Text = x.Message
End Try

Try
        'Fill the Table with non-member sites
        If ShowAllSites = True Then

            For Each objSubSite In objAllSites

                'Get the user collection for each sub site
                Dim objUsers As SPUserCollection = objSubSite.Users
                Dim objUser As SPUser
                Dim blnMember As Boolean

                'Skip the parent site
                If objMainSite.Name <> objSubSite.Name Then

                    blnMember = False

                    'Look through user list
                    For Each objUser In objUsers
                        If objUser.LoginName.Trim = strUsername.Trim Then
                            blnMember = True
                        End If
                    Next

                    If blnMember = False Then

                        'If the current user is not a member add a record
                        Dim objRow As DataRow = objTable.NewRow()
                        With objRow
                            .Item("Role") = "Not a Member!"
                            .Item("Name") = objSubSite.Name
                            .Item("Description") = objSubSite.Description
                            .Item("URL") = objSubSite.Url
                            .Item("Author") = objSubSite.Author.Name
                            .Item("eMail") = "mailto:" + objSubSite.Author.Email
                        End With
                        objTable.Rows.Add(objRow)
```

```
                End If

           End If

           objSubSite.Close()

      Next

    End If

    'Close sites
    objMainSite.Close()
    objSite.Close()

    'Tear down context
    objContext.Undo()

Catch x As Exception
    lblMessage.Text = x.Message
End Try
```

Once all of the sites are enumerated, the DataSet can be bound to the grid. Add the code from Listing 9-22 to complete the RenderWebPart method.

Listing 9-22. Displaying the Subsites

```
'Bind dataset to grid
output.Write("<p>Current user: " + objMainSite.CurrentUser.Name + "<br>" _
+ "Collection owner: <a href=""mailto:" + objSite.Owner.Email + """>" _
+ objSite.Owner.Name + "</a></p>")
With grdSites
    .DataSource = objDataset
    .DataMember = "Sites"
    .DataBind()
End With

'Show grid
grdSites.RenderControl(output)
output.Write("<br>")
lblMessage.RenderControl(output)
```

Using the Web Part

Before you can compile the web part, you must give it a strong name and modify the AssemblyInfo file with the name of the key pair file. Just as you have done with every web part, you must also modify the web.config file for SPS to mark the web part as safe. You have already accomplished these tasks several times, so I won't repeat the steps here. Once you have finished compiling the web part, import it onto the home page of a top-level site and verify that it enumerates the subsites below.

Exercise 9-3: Building a Global Task Web Part

Along with the proliferation of sites in SPS, the proliferation of task items can rapidly become overwhelming. Because tasks can be assigned at any site, end users rapidly lose track of their tasks. In this project, you will build a global task list web part that will be deployed on the master My Site so that it is available for every user in the portal. The web part will search for tasks throughout all sites and collect them in a single list. Figure 9-2 shows a view of the final project.

Host Site	Task
Capacity Planning	Perm Application
Capacity Planning	Board Portal
Capacity Planning	Advisory Platform
Capacity Planning	Training for Board Portal
SharePoint Development Book	Fix Chapter 8 code
SharePoint Development Book	Audience Rules Using Datalannt Domain Cannot Connect to Datalannt
SharePoint Issues	Cannot view Calendar
SharePoint Issues	Calendar on MySite shows Scot Hillier's Calendar
SharePoint Issues	Addendum Management link always uses internal server name
SharePoint Issues	Enumerate Child Sites
SharePoint Issues	Enhanced Task List
SharePoint Issues	Set up crawling of portal sites

Your Global Task List

Figure 9-2. The global task list

Prerequisites

As in the previous project, this project interacts with several sites and lists that an individual user may not have permission to access. Therefore, you must change the identity of the web part to that of an administrator. To accomplish this, you will use credentials stored in the SSO database.

To configure SSO credentials:

1. Log in to SPSPortal as a member of the MSSSOAdmins group.

2. Select Start ➤ All Programs ➤ SharePoint Portal Server ➤ SharePoint Portal Server Single Sign-On Administration.

3. On the Manage Settings page, select Enterprise Application Definition Settings ➤ Manage Settings for Enterprise Application Definitions.

4. On the Manage Enterprise Application Definitions page, click the New Item link.

5. On the Create Enterprise Application Definition page, enter **SPSAuthority** in the Display Name box.

6. Enter **SPSAuthority** in the Application Name box.

7. Enter **administrator@sps.local** in the Contact E-mail Address box.

8. Enter **UserName** in the Field 1: Display Name box.

9. Enter **Domain** in the Field 2: Display Name box.

10. Enter **Password** in the Field 3: Display Name box.

11. Select Yes for the Mask option associated with Field 3.

12. Click OK.

13. Return to the Manage Settings page and select Enterprise Application Definition Settings ➤ Manage Account Information for Enterprise Application Definitions.

14. In the Account Information section, choose SPSAuthority from the drop-down list.

15. Type **sps\Domain Users** in the Group Account Name box.

16. Click OK.

17. On the "Provide workflow engine account information" page, type **administrator** in the UserName box.

18. Type **sps** in the Domain box.

19. Type the administrator password in the Password box.

20. Click OK.

Creating the Project

Open Visual Studio and create a new web part project in VB.NET named
SPSTasks. When the project is created, rename the class file and the web part
description file as **SPSTasks.dwp** and **SPSTaskss.vb** respectively. Then, open
SPSTasks.dwp from the Solution Explorer and change the file to appear as shown
in Listing 9-23.

Listing 9-23. The Web Part Description File

```
<?xml version="1.0" encoding="utf-8"?>
<WebPart xmlns="http://schemas.microsoft.com/WebPart/v2" >
    <Title>Your Global Task List</Title>
    <Description>A web part to collect all tasks for a user</Description>
    <Assembly>SPSTasks</Assembly>
    <TypeName>SPSTasks.Lister</TypeName>
</WebPart>
```

Before you begin to modify the web part code, you must add two references
to the project. This web part uses a different identity to get permission to examine lists on all the sites. Therefore, you need access to the SSO system. You also
have to set a reference to the SharePoint Services namespace.

To set the references, follow these steps:

1. Select Project ➤ References from the Visual Studio menu.

2. In the Add References dialog, double-click Microsoft.SharePoint.
   Portal.SingleSignon.dll and Windows SharePoint Services.

3. Click OK.

Once the references are added, open the SPSTasks.vb file for editing. You will
add several Imports statements to the file and modify the class name. Change
your web part to appear as shown in Listing 9-24.

Listing 9-24. The Initial Class Code

```
Option Explicit On
Option Strict On
Option Compare Text

Imports System
Imports System.ComponentModel
Imports System.Web.UI
Imports System.Web.UI.WebControls
Imports System.Xml.Serialization
Imports Microsoft.SharePoint
Imports Microsoft.SharePoint.Utilities
Imports Microsoft.SharePoint.WebPartPages
Imports Microsoft.SharePoint.WebControls
Imports Microsoft.SharePoint.Administration
Imports System.Security.Principal
Imports System.Runtime.InteropServices
Imports Microsoft.SharePoint.Portal.SingleSignon

<DefaultProperty(""), ToolboxData("<{0}:Lister runat=server></{0}:Lister>"), _
XmlRoot(Namespace:="SPSTasks")> _
  Public Class Lister
      Inherits Microsoft.SharePoint.WebPartPages.WebPart
```

Creating the Child Controls

Just like several other web parts you have created, this web part displays a grid. The web part creates the global task list by filling a `DataSet`, which is subsequently bound to a grid for display. When you build the task list, you provide hyperlinks to both the site that hosts the task list and the task list itself. Add the code from Listing 9-25 to define the child controls for the web part.

Listing 9-25. Creating the Child Controls

```
Protected WithEvents grdTasks As DataGrid
Protected WithEvents lblMessage As Label

Protected Overrides Sub CreateChildControls()

    'Grid to display results
    grdTasks = New DataGrid
```

```
With grdTasks
    .AutoGenerateColumns = False
    .Width = Unit.Percentage(100)
    .HeaderStyle.Font.Name = "arial"
    .HeaderStyle.Font.Size = New FontUnit(FontSize.AsUnit).Point(10)
    .HeaderStyle.Font.Bold = True
    .HeaderStyle.ForeColor = System.Drawing.Color.Wheat
    .HeaderStyle.BackColor = System.Drawing.Color.DarkBlue
    .AlternatingItemStyle.BackColor = System.Drawing.Color.LightCyan
End With


Dim objHyperColumn As HyperLinkColumn

'Host Site Name Column
objHyperColumn = New HyperLinkColumn
With objHyperColumn
    .HeaderText = "Host Site"
    .DataTextField = "SiteName"
    .DataNavigateUrlField = "SiteURL"
    grdTasks.Columns.Add(objHyperColumn)
End With


'Host Site Name Column
objHyperColumn = New HyperLinkColumn
With objHyperColumn
    .HeaderText = "Task"
    .DataTextField = "TaskTitle"
    .DataNavigateUrlField = "ListURL"
    grdTasks.Columns.Add(objHyperColumn)
End With
Controls.Add(grdTasks)

'Label for error messages
lblMessage = New Label
With lblMessage
    .Width = Unit.Percentage(100)
    .Font.Name = "arial"
    .Font.Size = New FontUnit(FontSize.AsUnit).Point(10)
    .Text = ""
End With
Controls.Add(lblMessage)


End Sub
```

Changing the Identity

As you have done in several web parts, this web part must change identity in order to access the task lists. This code never changes from part to part, but it is essential for the web part to function. Add the code from Listing 9-26 to create this helper function.

Listing 9-26. Changing the Web Part Identity

```
Protected Shared Function CreateIdentity(ByVal User As String, _
ByVal Domain As String, ByVal Password As String) As WindowsIdentity

    Dim objToken As New IntPtr(0)
    Dim ID As WindowsIdentity
    Const LOGON32_PROVIDER_DEFAULT As Integer = 0
    Const LOGON32_LOGON_NETWORK As Integer = 3

    'Initialize token object
    objToken = IntPtr.Zero

    ' Attempt to log on
    Dim blnReturn As Boolean = LogonUser(User, Domain, Password, _
LOGON32_LOGON_NETWORK, LOGON32_PROVIDER_DEFAULT, objToken)

    'Check for failure
    If blnReturn = False Then
        Dim intCode As Integer = Marshal.GetLastWin32Error()
        Throw New Exception("Logon failed: " & intCode.ToString)
    End If

    'Return new token
    ID = New WindowsIdentity(objToken)
    CloseHandle(objToken)
    Return ID

End Function


<DllImport("advapi32.dll", SetLastError:=True)> _
    Private Shared Function LogonUser(ByVal lpszUsername As String, _
ByVal lpszDomain As String, _
ByVal lpszPassword As String, ByVal dwLogonType As Integer, _
ByVal dwLogonProvider As Integer, _
        ByRef phToken As IntPtr) As Boolean
End Function
```

```
<DllImport("kernel32.dll", CharSet:=CharSet.Auto)> _
    Private Shared Function CloseHandle(ByVal handle As IntPtr) As Boolean
End Function
```

Rendering the Web Part

Once the helper function is complete, you may begin to code the main body of the web part. Most of the work is embodied in a function that enumerates the tasks and fills the DataSet. The web part identifies a task when a list item has an Assigned To field and that field contains either the user's login name or display name. Add the code from Listing 9-27 to create the global task list.

Listing 9-27. Enumerating the Tasks

```
Protected Function GetGlobalTasks(ByVal objUser As SPUser) As DataSet

    'Purpose: Walk all sites and collect pointers to the tasks

    'Context for the new identity
    Dim objContext As WindowsImpersonationContext
    Dim arrCredentials() As String
    Dim strUID As String
    Dim strDomain As String
    Dim strPassword As String
    Dim objDataSet As DataSet

    Try

        'Try to get credentials
        Credentials.GetCredentials( _
Convert.ToUInt32("0"), "SPSAuthority", arrCredentials)
        strUID = arrCredentials(0)
        strDomain = arrCredentials(1)
        strPassword = arrCredentials(2)
        'Change the context
        Dim objIdentity As WindowsIdentity
        objIdentity = CreateIdentity(strUID, strDomain, strPassword)
        objContext = objIdentity.Impersonate

    Catch x As SingleSignonException
        lblMessage.Text += "No credentials available." + vbCrLf
    Catch x As Exception
```

```vbnet
            lblMessage.Text += x.Message + vbCrLf
    End Try

    Try
        'Create new DataTable for tasks
        objDataSet = New DataSet("root")
        Dim objTable As DataTable = objDataSet.Tables.Add("Tasks")

        'Design Table
        With objTable.Columns
            .Add("SiteName", Type.GetType("System.String"))
            .Add("SiteURL", Type.GetType("System.String"))
            .Add("TaskTitle", Type.GetType("System.String"))
            .Add("ListURL", Type.GetType("System.String"))
        End With

        'Fill DataTable with tasks for the current user
        Dim objAdmin As New SPGlobalAdmin
        Dim objServer As SPVirtualServer = objAdmin.VirtualServers(0)
        Dim objSites As SPSiteCollection = objServer.Sites
        Dim objSite As SPSite

        'Walk every site in the installation
        For Each objSite In objSites

            Dim objWeb As SPWeb = objSite.OpenWeb()
            Dim objLists As SPListCollection = objWeb.Lists
            Dim objList As SPList

            'Walk every list on a site
            For Each objList In objLists

                If objList.BaseType = SPBaseType.GenericList _
                OrElse objList.BaseType = SPBaseType.Issue Then

                    For i As Integer = 0 To objList.ItemCount - 1
                        Try
                            Dim objItem As SPListItem = objList.Items(i)

                            'Check to see if this task is assigned to the user
                            Dim strAssignedTo As String = _
                            UCase(objItem.Item("Assigned To").ToString)
```

```
                              If strAssignedTo.IndexOf( _
                              UCase(objUser.LoginName)) > -1 _
                              OrElse strAssignedTo.IndexOf( _
                              UCase(objUser.Name)) > -1 Then

                                  'If so, add it to the DataSet
                                  Dim objRow As DataRow = objTable.NewRow()
                                  With objRow
                                      .Item("SiteName") = objList.ParentWeb.Title
                                      .Item("SiteURL") = objList.ParentWeb.Url
                                      .Item("TaskTitle") = objItem("Title")
                                      .Item("ListURL") = objList.DefaultViewUrl
                                  End With
                                  objTable.Rows.Add(objRow)
                              End If

                    Catch
                    End Try

                Next
            End If
        Next

        objWeb.Close()

    Next

    'Tear down the context
    objContext.Undo()

Catch x As Exception
    lblMessage.Text += x.Message + vbCrLf
End Try

Return objDataSet

End Function
```

The `RenderWebPart` method retrieves the current user and makes a call to the `GetGlobalTasks` method. Once the tasks are all enumerated and contained in the `DataSet`, you can bind the `DataSet` to the grid for display. Add the code from Listing 9-28 to show the task list.

Listing 9-28. Displaying the Task List

```
Protected Overrides Sub RenderWebPart( _
ByVal output As System.Web.UI.HtmlTextWriter)

    'Get the site collection
    Dim objSite As SPSite = SPControl.GetContextSite(Context)
    Dim objWeb As SPWeb = objSite.OpenWeb
    Dim objUser As SPUser = objWeb.CurrentUser

    'Get the DataSet of Tasks
    Dim objDataSet As DataSet = GetGlobalTasks(objUser)

    'Display Tasks
    With grdTasks
        .DataSource = objDataSet
        .DataMember = "Tasks"
        .DataBind()
    End With

    'Show grid
    grdTasks.RenderControl(output)
    output.Write("<br>")
    lblMessage.RenderControl(output)

End Sub
```

Using the Web Part

Before you can compile the web part, you must give it a strong name and modify the AssemblyInfo file with the name of the key pair file. Just as you have done with every web part, you must also modify the web.config file for SPS to mark the web part as safe. Additionally, you should ensure that the trust level is set to Full. You have accomplished these tasks several times, so I will not repeat the steps here.

Once the web part is compiled, you will want to place it on the shared view for My Site. If you have administrator permissions and modify the shared view, the web part will be available to all users of the portal.

To add the web part, follow these steps:

1. Log in to SPS as a member of the Administrator site group.

2. From the portal home page, click the My Site link.

3. On the My Site home page, select Modify My Page ➤ Shared View.

4. On the shared view, select Modify Shared Page ➤ Add Web Parts ➤ Import.

5. Add the global task list web part to the shared page to make it available to all portal users.

 NOTE   *The task list aggregates tasks for an individual based on the logon name and the display name. Errors in either of these values can negatively impact the accuracy of the final task list. See the next project for more details on this issue.*

Exercise 9-4: Building an Identity Web Part

Another issue that comes up early in a SharePoint Services deployment is the management of display names and e-mail addresses associated with individual sites. Because all top-level sites are independent, it is easy for the site creator to misspell a name or address. Furthermore, end users have no simple way to correct their information. In this exercise, you will create a simple web part that will allow users to change their personal information directly in a site. Figure 9-3 shows a view of the final project.

Figure 9-3. Displaying personal information

Creating the Project

This web part project will be written in C#. Open Visual Studio and create a new web part project in C# named SPSIdentity. When the project is created, rename the class file and the web part description file as **SPSIdentity.dwp** and **SPSIdentity.cs** respectively. Then, open SPSIdentity.dwp and change the file to appear as shown in Listing 9-29.

Listing 9-29. The Web Part Description File

```xml
<?xml version="1.0" encoding="utf-8"?>
<WebPart xmlns="http://schemas.microsoft.com/WebPart/v2" >

    <Title>Your Information</Title>
    <Description>A web part that shows identity information</Description>
    <Assembly>SPSIdentity</Assembly>
    <TypeName>SPSIdentity.Reporter</TypeName>
</WebPart>
```

Before you begin to modify the web part code, you must add a reference to the SharePoint Services namespace. Once the reference is added, open the SPSIdentity.cs file for editing. You will add several using statements to the file, modify the class name, and remove the default property. Change your web part to appear as shown in Listing 9-30.

Listing 9-30. Starting the Project

```csharp
using System;
using System.ComponentModel;
using System.Web.UI;
using System.Web.UI.WebControls;
using System.Xml.Serialization;
using Microsoft.SharePoint;
using Microsoft.SharePoint.Utilities;
using Microsoft.SharePoint.WebPartPages;
using Microsoft.SharePoint.WebControls;


namespace SPSIdentity
{

    [DefaultProperty(""),
    ToolboxData("<{0}:Report runat=server></{0}:Report>"),
    XmlRoot(Namespace="SPSIdentity")]
    public class Reporter : Microsoft.SharePoint.WebPartPages.WebPart
    {
```

Creating the Child Controls

This web part has no properties. It simply displays the user's information and allows the user to make changes. The user interface for this web part is more involved than others you have created, but it still follows the same general development principles. Add the code from Listing 9-31 to the project to create the user interface for the web part.

Listing 9-31. Creating the Child Controls

```
protected Label userNameLabel;
protected TextBox displayNameText;
protected TextBox emailText;
protected Button updateButton;
protected Label messageLabel;

protected override void CreateChildControls()
{

    //UserName Label
    userNameLabel = new Label();
    userNameLabel.Width = Unit.Percentage(100);
    userNameLabel.Font.Size = FontUnit.Point(10);
    userNameLabel.Font.Name = "arial";
    Controls.Add(userNameLabel);

    //DisplayName Text
    displayNameText = new TextBox();
    displayNameText.Width = Unit.Percentage(100);
    displayNameText.Font.Name = "arial";
    displayNameText.Font.Size = FontUnit.Point(10);
    Controls.Add(displayNameText);

    //E-Mail Text
    emailText = new TextBox();
    emailText.Width = Unit.Percentage(100);
    emailText.Font.Name = "arial";
    emailText.Font.Size = FontUnit.Point(10);
    Controls.Add(emailText);

    //Submit Button
    updateButton = new Button();
    updateButton.Font.Name = "arial";
```

```
updateButton.Font.Size = FontUnit.Point(10);
updateButton.Text = "Change";
Controls.Add(updateButton);
updateButton.Click +=new EventHandler(update_Click);

//Message Label
messageLabel = new Label();
messageLabel.Width = Unit.Percentage(100);
messageLabel.Font.Size = FontUnit.Point(10);
messageLabel.Font.Name = "arial";
Controls.Add(messageLabel);
}
```

Rendering the Web Part

When the web part runs, it displays the logon name, display name, and e-mail address for the current user. The display name and e-mail address are presented in text boxes so that they can be edited directly. Add the code from Listing 9-32 to display the current user information.

Listing 9-32. Displaying Current User Information

```
protected override void RenderWebPart(HtmlTextWriter output)
{
    //Get current user information before the context is changed
    SPSite site = SPControl.GetContextSite(Context);
    SPWeb web = site.OpenWeb();
    SPUser user = web.CurrentUser;

    //Show user information
    userNameLabel.Text = user.LoginName;
    displayNameText.Text = user.Name;
    emailText.Text = user.Email;

    //Create output
    output.Write("<TABLE Border=0>");
    output.Write("<TR>");
    output.Write("<TD>User name: ");
    userNameLabel.RenderControl(output);
    output.Write("</TD>");
    output.Write("</TR>");
    output.Write("<TR>");
```

```
output.Write("<TD> Display name: ");
displayNameText.RenderControl(output);
output.Write("</TD>");
output.Write("</TR>");
output.Write("<TR>");
output.Write("<TD>e-Mail: ");
emailText.RenderControl(output);
output.Write("</TD>");
output.Write("</TR>");
output.Write("<TR>");
output.Write("<TD>");
updateButton.RenderControl(output);
output.Write("</TD>");
output.Write("</TR>");
output.Write("<TR>");
output.Write("<TD>");
messageLabel.RenderControl(output);
output.Write("</TD>");
output.Write("</TR>");
output.Write("</TABLE>");

//close
web.Close();
site.Close();
}
```

Updating the User Information

The user interface for the web part displays a button that can be clicked to edit
the user information. End users simply type the changes directly into the web
part and click the button. The changes are then written back to SharePoint
Services. Add the code from Listing 9-33 to update the credentials.

Listing 9-33. Updating the User Information

```
private void update_Click(object sender, EventArgs e)
{
    //Get current user information before the context is changed
    SPSite site = SPControl.GetContextSite(Context);
    SPWeb web = site.OpenWeb();
    SPUser user = web.CurrentUser;
```

```
//Update current user information
user.Email=emailText.Text;
user.Name=displayNameText.Text;
user.Update();
web.Close();
site.Close();

}
```

Using the Web Part

Using the web part is no different than using any other web part. Give the web part a strong name and compile it. Add the web part to the <SafeControls> section of the web.config file and import it into a page. The web part should then display the information for the current user. The best way to use this part is to place it on a top-level site to ensure the credentials are correct for the entire site collection.

CHAPTER 10

SharePoint Portal Server Administration

THROUGHOUT THIS BOOK, YOU HAVE USED the SharePoint Portal Server (SPS) Central Administration site to manage sites and users. However, administration and maintenance in SPS2003 go beyond simply setting up user accounts and team sites. Although the intent of this chapter is not to act as a substitute for the Administrator's Guide, we will examine the major administrative tasks you must perform to keep an SPS installation healthy.

Back Up and Restore

One of the first things that you will want to configure in a production environment is proper backup of the SPS installation. SPS ships with a backup and restore tool that is accessible by selecting Start ➤ All Programs ➤ SharePoint Portal Server ➤ SharePoint Portal Server Data Backup and Restore. Figure 10-1 shows the utility.

The backup and restore utility backs up every aspect of your SPS installation with the exception of custom web parts. Therefore, you should back up the Windows 2003 system in conjunction with the backup and restore utility. Additionally, several prerequisites must be met before the utility can run correctly:

- SQL Server 2000 client tools must be installed on the server where the utility runs.

- The service account for SQL Server must have write access to the backup directory.

- The search service must have write access to the backup directory.

- The search database access accounts must have write access to the backup directory.

- The user configuring backup and restore must have write access to the backup directory.

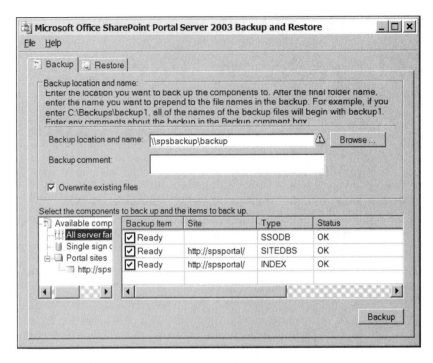

Figure 10-1. The backup and restore utility

Back up and restore in SPS is simple because you can only perform the operation for the entire portal as a whole. Although the task itself is simple, you pay the price in flexibility. For example, you cannot recover a single lost file from a document library. Instead, you have to rebuild the server and restore the entire portal. This is a significant drawback, to say the least. We can only hope that a third party produces a better set of tools that will allow more granular restorations.

Here are the steps to follow to perform a backup:

1. Log in to SPSPortal as a local administrator.

2. Open Windows Explorer.

3. Create a new directory at the location c:\backup.

4. Select Start ➤ SharePoint Portal Server ➤ SharePoint Portal Server Data Backup and Restore.

5. In the "Microsoft Office SharePoint Portal Server 2003 backup and restore" dialog, click Browse.

6. In the "File prefix for all backup images" dialog, navigate to the
   c:\backup directory and type the prefix **backup1** in the File Name field.

7. Click Open.

8. In the Backup Comment field, type **A test backup**.

9. In the Available Components list, expand the tree and ensure that all of
   the components are selected.

10. Click Backup to run the backup.

Site Usage Analysis

The distributed model of SPS potentially allows any user in the organization to
create sites. This is particularly true when you enable Self-Service Site Creation
(SSSC) mode. The result of this approach is that an organization can rapidly have
hundreds of team sites created. This situation not only increases the complexity
of site navigation for all users, but it also increases the resources required to
maintain backups. Therefore, you will want to take steps to ensure that the available sites are bringing significant value to end users.

Site usage analysis gives you a way to track the use of sites within SPS and to
identify those that are bringing the most value. Site usage analysis is not configured by default in SPS. You must begin by configuring it at the server level.

To enable site usage analysis, follow these steps:

1. Log in to SPSPortal as a local administrator.

2. Select Start ➤ All Programs ➤ SharePoint Portal Server ➤ SharePoint
   Central Administration.

3. On the SharePoint Portal Server Central Administration page, select
   Component Configuration ➤ Configure Usage Analysis Processing.

4. On the Configure Usage Analysis Processing page, check the box labeled
   Enable Logging.

5. Check the box labeled Enable Usage Analysis Processing.

6. Set appropriate parameters.

7. Click OK.

Once usage analysis is configured, it must run before any information is available. After it runs, however, you will be able to view usage information at either the collection or site level. The statistics provide information on such things as the number of page hits and number of unique users.

Here is what you need to do to view usage statistics:

1. Log in to SPS as a member of the Administrator site group.

2. Navigate to any top-level site in the portal.

3. From the site home page, click the Site Settings link.

4. On the Site Settings page, select Administration ➤ Go to Site Administration.

5. On the Top-Level Site Administration page, select Site Collection Administration ➤ View Site Collection Usage Summary.

6. On the Site Collection Usage Summary page, view the statistics and click OK.

7. On the Top-Level Site Administration page, select Management and Statistics ➤ View Site Usage Data.

8. On the Site Usage Report page, view the statistics for this individual site.

Cleaning Up Unused Sites

Along with ensuring the quality of available sites, another problem with site pro-liferation is that there is really no motivation for any user to delete a site after it has served its purpose. If a user creates a site for the annual company sales meet-ing, they are unlikely to care about the site after the meeting is over. In fact, this is just a larger version of the same issues that affect all file systems. If you were to examine the file system backups at most organizations, you would find that a sig-nificant number of the documents being backed up no longer have any use.

The solution in SPS is to implement site use confirmation and deletion. This facility allows SPS to query site owners and determine if a site is still in use. The owners confirm sites that are still in use, whereas sites that are no longer useful may be deleted. If you want, you can even set up SPS to automatically delete sites that have not been confirmed over a period of time.

Site use and confirmation is configured to send e-mail notifications to the owner of a site collection that has not been used for a specified period of time. When the e-mail is received, the owner will have a set of hyperlinks in the e-mail that will allow the owner to confirm that the site is in use or delete the site. If you have enabled automatic site deletion, then the site will automatically be deleted if the site collection owner fails to respond to the request after a configured number of notifications.

To enable site use confirmation and deletion, take these steps:

1. Log in to SPSPortal as a local administrator.

2. Select Start ➤ All Programs ➤ SharePoint Portal Server ➤ SharePoint Portal Server Central Administration.

3. On the SharePoint Portal Server Central Administration page, select Portal Site and Virtual Server Configuration ➤ Configure Virtual Server Settings from the Virtual Server List.

4. On the Virtual Server List page, select Default Web Site.

5. On the Virtual Server Settings page, select Automated Web Site Collection Management ➤ Configure Site Collection Use Confirmation and Deletion.

6. On the "Configure site collection use confirmation and auto-deletion" page, check the box labeled "Send e-mail notifications to owners of unused site collections."

7. Set the notification parameters.

8. Check the box labeled "Automatically delete the site collection if use is not confirmed" if you want to enable automatic site deletion.

9. Click OK.

Enabling automatic site deletion ensures that unneeded sites are always removed from the SPS installation. However, automatically deleting sites can result in the removal of sites that are seldom used but contain valuable information. For this reason, you should always set reasonable notification intervals that give plenty of opportunity for site collection owners to respond. Finally, you should require that all site collections have a designated secondary owner who can respond to the notifications if the primary owner is unavailable.

In order to make sure that all site collections have a secondary site collection contact, follow these steps:

1. Log in to SPSPortal as a local administrator.

2. Select Start ➤ All Programs ➤ SharePoint Portal Server ➤ SharePoint Portal Server Central Administration.

3. On the SharePoint Portal Server Central Administration page, select Portal Site and Virtual Server Configuration ➤ Configure Virtual Server Settings from the Virtual Server List.

4. On the Virtual Server List page, select Default Web Site.

5. On the Virtual Server Settings page, select Automated Web Site Collection Management ➤ Configure Self-Service Site Creation.

6. On the Configure Self-Service Site Creation page, ensure that Self-Service Site Creation mode is On.

7. Check the box labeled Require Secondary Contact.

8. Click OK.

The site use confirmation and deletion system uses two different message texts to send notifications: one text is used when you enable site confirmation; the other text is used if you have also enabled automatic deletion. Administrators may customize these notices, which are located in C:\Program Files\Common Files\Microsoft Shared\Web Server Extensions\60\TEMPLATE\1033\XML\DeadWeb.xml. Listing 10-1 shows the contents of the notification file.

Listing 10-1. The Site Notification Message

```
<?xml version="1.0" encoding="utf-8" ?>
<!- _lcid="1033" _version="11.0.5510" _dal="1" ->
<!- _LocalBinding ->
<Email>
    <Confirmation>
        <ConfirmationSubject>
        Confirm SharePoint Web site in use
    </ConfirmationSubject>
        <ConfirmationBody>
```

```
        <![CDATA[Please follow the link below
    to your SharePoint Web site to confirm that it is still in use.
            <br><a href="|0">|0</a><br><br>
            If the site is not being used, please go to <a href="|1">|1</a>,
            and select "Delete This Site" to remove the Web site.
            <br><br>
            You will receive reminders of this until you confirm the site is in
use, or delete it.]]>
        </ConfirmationBody>
    </Confirmation>
    <AutoDeleteWarning>
        <AutoDeleteSubject>
        ACTION REQUIRED: Your SharePoint site collection is about to expire
        </AutoDeleteSubject>
        <AutoDeleteBody>
        <![CDATA[To extend the expiration date for this site
        collection, click the link below:<br><a href="|0">|0</a><br><br>
        Otherwise this site collection, including all of its subsites, might be
deleted.<br><br>
            If this site collection is no longer needed, you can delete it by
going to <a href="|1">|1</a>, and selecting
            "Delete this site".<br><br>
            Please note - When a SharePoint Web site collection is deleted, all Web
sites, content and information which
            were part of the site collection are completely erased. The site can
only be restored if a backup exists.]]>
        </AutoDeleteBody>
    </AutoDeleteWarning>
</Email>
```

Managing the Search Service

Although SPS provides several ways to locate information, such as area and personal links, there is no substitute for a healthy search engine. The quality of searches performed within the portal is dependent upon properly scheduling and building indexes of content on key sources. Early in the book, I specified the account to use when crawling data sources, but it is important to remember that the account used must have permission to access the data sources you want to include in the index.

To change the access account, you need to follow this procedure:

1. Log in to SPSPortal as a local administrator.

2. Select Start ➤ All Programs ➤ SharePoint Portal Server ➤ SharePoint Portal Server Central Administration.

3. On the SharePoint Portal Server Central Administration page, select Server Configuration ➤ Configure Server Farm Account Settings.

4. On the "Configure server farm account settings" page, locate the Default Content Access Account section.

5. Check the Specify Account box.

6. Type the user name and password of an account that has permission to access the sources you wish to include in your index and search process.

Defining External Content Sources

In most organizations, searchable content will not be strictly limited to sites, documents, and lists contained within SPS. Instead, there are likely to be several external sources that contain documents that you will want to make accessible through searching. Along with site content already contained in the portal, SharePoint can index Microsoft Exchange servers, Lotus Notes databases, web sites, and file servers.

To add a content source, follow these steps:

1. Log in to SPS as a member of the Administrator site group.

2. From the portal home page, click the Site Settings link.

3. On the Site Settings page, select Search Settings and Indexed Content ➤ Configure Search and Indexing.

4. On the Configure Search and Indexing page, select General Content Settings and Indexing Status ➤ Add Content Source.

5. On the Add Content Source page, select the type of content to crawl and click Next.

6. Specify the particular parameters necessary to crawl the source.

7. Click OK.

8. Establish a full and incremental update schedule for the source.

Scheduling Content Crawls

Regardless of whether the content is a direct part of SPS or an external source, you will need to schedule content crawls to make the source available in search results. SPS's search service supports Full, Incremental, and Adaptive updates of the content indexes.

A Full update crawls the entire content source and updates the search index for every document. A Full update will add new information to the index, modify existing information, and delete obsolete information. A Full update is an intensive operation that should be scheduled for off-peak hours and performed only occasionally. Generally, a Full update is warranted under the following conditions:

- Whenever the index update rules are changed

- Whenever the server crashes

- When the portal structure changes significantly

- When the noise word file is changed

- When an index is manually reset

An Incremental update, on the other hand, only indexes content that has changed since the last crawl. This makes an Incremental update much more efficient. You can schedule such updates daily during off-peak hours to ensure that the search results are always up to date.

An Adaptive update uses historical analysis to try and perform a more efficient update than even that achieved with an Incremental update. The analysis uses information from previous updates to determine which documents are likely to have changed. The update then focuses on this set of documents.

To create an update schedule, follow these steps:

1. Log in to SPS as a member of the Administrator site group.

2. From the portal home page, click the Site Settings link.

3. On the Site Settings page, select Search Settings and Indexed Content ➤ Configure Search and Indexing.

4. On the Configure Search and Indexing page, select General Content Settings and Indexing Status ➤ Manage Search Schedules.

5. If the content source already has a schedule defined, you may select Edit from the drop-down menu associated with the item.

6. If the content source does not have a schedule defined, click the New Search Schedule link.

Creating Keywords

Keywords are used by the search engine to show results more prominently when a search result includes such words. Administrators can create and manage key words by selecting Site Settings ➤ Search Settings and Indexed Content ➤ Manage Keywords. In this section, you can create keywords, identify synonyms, and associate them with a Best Bet URL. Figure 10-2 shows a sample results page with a Best Bet prominently displayed using a star icon.

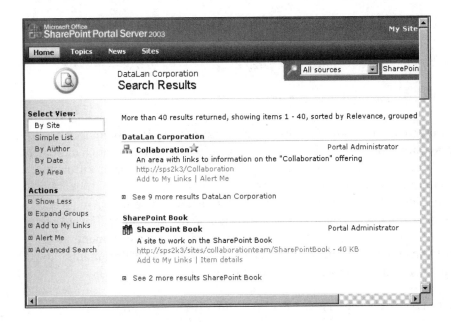

Figure 10-2. Displaying Best Bets

Enabling Online Presence

Wherever a user is referenced throughout SPS, you can provide *presence information*. Presence information is used to identify who is online and send instant messages to them. Presence information is available only when the client machine has Office 2003 installed along with either the Microsoft Messenger or the MSN Messenger. Figure 10-3 shows an example of presence information displayed in the portal.

Figure 10-3. Displaying presence information

To enable online presence, follow these steps:

1. Log in to `SPSPortal` as a local administrator.

2. Select Start ➤ All Programs ➤ SharePoint Portal Server ➤ SharePoint Portal Server Central Administration.

3. On the SharePoint Portal Server Central Administration page, select Portal Site and Virtual Server Configuration ➤ Configure Virtual Server Settings from the Virtual Server List Page.

4. On the Virtual Server List page, select Default Web Site.

5. On the Virtual Server Settings page, select Virtual Server Management ➤ Virtual Server General Settings.

6. On the Virtual Server General Settings page, select Yes to "Enable person name Smart Tag and online status for members."

7. Click OK.

Managing Quotas and Locks

As an organization uses SPS, it will consume more and more resources. To ensure that the installation remains healthy, you need to specify limits—called *quotas*—surrounding the resources that any site can use. If usage gets out of hand, you may even need to lock the site so that no additional resources can be consumed.

Quotas are not enabled by default in SPS. To enable them, you must define a quota template that contains the restrictions you wish to impose. Quota values are maintained in the configuration database and are typically applied to site collections when they are first created. The quota template is used to apply a set of restrictions to a site collection all at once.

Follow these steps to create and apply a quota template:

1. Log in to SPSPortal as a local administrator.

2. Select Start ➤ All Programs ➤ SharePoint Portal Server ➤ SharePoint Portal Server Central Administration.

3. On the SharePoint Portal Server Central Administration page, select Portal Site and Virtual Server Configuration ➤ Configure Site Quotas and Locks from the Virtual Server List.

4. On the Manage Quotas and Locks page, select Manage Quotas ➤ Manage Quota Templates.

5. On the Manage Quota Templates page, select "Create a new quota template."

6. Name the quota **Test Template**.

7. Click OK.

8. Return to the Manage Quotas and Locks page.

9. Select Manage Quotas ➤ Manage Site Collection Quota and Locks.

10. On the "Manage site collection quotas and locks" page, type the URL of a top-level site you have created.

11. Click View Data.

12. In the Current Quota Template list, select the Test Template.

13. Click OK.

Exercise 10-1: Establishing Secure Access

The work we have completed so far in this book has all been accomplished as if SPS was only accessible from an internal server. Typically, we have used the machine name of the server directly in the browser. If you want to include external access to SPS as part of your solution, however, you will have to make some changes.

The first thing you'll have to do is give your portal a name that's accessible from outside the firewall. Typically, you use portal or sharepoint as a prefix in the domain name (e.g., portal.datalan.com) and make a new entry in the Domain Name Service (DNS) for the enterprise. You'll also have to ensure that the server running the portal has an Internet Protocol (IP) address that can be exposed on the Internet, unlike the default setup this book uses.

Although these steps are enough to expose the portal externally, they are not enough to guarantee security. At a minimum, you should enable Secure Socket Layers (SSL) for the portal. You may also choose to implement a more significant authentication scheme such as the use of tokens. In this exercise, you will give your portal an alias name and enable SSL.

Creating an Alias

Creating an alias for your web site is a simple matter of making a new record entry in the DNS for the network. Creating an alias will allow you to use a name like sharepoint.sps.local when accessing SPS instead of SPSPortal. Although you will create your alias solely for internal use, you can create an alias for external use and map it to an IP address that will expose the portal on the Internet.

Here is what you should do to create an alias for SPSPortal:

1. Log in to SPSController as the domain administrator.

2. Select Start ➤ Administrative Tools ➤ DNS.

3. In the dnsmgmt dialog, expand the Forward Lookup Zones folder.

4. Right-click the sps.local folder and select New Alias (CNAME) from the pop-up menu.

5. In the New Resource Record dialog, type **sharepoint**.

6. Click Browse.

7. Double-click the SPSController node.

8. Double-click the Forward Lookup folder.

9. Double-click the `sps.local` folder.

10. Select the spsportal entry from the list and click OK.

11. In the New Resource Record dialog, click OK. Figure 10-4 shows the new entry in the DNS system.

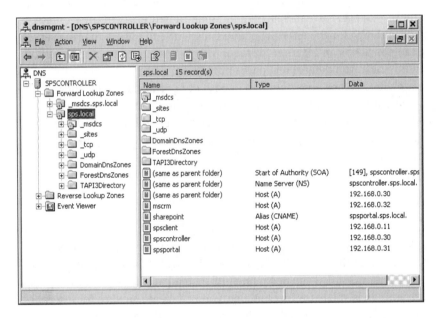

Figure 10-4. Creating an alias

One problem with using alias names to access the portal is that users will be presented with a log-in box regardless of whether they are inside or outside the firewall. There is no way to prevent this behavior. Users can also expect to be prompted occasionally when documents are accessed. You should be careful about how you configure and access SPS to minimize unnecessary logon prompts.

To test the alias name, follow this procedure:

1. Log in to `SPSClient` as an end user of the portal.

2. Open Internet Explorer and navigate to `sharepoint.sps.local`.

3. When prompted, log in and verify the portal home page is visible.

Another problem with using alias names lies in the proper resolution of addresses. Hard-coded addresses that reference internal resources can become unavailable when accessed externally through the alias name. SPS helps somewhat in this regard by providing a place for you to list alias names that are in use. When you list alias names for SharePoint, it will use the alias with search results to ensure that the address links are always valid.

Here is what to do to list the alias name with SharePoint Services:

1. Log in to SPSPortal as a portal administrator.

2. Select Start ➤ All Programs ➤ SharePoint Portal Server ➤ SharePoint Central Administration.

3. On the SharePoint Portal Server Central Administration page, select Portal Site and Virtual Server Configuration ➤ Configure Alternate Portal Site URLs for Intranet, Extranet, and Custom Access.

4. On the "Configure alternate portal access settings" page, select Edit from the drop-down menu associated with the Default Web Site entry.

5. In the Intranet URL field, type http://sharepoint.sps.local.

6. Click OK.

Enabling Secure Sockets Layer (SSL)

Enabling SSL for your portal affords an extra level of security based on certificates and encryption. In order to enable SSL for your portal, you must have a certificate for the server. Once the certificate is available, you can install it on the server and enable SSL.

Installing Certificate Services

Server certificates can be purchased commercially from a trusted source such as VeriSign, or you can create your own using Microsoft Certificate Services. In this exercise, you will install and use Microsoft Certificate Services. Making your own certificates is fine for testing and limited production use, but if you are going to allow access to the portal to a wide audience, you should consider getting a certificate from a trusted provider.

To install Certificate Server, follow these steps:

1. Log in to SPSController as a domain administrator.

2. Select Start ➤ Control Panel ➤ Add or Remove Programs.

3. In the Add or Remove Programs dialog, click Add/Remove Windows Components.

4. In the Windows Components dialog, check the Certificate Services box.

5. Respond to the warning dialog by clicking Yes.

6. Uncheck the "Internet Explorer enhanced security configuration" box.

7. In the Windows Components dialog, click Next.

8. In the CA Type step, select Stand-Alone Root CA.

9. Click Next.

10. In the CA Identifying Information step, type **spscontroller** into the "Common name for this CA" text box.

11. Click Next.

12. In the Certificate Database Settings step, accept the default values and click Next.

13. Click Finish to complete the operation.

Creating the New Certificate

You begin creating a certificate by preparing a request using the virtual server that you want to secure. This server prepares a text file that may then be submitted to Certificate Services. In this case, you will create a request for SPSPortal:

1. Log in to SPSPortal as a local administrator.

2. Open Windows Explorer.

3. Create a new directory at `c:\certificates\spsportal`.

4. Select the `c:\certificates` directory, right-click it, and select Sharing and Security from the pop-up menu.

5. On the Sharing tab, select Share This Folder.

6. Click Permissions.

7. Grant everyone full control and click OK.

8. Click OK again.

9. Select Start ➤ Administrative Tools ➤ Internet Information Services (IIS) Manager.

10. Expand the SPSPortal node and open the Web Sites folder.

11. Right-click the Default Web Site node and select Properties from the pop-up menu.

12. On the Directory Security tab, click Server Certificate.

13. In the Web Server Certificate wizard, click Next.

14. In the Server Certificate step, select the Create a New Certificate option, and click Next.

15. In the Delayed or Immediate Request step, select the "Prepare the request now, but send it later" option, and click Next.

16. In the Name and Security Settings step, leave the values as they are and click Next.

17. In the Organization Information step, type your company name in the Organization field and your company unit in the Organizational Unit field.

18. Click Next.

19. In the Your Site's Common Name step, type **spsportal** in the Common Name field.

20. Click Next.

21. In the Geographical Information step, enter the appropriate information and click Next.

22. In the Certificate Request File Name step, click Browse.

23. In the Saves As dialog, navigate to the `c:\certificates\spsportal` directory and click Save.

24. In the Certificate Request File Name step, click Next.

25. In the Request File Summary step, click Next.

26. Click Finish to complete the operation.

Once the request is prepared, you may use it to create a new certificate. Certificate Services uses the text file created under `SPSPortal` to generate the certificate. The new certificate may then be installed on the portal server.

Here you will create the new server certificate:

1. Log in to `SPSController` as the domain administrator.

2. Open Internet Explorer and navigate to `spscontroller/certsrv/default.asp`.

3. Click the Request a Certificate link.

4. Click the Advanced Certificate Request link.

5. Click the link labeled "Submit a certificate request by using a base-64-encoded CMC or PKCS #10 file, or submit a renewal request by using a base-64-encoded PKCS #7 file".

6. Open the certificate text file in NotePad that you previously saved at `\\spsportal\certificates\spsportal`.

7. Copy the entire contents of the certificate file and paste them into the Saved Request.

8. Click Submit.

9. Select Start ➤ Administration Tools ➤ Certification Authority.

10. In the Certification Authority dialog, expand the tree and open the Pending Requests folder.

11. Locate the pending request, right-click it, and select All Tasks ➤ Issue from the pop-up menu.

12. Open Internet Explorer and navigate to `spscontroller/certsrv/default.asp`.

13. Click the "View the status of a pending certificate request" link.

14. Click the link for the pending certificate.

15. On the Certificate Issued page, click the Download Certificate link.

16. In the File Download dialog, click Save.

17. Save the file into the `\\spsportal\certificates\spsportal` directory.

18. On the Certificate Issued page, click the Download Certificate Chain link.

19. In the File Download dialog, click Save.

20. Save the file into the `\\spsportal\certificates\spsportal` directory.

Installing the New Certificate

Once the new certificate is created, then you can install it on the portal server. When using the Microsoft Certificate Services, you must install the certificate file with the `.p7b` extension. This file will establish the appropriate trusts to ensure that you can view the portal.

To install the new certificate, follow these steps:

1. Log in to `SPSPortal` as the local administrator.

2. Select Start ➤ Administrative Tools ➤ Internet Information Services (IIS) Manager.

3. Expand the SPSPortal node and open the Web Sites folder.

4. Right-click the Default Web Site node and select Properties from the pop-up menu.

5. On the Directory Security tab, click Server Certificate.

6. In the Web Server Certificate Wizard, click Next.

7. In the Pending Certificate Request step, select "Process the pending request and install the certificate."

8. Click Next.

9. In the Process a Pending Request step, click Browse.

10. In the Open dialog, navigate to the `c:\certificates\spsportal` directory and select the file with the `.cer` extension.

11. Click Open.

12. In the Process a Pending Request step, click Next.

13. In the SSL Port step, accept the default value and click Next.

14. In the Certificate Summary step, view the details and click Next.

15. Click Finish to complete the operation.

16. In the Default Web Site Properties dialog, click View Certificate.

17. In the Certificate dialog, verify that the certificate is valid by viewing the Certification Path tab.

18. Click OK.

19. In the Default Web Site Properties dialog, click Edit under the Secure Communications section.

20. In the Secure Communications dialog, check the Require Secure Channel box and click OK.

21. In the Default Web Site Properties dialog, click OK.

22. When the Inheritance Overrides dialog appears, click OK.

Testing Secure Access

Once the certificate is installed on the portal server, you are ready to utilize SSL. When users access the portal through SSL, they will initially see the certificate warning; you can subsequently install the certificate on their machine and trust your root authority. This will allow them to access the portal without acknowledging the certificate each time.

Here is what you need to do to test secure communications:

1. Log in to SPSClient as a portal end user.

2. Open Internet Explorer and navigate to https://sharepoint.sps.local.

3. When the Security Alert dialog appears, click View Certificate.

4. On the Certification Path tab, select the root certificate named spscontroller and click View Certificate.

5. In the Certificate dialog, click Install Certificate.

6. In the Certificate Import Wizard, click Next.

7. In the Certificate Store step, select to Automatically Select the Certificate Store Based on the Type of Certificate and click Next.

8. Click Finish to complete the operation.

9. In the Root Certificate Store dialog, click Yes.

10. In the Certificate dialog, click OK.

11. In the other Certificate dialog, click OK.

12. In the Security Alert dialog, click Yes.

CHAPTER 11

Office Solution
Accelerators

THE LARGER TREND AWAY FROM PRODUCT FEATURES and benefits and toward complete solutions in the IT industry has been under way for several years, but it is really just taking hold at Microsoft. Previously, Microsoft was focused solely on license revenue and was driven by the prospect of selling yet another copy of Office. At this point, however, customers are right to ask why they need another version of Office when the current product is already reasonably mature. Microsoft's answer is to make the new version of Office part of a total solution and not just a product.

The Microsoft Office Solution Accelerators are frameworks for building specific solutions designed to showcase the value of the Microsoft Office System, and are targeted at solution developers and independent software vendors (ISV). The accelerators use many of the products and technologies I have presented—from Smart Documents to web parts. They are distributed as free downloads available from `www.microsoft.com/office/solutions/accelerators/default.mspx` and come with a reasonable set of guides and manuals to get started. Not all of the accelerators are available as of this writing. Microsoft is posting the accelerators as they are completed and will eventually produce all of the following:

- Office Solution Accelerator for Recruiting

- Office Solution Accelerator for Proposals

- Office Solution Accelerator for Six Sigma

- Office Solution Accelerator for Sarbanes-Oxley

- Office Solution Accelerator for Extensible Business Reporting Language

- Office Solution Accelerator for Business Scorecards

- Office Solution Accelerator for Excel Reporting

The first two accelerators completed are for recruiting and proposal writing. These accelerators are intended to streamline the recruiting and proposal writing processes within any organization, but they are not meant to be deployed without customization. In fact, most organizations will probably want to use the accelerators only as a starting point for their own solution.

In this chapter, we will examine the proposal and recruiting accelerators in detail. We will look at not only the technology upon which they are founded, but also the processes they embody. Finally, we will discuss how to customize the solutions for your own organization.

The Microsoft Office System Accelerator for Proposals

The proposal accelerator is a generalized solution designed so that you can use it horizontally across many different industries. Essentially, any organization that must prepare proposals, scopes of work, or detailed written plans can use the proposal accelerator. It is perhaps the most generic of all solutions because it works for any team that must prepare a document.

The first challenge any team faces when preparing a proposal is locating the document templates and company boilerplate materials that go into every document. In most organizations, these elements are kept in various file shares with cryptic names or mapped drives. Consequently, they are difficult to find. Most of the time, teams simply locate the person responsible for the documents and ask that person to forward them by e-mail. In other cases, individuals copy templates to their local machines and use them again and again only to discover that the actual company template changed long ago.

The proposal accelerator attempts to solve this problem by providing the centralized Content Library in the form of a SharePoint Services document library. This centralized library is integrated into the accelerator to ensure that only the most recent templates and boilerplate information is used. The Content Library is available to all proposal writers using the solution.

The next major challenge is to coordinate the work of several people and incorporate it into the final document. In most organizations, such coordination is handled in an ad-hoc way using e-mail notification. For example, if a proposal writer needs an estimate of effort from an engineer, they send an e-mail requesting the estimate. In some cases, the engineer may receive the proposal document as an attachment, but most likely they simply respond with the information in an e-mail. The proposal writer must then lift the content out of the e-mail and paste it into the document.

For small documents, this method may work fine, but problems arise when several people become involved in the proposal process. Some people have a copy of the proposal, others send e-mails with information, and still others might send spreadsheets. It becomes nearly impossible for the efforts to be coordinated and the results to be tracked.

The proposal accelerator helps with this problem by allowing a proposal writer to assign sections of the proposal to various team members and associate tasks with that assignment. The writer can literally assign responsibility directly from a section of the document in Microsoft Word. That assignment is tracked as part of a document workspace and is associated with the document through an XML schema.

Another challenge facing teams is locating documents that were successful proposals in the past. Quite often, proposal writers will ask others for a copy of a successful proposal. In many cases, these documents cannot be found. Because proposal writers have to manage the writing process alone, they typically keep the proposal on their personal computer. More often than not, this document is never moved to a searchable centralized document store.

The proposal accelerator solves this problem by managing all proposals from a central location. When the proposal is finished, it is stored in a document library that is searchable by future teams. Furthermore, the central management of proposals allows management to ensure a level of consistent quality across all proposals. At any time, a manager may look into the progress of a team and look across the organization to evaluate uniformity.

The Proposal Process

The proposal accelerator is designed to implement a simple business process that creates a new site with a new proposal document. The document can then be opened directly from the web site, and the author can immediately begin assigning tasks to the proposal team. Team members subsequently edit the document to complete their tasks.

Creating a new site for a proposal is accomplished from the Proposals Home page. From this page, users will see a link to the Proposal Library. Clicking this link displays a list of all individual proposal sites. The user may create a new proposal site by clicking the Create Proposal Site link. When creating the site, the user is asked to supply some basic information such as the site name and location, and then the site is created. Figure 11-1 shows a new proposal site.

When the new proposal site is created, a template proposal document is also created. The template proposal document is a Smart Document placed in the document library associated with the site. This document can then be opened in Microsoft Word for editing using the drop-down menu associated with the document.

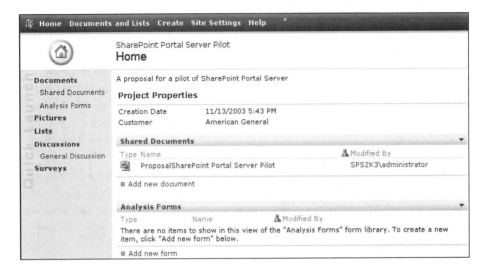

Figure 11-1. A new proposal site

When the document opens in Microsoft Word, the task pane for the Smart Document appears with the tools necessary to assign tasks to team members. The proposal author simply highlights the section to assign and clicks the "Assign a new section" link in the task pane. This action opens a dialog where the author can select the section name and team member to assign. Figure 11-2 shows the assignment dialog in Microsoft Word.

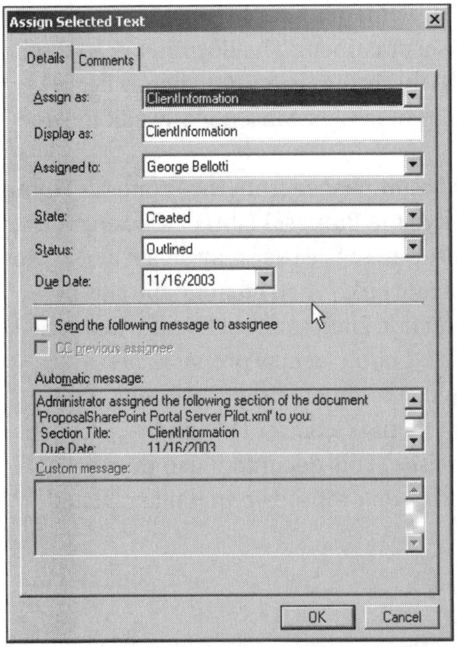

Figure 11-2. Assigning sections to team members

In addition to assigning sections, the task pane also allows the author to search the Content Library for boilerplate information to include in the proposal. The author simply clicks the Library link in the task pane and types a keyword for the search. The search results return documents in the Content Library that match the keyword. The author may then preview the resulting documents and paste the desired text directly into the proposal. Figure 11-3 shows the task pane with results from a Content Library search.

Figure 11-3. Searching the Content Library

Solution Architecture

Figure 11-4 shows a diagram of the underlying architecture upon which the proposal accelerator is based. The client-side components consist of a Smart Document that forms the foundation of the proposal. When loaded, the Smart Document brings along an XML expansion pack that ties the proposal into a web service. The web service is the backbone of the server-side solution together with SharePoint Services and a Metadata database.

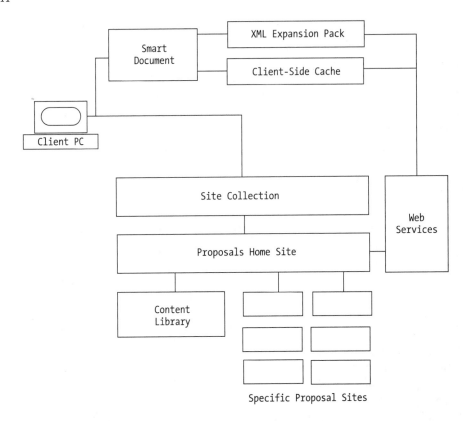

Figure 11-4. The accelerator architecture

SharePoint Services Components

The SharePoint Services components of the proposal accelerator are composed of three site templates. These templates allow you to create a site collection for proposals, a site for each individual proposal, and the Content Library to hold all of the templates and boilerplate information.

All proposal sites are created under a single top-level site. Within this site collection, you create a home page for proposals. This page acts as the starting point for any team that needs to create a proposal. The Proposals Home site is created using a template from the accelerator installation, and consists of little more than some instructions and a link to the Proposal Library.

The Proposal Library is also created from a template associated with the accelerator. It is a modified site creation page, which lists all of the individual proposal sites that exist in the collection. From this list, a user may create a new site for a specific proposal. The Proposal Library also acts as a very simple tool to manage the overall proposal process within an organization. Managers can, for example, filter the view based on any field defined in the list.

When a new individual proposal site is created, the accelerator builds the site based on another template. This template creates a new site with a Smart Document already available in the document library. The Smart Document is the template for the new proposal and is already associated with an XML expansion pack. Assuming the client-side installation is complete, the proposal process can begin when the template is opened in Microsoft Word.

The last site created for the accelerator is the Content Library. The Content Library is designed to hold all of the templates, boilerplate, and other data that may be important to proposal creation. Through the use of the Proposals Web Service, the Content Library is searchable directly from the task pane of Microsoft Word.

The Metadata Database

The Metadata database is a SQL Server database that keeps configuration information for the accelerator. You can access the database directly using SQL Server client tools, but there is very little you would ever want to do with this data. Be careful not to change any of the data should you choose to examine it.

The Proposals Web Service

The accelerator ships with a web service that facilitates the search and retrieval of information from SharePoint Services necessary to work within the document sections of the proposal. Unfortunately, almost no documentation on the web service ships with the accelerator. Furthermore, the web methods are not initially exposed through Web Service Description Language (WSDL), and you cannot set a reference to the web service in Visual Studio. In order to solve this problem, you must modify the web.config file associated with the web service to allow WSDL to be automatically generated.

To modify the web.config file, follow these steps:

1. Log in to SPSPortal as a local administrator.

2. Open the file C:\Program Files\Microsoft Solutions\Information Worker\Proposals\MSProposals\web.config in Visual Studio.

3. Remove the following code from the file:

```
<webServices>
    <protocols>
        <remove name="Documentation"/>
        <!- This removes WSDL and help from being autogenerated ->
```

```
        </protocols>
    </webServices>
```

4. Save and close the file.

5. Select Start ➤ Administrative Tools ➤ Internet Information Services (IIS) Manager.

6. In the IIS Manager dialog, right-click the SPSPortal node and select All Tasks ➤ Restart IIS.

7. In the Start/Stop/Restart dialog, click OK.

Once the `web.config` file is modified, you can return the WSDL and set references to the web service. You can examine the members of the web service directly from a browser by navigating to the URL `http://spsportal:6002/MSProposals.asmx`. Table 11-1 lists the web service members and a brief description of each.

Table 11-1. Proposals Web Service Members

WEB METHOD	DESCRIPTION
SearchForSections	Searches Content Library for documentation that matches the given set of search properties.
Publish	Publishes files to a SharePoint site.
SendWmiEvent	Sends notifications to WMI. Used when section changes occur in the document.
SendNotificationEmail	Sends notifications via e-mail. Used when section ownership changes in the document.
GetUsers	Gets the list of users (including users from cross groups) for the site.
GetFilesProperties	Retrieves one or more file properties from a SharePoint site.
GetSolutionConfiguration	Gets the configuration information that corresponds to the config file for a particular solution namespace (e.g., `microsoft.com/Solutions/InformationWorker/Proposals/`)
GetLibraries	Gets all SharePoint document libraries from the SharePoint server.

The Smart Document

The client side of the application consists primarily of a Smart Document that is associated with an XML schema and a task assignment utility. Using the associated XML schema, you can assign sections of the proposal to various team members directly from Microsoft Word. Users receive an e-mail notifying them that they have been assigned a section of the document to complete. A link to the document is included in the e-mail.

Customizing the Accelerator

Although you can perform some limited customization of the client installation, such as changing the logo associated with the solution, most of your customization efforts will be directed toward items on the server. When you first install the solution, it has a proposal template, but the template is blank. Additionally, the XML schema for the Smart Document has predefined sections that are unlikely to be immediately useful to your organization. Therefore, you will want to change these items as a first order of business.

The proposal template used by the solution can be located from the Proposals Home site. Clicking the Documents and List link on the home page will show the three document libraries used by the accelerator when creating new sites. Table 11-2 lists the available document libraries and provides a brief description.

Table 11-2. The Proposal Accelerator Libraries

LIBRARY NAME	DESCRIPTION
Help	A library containing the Help documents displayed in the solution
Manifests	A library containing the solution manifest and Smart Document schema
Templates	A library containing the proposal template for the solution

The simplest way to customize the template associated with the solution is to open it in Microsoft Word for editing. Once you open it in Word, you can edit the document or copy the contents of your organization's proposal template directly into the document. Then simply save the template back into the Templates document library.

After the template is customized, you will need to edit the Smart Document schema to reflect the document sections in your new proposal template. The schema is located in the Manifests document library, but the best way to edit it is to edit the file that was used for installation and then upload it again into the Manifests library.

The schema file can be found on the client at C:\Program Files\Microsoft Solutions\Information Worker\Proposals\ProposalsSchema.xsd. You can open this file directly in Visual Studio to edit the sections. Several default document elements are listed under a single General Section. Listing 11-1 shows a truncated example of how a section and its attributes are defined in the file.

Listing 11-1. Defining a Document Section and Attributes

```
<xsd:complexType name="GeneralSection" mixed="true">
    <xsd:attributeGroup ref="SectionAttributeGroup" />
</xsd:complexType>

<xsd:attributeGroup name="SectionAttributeGroup">
    <xsd:attribute name="Title" type="xsd:string" use="optional" />
    <xsd:attribute name="ID" type="xsd:string" use="required" />
    <xsd:attribute name="CreatedBy" type="xsd:string" use="optional" />
    <xsd:attribute name="DateCreated" type="xsd:long" use="optional" />
    <xsd:attribute name="ModifiedBy" type="xsd:string" use="optional" />
</xsd:attributeGroup>
```

CAUTION *The attributes defined in the schema file should never be modified. The proposal accelerator expects these attributes to be present and can fail if they are deleted or changed.*

Underneath each section, you can define document elements that may be assigned to team members. These are defined using a simple single-line element. The element is then tied back to the section. The following code shows a truncated example of how the document elements are defined in the schema.

```
<xsd:element name="LegalNotice" type="GeneralSection" />
<xsd:element name="TableOfContents" type="GeneralSection" />
<xsd:element name="Overview" type="GeneralSection" />
```

The Microsoft Office System Accelerator for Recruiting

The recruiting accelerator is a solution designed for larger organizations with permanent human resources staff engaged in regular recruitment cycles. The accelerator is useful for scheduling interviewers and collecting feedback, but it is formal and requires adherence to a rather strict process. For this reason, smaller organizations may find it too stodgy to implement. For organizations that do engage in significant recruiting, however, the solution does have value. It is these larger organizations where most of the recruiting challenges are found.

Once applicants have been identified, an organization faces significant challenges when guiding individuals through the recruiting process. Criteria must be developed against which to judge candidates. Internal resources must be scheduled to interview the applicants for various competencies, and their feedback must be collected so a hiring decision can be made.

The recruiting accelerator attempts to solve these problems by creating a centralized site where all resources are coordinated and feedback is collected.

The Recruiting Process

The accelerator provides a SharePoint Services team site as a home for the recruiting process. The site is designed to recognize the role that an individual plays in the recruiting process. The web parts display available job openings, candidates currently interviewing for the positions, and interview feedback. Figure 11-5 shows a portion of a typical recruiting site.

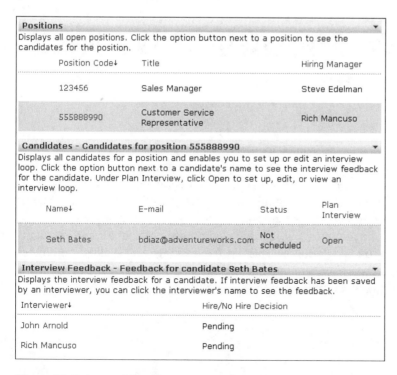

Figure 11-5. A recruiting site

From the recruiting site, the hiring manager selects positions and reviews candidates. A link is associated with each candidate that allows the hiring manager to plan the interview process. The form allows the hiring manager to set up the competency areas that will be investigated during the interview process and schedule company personnel to perform interviews. Figure 11-6 shows part of the InfoPath form for selecting competencies.

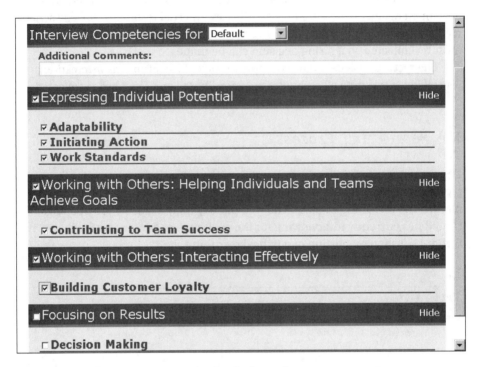

Figure 11-6. Selecting competencies for the interview process

Personnel who are scheduled to interview the candidates receive a meeting request generated by the accelerator. The meeting request contains a link back to an InfoPath form for providing feedback and evaluating the candidates against the competency areas. When all of this information is collected, interviewers may make hiring recommendations that can be viewed at the recruiting site.

Along with the recruiting site, the accelerator also provides a somewhat separate solution for tracking resumes. This resume tracking facility allows candidates to utilize a web service and an InfoPath form to submit resumes to an organization. These resumes can subsequently be made available to interviewers.

Solution Architecture

The recruiting accelerator is built upon a foundation of InfoPath forms, web parts, web services, and two SQL databases. The client uses the InfoPath and the web parts to interact with the recruiting accelerator. The web services are responsible for all the data manipulation behind the scenes. Figure 11-7 shows a conceptual drawing of the accelerator architecture.

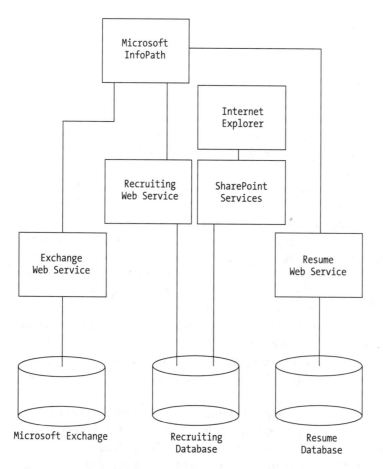

Figure 11-7. The accelerator architecture

Data Stores

The recruiting accelerator consists of three data stores. Two of these stores are SQL Server databases—named Recruiting and Resume —and one is the Exchange 2003 store. The Recruiting database is the store for information regarding open positions, scheduled interviewers, and interview feedback. The accelerator uses Exchange 2003 to retrieve free/busy information and send meeting requests to interviewers.

Web Services

The recruiting process is broken down into four main stages: resume submission, selecting competencies, scheduling interviewers, and receiving feedback. The recruiting accelerator consists of four web services that facilitate all aspects of the resume submission and interview process. In each case, you must properly customize and configure the web service to successfully utilize the recruiting accelerator.

Resume submission is handled by the web service Submit.asmx, which is designed to submit resumes to the back-end data store. The web service that ships with the recruiting accelerator is sophisticated, but unsupported. The documentation on the service is poor. Furthermore, it uses special web service extensions and is configured primarily to support the Microsoft demonstration for which it was originally created. As a result, you are most likely going to create your own web service specifically designed to meet your needs. Later in the chapter, you will create a simple web service to fill this need.

Competency management is handled by a web service that can download standard competencies and make them available for the interview process. The web service that ships with the accelerator provides some default functionality, but it must be customized for your organization to receive the correct competencies.

Interview scheduling is accomplished through a web service that works with Exchange 2003. Free/busy information is retrieved for selected interviewers and the hiring manager creates a schedule based on this information. When the schedule is created, the hiring manager can send out meeting invitations using the web service.

InfoPath Forms

InfoPath forms are used throughout the accelerator solution as front ends to the web services. When candidates create a resume, they do so using an InfoPath form. The form is then submitted and stored in the Resume database. Similarly, when hiring managers plan the interview process, they use an InfoPath form to set up competencies and schedule interviewers. Interviewers use an InfoPath form to provide feedback on the candidate.

Customizing the Accelerator

As I have pointed out already, the recruiting accelerator must be customized to work correctly in your environment. In fact, the installation, customization, and configuration of this accelerator is not trivial. Nearly every aspect of the solution must be customized and configured by hand. You can easily imagine attending a weeklong training class focusing on customization and configuration—although no such class exists as of this writing.

Exercise 11-1: The Accelerator for Proposals

The Microsoft Office Solution Accelerator for Proposals is intended to deploy a foundation for teams creating proposal documents with the Microsoft Office System. In general, all of the accelerators that Microsoft produces must be customized for an organization before they are truly useful. In this exercise, you will install, customize, and use the proposal accelerator with your portal.

Prerequisites

Before beginning this exercise, you should download the installation files for the accelerator from www.microsoft.com/office/solutions/accelerators/default.mspx. You must also download the installation files for the XML Content Filter from www.microsoft.com/sharepoint/server/techinfo/reskit/xml_filter.asp. Copy the installation files to a directory and extract them. All of the installation steps in this exercise assume you have extracted the files. Once the packages are unpacked, you will find the following key items:

Microsoft.Solutions.InformationWorker.Proposals.Server.msi: An installation package for elements that belong on the SharePoint Services servers.

Microsoft.Solutions.InformationWorker.Proposals.Client.msi: An installation package for elements that belong on each client machine.

Proposals_Overview_Guide.doc: An overview of the accelerator.

Proposals_Build_Test_Guide.doc: A document outlining the accelerator installation process.

Proposals_Planning_and_Architecture_Guide.doc: A document to use for planning your rollout of the accelerator to an organization.

Proposals_Customization_Guide.doc: A document to assist in customizing the accelerator.

XMLFilter.dll: The XML Content Filter component.

Installing the Accelerator

The proposal accelerator ships with generalized installation instructions. The installation in this exercise has been adapted to work with the test configuration used throughout this book. Initially, you will install the XML Content Filter. Then you will perform the server-side setup followed by the client-side setup.

Installing the XML Content Filter

The XML Content filter is required for the proposal accelerator to function correctly, but it does not ship as part of the accelerator. The XML Content Filter allows the search and indexing service to crawl documents with an `.xml` extension. This is important to the solution because the proposal template is an XML document.

To install the XML Content Filter, here is what you need to do:

1. Log in to SPSPortal as a local administrator.

2. Open Windows Explorer and copy the file XMLFilter.dll into the directory c:\windows\system32.

3. Select Start ➤ All Programs ➤ Accessories ➤ Command Prompt.

4. In the Command Prompt window, change to the directory where the XMLFilter.dll file is installed by typing the following:

    ```
    cd c:\windows\system32
    ```

5. Register the dynamic-link library by typing the following into the Command Prompt window:

    ```
    regsvr32 xmlfilter.dll
    ```

6. Select Start ➤ Administrative Tools ➤ Services.

7. In the Services dialog, right-click the Microsoft Search service and select Restart from the pop-up menu.

Setting Up the Server

Once the XML Content Filter is installed, you may perform the general setup of the server. The server setup consists primarily of running an MSI file that executes a setup wizard. The setup is fairly straightforward, but you should pay special attention to the Content Site URL entry to ensure that the setup routine understands correctly where you intend to set up the Content Library for the solution. You must provide this URL before the library is actually set up.

To set up the server, follow these steps:

1. Log in to SPSPortal as a local administrator.

2. Select Start ➤ Run.

3. In the Run dialog, click Browse.

4. Select the file Microsoft.Solutions.Informationworker.Proposals. Server.msi and click Open.

5. In the Run dialog, click OK.

6. In the Microsoft Office Solution Accelerator for Proposals wizard, click Next.

7. In the License Agreement step, accept the license agreement and click Next.

8. In the Select Installation Folder step, accept the default settings and click Next.

9. In the "Microsoft Proposals web service location" step, change the Content Site URL to **http://SPSPortal/sites/Sales/ProposalsHome/ ContentLibrary** and click Next.

10. Click Install to begin the installation.

11. Select Start ➤ Administrative Tools ➤ Internet Information Services (IIS) Manager.

12. In the IIS Manager dialog, expand the SPSPortal node.

13. Right-click the Application Pools folder and select New ➤ Application Pool.

14. In the Add New Application Pool dialog, name the new pool **PropAccPool**.

15. Select to use MSSharePointPortalAppPool as a template.

16. Click OK.

17. Open the Web Sites folder.

18. Right-click the Microsoft Office Solution Accelerator for Proposals virtual directory and select Properties from the pop-up menu.

19. On the Home Directory tab, select PropAccPool from the drop-down list of application pools.

20. Click OK.

21. Right-click the SPSPortal node and select All Tasks ➤ Restart IIS from the pop-up menu.

22. In the Stop/Start/Restart menu, click OK.

Setting Up the Proposal Site

After the general server setup is complete, you must manually construct sites in SharePoint Portal Server (SPS). This requires you to create a new site collection—or identify an existing one—under which you will create the Proposals Home page. You must also define special cross-site groups for the solution and add members. Finally, you must create the Content Library site at the location you specified during the server setup.

Creating the Sales Site Collection

The proposal accelerator relies on several templates to create the sites necessary to support the designed workflow. Templates such as these can be added to SPS, but only under a site collection. If you want to make templates available at the portal level so that they can be used to create new sites, you must use the STSADM tool. In this exercise, you will keep it simple and create a site collection under which you can install the required templates.

To create the site collection, follow these steps:

1. Log in to SPSPortal as a member of the Administrator site group.

2. Open Internet Explorer and browse to the portal home page.

3. On the portal home page, click the Sites link.

4. On the Sites page, click the Create Site link under the Actions list.

5. On the New SharePoint Site page, name the new site **Sales**.

6. Ensure the web site address for the new site is http://SPSPortal/ sites/Sales.

7. Click OK.

8. On the Add Link to Site page, click OK.

9. On the Template Selection page, select Blank Site from the list.

10. Click OK.

Adding New Site Members

Once the top-level site is created, you should immediately add members to it. When you later create the proposal sites beneath this collection, you will inherit permissions from the site collection. Therefore, you should add users to the site collection who are eligible to contribute to the proposal. Generally, you should add users to the site collection as members of the Contributor site group at a minimum so that they can participate in the process.

To add new members, follow these steps:

1. Navigate to the Sales site collection.

2. From the site home page, click the Site Settings link.

3. On the Site Settings page, select Administration ➤ Manage Users.

4. On the Manage Users page, click the Add Members link.

5. Type the user names of the people to add to the site collection.

6. Assign them to appropriate groups.

7. Click Next.

8. Click Finish.

Creating the New Cross-Site Groups

The proposal accelerator uses a specific set of cross-site groups to track roles within the proposal process. Using these cross-site groups allows you to assign more granular permissions to the group of people who have access to the site collection.

Complete these steps to add new cross-site groups:

1. Navigate to the Sales site collection.

2. From the site home page, click the Site Settings link.

3. On the Site Settings page, select Administration ➤ Go to Site Administration.

4. On the Top-Level Site Administration page, select Users and Permissions ➤ Manage Cross-Site Groups.

5. On the My Cross-Site Groups page, click the New Cross-Site Group link.

6. On the New Cross-Site Group page, name the new group **Authors** and give it the description "**The group that provides content for the proposal**."

7. Click Create.

8. On the Members page, click the Add Members link.

9. Add members to the site group.

10. On the My Cross-Site Groups page, click the New Cross-Site Group link.

11. On the New Cross-Site Group page, name the new group **Coordinators** and give it the description "**The group that manages the content for the proposal.**"

12. Click Create.

13. On the Members page, click the Add Members link.

14. Add members to the site group.

Setting Up Site Templates

Once the site collection is created, you may install the required templates beneath the collection. When you run the server-side setup, the proposal accelerator extracts three templates that must be added to the site collection. These templates are then used to create the Proposals Home, each individual proposal site, and the Content Library.

To set up site templates, follow these steps:

1. Navigate to the Sales site collection.

2. From the site home page, click the Site Settings link.

3. On the Site Settings page, select Administration ➤ Go to Site Administration.

4. On the Top-Level Site Administration page, select Site Collection Galleries ➤ Manage Site Template Gallery.

5. On the Site Template Gallery Page, click the Upload Template link.

6. On the Upload Template page, click the Upload Multiple Files link.

7. Navigate to `C:\Program Files\Microsoft Solutions\Information Worker\Proposals\SharePoint`.

8. Select to upload the three template files found in this directory.

9. Click the Save and Close link.

Creating the Proposal Home Site

Once the templates are uploaded, they can be used to create the required sites. The Proposals Home will be created directly underneath the site collection. All other sites will be created beneath the Proposals Home site. You should pay close attention to the location of sites and ensure that they follow the URL hierarchy entered during the server-side setup.

Follow this procedure to create the home site:

1. Navigate to the Sales site collection home page.

2. From the home page, click the Create link.

3. On the Create page, select Web Pages ➤ Sites and Workspaces.

4. On the New SharePoint Site page, name the new site **Proposals Home**.

5. Ensure the URL for new site is `http://SPSPortal/Sites/Sales/ProposalsHome`.

6. Click Create.

7. From the Template list, select Microsoft Proposals Home Portal.

8. Click OK.

Creating the Content Library

The Content Library is where all boilerplate information is stored. Teams may also use the Content Library to store reusable blocks of text for multiple proposals. The library can also be searched directly from Microsoft Word in the task pane.

Here is what to do to create the Content Library:

1. Navigate to the Proposals Home site.

2. From the home page, click the Create link.

3. On the Create page, select Web Pages ➤ Sites and Workspaces.

4. On the New SharePoint Site page, name the new site **Content Library**.

5. Ensure the URL for new site is `http://SPSPortal/Sites/Sales/ProposalsHome/ContentLibrary`.

6. Click Create.

7. From the Template list, select Microsoft Proposals Content Library.

8. Click OK.

Setting Up the Client

After the server is completely configured, you must set up the client. Each client that will use the proposal accelerator must have the installation files run on it. The best way to accomplish this task is to create a group policy in Active Directory that will make the software available to users through the Add or Remove Programs dialog.

Here are the steps to follow to create a group policy:

1. Log in to `SPSController` as the domain administrator.

2. Open Windows Explorer and create a new directory named `C:\SoftwareDistribution`.

3. Right-click the new folder and select Properties from the pop-up menu.

4. On the Sharing tab, select the option Share This Folder.

5. Click OK.

6. Copy the file `Microsoft.Solutions.Informationworker.Proposals.Client.msi` into the directory `C:\SoftwareDistribution`.

7. Select Start ➤ Administrative Tools ➤ Active Directory Users and Computers.

8. In the Active Directory Users and Computers dialog, right-click the `sps.local` node and select Properties from the pop-up menu.

9. On the Group Policy tab, click New.

10. Rename the new policy object **Proposal Accelerator Client**.

11. Select the Proposal Accelerator Client object and click Edit.

12. In the Group Policy Object Editor dialog, expand the tree to locate the Proposal Accelerator Client ➤ User Configuration ➤ Software Settings ➤ Software Installation Node.

13. Right-click the Software Installation node and select Properties from the pop-up menu.

14. On the General tab, type **\\SPSController\SoftwareDistribution**.

15. Click OK.

16. Right-click the Software Installation node and select New ➤ Package from the pop-up menu.

17. In the Open dialog, specify the path to the client install using Universal Naming Convention (UNC) convention by typing `\\SPSController\SoftwareDistribution\Microsoft.Solutions.Informationworker.Proposals.Client.msi`.

18. Click Open.

19. In the Deploy Software dialog, select the Published option and click OK.

 CAUTION   *The client installation package is dependent upon the Microsoft .NET Framework version 1.1 and Microsoft Word .NET programmability support. Be sure to upgrade* `SPSClient` *or the proposal accelerator installation package will fail.*

Once the group policy is created, the client software will be available from the Add or Remove Programs dialog on `SPSClient`. When applications are published through a group policy, each individual user must choose whether or not to install the package.

To install the client software, you will need to take these steps:

1. Log in to SPSClient as a local administrator.

2. Select Start ➤ Control Panel.

3. In the Control Panel, double-click Add or Remove Programs.

4. In the Add or Remove Programs dialog, click Add New Programs.

5. Select the "Microsoft Office Solution Accelerator for Proposals—Client v1,0" item and click Add.

6. In the Microsoft Office Solution Accelerator for Proposals wizard, click Next.

7. In the License Agreement step, accept the license agreement and click Next.

8. In the Select Installation Folder step, accept the default settings and click Next.

9. In the "Microsoft proposals web service location" step, change the location to http://spsportal:6002/MSProposals.asmx and click Next.

10. Click Install to begin installation.

Customizing the Accelerator

Before the accelerator can be used, you must customize the proposal template, modify the Smart Document schema, and load some items into the Content Library. In this exercise, you will use standard Microsoft Word templates to create your proposal template. Then you will modify the schema to match the new template.

To modify the proposal template, follow these steps:

1. Log in to SPSClient as a member of the Administrator site group for the Proposals Home site.

2. Navigate to the Proposals Home page.

3. On the home page, click the Documents and Lists link.

4. On the Documents and List page, select Document Libraries ➤ Templates.

5. On the Templates page, select Edit in Microsoft Office Word from the drop-down menu associated with the proposal template.

NOTE *If you receive an error indicating that the XML expansion pack for the Smart Document cannot be found, then the client installation was not performed correctly. Check your group policy or install the client software manually before proceeding.*

---

6. When the proposal template is open in Microsoft Word, select File ➤ New from the menu.

7. In the New Document pane, select Templates ➤ On My Computer.

8. On the Reports tab, select the Professional Report template.

9. Click OK.

10. When the new document opens, select Edit ➤ Select All and then select Edit ➤ Copy from the menu.

11. Switch to the proposal template and select Edit ➤ Paste from the menu.

12. When you have pasted the report text into the proposal template, select File ➤ Save.

13. Close Microsoft Word.

Once the template is changed, you must modify the schema to reflect the changes. In the following procedure, you will modify the schema directly on the server and then upload the changes to the Manifests library.

1. Log in to SPSClient as the local administrator.

2. Open the file at C:\Program Files\Microsoft Solutions\Information Worker\Proposals\ProposalsSchema.xsd in Visual Studio for editing.

3. Remove several of the document elements from the schema so that your final schema appears as shown in Listing 11-2, which follows this procedure.

4. Save and close the file.

5. Navigate to the Proposals Home page in Internet Explorer.

6. From the home page, click the Documents and Lists link.

7. On the Documents and Lists page, select Document Libraries ➤ Manifests.

8. On the Manifests page, click the Upload Document link.

9. On the Upload Document page, click Browse.

10. In the Choose File dialog, navigate to `C:\Program Files\Microsoft Solutions\Information Worker\Proposals\ProposalsSchema.xsd`.

11. Click Open.

12. Click the Save and Close link.

 NOTE *Microsoft Word caches the Smart Document schema based on the* updateFrequency *element in the* Manifest.xml *file. If you open a proposal template and then subsequently edit the schema, the updates may not be available for a significant time.*

Listing 11-2. The Document Schema

```xml
<?xml version="1.0" encoding="utf-8" ?>
<xsd:schema xmlns:xsd="http://www.w3.org/2001/XMLSchema"
xmlns="http://microsoft.com/Solutions/InformationWorker/Proposals/"
targetNamespace="http://microsoft.com/Solutions/InformationWorker/Proposals/"
elementFormDefault="qualified" version="1.0">

<xsd:complexType name="GeneralSection" mixed="true">
    <xsd:attributeGroup ref="SectionAttributeGroup" />
```

```
    </xsd:complexType>

    <xsd:element name="Title" type="GeneralSection" />
    <xsd:element name="Customer" type="GeneralSection" />
    <xsd:element name="CompanyInformation" type="GeneralSection" />

    <xsd:attributeGroup name="SectionAttributeGroup">
        <xsd:attribute name="Title" type="xsd:string" use="optional" />
        <xsd:attribute name="ID" type="xsd:string" use="required" />
        <xsd:attribute name="CreatedBy" type="xsd:string" use="optional" />
        <xsd:attribute name="DateCreated" type="xsd:long" use="optional" />
        <xsd:attribute name="ModifiedBy" type="xsd:string" use="optional" />
        <xsd:attribute name="NotificationSentBy" type="xsd:string" use="optional" />
        <xsd:attribute name="DateModified" type="xsd:long" use="optional" />
        <xsd:attribute name="DueDate" type="xsd:long" use="optional" />
        <xsd:attribute name="CurrentOwner" type="xsd:string" use="optional" />
        <xsd:attribute name="CurrentOwnerEmail" type="xsd:string" use="optional" />
        <xsd:attribute name="OriginalOwner" type="xsd:string" use="optional" />
        <xsd:attribute name="OriginalOwnerEmail" type="xsd:string" use="optional" />
        <xsd:attribute name="NotificationCustomBody" type="xsd:string"
            use="optional" />
        <xsd:attribute name="NeedNotify" type="xsd:boolean" use="optional" />
        <xsd:attribute name="NotifyPreviousOwner" type="xsd:boolean"
            use="optional" />
        <xsd:attribute name="IsChangePublicationPending"
            type="xsd:boolean" use="optional" />
        <xsd:attribute name="DateNotified" type="xsd:long" use="optional" />
        <xsd:attribute name="DateWmiEventSent" type="xsd:long" use="optional" />
        <xsd:attribute name="Notes" type="xsd:string" use="optional" />
        <xsd:attribute name="Status" type="xsd:string" use="optional" />
        <xsd:attribute name="State" type="xsd:string" use="optional" />
    </xsd:attributeGroup>

</xsd:schema>
```

Using the Accelerator

Once you have finished the customization, you are ready to use the accelerator. Using the accelerator begins with creating a new proposal site. After the site is created, you can open the template proposal and assign tasks.

Follow these steps to create a new proposal:

1. Log in to SPSClient as a member of the Coordinators cross-site group associated with the proposals site collection.

2. Open Internet Explorer and navigate to the Proposals Home site.

3. From the home page, click the Proposal Library link.

4. On the Proposal Library page, click the link Create Proposal Site.

5. Name the site **Book Proposal** and give it a description.

6. Fill in an appropriate URL for the new site.

7. Type **New Moon Books** into the Customer field.

8. Click Create.

9. On the New SharePoint Site page, click the link to go to your new site.

10. On the Book Proposal home page, select Documents ➤ Shared Documents from the Quick Launch bar.

11. On the Shared Documents page, select to open the proposal document by selecting "Edit in Microsoft Office Word" from the drop-down menu.

12. When the proposal opens, highlight the document title Proposal and Marketing Plan.

13. In the task pane, click "Assign a new section link."

14. Select to assign the proposal title section to a team member.

Exercise 11-2: The Accelerator for Recruiting

The Microsoft Office Solution Accelerator for Recruiting deploys a solution to manage both resumes and interviews. The Resume Builder provides a set of tools for managing resumes, and the Interview Manager creates a central location for managing the interview process. The Resume Builder and Interview Manager both come with setup and customization documentation, but for this exercise, you will use your own version, which has been adapted to your particular environment.

Prerequisites

Before beginning this exercise, you should download the installation files for the accelerator from www.microsoft.com/office/solutions/accelerators/default.mspx. Both the Resume Builder and the Interview Manager ship as part of a single installation package. The installation files should be copied to a directory and extracted. All of the installation steps in this exercise assume you have extracted the files. Once the packages are unpacked, you will find the following key items:

> **Microsoft.Solutions.InformationWorker.Recruiting.msi:** The accelerator installation package.
>
> **InterviewManager_DeploymentGuide.doc:** A document with installation and customization instructions for the Interview Manager solution.
>
> **InterviewManager_PlanningGuide.doc:** A document to assist in the design and deployment planning of the Interview Manager solution.
>
> **ResumeBuilder_BuildandTestGuide.doc:** A document with installation and customization instructions for the Resume Builder solution.
>
> **ResumeBuilder_PlanningGuide.doc:** A document to assist in the design and deployment planning of the Resume Builder solution.

Installing the Accelerator

The recruiting accelerator ships with a set of generalized instructions designed to work under a variety of conditions. Quite often the instructions require some interpretation for a particular environment. In this exercise, the instructions have been modified to work with your configuration.

The Basic Installation

Both the Interview Manager and the Resume Builder solution are part of the same installation package. This single installation package must be run on the server where SharePoint Services is installed. Although this process is fairly simple, it represents just the beginning of the effort required to successfully install the accelerator.

To perform the basic installation, take these steps:

1. Log in to `SPSPortal` as a local administrator.

2. Select Start ➤ Run.

3. In the Run dialog, click Browse.

4. Select the `Microsoft.Solutions.InformationWorker.Recruiting.msi` file and click Open.

5. In the Run dialog, click OK.

6. In the Microsoft Office Solution Accelerator for Recruiting wizard, click Next.

7. In the License Agreement step, accept the license agreement and click Next.

8. In the Select Installation Folder step, accept the default settings and click Next.

9. Click Install to begin installation.

10. Open Windows Explorer and navigate to the folder `C:\Program Files\Microsoft Solutions\Information Worker\Recruiting\Shared Components`.

11. Drag the following assemblies into the Global Assembly Cache (GAC) located at `C:\Windows\Assembly`:

    - `Microsoft.ApplicationBlocks.ExceptionManagement.dll`

    - `Microsoft.ApplicationBlocks.ExceptionManagement.Interfaces.dll`

    - `Microsoft.Solutions.InformationWorker.Security.dll`

    - `Microsoft.Solutions.InformationWorker.Common.dll`

    - `Microsoft.Solutions.InformationWorker.SoapExceptions.dll`

    - `RecruitingCommon.dll`

Installing the Interview Manager Database

The Interview Manager uses a SQL Server database to keep track of open job positions, candidates, and interview assignments. The accelerator ships with a set of sample data that you can use in your exercise; however, you will need to modify this data because the employee data is specific to a Microsoft demonstration. You should take care when working with this data because many different errors can be caused by bad data not properly associated with portal users.

Here are the steps to follow to build the Recruiting database:

1. Log in to `SPSPortal` as a local administrator.

2. Select Start ➤ Run.

3. In the Run dialog, click Browse.

4. Locate the file `C:\Program Files\Microsoft Solutions\Information Worker\Recruiting\Interview Management\Database Components\Sample Database\BuildandFillDB.cmd` and click Open.

5. In the Run dialog, click OK.

6. When the batch program has finished running, select Start ➤ All Programs ➤ SharePoint Portal Server ➤ SharePoint Central Administration.

7. On the SharePoint Portal Server Central Administration page, select Server Configuration ➤ Configure Server Farm Account Settings.

8. On the "Configure server farm account settings" page, note the account listed in the Portal Site Application Pool Identity text box.

 NOTE *If you have configured your environment as described in this book, the above account should already have SQL Server access. The following steps assume a log-in for SQL Server exists for the above account. If the account does not have a SQL Server log-in, you must create one.*

---

9. Select Start ➤ All Programs ➤ Microsoft SQL Server ➤ Enterprise Manager.

10. In the SQL Server Enterprise Manager, select Console Root ➤ Microsoft SQL Servers ➤ SQL Server Group ➤ (local)(Windows NT) ➤ Security ➤ Logins.

11. Locate the account you identified earlier as the "Portal site application pool identity" from SharePoint Portal Server Central Administration.

12. Right-click the account and select Properties from the pop-up menu.

13. On the Database Access tab, locate the Recruiting database.

14. Ensure that the account has access to the Recruiting database with at least the Public role checked.

15. On the General tab, set the default database to Recruiting.

16. Click OK.

17. In the SQL Server Enterprise Manager, select Console Root ➤ Microsoft SQL Servers ➤ SQL Server Group ➤ (local)(Windows NT) ➤ Databases ➤ Recruiting ➤ Users.

18. Locate the account you identified earlier as the "Portal site application pool identity" from SharePoint Portal Server Central Administration.

19. Right-click the account and select Properties from the pop-up menu.

20. In the Database User Properties dialog, click Permissions.

21. On the Permissions tab, ensure that Exec permission is enabled for the following objects:

- add_CompetencyToJobDescription

- add_HiringManagerFavoriteInterviewer

- add_NewCompetency

- admin_AddCompetency

- admin_AddCompetencyScale

- admin_AddJobAssociationDetail

- admin_AddJobCategory

- admin_AddJobDescription

- delete_Competency

- find_Employee

- get_Competencies

- get_Competency

- get_CompetencyWeight

- get_CompetencyWeightTypes

- get_EmployeeIDFromEmail

- get_EmployeePositions

- get_EntityOwners

- get_FeedbackDetail

- get_FeedbackHeader

- get_HiringManagerFavoriteInterviewers

- get_InstanceID

- get_InterviewFeedback

- get_InterviewHeader

- get_InterviewInstanceCompetencies

- get_Interviewers

- get_InterviewersSummary

- get_JobCompetencies

- get_Jobs

- get_PositionCandidates

- remove_CompetencyFromJobDescription

- remove_CompetencySelectionFromJobDescription

- remove_HiringManagerFavoriteInterviewers

- update_Competency

- update_FeedbackDetail

- update_FeedbackHeader

- update_Interview

- update_InterviewInstanceCompetencySelection

- update_InterviewInstanceStatus

- update_InterviewStatus

- update_InterviewerInstance

- update_InterviewInstanceComplete

- update_JobCompetencySelection

Setting Up the User Information

Because the data contained in the Interview Manager database is particular to a Microsoft demonstration, you will have to edit it by hand to make it work in your environment. Be careful when editing to maintain database integrity. Do not add or remove rows from the database. Instead, just make changes to the existing records as described in the following procedure:

1. Select Start ➤ All Programs ➤ Microsoft SQL Server ➤ Enterprise Manager.

2. In the SQL Server Enterprise Manager, select Console Root ➤ Microsoft SQL Servers ➤ SQL Server Group ➤ (local)(Windows NT) ➤ Database ➤ Recruiting ➤ Tables.

3. Right-click the `Employee` table and select Open Table ➤ Return All Rows.

4. In the `Employee` table, modify the `AccountName` and `Email` fields to match accounts already defined on your system.

5. Right-click the `PersonName` table and select Open Table ➤ Return All Rows.

6. In the `PersonName` table, modify the names to match the records previously defined in the `Employee` table. Figure 11-8 shows an example configuration for both tables.

NOTE   *The* `PersonNameID` *field joins the* `Employee` *table to the* `PersonName` *table. Ensure your modified entries maintain the database integrity.*

PersonNameID	GivenName	PreferredGivenName	M	FamilyName	Far	Fa	LegalName	FormattedName
1	John	John		Arnold	0	<I	John Arnold	John Arnold
2	Scot	Scot		Hillier	0	<I	Scot Hillier	Scot Hillier
3	Steve	Steve		Edelman	0	<I	Steve Edelman	Steve Edelman
4	Robin	Robin		Williams	0	<I	Robin Williams	Robin Williams
5	Mark	Mark		Marotta	0	<I	Mark Marotta	Mark Marotta
6	Dave	Dave		Wallen	0	<I	Dave Wallen	Dave Wallen
7	Rich	Rich		Manucuso	0	<I	Rich Mancuso	Rich Mancuso
8	Tony	Tony		Smith	0	<I	Tony Smith	Tony Smith

Data in Table 'Employee' in 'Recruiting' on '(local)'

EmployeeCode	PersonNameID	AccountName	Email	Phone	OfficeLocation
1	1	sps\JohnArnold	JohnArnold@sps.loc	(425) 555-1111	1-1111
2	2	sps\ScotHillier	ScotHillier@sps.loca	(425) 555-2222	1-2222
3	3	sps\SteveEdelman	SteveEdelman@sps.	(425) 555-3333	1-3333
4	4	sps\RobinWilliams	RobinWilliams@sps.	(425) 555-4444	1-4444
5	5	sps\MarkMarotta	MarkMarotta@sps.lc	(425) 555-5555	1-5555
6	6	sps\DaveWallen	DaveWallen@sps.lo	(425) 555-6666	1-6666
7	7	sps\RichMancuso	RichMancuso@sps.l	(425) 555-7777	1-7777
8	8	sps\TonySmith	TonySmith@sps.loc	(425) 555-8888	1-8888

Figure 11-8. The Employee and PersonName tables

Installing the Resume Database

The Resume database provides a central store where all submitted resumes reside. Resumes are stored in XML format in a single field. Job candidates will use an InfoPath form to submit resumes to the database.

Here are the steps for creating the Resume database:

1. In the SQL Server Enterprise Manager, select Console Root ➤ Microsoft SQL Servers ➤ SQL Server Group ➤ (local)(Windows NT) ➤ Databases.

2. Right-click the Databases folder and select New ➤ Database from the pop-up menu.

3. In the Database Properties dialog, name the new database **Resume** and click OK.

4. Select Tools ➤ SQL Query Analyzer from the menu.

5. In the SQL Query Analyzer, select File ➤ Open.

6. In the Open Query File dialog, navigate to `C:\Program Files\Microsoft Solutions\Information Worker\Recruiting\Resume Builder\Database Components\Sample Database\resume.sql`.

7. Click Open.

8. Select Query ➤ Execute from the menu.

Configuring Web Services

Both the Interview Manager and the Resume Builder rely on web services to perform correctly. The Interview Manager uses web services extensively to manage the interview competencies, scheduling, and feedback. The Resume Builder uses a web service to facility the submittal of resumes. The following sections configure web services for both solutions.

Configuring the Interview Manager Web Services

Configuring the web services for the Interview Manager is not trivial. To successfully configure these services, you must create several new web sites and modify several configuration files. You should take extra care when performing these steps.

Creating a New Application Pool

The web services associated with the Interview Manager need access to the SQL Database for managing positions, candidates, and interviewers. Therefore, you need to create a new application pool for the web services running under an account that has database access permissions. In this exercise, you will base the new pool on the existing one running your SharePoint Services installation.

Here are the steps to follow to create the new application pool:

1. Log in to SPSPortal as a local administrator.

2. Select Start ➤ Administrative Tools ➤ Internet Information Server (IIS) Manager.

3. In the IIS Manager dialog, expand the SPSPortal node.

4. Right-click the Application Pools folder and select New ➤ Application Pool from the pop-up menu.

5. In the Add New Application Pool dialog, type **RecruitingPool**.

6. Select to base the new pool on the existing MSSharePointPortalAppPool pool.

7. Click OK.

Creating a New Web Site

The web services associated with the Interview Manager will all run from a new web site. In most cases, services like these will run separately from the SharePoint Services installation. Therefore, you must create a new site running under an unused port number.

1. Log in to SPSPortal as a local administrator.

2. Select Start ➤ Administrative Tools ➤ Internet Information Server (IIS) Manager.

3. In the IIS Manager dialog, expand the SPSPortal node.

4. Right-click the Web Sites folder and select New ➤ Web Site from the pop-up menu.

5. In the Web Site Creation wizard, click Next.

6. In the Web Site Description step, type **Recruiting** and click Next.

7. In the IP Address and Port Settings step, change the "TCP port this Web site should use" field to 81.

8. Click Next.

9. In the Web Site Home Directory step, click Browse.

10. In the Browse for Folder dialog, navigate to the directory `C:\Program Files\Microsoft Solutions\Information Worker\Recruiting\Interview Management\Server Components\Web Services`.

11. Click OK.

12. In the Web Site Home Directory step, uncheck the Allow Anonymous Access box.

13. Click Next.

14. In the Web Site Access Permissions step, accept the default values and click Next.

15. Click Finish to complete the operation.

16. In the IIS Manager dialog, right-click the new Recruiting web site node and select Properties from the pop-up menu.

17. On the Home Directory tab, select RecruitingPool from the Application Pool drop-down list.

Creating the Web Applications

The web services associated with the Interview Manager need to have some specific web site configurations in place to work correctly. Each of the services must first function as a separate application. Each of these separate applications must run in the pool you created earlier.

1. In the IIS Manager dialog, right-click the Competencies folder under the Recruiting web site and select Properties from the pop-up menu.

2. On the Directory tab, click Create.

3. Select RecruitingPool from the Application Pool drop-down list.

4. Click OK.

5. Repeat steps 1 through 4 for the following folders:

   - Interview_Data

   - Interview_Exchange

   - Interview_LoopData

Configuring the Interview_Data Application

The Interview_Data web application allows access to the primary user interface for managing interview information. This application requires some specific customizations to function correctly.

1. In the IIS Manager dialog, right-click the Interview_Data folder under the Recruiting web site and select Properties from the pop-up menu.

2. On the Directory tab, click Configuration.

3. In the Application Extensions list, select .aspx and click Edit.

4. In the Add/Edit Application Extension Mapping dialog, select the All Verbs option.

5. Click OK.

6. In the Application Configuration dialog, click OK.

7. In the Properties dialog, click the HTTP Headers tab.

8. In the Custom HTTP Headers section, click Add.

9. In the Add/Edit Custom HTTP Header dialog, type **MS-Author-Via** into the Custom Header Name field.

10. Type **DAV** into the Custom Header Value field. Figure 11-9 shows the completed dialog.

11. Click OK.

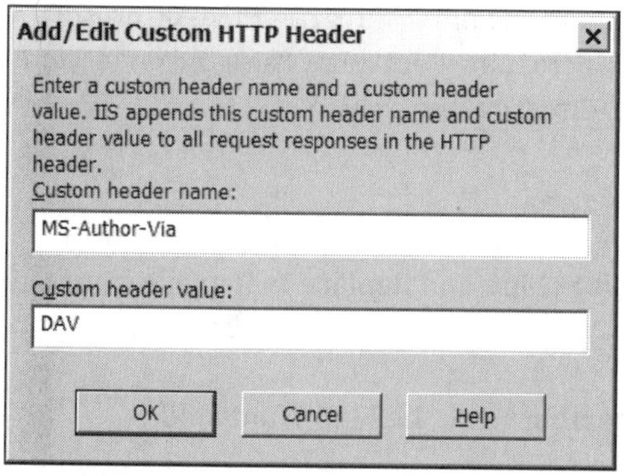

Figure 11-9. The Add/Edit Custom HTTP Header dialog

12. In the Custom HTTP Headers section, click Add.

13. In the Add/Edit Custom HTTP Header dialog, type **DAV** into the Custom Header Name field.

14. Type **1,2** into the Custom Header Value field.

15. Click OK.

16. In the Properties dialog, click OK.

17. In the IIS Manager dialog, open the Web Service Extensions folder.

18. Right-click the WebDAV Web service extension and select Prohibit from the pop-up menu.

Modifying the Configuration Files

All of the web services and applications associated with the Interview Manager solution have configuration files that must be modified. In most cases, it is simply a matter of replacing the default web server name with your particular web server. Make these changes carefully to ensure the solution functions correctly.

To modify the configuration files, follow these steps:

1. Select Start ➤ All Programs ➤ Microsoft Visual Studio .NET 2003 ➤ Microsoft Visual Studio .NET 2003.

2. In Visual Studio, select File ➤ Open ➤ File.

3. In the Open File dialog, navigate to the file `C:\Program Files\Microsoft Solutions\Information Worker\Recruiting\Interview Management\Server Components\Web Services\Interview_Data\Web.config`.

4. Click Open.

5. When the file opens, select Edit ➤ Find and Replace ➤ Replace from the menu.

6. In the Replace dialog, enter **localhost** into the Find What field.

7. Enter **SPSPortal:81** into the Replace With field.

8. Click Replace All.

9. When the replacements have been made, click Close.

10. Save and close the file.

11. In Visual Studio, select File ➤ Open ➤ File.

12. In the Open File dialog, navigate to the file `C:\Program Files\Microsoft Solutions\Information Worker\Recruiting\Interview Management\Server Components\Web Services\Interview_Exchange\Web.config`.

13. Click Open.

14. When the file opens, select Edit ➤ Find and Replace ➤ Replace from the menu.

15. In the Replace dialog, enter **Exchange_server_name** into the Find What field.

16. Enter **SPSController** into the Replace With field.

17. Click Replace All.

18. In the Replace dialog, enter **Domain_name_in_use** into the Find What field.

19. Enter **sps** into the Replace With field.

20. Click Replace All.

21. In the Replace dialog, enter [**ExchangeResourcesDirectory**] into the Find What field.

22. Enter `C:\Program Files\Microsoft Solutions\Information Worker\ Recruiting\Interview Management\Server Components\Web Services\ Interview_Exchange` into the Replace With field.

23. Click Replace All.

24. When the replacements have been made, click Close.

25. Save and close the file.

26. In Visual Studio, select File ➤ Open ➤ File.

27. In the Open File dialog, navigate to the file `C:\Windows\Microsoft.NET\Framework\v1.1.4322\CONFIG\machine.config`.

28. Click Open.

29. Locate the following code in the file:

```
<!- use this section to add application specific configuration
       example:
    <appSettings>
            <add key="XML File Name" value="myXmlFileName.xml" />
    </appSettings>
->
```

30. Modify this code section to appear as follows:

```
<appSettings>
    <add
key="Microsoft.Solutions.InformationWorker.Recruiting.Exchange.UserID"
value="sps\Exchange_account_name"/>
    <add
key="Microsoft.Solutions.InformationWorker.Recruiting.Exchange.Password"
value="Exchange_account_password"/>
</appSettings>
```

31. Replace `Exchange_account_name` and `Exchange_account_password` with a user name and password that will act as the master meeting organizer for the system.

NOTE *You can use any existing account to coordinate the meetings. In an actual deployment, you would create an account specifically for this task.*

32. Save and close the file.

33. Restart IIS.

Creating the Resume Builder Web Service

The recruiting accelerator ships with a web service specifically for the Resume Builder component, but the service is unsupported. Furthermore, the service uses customizations that were intended for a Microsoft demonstration. It is exceedingly difficult to get the service to work. Therefore, you will create your own simple service in this exercise.

Creating a New Web Site

Your web service will be a simple one to populate the Resume database. It will use a new site separate from the other components. Therefore, you must create a new site for the service.

1. In the IIS Manager dialog, right-click the Web Sites folder and select New ➤ Web Site from the pop-up menu.

2. In the Web Site Creation wizard, click Next.

3. In the Web Site Description step, type **Resume** and click Next.

4. In the IP Address and Port Settings step, change the "TCP port this Web site should use" field to 88.

5. Click Next.

6. In the Web Site Home Directory step, click Browse.

7. In the Browse for Folder dialog, navigate to the directory C:\.

8. Click Make a new Folder.

9. Name the new folder **ResumeService**.

10. Click OK.

11. In the Web Site Home Directory step, click Next.

12. In the Web Site Access Permissions step, click Next.

13. Click Finish to complete the operation.

Creating the Web Service

Your custom web service will use a single method to accept XML and save it out to the Resume database. The database has some required fields and a dependency between the two tables that it contains. Your web service will consist mainly of an insert operation necessary to upload the resume and maintain the database integrity.

To create the custom web service, follow this procedure:

1. Select Start ➤ All Programs ➤ Microsoft Visual Studio .NET 2003 ➤ Microsoft Visual Studio .NET 2003.

2. In Visual Studio, select File ➤ New ➤ Project.

3. In the Add New Project dialog, click the Visual Basic Projects folder.

4. Select ASP.NET Web Service from the Templates list.

5. In the Location text box, type `http://SPSPortal:88/ResumeWebService`.

6. Click OK.

7. When the new project is created, rename the file `Service1.asmx` as `Submit.asmx`.

8. Open `Submit.asmx` in Visual Studio for editing.

9. Rename the web class `Submit`.

10. Create a single web method in your web service to submit the resume. Listing 11-3 shows how your final web service code should appear.

11. Build the web service.

12. Close Visual Studio.

Listing 11-3. Web Service for Resume Submittal

```vb
Imports System.Web.Services

<System.Web.Services.WebService
(Namespace:="http://tempuri.org/ResumeWebService/Service1")> _
Public Class Submit
    Inherits System.Web.Services.WebService

    <WebMethod()> _
    Public Function SubmitResume(ByVal strXML As String) As String

        Try
            Dim UserName As String = "sa"
            Dim Password As String = ""

            'Set up connection string from custom properties
            Dim strConnection As String
            strConnection += "Password=" & Password
            strConnection += ";Persist Security Info=True;User ID="
            strConnection += UserName + ";Initial Catalog=Resume"
            strConnection += ";Data Source=(local)"

            'Create the insert statement
            Dim ResumeName As String = "Admin" + Now.ToString
            Dim strSQL As String = _
            "INSERT INTO tblUser (username,password) " + _
"VALUES('" + ResumeName + "','password')"

            'Insert user name
            Dim objCommand As New System.Data.SqlClient.SqlCommand

            With objCommand
                .Connection = New _
System.Data.SqlClient.SqlConnection(strConnection)
                .Connection.Open()
                .CommandText = strSQL
                Dim intRows = .ExecuteNonQuery()
                .Connection.Close()
            End With

            strSQL = _
            "INSERT INTO tblResume " + _
" (owner,name,description,lastChanged,DocData) VALUES('" + _
```

```
ResumeName + "','" + _
ResumeName + "','test resume','" + Now + "','" + strXML + "')"

                'Insert resume
                With objCommand
                    .Connection.Open()
                    .CommandText = strSQL
                    Dim intRows = .ExecuteNonQuery()
                    .Connection.Close()
                End With

                Return ""

        Catch x As Exception
            Return x.Message
        End Try

    End Function

End Class
```

Configuring InfoPath Forms

All of the InfoPath forms associated with the recruiting accelerator need to be customized to work properly. In some cases, all you have to do is substitute some particular values for placeholders in the configuration. In other cases, you have to make significant changes.

Configuring the Interview Manager InfoPath Forms

The Interview Manager uses InfoPath forms extensively to manage the competencies, scheduling, and feedback of interview information. In order for members of the interview team to have access to the forms, they must be part of the web site. After that, some specific changes must be made to each form so that they will function in your environment.

Creating the InfoPath Web

The site for the Interview Manager InfoPath forms is created as a virtual directory on the Recruiting web site. The key to providing access to these forms is to ensure that the physical directory has the proper access permissions. In this exercise, you must give all users read and write access to the virtual directory.

To create the InfoPath web, follow these steps:

1. In the IIS Manager dialog, right-click the new Recruiting web site node and select New ➤ Virtual Directory from the pop-up menu.

2. In the Virtual Directory Creation wizard, click Next.

3. In the Virtual Directory Alias step, type **Solutions** and click Next.

4. In the Web Site Content Directory step, click Browse.

5. In the Browse for Folder dialog, navigate to the directory `C:\Program Files\Microsoft Solutions\Information Worker\Recruiting\Interview Management\Client Components\InfoPath Forms`.

6. Click OK.

7. In the Web Site Content Directory step, click Next.

8. In the Virtual Directory Access Permissions step, accept the default values and click Next.

9. Click Finish to complete the operation.

10. Open Windows Explorer and navigate to the directory `C:\Program Files\Microsoft Solutions\Information Worker\Recruiting\Interview Management\Server Components\Web Services\Interview_Data`.

11. Right-click the `Interview_Data` folder and select Properties from the pop-up menu.

12. In the Properties dialog, click the Security tab.

13. On the Security tab, click Add.

14. In the Select Users, Computers, or Groups dialog, type **Everyone**.

15. Click OK.

16. In the Permissions for Everyone list, check the following permissions:

    • Read & Execute

    • List Folder Contents

    • Read

    • Write

17. Click OK.

Configuring the InfoPath Forms

The Interview Manager InfoPath forms are all configured for a generic localhost server. In order for them to work properly, you must modify them to work with your particular server. This requires you to edit a resource file for the forms by hand.

Here is what you need to do to configure the InfoPath forms:

1. Open Windows Explorer and navigate to the directory C:\Program Files\Microsoft Solutions\Information Worker\Recruiting\Interview Management\Client Components\InfoPath Forms.

2. Right-click the file CompetencySolution.xsn and select Design from the pop-up menu.

3. On the Microsoft InfoPath menu, select Tools ➤ Resource Manager.

4. In the Resource Manager dialog, select the file resource.xml and click Export.

5. In the Export dialog, navigate to My Documents and click Save.

6. In the Resource Manager dialog, click OK.

7. Select Start ➤ All Programs ➤ Microsoft Visual Studio .NET 2003 ➤ Microsoft Visual Studio .NET 2003.

8. In Visual Studio, select File ➤ Open ➤ File.

9. In the Open File dialog, navigate to the resource.xml file and click Open.

10. When the file opens, select Edit ➤ Find and Replace ➤ Replace from the menu.

11. In the Replace dialog, enter **localhost** into the Find What field.

12. Enter **SPSPortal:81** into the Replace With field.

13. Click Replace All.

14. Save and close the file.

15. On the Microsoft InfoPath menu, select Tools ➤ Resource Manager.

16. In the Resource Manager dialog, click Add.

17. In the Add File dialog, navigate to the `resource.xml` file and click OK.

18. When prompted, select to replace the existing file.

19. Save and close the file.

20. Repeat steps 2 through 19 for the files `Interview_FeedbackSolution.xsn` and `Interview_ManagerSolution.xsn`.

Configuring the Resume Builder InfoPath Form

The Resume Builder provides an InfoPath form that candidates can use to submit resumes online. For this exercise, you will need to edit the resource file to make it work with your configuration. Then you will copy it to the Recruiting web site.

1. Open Windows Explorer and navigate to the directory `C:\Program Files\Microsoft Solutions\Information Worker\Recruiting\Resume Builder\Templates\InfoPath Form`.

2. Right-click the file `Resume_InfoPath.xsn` and select Design from the pop-up menu.

3. From the InfoPath menu, select Tools ➤ Submitting Forms.

4. In the Submitting Forms dialog, click the option Enable Submit.

5. Click Select a Web Service.

6. In the Submit to Web Services wizard, type `http://spsportal:88/ResumeWebService/Submit.asmx?WSDL`.

7. Click Next.

8. Select the `SubmitResume` operation and click Next.

9. Click Modify.

10. In the Select a Field or Group dialog, open the `StructuredXMLResume` folder and select the ExecutiveSummary node.

11. Click OK.

12. Click Next.

13. Click Finish to complete the operation.

14. In the Submitting Forms dialog, click OK.

15. Save and close the file.

16. Copy the `Resume_InfoPath.xsn` file to the directory `C:\Program Files\Microsoft Solutions\Information Worker\Recruiting\Interview Management\Client Components\InfoPath Forms`.

Installing Web Parts

The Recruiting site relies heavily on three different web parts to present open job positions, candidate information, and interview feedback. These web parts must be installed and marked as safe before you can use them in the site. This process should be familiar by now, as it is similar to work you have done throughout the book.

1. Log in to `SPSPortal` as a local administrator.

2. Open Windows Explorer and navigate to the directory `C:\Program Files\Microsoft Solutions\Information Worker\Recruiting\Interview Management\Server Components\webparts\assemblies`.

3. Drag the two assemblies located in this folder to the GAC located in `C:\Windows\assembly`.

4. Create a new folder for the web part resources at `C:\Program Files\ Common Files\Microsoft Shared\web server extensions\wpresources\ InterviewWebParts\1.0.0.0__31bf3856ad364e35`.

5. Copy the GIF files located in `C:\Program Files\Microsoft Solutions\ Information Worker\Recruiting\Interview Management\Server Components\ webparts\InterviewWebParts\resources` to the resource folder you just created.

6. Select Start ➤ All Programs ➤ Microsoft Visual Studio .NET 2003 ➤ Microsoft Visual Studio .NET 2003.

7. In Visual Studio, select File ➤ Open ➤ File.

8. In the Open dialog navigate to the file `C:\inetpub\wwwroot\web.config` and click Open.

9. In the `<SafeControls>` section, add the following entry to allow the web parts to run:

```
<SafeControl Assembly="InterviewWebParts,
Version=1.0.0.0, Culture=neutral,
PublicKeyToken=31bf3856ad364e35"
Namespace="Microsoft.Solutions.InformationWorker.Recruiting"
TypeName="*" Safe="True" />
```

10. Save and close the file.

11. In Visual Studio, select File ➤ Open ➤ File.

12. In the Open dialog, navigate to the file `C:\Program Files\Microsoft Solutions\Information Worker\Recruiting\Interview Management\Server Components\webparts\InterviewWebParts\dwp\Candidates.dwp` and click Open.

13. When the file opens, select Edit ➤ Find and Replace ➤ Replace from the menu.

14. In the Replace dialog, enter **localhost** into the Find What field.

15. Enter **SPSPortal:81** into the Replace With field.

16. Click Replace All.

17. In the Replace dialog, enter `c:\inetpub\wwwroot\webparts\` `InterviewWebParts\resources` into the Find What field.

18. Enter `C:\Program Files\Microsoft Solutions\Information Worker\` `Recruiting\Interview Management\Server Components\webparts\` `InterviewWebParts\resources` into the Replace With field.

19. Click Replace All.

20. Save and close the file.

21. Repeat steps 13 through 20 for the files `InterviewFeedback.dwp` and `Positions.dwp`.

22. Restart IIS.

Creating the Recruiting Site

Once all the components of the accelerator are installed and configured, you can create the Recruiting site. The site consists of three web parts to display the key information and links to access the InfoPath forms. All aspects of the recruiting process begin by accessing the site.

To create the Recruiting site, take these steps:

1. Log in to SPSPortal as a member of the Administrator site group.

2. Open the portal home page in Internet Explorer.

3. On the portal home page, click the Sites link.

4. From the Site Directory, click the Create Site link under the Actions list.

5. On the New SharePoint Site page, give your new site the title **Recruiting** and designate a URL.

6. Click Create.

7. On the Add Link to Site page, fill in any options you want and click OK.

8. On the Template Selection page, select Team Site and click OK.

9. On the Recruiting site home page, select Modify Shared Page ➤ Add Web Parts ➤ Import.

10. In the Add Web Parts pane, click Browse.

11. In the Choose File dialog, navigate to the file `C:\Program Files\Microsoft Solutions\Information Worker\Recruiting\Interview Management\Server Components\webparts\InterviewWebParts\dwp\Positions.dwp`.

12. Click Open.

13. In the Add Web Parts pane, click Upload.

14. Drag the web part into a pane on the page.

15. Repeat steps 10 through 14 for the files `Candidates.dwp` and `InterviewFeedback.dwp`.

16. On the Candidates web part, select Modify Shared Web Part from the drop-down menu.

17. When the Candidates web part enters design mode, select Connections ➤ Candidate Consumer ➤ Positions from the drop-down menu.

18. On the Interview Feedback web part, select Connections ➤ Interview Feedback Consumer ➤ Candidates from the drop-down menu.

19. Close the Web Part pane.

20. Using the Links web part, add a link to the online resume at `http://spsportal:81/Solutions/Resume_InfoPath.xsn`.

21. On the Recruiting home page, click the Site Settings link.

22. On the Site Settings page, select Administration ➤ Manage users.

23. On the Manage Users page, click the link Add Users.

24. On the Add Users page, enter the user names for the accounts to access the Recruiting site.

25. Check the Contributor site group.

26. Click Next.

27. On the Add Users page, click Finish.

Using the Recruiting Site

Once the site is created, you are ready to initiate a mock interview process. The site you have created can be used to submit resumes and manage the interview process. Here is a simple series of steps to get started with the process:

1. Log in to SPSPortal as the local administrator.

2. Select Start ➤ All Programs ➤ Microsoft SQL Server ➤ Enterprise Manager.

3. In the SQL Server Enterprise Manager, select Console Root ➤ Microsoft SQL Servers ➤ SQL Server Group ➤ (local)(Windows NT) ➤ Databases ➤ Recruiting ➤ Tables.

4. Right-click the Employee table and select Open ➤ Return All Rows from the pop-up menu.

5. In the Employee table, identify the account that is associated with the PositionID of 6. This is the hiring manager for the exercise.

6. Log in to SPSClient as the hiring manager.

7. Open the portal in Internet Explorer and navigate to the Recruiting site.

8. On the Recruiting home page, click Customer Service Representative.

NOTE *If you do not see the Customer Service Representative position, then you are not logged in as the hiring manager.*

9. In the Candidates web part, click the Open link in the Plan Interview column. Figure 11-10 shows the Candidates web part.

10. In the "Select interviewers for this interview loop" section of the InfoPath form, click Select All.

11. In the task pane, click the link "Save or send interview notices."

12. In the Save or Send Interview Notices dialog, select the option to Save the Form Only.

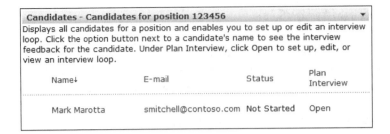

Figure 11-10. *The Candidates web part*

13. Uncheck the Close Interview Manager box and click OK.

14. In the task pane, select the Schedule Interviewers link.

15. Create an interview schedule using the scheduling tools.

16. In the task pane, click the link "Save or send interview notices."

17. In the Save or Send Interview Notices dialog, select the option to "Save the form and send interview notices."

18. Uncheck the Close Interview Manager box and click OK.

19. In the task pane, click the link Select Competencies.

20. Check all of the competencies on the form.

21. In the task pane, click the link "Save or send interview notices."

22. In the "Save or send interview notices" dialog, select the option to Save the Form Only.

23. Click OK.

24. Return to the hiring portal and refresh the page. Verify that the interviewers are set up in the page.

25. Log in to SPSClient using one of the accounts that you scheduled for as an interviewer.

26. Open Microsoft Outlook and accept the interview meeting.

27. In the meeting request form, click the link to provide interview feedback.

28. From the Recruiting site, click the link for the online resume.

29. When the online resume appears, fill out the form.

30. When you have filled out the form, select File ➤ Submit.

Index

A

<AboutPath> element, 304
Accelerator for Proposals, 416–24,
  429–43
  customizing, 421–22, 437–40
  installing, 428–30
  prerequisites, 427–28
  proposal process, 415–17
  setting up client, 435–37
  setting up Proposal site, 430–35
    adding new site members, 431–32
    creating Content Library, 434–35
    creating new cross-site groups,
      432–33
    creating Proposal Home site, 434
    creating Sales site collection, 431
    setting up site templates, 433–34
  solution architecture, 417–21
    Metadata database, 419
    proposals web service, 419–20
    SharePoint Services components,
      418–20
    Smart Document, 421
  using, 440–41
Accelerator for Recruiting, 422–27,
  441–70
  configuring InfoPath forms, 459–63
    Interview Manager forms, 459–62
    Resume Builder form, 462–63
  configuring web services, 449–59. *See
    also* Interview Manager,
    configuring web services for
  creating Resume Builder web
    service, 456–59
  creating Recruiting site, 465–66,
    467–70
  customizing, 427
  installing, 442–49
    basic installation, 442–43

    Interview Manager database,
      444–47
    Resume database, 448–49
    setting up user information,
      447–48
  installing web parts, 463–65
  prerequisites, 442
  recruiting process, 423–24
  solution architecture, 425–27
access
  to applications, 14–15
  code access security, 155–56
    customizing policy files, 159–64
    marking web parts as safe, 164–65
  external, allowing, 13–14
  modifying rights, 97–101
Active Directory Account Creation
  (ADAC), 66–67
ActiveX controls, 223–24
ADAC (Active Directory Account
  Creation), 66–67
Adaptive update, of content indexes,
  399
Add and Customize Pages right, 62, 64
Add Items right, 62, 63
Add Link to Site page, 58
Add Project Output Group dialog box,
  166, 167
Add Users page, 66
Add/Remove Personal Web Parts right,
  62, 63
ad-hoc sites, 277–78
Administer permission, 199
Administrator site group, 61, 69, 97, 105
agreements, service-level, 14
alerts, 86–87
<alias> element, 299
announcements, 84
Application class, 201, 205–6

Application Pool Identity, 336, 337
Application Portals, 2–3
ApplicationCollection class, 206
ApplicationField class, 206
ApplicationFieldCollection class, 206, 207
ApplicationInfo class, 206
applications
    accessing, 14–15
    complexity of, 4–6
Apply Style Sheets right, 62, 64
ApplyChanges method, 242
approval routing, 80–81
Approval Status property, 343, 344–45
Area settings page, 94–95
area templates, 113
areas, 53–58
    designing structure, 91–92
    news areas, 57–58
    removing, 91
    sites areas, 58
    topics areas, 55–57
AspNetHostingPermission, 156, 158
Assembly attribute, 165
<Assembly> element, 154, 172, 179
AssemblyCulture attribute, 154
AssemblyDelaySign attribute, 153
AssemblyInfo file, 152, 154, 321, 338, 375, 384
AssemblyInfo.cs file, 139, 176, 359–60
AssemblyInfo.vb file, 139
AssemblyKeyFile attribute, 152, 359
AssemblyVersion attribute, 360
audiences, 15–17, 101–4
audit log, 209–10
Author role, 77

B

back up and restore, 391–93
backward-compatible document libraries, 73–81
    administering users, roles, and rights, 76–77
    alerts, 86–87
    discussions, 87–88
    document management features, 76–81
    form libraries, 81–83
    image libraries, 83
    installation, 73–76
    lists, 84
    searching, 89
    surveys, 88–89
BaseType property, 347
Boolean properties, 240
booting from CD-ROM, 35
BoundColumns, 367
Browsable attribute, 145
Browse Directories right, 62, 64
browsers, and FrontPage, 116
business solutions, 1–19
    analysis and design considerations, 11–18
        documenting business vision, 12
        documenting policies and practices, 12–15
        managing change, 17–18
        working with audiences, processes, and web parts, 15–17
    end-user challenges, 4–8
    history of portals, 1–4
    overview, 1
    scenarios, 8–11
    technical considerations, 18–19

C

calendar, 114–15
Cancel Check Out right, 62, 63
CancelChanges method, 243
CanRunAt method, 233
Category attribute, 145
<Category> element, 304
CD-ROM, booting from, 35
CellConsumerInit event, 236
CellProviderInit method, 261
CellReady event, 237, 261
certificates
    creating new, 406–9
    installing Certificate Services, 405–6

installing new, 409–10

challenges, end-user, 4–8

Change Anonymous Access Settings page, 100–101

Change Component Assignments page, 47

Change Document Library Settings page, 76, 78

Change Settings page, 93

child controls

  creating

    when building global task web part, 378–79

    when building identity web part, 387–88

    when building site collection web part, 367–69

  defining, 215

child controls, adding to web parts, 178–89

  coding web part, 180–85

    defining child controls, 183–84

    defining properties, 181–83

    rendering web part, 184–85

  creating new project, 178–79

  deploying web part, 186–89

    compiling web part, 186–87

    creating strong names, 186

    modifying web.config file, 187–88

    using web part, 188–89

  modifying web part description file, 179–80

cleaning up unused sites, 394–97

client requirements, 19

ClientReference parameter, 232

client-side web parts, 223–26

  using ActiveX controls, 223–24

  using script files, 225–26

CLR (Common Language Runtime), 159

<CLSNAME> element, 299

code access security, 155–56

  customizing policy files, 159–64

  marking web parts as safe, 164–65

  understanding configuration files, 156–59

<CodeGroup> section, 161

Common Language Runtime (CLR), 159

<compilation> element, 169

compiling

  audiences, 102

  web parts, 176, 186–87, 219

  workflow engine, 359–60

Component Assignments, 47

conditional formatting, 123–24

Configuration Database Settings, 46

configuration files, 156–59

<configuration> element, 169, 170

Configure Profile Import page, 67, 68

Configure Server Farm Account Settings page, 44

Configure Server Topology page, 47, 74

configuring

  ASP.NET, 41–42

  InfoPath forms, 459–63

    Interview Manager forms, 459–62

    Resume Builder form, 462–63

  Internet Explorer, 42–44

  Interview_Data application, 452–53

  prerequisites, 38

  Remote Desktop Administration on SPSController, 40–41

  Resume Builder InfoPath forms, 462–63

  Server Farm Account Settings, 44–46, 46–47

  Terminal Services, 246

  web services, 449–59. *See also* Interview Manager, configuring web services for

  creating Resume Builder web service, 456–59

connectable web parts, 108–10, 251–68

  coding web part life cycle, 255–63

    communicating schema information, 259–60

    connection notification, 257–58

    implementing transformers, 258–59

    receiving data, 261–63

    registering interfaces, 256

    rendering web part, 263

    run location, 257

    sending data, 260–61

  creating child controls, 254–55

creating project, 252
defining properties, 253
implementing interfaces, 253
using web part, 264–68
connectable web parts, building, 226–40
connection interfaces, 226–29
connection life cycle, 230–38
broadcasting schema information, 235–36
connection notifications, 234–35
exchanging data, 236–38
registering interfaces, 231–33
running on client or server, 233–34
using transformers, 238–40
contacts, 85
content development, 97–138. *See also* customizing portal content
building Executive Dashboard, 128–38
accessing site from SPS, 137–38
building team site, 131–36, 132–33, 134–36
preparing data sources, 129–31
customizing with FrontPage, 116–28
creating and consuming web services, 125–28
designing new pages, 117–20
using web components, 128
working with data sources, 120–23
working with data views, 123–25
overview, 97
personalization with My Site, 113–16
Content Library, 414, 417, 418, 419, 434–35
Content Manager site group, 61, 69, 72, 93, 105
Context variable, 346
Contributor site group, 61, 71, 93, 98
control sets
building, 293–97
creating, 310–19
working with, 297
ControlCaptionFromID property, 314
ControlCount property, 294, 312
ControlID property, 295, 296, 297, 313

ControlNameFromID property, 296, 313
Controls collection, 147–48, 215
ControlTypeFromID property, 296, 314–15
Coordinator role, 77
<Copyright> element, 304
<Count> element, 305
Create Area right, 62, 64
Create Personal Site right, 62, 64
Create Portal Site for SPSPortal page, 49
Create Sites right, 62, 64
CreateChildControls method
and connection notifications, 234
and creating child controls, 254
and defining child controls, 183, 215
and rendering web parts, 147–48
CreateDws method, 348
Credentials class, 201, 209
Credentials permission, 199
Culture attribute, 165
custom tool parts, 240–43, 270–74
adding, 273–74
building basic web part, 269–70
coding property pane events, 271–73
creating child controls, 271
creating new class, 270
creating tool parts, 241–43
default tool parts, 240–41
rendering tool part, 273
customers, integrating SharePoint solutions with, 11
customizing
Accelerator for Proposals, 423–24, 439–42
Accelerator for Recruiting, 429
My Site, 115–16
policy files, 159–64
customizing portal content, 97–113
audiences, 101–4
site membership, 97–101
templates, 110–13
area templates, 113
list templates, 112–13
site templates, 111–12
understanding web parts, 104–10

connecting web parts, 108–10
modifying web part pages, 105–8
CustomPropertyToolPart object, 240

D

Data Source Catalog, 120–22, 128
Data Source Properties dialog, 128
data sources
adding to catalog, 132–33
preparing, 129–31
working with using FrontPage,
120–23
data views
creating, 134–36
working with using FrontPage,
123–25
database property, 253
DataGrid control, 181, 215, 254
DataSet objects, 126, 372, 374, 378, 381
db_owner right, 192
DCOM (Distributed Component Object
Model), 125
debug attribute, 169
debugging web part pages, 168–70
Default Content Access Account setting,
44
DefaultProperty attribute, 141, 173, 180
DefaultValue attribute, 145–46
Delete Items right, 62, 63
deploying smart documents, 298–99,
319–22
deploying web parts, 151–68, 175–78
building the web part, 153–55
code access security, 155–66
customizing policy files, 159–64
marking web parts as Safe, 164–65
understanding configuration files,
156–59
compiling web part, 176
creating strong names, 175–76
deployment packages, 166–67
marking web part as safe, 177
SSO service, 217–20
compiling web parts, 219
creating strong names, 217–19

modifying web.config File, 220
understanding strong names, 151–53
using web parts, 177–78
deployment packages, 166–67
Description attribute, 146
Description parameter, 232
<Description> element, 154, 172, 179,
304
designing area structure, 91–92
desktop, complexity of, 4–6
Desktop Database Engine, 43
DesktopHeight property, 249, 251
DesktopWidth property, 249
Detail class, 253
development environment, creating,
34–50. *See also* SPSPortal
configuring Remote Desktop
Administration on
SPSController, 40–41
installing Exchange 2003 on
SPSController, 38–40
installing SQL Server 2000 on
SPSPortal, 43–44
installing Visual Studio.NET 2003 on
SPSPortal, 51
installing Windows Server 2003 on
SPSController, 35–37
installing Windows Server 2003 on
SPSPortal, 41–43
preparing SPSClient, 51
prerequisites, 34–35
development of web parts, 223–74. *See
also* connectable web parts,
building
client-side web parts, 223–26
using ActiveX controls, 223–24
using script files, 225–26
connectable web parts, 251–68
custom tool parts, 240–43
adding custom tool part, 273–74
building basic web part, 269–70
coding property pane events,
271–73
creating child controls, 271
creating new class, 270
creating tool parts, 241–43
default tool parts, 240–41

rendering tool part, 273
overview, 223
using Terminal Services, 243–51
  creating new web page, 247–48
  creating web part, 248–50
  deploying web part, 250–51
  setup, 243–46
DHCP service, 36
Directory Service permission, 157, 159
discussion forum, threaded, 10
discussions, 87–88
<Display> element, 304
DisplayHeight property, 249
DisplayWidth property, 249, 251
Dispose event, 143
Distributed Component Object Model
  (DCOM), 125
distributed file system, 23–24
.dll extension, 154
DNS permission, 157, 159
Document Information tab, 282
document libraries, 69–73
Document Library page, 70
Document Library Settings page, 72, 73
document taxonomy, 91–92
document workflow, 333–45
  capturing events, 334–39
    connecting to target library,
      338–39
    creating event handler, 335–38
    enabling events handlers, 334–35
  manipulating documents, 339–45
    accessing document properties,
      341–44
    acting on documents, 344–45
    referencing event information,
      339–41
document workspaces, 26–27, 277–82
  Document Information tab, 282
  Documents tab, 281–82
  Links tab, 282
  Membership tab, 279–80
  Status tab, 280
  Tasks tab, 281
documenting management features,
  76–81

documents, loading, 94–96
Documents tab, 281–82
<documentSpecific> element, 299
domain attribute, 327
domain controller, creating, 36
domains
  adding users and groups to, 37
  not joining, 36
.dwp extension, 153, 172, 179

E

Edit Items right, 62, 63
encrypting file system, 23
end-user challenges, 4–8
Engine class, 354–55
EnsureInterfaces method, 232, 256
Enterprise Information Portals, 3
Environment permission, 156, 158
event information, referencing, 339–41
EventLog permission, 157, 159
events, 85
events handlers
  creating, 335–38
  enabling, 334–35
Exchange 2003, installing on
  SPSController, 38–40
Executive Dashboard, building, 128–38
  accessing site from SPS, 137–38
  building team site, 131–36
    adding data sources to catalog,
      132–33
    creating data views, 134–36
    preparing data sources, 129–31
external access, 13–14

F

"Failed to retrieve the current domain
  name.." error message, 68
features, of SharePoint, 7
file system
  distributed, 23–24
  encrypting, 23
FileIO permission, 156, 158
filename switch, 167

<filePath> element, 299
Filter Criteria dialog, 123
Folder Redirection feature, 22–23
force switch, 167
form libraries, 81–83
formatting
    conditional, 123–24
    partitions, 36
FriendlyName attribute, 146
FrontPage, 116–28
    creating and consuming web
        services, 125–28
    designing new pages, 117–20
    using web components, 128
    working with data sources, 120–23
    working with data views, 123–25
Full update, of content indexes, 399
FullScreen property, 249, 251

G

GAC (Global Assembly Cache), 160, 338,
    445
gacutil.exe utility, 160, 338
galleries, 106
GetContextSite method, 346
GetCredentialEntryUrl method, 204
GetCredentials method, 202
GetFilesProperties method, 420
GetGlobalTasks method, 383
GetInitEventArgs method, 239, 258
GetLibraries method, 420
GetSolutionConfiguration method, 420
GetSubwebsForCurrentUser method,
    348
GetToolParts method, 240–41, 273
GetUsers method, 420
Global Assembly Cache (GAC), 160, 338,
    443
Global E-mail Settings, 47–49
global task web part, building, 375–85
    changing identity, 380–81
    creating child controls, 378–79
    creating project, 377–78
    prerequisites, 375–77
    rendering web part, 381–84

using web part, 384–85
globalinstall switch, 167
Group Policy object, 23

H

Hashtable object, 341, 343
Help library, 423
helper functions, 369–70
home page. *See* portal home page
HtmlTextWriter class, 149
HyperLinkColumns, 367

I

ICellConsumer interface, 231
    CellProviderInit method, 261
    and child controls, 254
    compatibility of, 227, 258
    example of, 236
    implementing, 253
ICellProvider interface, 227, 228, 231,
    237
<Id> element, 304, 327
identity web part, building, 385–90
    creating child controls, 387–88
    creating project, 385–86
    rendering web part, 388–89
    updating user information, 389–90
    using web part, 390
IFilterConsumer interface, 227, 228, 239
IFilterProvider interface, 227
<IFRAME>...</IFRAME> tags, 174
IIS. *See* Internet Information Server (IIS)
IListConsumer interface, 227, 228
IListEventSink interface, 354, 357–59
IListProvider interface, 227, 228
image libraries, 83
images, 108, 117–18
Imports statements, 377–78
Incremental update, of content indexes,
    399
InfoPath application, 27, 82, 125, 426,
    425
Information Worker Infrastructure
    (IWI), 21–24

InitEventArgs class, 239
initialization phase, 142
InitialSelected argument, 316
installing
  Accelerator for Proposals, 428–30
  Accelerator for Recruiting, 442–49
    basic installation, 442–43
    installing Interview Manager
      database, 444–47
    installing Resume database,
      448–49
    setting up user information,
      447–48
  backward-compatible document
    library components, 73–76
  Certificate Services, 405–6
  Exchange 2003, 39–40
  Exchange 2003 on SPSController,
    38–40
  new certificates, 409–10
  SharePoint Portal Server (SPS)
    deployment architectures, 30–33
    limitations, 30
    shared services, 33
    and upgrading, 33–34
    user capacity, 29
  SPS on SPSPortal, 44–51
    adding new users, 49–50
    Component Assignments, 47
    Configuration Database Settings,
      46
    configuring Server Farm Account
      Settings, 44–46, 46–47
    creating portal, 49
    global e-mail settings, 47–49
  SQL Server 2000 on SPSPortal, 43–44
  Terminal Services, 243–44
  web client, 244–45
  Windows Server 2003
    on SPSController, 35–37
    on SPSPortal, 41–43
InterfaceName parameter, 232
InterfaceObject parameter, 232
interfaces
  implementing, 253
  registering, 256
InterfaceType parameter, 232

Internet Information Server (IIS), 160
  Application Pool Identity, 336, 337
  installing, 38–39, 244–45
  "lock down" mode, 42
Interview Manager, 441–42
  configuring InfoPath forms, 459–62
  configuring web services for, 449–56
    configuring Interview_Data
      application, 452–53
    creating new application pool, 450
    creating new web site, 450–51
    creating web applications, 451–52
    modifying configuration files,
      453–56
  database
    editing, 447–48
    installing, 444–47
Interview_Data application, 452–53
InterviewManager_DeploymentGuide.d
  oc file, 442
InterviewManager_PlanningGuide.doc
  file, 442
intranets, 2
IParametersInConsumer interface, 227,
  228
IParametersInProvider interface, 227
IParametersOutConsumer interface, 227
IParametersOutProvider interface, 227
<IPermission> element, 163, 200, 221
IRowConsumer interface, 227, 228
IRowProvider interface
  compatibility of, 228, 258
  example of, 229
  implementing, 253
  and PartCommunicationMain
    method, 260
  purpose of, 227
  testing, 266–67
IsClientScriptBlockRegistered method,
  226
ISmartDocument interface, 292, 293,
  297, 310
IsolatedStorage permission, 156, 158
issues, 86
IWI (Information Worker
  Infrastructure), 21–24

K

K2.net workflow engine, 334
Key Performance Indicators (KPI), 128
keywords, 400
K-Wise Deployer, 92

L

Label controls, 207–9, 271
large server farm, 33
LastErrorCode property, 202
layers, 119
layout tables, 118–20
libraries, 68–89. *See also* backward-
    compatible document libraries
    document libraries, 69–73
links, 84
Links for You section, 8
Links tab, 282
List and Manage Document Libraries
    page, 75, 76
List argument, 316
list templates, 112–13
ListBox control, 237
ListID property, 340
lists, 84
Live Meeting application, 282
loading documents, 94–96
LoadViewState method, 142
LoginName property, 348
LogonUser function, 337

M

machine.config file, 156, 158
MakeCert.exe tool, 300
Manage Access request page, 98
Manage Alerts right, 63, 64
Manage Area Permissions right, 62, 64
Manage Area right, 62, 64
Manage Audiences right, 63, 64
Manage Personal Views right, 62, 63
Manage Portal Site right, 63, 64
Manage Profile Database page, 67, 68
Manage Search right, 63, 64

Manage Settings for Single Sign-On
    page, 196
Manage User Profiles right, 63, 64
Manage Users page, 49, 65–66, 98
Manage Your Server applet, 36
<managed> element, 299
management features, documenting,
    76–81
Manifests library, 421, 438
Manifest.xml file, 139, 171, 179, 319–20,
    439
MaxConnections parameter, 232
medium server farm, 32
meeting workspace, 26, 27–28, 282
Member site group, 61, 70–71, 84, 93
Membership tab, 279–80
MenuItem parameter, 232
Message Queue permission, 157, 159
<Message> element, 304
Metadata database, 419
Microsoft Certificate Services, 405, 409
Microsoft Desktop Database Engine
    (MSDE), 43
Microsoft FrontPage. *See* FrontPage
Microsoft InfoPath application, 27, 82,
    125, 424, 425
Microsoft Live Meeting application, 282
Microsoft Office 2003, 26–28
Microsoft Office Solution Accelerators.
    See Accelerator for Proposals;
    Accelerator for Recruiting
Microsoft Office System. *See* Office
    System
Microsoft Outlook program, 6
Microsoft SharePoint Portal Server. *See*
    SharePoint Portal Server (SPS)
Microsoft Single Sign-On (SSO) service.
    See Single Sign-On (SSO) service
Microsoft SQL Server Desktop Engine
    (MSDE), 31
Microsoft Terminal Services. *See*
    Terminal Services
Microsoft Word application. *See* Word
    application
Microsoft.OfficeInterop.SmartTag
    namespace, 292
Microsoft.Office.Interop.SmartTag.C_TY
    PE, 296

Microsoft.SharePoint.IListEventSink interface, 335

Microsoft.SharePoint.WebControls namespace, 346

Microsoft.SharePoint.Portal namespace, 104, 205

Microsoft.SharePoint.Portal.SingleSigno n namespace, 200

Microsoft.SharePoint.Security namespace, 159

Microsoft.SharePoint.WebPartPages.Co mmunication namespace, 229

Microsoft.SharePoint.WebPartPages.We bPart class, 140, 141

Microsoft.Solutions.InformationWorker. Recruiting.msi package, 442

Microsoft.Solutions.InformtionWorker.P roposals.Client.msi installation package, 427

Microsoft.Solutions.InformationWorker. Proposals.Server.msi installation package, 427

Minimal permission, 199

Modify Shared Page, 90

MoveTo method, 345

MSDE (Microsoft Desktop Database Engine), 43

MSDE (Microsoft SQL Server Desktop Engine), 31

MSSSOAdmins group, 194, 210

My Calendar, 114–15

My Calendar Alerts Summary list, 115

N

Name property, 348

name switch, 167

<Name> element, 304, 305

<NamedPermissionSets> section, 161

Namespace attribute, 126, 165

naming servers, 36

Netscape browser, 5

network interface card (NIC), 19

Network Load Balancing (NLB), 19, 32, 33

New SharePoint Site page, 58

new users, adding, 49–50

news areas, 57–58

News page, 57–58

NIC (network interface card), 19

NLB (Network Load Balancing), 19, 32

O

o switch, 167

<OBJECT> tag, 224

Office 2003, 26–28

Office Solution Accelerators. *See also* Accelerator for Proposals; Accelerator for Recruiting

Office System, 275–332

developing Office solutions, 286–307. *See also* research service; smart documents

XML support, 287–89

Office integration, 275–86. *See also* document workspaces

document management, 275–77

linked lists, 284–86

meeting workspaces, 282–84

Outlook contacts and calendars, 284

overview, 275

Office Web Components (OWC), 223–24

OleDBPermission, 157, 159

OnEvent method, 335, 339, 357, 358

OnInit method, 142

Online Gallery, 107

OnLoad event, 142–43

OnPreRender event, 143

OnUnload event, 143

Open dialog, 275–76

Outlook program, 6

OWC (Office Web Components), 223–24

P

.p7b extension, 409

Page object

IsClientScriptBlockRegistered method, 226

RegisterClientScriptBlock method, 225

Page_Load event, 247

PageView.cs file, 173

PartCommunicationConnect method, 234, 257

PartCommunicationInit method, 235, 236, 259

PartCommunicationMain method, 236–37, 260

partitions, formatting, 36

partners, integrating SharePoint solutions with, 11

password property, 253

password restrictions, changing, 37

Performance Counters permission, 157, 159

permissions, assigning, 220–22

<PermissionSet> element, 221

personal identification number (PIN) number, 13

personal productivity, increasing, 8–9

Personal View, 105

PIA (primary Interop assemblies), 290, 292, 307–8

PIN (personal identification number) number, 13

policy files, customizing, 159–64

PopulateListOrComboContent method, 316

PopulateTextboxContent method, 317

portal content. *See* content development; customizing portal content

portal home page, 28–29

    clearing, 90

    granting users permissions from, 49

    Links for You section, 8

    set of topics within, 16

Portal Server Central Administration page, 47, 49

portal site, accessing, 345–49

Portal Site Application Pool Identity setting, 46

portal structure, 53–60

    areas, 53–58

        news areas, 57–58

        sites areas, 58

        topics areas, 55–57

Self-Service Site Creation (SSSC), 59–60

    sites, 58–59

portals (in general)

    creating, 49

    history of, 1–4

Power Users group, 32, 33

presence information, 401

primary Interop assemblies (PIA), 290, 292, 307–8

Printing permission, 157, 159

processes, 15–17

productivity, increasing, 8–10

profiles, 67–68, 114

programming SharePoint Services, 333–90. *See also* document workflow

    accessing portal site and user information, 345–49

    building global task web part, 375–85

        changing identity, 380–81

        creating child controls, 378–79

        creating project, 377–78

        prerequisites, 375–77

        rendering web part, 381–84

        using web part, 384–85

    building identity web part, 385–90

        creating child controls, 387–88

        creating project, 385–86

        rendering web part, 388–89

        updating user information, 389–90

        using web part, 390

    building site collection web part, 363–75

        creating child controls, 367–69

        creating helper functions, 369–70

        creating project, 365–66

        defining properties, 367

        prerequisites, 364–65

        rendering web part, 370–74

        using web part, 375

    creating workflow engine, 351–63, 354–60

        coding IListEventSink interface, 357–59

        compiling the engine, 359–60

connecting libraries, 360–62
creating new identity Helper, 355–56
creating XML document, 356–57
debugging the solution, 362–63
prerequisites, 352–53
overview, 333
using SharePoint web services, 349–51
programs. *See* applications
properties, defining, 213–14, 253, 367
Properties field, 339
PropertiesAfter property, 340
PropertiesBefore property, 340
Property Pages dialog, 155
Proposal Home site, creating, 434
Proposal Library, 418
proposals. *See* Accelerator for Proposals
Proposals Home page, 415, 418, 421
Proposals_Build_Test_Guide.doc file, 427
Proposals_Customization_Guide.doc file, 428
Proposals_Overview_Guide.doc file, 427
Proposals_Planning_ and_Architecture_Guide.doc file, 428
<Provider> element, 304
<Providers> element, 304
<ProviderUpdate> element, 304
PublicKeyToken, 165, 177, 187, 188
Publish method, 420

Q

Query method, 304–5, 324, 326, 327–28
<QueryPath> element, 304
QueryResponse.xml file, 327
<QueryText> element, 305, 327

R

Range object, 287
<Range> and </Range> tags, 306
RDA (Remote Desktop Administration), 40–41

Reader group, 61–62, 69
Reader role, 77
Reader site group, 84
recruiting. *See* Accelerator for Recruiting
RedirectDrives property, 249, 251
RedirectPrinters property, 249, 251
Reflection permission, 156, 158
RegisterClientScriptBlock method, 225
registering interfaces, 256
RegisterInterface method, 232, 233
RegisterInterfaces method, 234
RegisterScriptBlock method, 226
Registration method, 303, 324, 325, 326, 327
<RegistrationPath> element, 304
RegistrationResponse.xml template, 325
Registry permission, 156, 158
Remote Desktop ActiveX control, 251
Remote Desktop Administration (RDA), 40–41
remote workers, supporting, 11
RenderToolPart method, 242
RenderWebPart method, 370–71, 383
<OBJECT> tag in, 224
creating hyperlink in, 250
and drawing web part, 143, 147, 238
generating script code in, 224
and HtmlTextWriter class, 149, 175
redirecting users to logon form, 204
and sign-on code, 215
research service, building, 302–7
creating Query Response, 326–30
creating registration response, 325–26
prerequisites, 323
registering service, 303–4
responding to queries, 304–7
starting project, 324
using Custom Service, 331
<Response> element, 306, 327
restore, 391–93
Resume Builder, 441, 442
configuring InfoPath forms, 462–63
creating web service for, 456–59
Resume database, installing, 448–49

ResumeBuilder_BuildandTestGuide.doc file, 442
ResumeBuilder_PlanningGuide.doc file, 442
rights, 76–77
roles, 76–77
RowReady event, 260–61
RSA SecurID, 13
RunAt parameter, 232
<runFromServer> element, 299

S

Safe attribute, 165
<SafeControl> element, 164
<SafeControls> section, 164, 165, 169, 177, 187, 188, 220, 390
SaveViewState event, 143
script files, 225–26
Search right, 63, 64
search service, managing, 397–402
    creating keywords, 400
    defining external content sources, 398–99
    enabling online presence, 401–2
    managing quotas and locks, 402
    scheduling content crawls, 399–400
SearchForSections method, 420
secure access, establishing, 403–12
    creating an alias, 403–5
    enabling SSL, 405–12
        creating the new certificate, 406–9
        installing Certificate Services, 405–6
        installing the new certificate, 409–10
        testing secure access, 411–12
Secure Socket Layers (SSL), 403
SecurID, 13
Security permission, 158
Security Utility tool, 161
<SecurityClasses> section, 199, 221
SecurityException class, 233
<securityPolicy> section, 156, 162
SelectedWebPart property, 242
Self-Service Site Creation (SSSC), 59–60, 393

SendNotificationEmail method, 420
SendWmiEvent method, 420
Server Farm Account Settings, 44–47, 46–47
Server property, 249, 251
server requirements, 18–19
servers, naming, 36
Service Controller permission, 157, 159
Service Manager, 44
<Service> element, 304, 327
Service1.asmx file, 126
ServiceAction enumeration, 209
service-level agreements, 14
<Services> element, 304
SetCredentials method, 209
Shadow Copy folders, 21–22
Shared Links, 116
Shared View, 105
Shared Workspace Sites, 116
SharePoint namespace, 140
SharePoint Portal Server Central Administration page, 47, 49
SharePoint Portal Server (SPS), 28–34, 53–96, 89–96
    accessing site from, 137–38
    adding users, 92–93
    clean up, 90–91
    creating site structure, 93–94
    designing area structure, 91–92
    installation considerations, 28–34
        deployment architectures, 30–33
        limitations, 30
        shared services, 33
        upgrading, 33–34
        user capacity, 29
    libraries, 68–89. *See also* backward-compatible document libraries
        document libraries, 69–73
    loading documents, 94–96
    managing users, 61–68
        Active Directory Account Creation (ADAC), 66–67
        adding users, 64–66
        site groups, 61–64
        user profiles, 67–68
    Portal Structure, 53–60

Self-Service Site Creation (SSSC), 59–60

sites, 58–59

SharePoint Portal Server (SPS)
administration, 391–412. *See also*
secure access, establishing

back up and restore, 391–93

cleaning up unused sites, 394–97

managing search service, 397–402

creating keywords, 400

defining external content sources, 398–99

enabling online presence, 401–2

managing quotas and locks, 402

scheduling content crawls, 399–400

overview, 391

site usage analysis, 393–94

SharePoint Services. *See also*
programming SharePoint Services

accessing information via web services, 349–51

overview, 24–26

SharePointPermission, 159

ShowAllSites property, 367, 372

SignCode.exe utility, 300

Single Sign-On (SSO) service, 191–222, 210–22

assigning permissions, 220–22

creating application definition, 210–11

creating web part, 212–17

defining child controls, 215

defining properties, 213–14

rendering web part, 215–17

setting references, 212–13

deploying web parts, 217–20

compiling web parts, 219

creating strong names, 217–19

modifying web.config File, 220

entering credentials, 211–12

overview, 191

prerequisites, 210

programmatic administration, 205–9

as proxy for end users, 7

setting security policy, 199–200

setting up, 191–99

using in web parts, 200–205

viewing audit log, 209–10

SingleSignOn assembly, 200

SingleSignonException class, 201

SingleSignonException object, 202

SingleSignonLocator class, 204, 205

SingleSignonPermission class, 199, 200

SinkData property, 339, 340, 356

site collection web part, building, 363–75

creating child controls, 367–69

creating helper functions, 369–70

creating project, 365–66

defining properties, 367

prerequisites, 364–65

rendering web part, 370–74

using web part, 375

Site Directory, 137

site groups, 61–64

site membership, 97–101

Site property, 340

Site Settings page, 67, 96, 98, 104, 111

site structure, 93–94

site templates, 111–12

site usage analysis, 393–94

[Site] Gallery, 106–7

sites areas, 58

Sites page, 58

small server farm, 31–32

smart documents, 289–300

and Accelerator for Proposals, 421

building, 307–22

creating control sets, 310–19

creating XML schema, 309

deploying, 319–22

prerequisites, 307–8

setting up the project, 308–9

building control sets, 293–97

deploying, 298–99

deploying smart documents, 298–99

preparing environment, 290–92

relating schema and functionality, 292–93

security considerations, 300

working with control sets, 297

SmartDocInitialize method, 293

SmartDocXmlTypeCount method, 293–94

SmartDocXmlTypeCount property, 310, 311–12

sn.exe tool, 152, 154, 175, 186

Socket permission, 157, 158

<solutionID> element, 299

Sort and Group dialog, 123

SPBaseType enumeration, 347

SPControl class, 346

Specify Configuration Database Settings page, 46

SPFile object, 341, 342, 343, 345

SPList object, 347

SPListCollection object, 347

SPListEvent class, 339–40

SPListEvent object, 335, 339, 341

SPListEventType object, 344

SPListEventType.CheckIn event, 335

SPListEventType.CheckOut event, 335

SPListEventType.Copy event, 335

SPListEventType.Delete event, 335

SPListEventType.Insert event, 335

SPListEventType.Move event, 335

SPListEventType.UncheckOut event, 335

SPListEventType.Update event, 335, 344

SPListItem class, 343

SPListItem object, 341

SPS. *See* SharePoint Portal Server (SPS)

SPS_WPG group, 192

SPSController

    configuring Remote Desktop Administration on, 40–41

    installing Exchange 2003 on, 38–40

    installing Windows Server 2003 on, 35–37

SPSIdentity.cs file, 385, 386

SPSIdentity.dwp file, 385, 386

SPSite object, 346

sps.local domain, 41

SPSMaskTool.Part, 273

SPSPortal, 308, 323

    installing SPS on, 44–51

        adding new users, 49–50

        Component Assignments, 47

        Configuration Database Settings, 46

        configuring Server Farm Account Settings, 44–46, 46–47

        creating portal, 49

        Global E-mail Settings, 47–49

        installing SQL Server 2000 on, 43–44

        installing Windows Server 2003 on, 41–43

SPSSTaskss.vb file, 377

SPSSubSites.dwp file, 365

SPSSubSites.vp file, 366

SPSTasks.dwp file, 377

SPUser object, 348

SPWeb class, 348

SPWeb object, 341, 346

SQL Server, 129

SQL Server 2000, 43–44

SQL Server Desktop Engine, 31

SQL Server Service Manager, 44

SqlClientPermission, 157, 159, 161

sqlServer property, 253

SSL (Secure Sockets Layer), enabling, 405–12

    creating new certificate, 406–9

    installing Certificate Services, 405–6

    installing new certificate, 409–10

    testing secure access, 411–12

SSO. *See* Single Sign-On (SSO) service

SSO_Audit table, 209–10, 213

SSOReturnCodes class, 201

SSSC (Self-Service Site Creation), 59–60, 393

<StartAt> element, 305

Status property, 343

Status tab, 280

<Status> element, 304

String properties, 240

strong names, creating, 175–76, 186

Strong Name tool, 152, 154, 175, 186, 217–19

STS_WPG group, 192

STSADM tool, 433

StsAdm.exe tool, 167

<Submit>...</Submit> elements, 357

Submit.asmx web service, 426

surveys, 88–89

SyncChanges method, 242, 243

System.Data.dll assembly, 212

System.Security.Principal.WindowsIdentity object, 337

<system.web> section, 159, 162

System.Web.UI.Control class, 142, 143, 147

System.Web.UI.WebControls namespace, 147

System.Web.UI.WebControls.WebControl class, 140

T

<TABLE> tag, 150

target library, connecting to, 338–39

<targetApplication> element, 299

task pane, of FrontPage, 117

tasks, 85

Tasks tab, 281

team productivity, 9–10

Team Services. *See* SharePoint Services

team site, building, 131–36

   adding data sources to catalog, 132–33

   creating data views, 134–36

Template Selection page, 59

templates, 110–13

   area templates, 113

   list templates, 112–13

   site templates, 111–12

Templates and Add-Ins dialog, 299

Templates library, 423

Terminal Services, 14–15, 243–51

   creating new web page, 247–48

   creating web part, 248–50

   deploying web part, 250–51

   setup, 243–46

testing

   IRowProvider interface, 266–67

   secure access, 411–12

   web client, 245

TextBox controls, 207–9, 271

threaded discussion forum, 10

Title property, 340

<Title> element, 154, 172, 179

tool parts, custom, 269, 270–74

   adding, 273–74

   building basic web part, 269–70

   coding property pane events, 271–73

   creating, 241–43

   creating child controls, 271

   creating new class, 270

   default tool parts, 240–41

   rendering, 273

tool parts, default, 240–41

ToolboxData attribute, 141

"tool-only" approach, 12

ToolPart class, 241–42

Topic Assistant tool, 56, 95, 96

topics, 16

topics areas, 55–57

Top-Level Site Administration page, 98, 112

tracing images, 117–18

transformers, 228, 238–40, 258–59

<trust> element, 160, 162, 169, 170, 188, 220

<trustLevel> element, 156

two-factor authentication, 13

Type property, 340

<type> element, 299

<Type> element, 304

TypeName attribute, 165

<TypeName> element, 154, 172, 179

Tzunami K-Wise Deployer, 92

U

Uniform Resource Identifier (URI), 163

unused sites, cleaning up, 394–97

Update Personal Web Parts right, 62, 63

<updateFrequency> element, 299, 439

upgrading SPS, 33–34

URI (Uniform Resource Identifier), 163

<uri> element, 299

URL property, 249, 251

url switch, 167

UrlAfter property, 340

UrlBefore property, 340

urn:Microsoft.Search namespace, 324

Use Personal Features right, 63, 64

Use Topic Assistant page, 56

UserDisplayName property, 340
UserID property, 341
UserLoginName property, 341
userName property, 253
users, 61–68
   accessing information, 348–49
   Active Directory Account Creation
     (ADAC), 66–67
   adding, 49–50, 64–66, 92–93
   administering, 76–77
   profiles of, 67–68
   site groups, 61–64
   updating information, 389–90

V

Version attribute, 165
version history, 80
<version> element, 299
Versions page, 71
View Area right, 62, 63
View Pages right, 62, 63
View Styles dialog, 123
ViewState property, 142
virtual directories, 129–31
Virtual Server Gallery, 107
virtual servers, 126
Virtual Server Settings page, 59–60
Visual Studio Tools for Office loader, 300
VMware, 35

W

webconfig file, 419–20
Web Designer site group, 61, 69, 105
Web discussions, 87–88
Web Part Page Gallery, 106
web parts, 15–17. *See also* child controls,
   adding to web parts; connectable
   web parts; deploying web parts;
   development of web parts; Single
   Sign-On (SSO) service
   adding to pages, 168
   building
     coding web part, 172–75
     creating new project, 171

     modifying web part description
      file, 172
     overview, 139
     rendering web parts, 147–50
     web part life cycle, 142–44
     web part properties, 144–46
     webpart class, 140–42
   client-side, 223–26
     using ActiveX controls, 223–24
     using script files, 225–26
   coding life cycle, 255–63
     communicating schema
      information, 259–60
     connection notification, 257–58
     implementing transformers,
      258–59
     receiving data, 261–63
     registering interfaces, 256
     rendering web part, 263
     run location, 257
     sending data, 260–61
   debugging, 168–70
   modifying web part pages, 105–8
Web Service Description Language
   (WSDL), 419
web services, creating and consuming
   with FrontPage, 125–28
Web Storage System (WSS), 73, 74
web.config file
   <SafeControls> section, 169, 177, 390
   <securityPolicy>section, 158
   <system.web> section, 159–60
   and IIS, 264
   modifying, 187–88
WebForm1.aspx file, 247
<WebMethod( )> decoration, 126
WebPart class, 140–42, 147, 232, 240
WebPart1 class, 173, 180
WebPart1.cs file, 171
WebPart1.dwp file, 171
WebPart1.vb file, 179
WebPart.cs file, 139–40
WebPartPermission, 159
WebPartStorage attribute, 146
WebPartTemplatesforVSNetSample.exe
   template, 139
WebPartToolPart object, 240

WebPart.vb file, 139–40
WebPermission, 157, 158
WebUrl property, 340
WIDTH definition, 150
Windows integrated security, 130, 131
Windows Network Load Balancing
    (NLB), 19
Windows Server 2003
    Information Worker Infrastructure,
        21–24
    installing on SPSController, 35–37
    installing on SPSPortal, 41–43
Windows Terminal Services, 14–15
WindowsIdentity object, 355
WindowsImpersonationContext object,
    337
WithEvents keyword, 147
Word application
    creating document workspace from,
        278
    preserving formatting of, 287–89
WordML, 287
workflow engine, creating, 351–63,
    354–60
    coding IListEventSink interface,
        357–59
    compiling the engine, 359–60
    connecting libraries, 360–62
    creating new identity Helper, 355–56
    creating XML document, 356–57
    debugging the solution, 362–63

prerequisites, 352–53
Workflow.xml file, 356–57
workspace pane, 278–79
workspaces, 26–28
WSDL (Web Service Description
    Language), 421
WSS (Web Storage System), 73, 74
wss_mediumtrust.config file, 217, 220,
    221

X

XML Content filter, 428–29
XML Content Filter from, 427
XML data sources, 120–23
XML document, creating, 356–57
XML expansion pack, 298–99, 321–22
XML schema, creating, 309
XML Schema Document (XSD), 287
XML support, for Office System, 287–89
XML-based forms, 81–82
XMLFilter.dll file, 428
XmlRoot attribute, 141
XmlTextWriter object, 306
XSD (XML Schema Document), 287

Z

zones, placing web parts in, 107